Linguistic Structure and Language Dynamics in South Asia

Papers from the Proceedings of
SALA XVIII Roundtable

MLBD SERIES IN LINGUISTICS

General Editor
DHANESH JAIN

Volume XV

Linguistic Structure and Language Dynamics in South Asia

Papers from the Proceedings of
SALA XVIII Roundtable

Edited by
ANVITA ABBI
R.S. GUPTA
AYESHA KIDWAI

MOTILAL BANARSIDASS PUBLISHERS
PRIVATE LIMITED • DELHI

Reissued in 2010
First Edition: Delhi, 2001

ISBN: 978-81-208-1765-4

MOTILAL BANARSIDASS
41 U.A. Bungalow Road, Jawahar Nagar, Delhi 110 007
8 Mahalaxmi Chamber, 22 Bhulabhai Desai Road, Mumbai 400 026
203 Royapettah High Road, Mylapore, Chennai 600 004
236, 9th Main III Block, Jayanagar, Bangalore 560 011
Sanas Plaza, 1302 Baji Rao Road, Pune 411 002
8 Camac Street, Kolkata 700 017
Ashok Rajpath, Patna 800 004
Chowk, Varanasi 221 001

Printed in India
By Jainendra Prakash Jain at Shri Jainendra Press,
A-45 Naraina, Phase-I, New Delhi 110 028
and published by Narendra Prakash Jain for
Motilal Banarsidass Publishers Private Limited,
Bungalow Road, Delhi 110 007

Contents

PART IV
SYNTAX AND SEMANTICS

From the editors

The Eighteenth Round Table of South Asian Language Analysis (SALA) was organised by the Centre of Linguistics and English School of Languages, Jawaharlal Nehru University, New Delhi (India) during January 4-6, 1997. The conference was attended by scholars from all over the world and about 150 papers were presented in 20 parallel sessions and plenary sessions. This volume presents a selection from the papers that were submitted and found suitable for publication. The editors are grateful to all those who sent in their papers, and regret that constraints of finance, technology and space precluded the publication of a more exhaustive volume of the entire proceedings. Our selection in this volume aims at providing representation to the major areas covered during the conference, and at showcasing the breadth, variety and quality that characterises research in South Asian language and linguistics today.

ANVITA ABBI
R.S. GUPTA
AYESHA KIDWAI

Languages in contact: Where we have been and where we might go

JAMES W. GAIR
Cornell University

I am honoured to be here and to have the opportunity to give this address, and it is a considerable source of satisfaction that this SALA is being held once more in India, thus allowing the participation of a wider range of participants and especially of students. This is an especially gratifying occasion for me personally, because the primary organiser of this event, Professor Abbi, is one in whose career of graduate study I had the opportunity of participating, and I also learned much.

A colleague of mine who was engaged in Chinese linguistics once mentioned to me a saying to the effect that if the teacher is blue the student must be indigo, and I believe that there is no greater satisfaction than seeing one's students be productive and contribute to the field as both scholar and teacher. I, and all of us, should thank and congratulate Professor Abbi and her colleagues for planning and organising so successfully this exceptionally wide-ranging program and note especially the lively and enthusiastic group of students who have played such a vital part in the effort.

Originally, when invited, I was asked to comment on the 'state of the art'. However, now that the study of languages has taken so many branches and turns, I am not sure what the art is now, and even if I was, I could not comment on the state of all of it in the time available. What I will do, though, is to give a brief account of some highlights of South Asian Linguistics for the past forty or so years, and a brief and rather personal account of some directions that it might profitably take. I will concentrate primarily on the sub-areas of syntax, but that by no means should be taken to mean that I believe that other areas are unimportant.

In 1955, Murray Emeneau delivered a presidential address to the American Oriental Society entitled 'India and Linguistics'. His address offers an excellent starting point and point of reference for our account here. In it, he summed up the debt that Western linguistics owed to the Indian tradition, saying, in part,[1]

> It is clear that, however much may have been added by Western scholars to the general phonetic inventory and to an exact knowledge of the articulatory processes, the first long but slow steps away from the awkward fumblings of early European scholarship were taken only when Hindu phonetics had come to be generally known to Sanskrit scholars and had been introduced by them into the stream of European scholarship.

He went on to characterise the direct influence of the Indian tradition on modern, especially American, linguistics through Leonard Bloomfield who was the towering figure of the time and one who was, as Emeneau noted, 'intimately acquainted with Panini and the commentaries on Panini'.[2] Bloomfield's *Language* was the essential charter of American structural-descriptive linguistics, and as Emeneau stated:

> . . . linguistic method as stated by Bloomfield in his book *Language* shows much that is the result of his readings of the Hindu grammarians. It is not too much to say that his methods in phonemic analysis, and in morphology and syntax would hardly have been stated as they were, if Bloomfield had not been steeped in Hindu grammar, so that he became such a firm admirer of its 'scientific condensation, which places every feature into its proper settings' and of its 'completeness' (*Language*, vol. V, p. 274), as well as of its striving for brevity and stringency of statement.[3]

Emeneau was referring there primarily to American linguistics, but the influence of the Indian tradition went well beyond that, and I noticed happily that one paper to be given at this SALA is devoted to the influence of Indian linguistics on de Saussure, a topic well worth pursuing.

Emeneau then summarised the then-current state of Indian linguistics, pointing out especially the lack of descriptive statements for modern Indo-Aryan languages, while hoping that 'combined Indian, American and British efforts will make good at least a part of this want in the not too distant future'.[4] The situation for Dravidian languages was similar, and for other languages, work was virtually non-existent. He added, 'Present Indian plans for descriptive work include non-Indo-Aryan languages, and it is to be hoped that the many blank spots in the Indian linguistic map will soon be filled in'.[5] To anticipate my conclusions here, it is clear that considerable progress has been made in the interim. It is equally clear that much remains to be done. Providentially in this connection, the book edited by Professor Abbi that is being released this morning[6] testifies to ongoing work in the non-major languages, and holds out the prospect for more to be done.

Though exporting linguistics to India, with its long and rich scholarly tradition, might be seen as having had an element of preaching to the founders of the faith, a whole generation of South Asian linguists, both Indian and foreign, was created, and many lasting relationships, both collegial and personal, were forged that led to much productive work. Equally important, the alumni of these programs ultimately staffed to a great extent the major South Asian linguistics programs both here and abroad. Noteworthy also was the connection of linguistics with first-hand descriptive research on languages on the one hand and their teaching on the other – connections that have since been attenuated to a great degree, at least in the United States. In my view, this development is unfortunate, since the advances that progress from such an interaction have been, and can be, considerable in both directions.

Perhaps I may be permitted a personal note here. Though in many respects I am a member of that generation, I was not a participant in any of those programs, but came in later from another area: English linguistics. However, this occasion gives me an opportunity to acknowledge my own guru in South Asian linguistics, Gordon Fairbanks, who was very much involved in those activities. Once I had shifted, through Gordon's influence and example, I never turned back, and I have certainly never regretted it.

In a 1969 paper in the major *Current Trends* survey of South Asian linguistics, Ashok Kelkar referred to those 1950s efforts as inaugurating what he called the 'contemporary phase' of South Asian linguistics, stating:[7]

> Indian linguistics [he later added Pakistan, Ceylon and Nepal] was finally ready to catch up with the Saussure-Sapir-Bloomfield revolution in linguistics. Linguistics has been put back on the map of Indian scholarship.

The dominant paradigm in that phase was indeed that Bloomfeldian-Saussurean one in which most of us at the time had been trained, but by the time of Kelkar's paper the seeds of change had already been sown and were well sprouted. Kelkar noted that by then,[8]

> . . . South Asian linguistics does have its exhibits of classical American descriptions: Pike-tagmemics, Longacre-tagmemics, Harris-transformationalism, Firthian studies, Chomsky-generative presentations, Halliday-inspired descriptive grammars, even glossematic studies. Structuralism has some comparativist-historical work to its credit in the Indo-Aryan, Dravidian, and Munda fields.

Parenthetically, I may note that Kelkar includes a cogent note that we might still profitably attend to, in referring to the 'relatively lonely efforts' that were 'away from the network of institutions', adding that 'the fate of purely traditional pundits and maulvis has on the whole been that of playing third or fourth fiddle. The world will be the loser if individual efforts against heavy odds remain neglected'.[9] Kelkar's account of the general situation, though scarcely a quarter century old, already has a rather archaic ring. The competition that he described has devolved, since about 1970, into the increasing dominance at least in syntax, of whatever Noam Chomsky at MIT and his followers were developing. Whatever one's theoretical persuasion, or lack of it, I believe this observation to be sociologically correct, since there is no lack of either celebrations or condemnations of the situation that I have characterised in that way.

The earlier versions of transformational grammar, including the work of Chomsky's teacher Zellig Harris, appeared to many of us to offer a welcome set of powerful descriptive devices to account for data that had eluded or resisted standard descriptive treatment. As a result, a number of grammars, or portions of grammars, of South Asian languages were produced in versions of that paradigm, ranging from Chomsky's 1957 *Syntactic Structures*[10] to his 1965 *Aspects of a Theory of Syntax*.[11] Studies of this kind appeared both in India and abroad. Among them, we might mention, among others, published works such as those by Mahendra Verma and Yamuna Kachru for Hindi, Franklin Southworth and Mahadeo Apte for Marathi, S. Agesthialingom and Harold Schiffman on Tamil, and my own on Sinhala, along with a number of these and a quantity of works by A.K. Ramanujan, James Londholm, Colin Masica and others that were circulated in 'purple ink' or cyclostyled form.

As time passed, however, a reaction, or perhaps disillusion, set in and efforts in South Asia itself shifted largely to other areas and kinds of linguistics, such as socio-linguistics or applied linguistics, though generative syntax, sometimes in older forms, continued in some islands. There were a number of reasons for this change that I cannot go into here, but prominent among them was clearly the changing face of generative grammar itself.

Chomsky's fundamental concern has always been theory, and universal grammar in some form, not description. After all, the early work that he considered most important was not the 1957 *Syntactic Structures* through which most of us were introduced to the theory, but rather *The Logical Structure of Linguistic Theory*, incorporating his Ph.D. dissertation and written in 1955–56, but not published until 1985.[12] Over time, theory became more prominent in presentations of transformational-generative grammar, but there was also a real shift from a theory that held that a theory of language L (though as a part of a general explanatory of language) was a (presumably) possible device for generating all and only the sentences of L to a theory in which individual language systems and structures played less and less a role, to the point that universal grammar replaced them and rendered them epiphenomenal. Thus in characterising the Principles and Parameters model that led into the current Minimalist one, Chomsky stated:[13]

> This constituted a radical break from the rich tradition of thousands of years of linguistic inquiry, far more so than early generative grammar, which could be seen as a revival of traditional concerns and approaches to them (perhaps the reason why it was often more congenial to traditional grammarians than to modern structural linguists). In contrast, the P&P approach held that languages have no rules in anything like the familiar sense, and no theoretically significant grammatical constructions except as taxonomic artifacts. There are universal principles and a finite array of options as to how they apply (parameters), but no language-particular rules and no grammatical constructions of the traditional sort with and across languages.

Even before the point in the development of generative theory summarised in that quotation was arrived at, however, the theory seemed to many to be becoming less and less relevant to the description of specific languages, while at the same time technically and terminologically more complex and arcane. Moreover, it was often difficult of access, unless one was plugged into the network of those working in the forefront of the theory, and particularly for scholars in South Asia itself that could prove a significant hurdle.

Relatively recently, however, there has been a revived involvement of South Asian languages in generative grammar research, but approached from a different direction from the earlier efforts. Perhaps paradoxically, it arose from a recognition of the value, and in fact the necessity, of cross-language research in the attempt to arrive at a valid characterisation of Universal Grammar. That is, despite the view that specific grammars were epiphenomenal, there came a recognition that a correct theory of Universal Grammar as representing the fundamental and inherent human language capacity had to accord with the observably phenomena of languages and that English-based efforts would not suffice, even if extended to the more familiar European languages.[14] Put in more specific theoretical terms, in the search for explanatory adequacy, descriptive adequacy could not be jettisoned, though it might appear in a different form from that envisioned in early transformational theory.

Thus, we have witnessed the appearance recently of works on South Asian languages, and others, cast within a current theoretical framework. Characteristically, however, these efforts have not been entitled something like the earlier 'A transformational-generative analysis of Language L', but more like 'The X principle in L' or 'L-movement in L'. In short, they proceed from some general theoretical question or concern to the language, and not in the reverse direction.

I am certainly not downgrading such efforts. They can make a contribution to both general linguistics and our knowledge of the languages concerned, and I have myself made some attempts in that direction. I am happy also to see such work well represented in the program of this SALA, in contradistinction to a SAKA that I recall from the early 1980s in which only a handful of participants at best were interested in current syntax. This represents a real gain and a welcome widening and refreshing of the field.

Nevertheless, welcome as these developments are, they do not constitute South Asian linguistics *per se*, and as I now turn to sketch some kinds of directions that the field might profitably take, I would like to enter a plea for another kind of theoretically relevant work to be carried out in tandem with those theory-centred studies. What I would propose is more and fuller descriptions of our languages, in a mode that I would call 'principled descriptions'.

Those of us who attempt to work cross-linguistically know how difficult it is to locate comparable and dependable data for that task. Providentially, Murray Emeneau once more provides me with a relevant and cogent statement in the volume just released. He says, in relation to so-called 'tribal languages',

> We as linguistic scholars must make it our first duty to collect the languages of the tribes of the Indian subcontinent. We must collect data and present the learned world with descriptions of the languages, whether in an old-fashioned mode or in the newer transformational style. Whatever the mode adopted, we must strive to present all features of the language, phonological, morphological, syntactic, lexical. And, though this might seem elementary, texts are strongly needed (and not merely sentences).[15]

Parenthetically, we might note here that some progress is being made in this direction. The work being carried out on such languages at our host university JNU and the data-base being established here is a welcome development, as is the work at other institutions such as the Delhi University and the Central Institute of Indian Languages. One hopes that such efforts will receive the recognition and respect that they so richly deserve. In this connection, we might also note the welcome inclusion of the panels on lesser-known and endangered languages in the program of this SALA.

Though Emeneau was addressing the need for descriptive work in the 'tribal' languages, his remarks can be extended further and have wider application. Even for some major and official languages, detailed and accurate descriptions are not always available. For example, Colin Masica's important survey on the Indo-Aryan languages[16] can serve as a state-of-the-art volume, but at the same time, it is, as Masica recognises at many points, not only a compilation of what we do know but an indication of how much more we need to known in relation to information that is lacking, sketchy, or uncertain, even in that relatively well-studied family.

What I would like to propose is the production of what might be called 'principled descriptions'. In my view, there is no description without some kind of theory, expressed or implied, as Emeneau in fact suggests. A good description, in modern terms, is a kind of interrogation of a language, or a three-sided conversation between theory, the data and the investigator. It is essential, for that interaction to be truly effective and reliable, that the data be allowed to talk back to the other participants, and not have its contributions predetermined. In fact, some free conversation, in the form of texts, is a useful check on such limitation. Linguistics may not be a classificatory science as someone claimed, but it should be an empirical one. I am not suggesting here that 'empirical' means 'empiricist', since that would diminish one of the other participants', theory, in our three-cornered conversation, but it does mean that falsification should be possible. Pet theories have been known to bite their owners in embarrassing places when they are allowed to feed freely on the fats, and for a science, that is the way it should be.

I will not attempt to define 'principled description' here further except to characterise it as having a descriptive bend but with a constant eye to theoretical concerns. In short, we try to anticipate as well as we can what kind of questions a linguist working in different sub-areas from different points of view might ask. Also, in my own case, I have never been able to shed my deep-seated Saussurean-Bloomfeldian conviction that individual languages have system and structure, and, however constrained by Universal Grammar, the interaction of subsection and parts is a vital part of the individual architecture of a language. I thus have the strong conviction that in addition to providing ample and necessary information on which to base comparative and theoretical work, a really good description should capture that architecture as well.

The Lingua Descriptive Series, under several transformations, was an attempt in the general direction that I am indicating. Whatever its shortcomings, it made a real contribution, not the least of which was to indicate what was not satisfactory or what to follow, thus making it easier to formulate a better framework. We in South Asian linguistics have also profited from several works in this series, including Tamil, Kannada, Punjabi and Kashmiri, and I believe that one on Marathi is nearing completion. Unfortunately, that series is coming to an end.

The recent project on anaphora in South Asian languages, with which I was associated, provided a somewhat different model, in which a detailed questionnaire-outline was developed and revised by feedback from the investigators of the languages. The authors were then held to following it in their presentations to ensure comparability across the fourteen languages included, and the entire set was then edited as a unit. However, space was also left for individual analyses and the notation of problems arising from the intersection of the outline and the features of the individual languages, so as to insure that the outline did not limit as well as elucidating relevant information. The volume from that enterprise is now in its final stages and will, we hope, appear shortly. Again, we can learn from our mistakes as well as our findings when we evaluate that project.

In South Asian languages, many of the variables that we attempt to isolate and dissociate in language research, particularly of a topological kind, are naturally present, identifiable, and thus naturally dissociatable. I am thinking here of such factors as genetic relationship, areal features, and the presence of formal and functional varieties, as well as of structural features such as constituent order, morpho-syntactic processes and linkages, and devices for embedding and complementation, and the list is easily expanded. South Asia thus forms a natural and accessible laboratory for topological and historical-areal research, and we should use it as such, to the benefit of the field at large.

The potential for work on language contact is immense, and though some valuable work has been done and is continuing (at JNU and Delhi University among other places), the field still beckons further research. The work done so far has contributed significantly to our understanding of area formation and diffusion of features and their relation to social factors and bi- and multilingualism, but important answers remain to be found. A positive sign here is the inclusion in this SALA of several papers relating to this topic.

In 1978, just ten years after Kelkar's paper, D.P. Pattanayak, in the introduction to a bibliography on linguistic theses,[17] deplored the lack of interdisciplinary research in South Asian language studies. The program of this SALA, which includes papers on neurolinguistics and language disorders is a happy indication that this is being remedied, and it will have much to contribute to the field at large.

There are numerous other areas that I could mention in which work in South Asia could make a real contribution, including typology, applied linguistics, language pedagogy, first- and second-language acquisition, and so on. Fortunately, the SALA program itself, and the list of panels, provides a kind of map in itself, and I would like to conclude on another topic, and in another vein.

In a famous statement, the British jurist Justice Hewart said that 'justice should not only be done, but should manifestly and undoubtedly be seen to be done'.[18] I would suggest that we could properly transform this to apply to South Asian linguistics. Work in all of the areas that I have mentioned will avail little to the general field unless it is made known at large. This is, I fear, an area in which we are presently deficient. I am always shocked and disappointed to pick up a volume or encounter a general article on a topic on which our languages would have important things to say, and discover that they are only nodded at, or worse, completely lacking. For example, despite the great contribution that work in South Asia could make to areal, contact, and diffusion studies, alluded to above, they are greatly under-represented in the literature in proportion to their importance. Similarly, I noted that a book on 'discourse-configurational languages'[19] included work not only on western and central European languages, but also on East Asian and African ones, but nothing was included on South Asia, despite the rich variety of relevant phenomena here and the work that had already been accomplished.

A very recent article by B.A. Sarada and L. Devaki in the *International Journal of Dravidian Linguistics*[20] is instructive in this regard. It does not deal with publications in South Asian linguistics as a whole by all scholars, but rather tracks published productions by Indian scholars, whether located in India or abroad. The results are thus limited, but they are highly instructive. What their studies show, among other things, is that the most productive Indian linguists, in terms of publications abstracted in a general series *Language and Language Behaviour Abstracts* (LLBA), are largely residing abroad, mostly in the US. Out of the eleven scholars contributing ten or more articles to journals in the years surveyed, two contributed from India, and one from both India and abroad.

Sarada and Devaki's findings require some interpretation, since they are to a great extent a function of the methodology they employed, but that in itself is instructive. They tracked papers listed in LLBA from 1977 to 1990, for a total of 998 papers in all. Articles published but not listed there thus do not count, so that the figures are only a limited indication of productivity, but that makes them in turn a reasonably good indicator of general recognisability and availability, and we should take notice.

I, and I am sure all of you, know of much good work done in India and other countries of South Asia, not only at the institutions that I have mentioned, but at others as well that I will not venture to name, that has not found its way into the general stream. The fault here does not lie entirely, and perhaps not even primarily, with the scholars, but it is to a significant extent a product of the infrastructure. Outlets for publication and distribution in South Asia are insufficient, as are, as many of you are sadly aware, the resources for distribution, like photocopying and postage.

Also, as Sarada and Devaki note, Indian authors not residing abroad have contributed their work largely to Indian journals of which the number is limited (22 out of 229 journals in their study that included contributions). They have thus suggested, among other things, that the publication of Indian journals should be increased and their coverage in LLBA be encouraged so as to get wider international readership. Cooperative international publication efforts for books, along with increased publication of linguistic works by Indian publishers could also make a great contribution to the dissemination of South Asian linguistic research. This topic would, of course, make a study in its own right, and cannot be pursued here. I would also suggest that more editorial work is needed. In particular, having students submit papers to edited and referred journals is a most important and effective way of preparing the next generation of scholars for international participation. Encouraging student participation in conferences such as this one is an important step as well, and the extent of such participation in this SALA is a good sign for the development of the next generation on which the continuation of our field depends.

One obvious problem facing us is the lack of positions in which graduates can continue to be productive and teach. This is a problem not only here, but in the US and elsewhere, where we have lost some of the brightest and most promising prospects to other endeavours. That problem, however is not one for which I can suggest a practical solution that lies within our power, except to set a good example and make our voices heard as much as possible.

I began with a quotation from Murray Emeneau. Allow me to end with another from the same address, in which he said:

> In the dawn of western linguistics, light certainly came from India. With the present resurgence of interest in linguistics in India, we can look forward to a new flood of light from India.[21]

Let us hope that this SALA will signal another international resurgence of interest and a further expansion and brightening of that light.

NOTES AND REFERENCES

1. Reprinted in *Collected Papers*. Annamalainagar: Annamalai University. 1967. 187–200. The quotations here, including this one from p. 194, have been taken from this volume.
2. Ibid., p. 195.
3. Ibid., pp. 195–96.
4. Ibid., p. 198.
5. Ibid., p. 200.
6. Anvita Abbi (ed.), *Languages of tribal and indigenous peoples of India: The*

ethnic space. Delhi: Motilal Banarsidass. 1997.

7. p. 535 in General Linguistics in South Asia in Thomas Sebeok (ed.), *Current trends in linguistics*, vol. 5. *Linguistics in South Asia*. pp. 532–42.
8. Ibid., p. 538.
9. Ibid., pp. 537–38.
10. The Hague: Mouton.
11. Cambridge and London: MIT Press.
12. Chicago and London: The University of Chicago Press.
13. *The minimalist program*. Cambridge (USA) and London: MIT Press. 1995. pp. 5–6.
14. Thus, for example, Chomsky in 1986, in *Knowledge of language: Its nature, origin and use*. New York: Praeger. pp. 37–38:

> It is important to bear in mind that the study of one language may provide crucial evidence concerning the structure of some other language, if we continue to accept the plausible assumption that the capacity to acquire language, the subject matter of UG, is common across the species . . . A study of English is a study of the realisation of *the initial state* S_0 under particular conditions. Therefore it embodies assumptions, which should be made explicit, concerning S_0. But S_0 is a constant; therefore Japanese must be an instantiation of the same initial state under different conditions. Investigation of Japanese might show that the assumptions concerning S_0 derived from the study of English were incorrect; these assumptions might provide the wrong answers for Japanese, and after correcting them on this basis we might be led to modify the postulated grammar of English. Because evidence from Japanese can evidently bear on the correctness of a theory of S_0, can have indirect – but very powerful – bearing on the choice of the grammar that attempts to characterise the I-language attained by a speaker of English. This is standard practice in the study of generative grammar . . .
>
> If we are interested in discovering the real properties of the initial state of the language faculty and of its particular realisations as potential or actual I-languages . . . we must regard a theory of one language as subject to change on the basis of evidence concerning other languages (mediated through a theory of UG), or evidence of other sorts.

15. In A. Abbi (ed.), 1997. p. 28.
16. *The Indo-Aryan languages*. Cambridge: Cambridge University Press. 1991.
17. *Classified bibliography of linguistic dissertations on Indian languages*. Compiled by J. Sakuntala Sharma; Supervised by D.P. Pattanayak and E. Annamalai. Central Institute of Indian Languages. 1978.
18. *King's Bench Reports, 1924, Volume 1*. Quoted in *The Columbia Dictionary of Quotations*. Columbia University Press. 1993.
19. Katalin E. Kiss (ed.), *Discourage of configurational languages*. New York: Oxford University Press. 1995.
20. Indian linguistics at the international scene. *International Journal of Dravidian Linguistics,* 25. 2 June 1996, pp. 100–17.
21. Emeneau, 1955. p. 200.

I

LANGUAGE CONTACT AND RELATED ISSUES

1
Language endangerment and Indian languages: An exploration and a critique

MAHENDRA K. VERMA
University of York

In his paper on 'Bilingualism and Structural Borrowings' Emeneau (1962) makes a fundamental distinction between Western and Indian responses to linguistic diversity created by immigrant language contact. He observes:

> It is clear that in the West, specifically in the United States of America, the prestige of the old established English-speaking community work with such powerful pressure for conformity that the languages even of sizeable immigrant groups are generally wiped out in a very few generations. . . . in India immigrant situations often result otherwise than in America. After a period of at least fifteen centuries of migration Saurashtran still survives as the domestic language of the immigrant silk weavers in Madura [Tamil Nadu state].

The forces that have shaped these divergent responses in the East and the West have been driven by monolingual and monocultural ideologies aimed at assimilation and monolingual nationalism versus plurilingualism and pluriculturism aimed at diversity and multilingual and multicultural nationalism. Le Page and Keller (1985) have views similar to Emeneau's:

> There is a tendency in a number of modern Nation-States to wish to make ethnic consciousness synonymous, and language is frequently seen as a major tool for this purpose, via the education system. As against that, many have tried to defend and protect cultural pluralism and to ensure that provision is made for the retention of 'minority' languages and cultures within the national education system – both out of respect for the individual and groups who use them and

from the argument that cultural pluralism is a source of strength rather than weakness in a society.

In the Indian sociolinguistic situation, inter-language boundaries could be highly fluid. Mobility and migration of groups of people across language and state boundaries is quite common. Consider, for example, the Maithili-speaking migrant Bihari rickshaw-pullers in Delhi, the Awadhi-speaking UP milkmen in Bombay, the Marwari-speaking Rajasthani businessmen in Calcutta, and the Punjabi-speaking Sikh taxi drivers in Calcutta – such a language situation is quite common in these cases.

In these kinds of linguistically diverse cities, individuals and groups do not simply develop multilingualism but often acquire a plurality of mother tongues. However, the forces affecting mother-tongue maintenance resulting in language shift are also beginning to emerge.

This paper describes and interprets the concept of language endangerment in the context of the linguistic situation in India since Independence and that of transplanted Indian languages abroad.

In spite of apparently liberal provision and safeguards in the Indian Constitution for the minority tribal and non-tribal languages, the forces of economic and social change, the patterns of industrially driven migration, the prospects of stable bilingualism and mother-tongue maintenance are bleak. As Dua (1986) observes:

> . . . while the spirit and content of the constitutional rights of the minorities has been upheld, the implementation of safeguards for use of minority languages in education and administration has been slow, and the agencies to implement the safeguards have been constrained by various factors. . . . the forces of change within the minority community and the society at large may be too strong for it as well as the government to effectively implement the constitutional safeguards and develop the minority languages for education, administration, and mass communication.

This is confirmed by the Annual Report of the Deputy Commissioner for Linguistic Minorities in regard to the tribal languages in Bihar, which remarks that

> in practice the state government has not taken any action to introduce Oraon, Ho, Santali and Mundari as media of instruction in areas where the speakers of these languages are in sizeable majority (1981-82).

Although the architects of the Indian Constitution tried to build a supposedly multilingual edifice which could offer the window of opportunity and equality to all linguist groups to maintain and develop their mother tongues alongside the regional and national dominant languages, they have unwittingly weakened its foundation by creating a list of privileged languages in the Eighth Schedule. Gupta and Abbi (1995) observe:

> It is our contention that rather than assuring any semblance of equality, the ES has succeeded only in creating new cleavages, new hierarchies and new conflicts. The ES has accorded differential status to Indian languages, and this discriminatory dispensation, in turn, has been reflected in differential institutional and societal support for and attitudes towards different languages within the polity. This in turn has given rise to cleavages such as majority-minority, dominant-subordinate, privileged-underprivileged.

Non-schedule languages, like Bhojpuri, Maithili, Magahi, Awadhi, Braj and other kin languages spoken in the states where Hindi is the language of administration and education, were legally absorbed under the superordinate label of HINDI in the 1961 Census. This raises the question whether such state and national policies, together with the rapid globalisation of the media and satellite television and the increasingly computer-driven urban ecology of India, are creating conditions for language endangerment.

In his appraisal of Indian languages from the point of view of endangerment Mahapatra (1991) said,

> ... the threatened languages of India are not on a similar footing. Some are dead, some others are dying and some are waiting to die. There is no single set of circumstances for these languages; they may become extinct by more than one means.

This grim picture of the endangered languages of India is not much dissimilar to that of the native North American, native Latin American and native Australian languages (generally referred to as aboriginal languages), and to that of other threatened languages in the world. The arrival of the Anglo-Saxons in Britain and the rising supremacy of English led to the decline of Celtic languages in the UK. Dolly Pentreath of Mousehole, the last person who spoke only Cornish, died in 1778.

Sociolinguists have often raised the question of the validity of the assumption that there is a necessary and sufficient cause-and-effect relationship between the death of a group and the last member of a speech community and the extinction of its language. 'For the death of a language, however, it would seem that an entire group of "hosts" must perish, either literally or by way of language shift' (Edwards 1994). Both numerical and demographic strengths have been claimed to be important contributory factors to the survival of a language. But the growth or decline in the population of individual language speakers is inextricably linked with the socioeconomic, political and educational policies of states or nations, which have not only colonised territories resulting in rootlessness, slavery, indenturement but have also engineered the colonisation of the minds of powerless and linguistically defranchised minorities.

Mahapatra (1991), highlighting the importance of the numerical and demographic strength of some of the languages banished to the dustbin of the 'non-scheduled' list in India, states that they do not only not demonstrate growth but actually register substantial losses (see Table 1). However, the major and privileged languages enshrined in the Eighth Schedule registered steady growth according to the 1981 Census. The decadal growth or decline figures should be studied with caution though because of the politically driven ways in which the Indian census often provides statistics.

The design of the questionnaire, the attitudes of the respondents, the belief and ideology of the researcher and the method of analysis could result in surface figures which may be divorced from reality: 'Shifts in declarations of mother-tongue from one language to another in successive censuses, seem to be a frequent feature among such speech groups in India' (Khubchandani 1983).

TABLE 1

LANGUAGE	LOSS
Halam	-10.57%
Hmar	-35.87%
Jatapu	-67.19%
Konda	-42.11%
Kuki	-21.83%
Lepcha	-02.41%
Mundari	-55.23%
Parji	-01.70%

The figures displaying language decline, nevertheless, should be a matter of concern. According to Mahapatra (1991), these are the endangered languages of India:

> Many of these languages are in immediate danger of extinction through their lack of demographic strength. To this group belongs the whole family of the Andaman islands. . . . Not only these languages, but the primitive Negrito tribes themselves who speak them are on the verge of extinction.

Another group often languages cited as 'endangered' are the Indo-Aryan languages – Bhojpuri, Maithili, Braj, Awadhi, Rajasthani, Pahari, and others spoken in the states in which Hindi is the official language and language of education and commerce. The fluidity and instability in respondents' reported choice of language labels in the census in these regions is vividly described by Mitra (1964).

> The big fish make bids to gobble up the small fish, that for some time some small fish feel content to stay inside the belly of a big fish, but at other moments they kick back and get out of the belies again; their strength diminished or increased for no apparent reason whatever.

However, there is no overwhelming empirical research evidence that suggests that the processes of language shift are affecting the Indo-Aryan minority language groups in the Hindi states in any significant way. Is Hindi, like the big fish, preying on them? In order to answer this question we will look at two case studies. The ethnographic sociolinguistic researches that are available, Simon (1986) and Jha (1994), suggest that the local indigenous mother tongues are fostering partnership bilingualism with Hindi in Varanasi and Darbhanga.

In her research into bilingualism and language maintenance in Banaras (Varanasi), Simon (1986) observes:

> Banarasi Boli, the speech variety that identifies the Banarasi community, has been maintained over a great many generations. This maintenance of a non-dominant language is in combination with a pervasive and stable bilingualism that community members do not find remarkable. Banarasi Boli as a speech variety identifies the community linguistically; the amount, stability, unremarkableness, and pervasiveness of Banarasi Boli/Hindi bilingualism identifies the community socially. . . . There are two lingua franca for economic interaction: Banarasi Boli and Hindi. Finally, public compulsory education is provided in Hindi. This has been a deciding factor in establishing the importance, continuance, and expansion, of Hindi in the Banarasi's sociolinguistic spectrum. . . . The result is not a loss of the local speech and replacement by the more prestigious and prominent Hindi, but rather a utilization of Hindi features to expand the language repertoire.

Simon's research is complemented by the emotional forecasts of Waseem (1995):

> Fortunately, however, Bhojpuri is not an 'endangered language' to depend on Government support for its survival. It is a growing language and the number of its speakers exceeds that of many privileged languages.

Jha's (1994) study of the Maithili speech community in Darbhanga confirms the complex and fluid situation that one finds in other similar Hindi – local kin language (Bhojpuri, Awadhi) – sociolinguistic contexts in India. His research findings suggest that in the settled community under focus there is plenty of evidence of both the impact of Hindi resulting in some degree of shift away from Maithili in certain domains, and of secure, dynamic societal and individual bilingualism. Jha (1994) concludes that

> the use of Maithili and Hindi which permeates the sociolinguistic setting of the speech community of Darbhanga does not lend itself to the idea that any of these languages is in imminent precarious situation.

The Maithili language movement in Bihar should be viewed more as an elite language awareness and language preservation movement than as a saviour of an endangered language. Pattanayak (1981) makes a general observation in regard to such pan-Indian language contact situations.

> In India the teaching of standard Hindi has not resulted in the loss of Bhojpuri, Maithili, Magahi, Braj and Rajasthani. Acceptance of Kannada by Tulu speakers and Marathi/Kannada by Konkani speakers as culture languages has not led to the assimilation of these languages.

However, it is not the teaching of a dominant regional language that results in the assimilation of numerically smaller languages. It is the exclusion of these languages from the school curriculum that is likely to lead to their decline. In their own natural environment, demographic strength and a strong cultural tradition have helped the smaller languages preserve their identity and create new bilingual identities. Once communities become uprooted in migrant transplanted situations they become victims to pressures to assimilate. It is in the 'migrant cities' – cosmopolitan, capital or industrial – that immigrant languages feel threatened as soon as they come in contact with the preying big fish – the dominant official language. A migrant language with no dense enclaves or islands to maintain and develop its heritage mother tongue in its new habitat begins to feel dehydrated and shows signs of language striation and death.

We have anecdotal information based on personal observation about the lack of motivation among the younger generation of the children of Bhojpuri-speaking parents to acquire competence in Bhojpuri language and its appropriate use in Patna and Delhi.

Pattanayak (1981) reports that some of the uprooted communities like the Sindhis and the Marathis settled in different parts of the country have lost their heritage mother tongues. In his study of the patterns of language use among a sample of undergraduate women students of the upper and middle classes in the Punjabi migrant community in Delhi, Pandit (1978) indicated the process of shift to Hindi:

> . . . when Hindi enters the domestic domain of a Punjabi speaker, it makes the beginning of the shift from Punjabi to Hindi as the 'mother-tongue': here the girls who used Hindi with their parents would wish their children to speak with them in Hindi.

Mukherjee (1981) showed how the Bengali and Punjabi refugee communities which migrated to Delhi in India after the partition reacted differently to the pressures from the host Hindi community. Although both the communities showed tendencies to shift and assimilate, the Bengalis maintained their language in greater degree than the Punjabis.

However, Satyanath's (1982) research into the patterns of language use among the migrant Kannadigas in Delhi showed that Hindi was intruding into the home domain. Lal's (1986) research also suggests that the Tamil-speaking Iyengar immigrant community settled in Bangalore are going through similar processes of heritage mother tongue change and shift. Kannada has become their dominant language, and may be characterised as their new mother tongue:

> The younger generation speaks Tamil very little and converse mostly in Kannada even with their parents in the family domain even though their parents speak to them in Tamil.

Among the non-scheduled minority languages in India are the languages of the *adivasis*, the original inhabitants of India, called the tribals. It is unfortunate that in the sociolinguistic hierarchy these *adivasis* have always been given the least educational, linguistic, and educational support. Even Chatterjee (1963) was not economical with his words in regard to some of these minority languages:

> Of the 179 'languages', so called, 116 are small tribal speeches belonging to the Sino-Tibetan speech family which are found in the north-central and north-eastern fringe of India, and these are generally without any numerical, political, commercial or cultural importance; and some two dozen more are either similar insignificant tribal dialects belonging to the other language groups (Dravidian and Austric), or are really languages not properly belonging to India, with wide plains making communication easy, it is these languages used by large civilized groups that matter.

The *adivasis* have had to go through periods of 'isolation' and linguistic and cultural exploitation in pre-colonial, colonial, and even in post-colonial India. But their political, linguistic, and cultural consciousness has been growing in independent India, and the Constitution does offer equal opportunities-based educational framework to a limited degree. However, the linguistic pressures of the major regional languages, which alone offer educational, occupational, and commercial opportunities, are so great that it is difficult to outwit linguistic assimilation completely.

There is plenty of evidence of variation in respect of language change and shift in the heterogeneous *adivasi* communities. In some parts the heritage language identity is preserved. Ishtiaque (1985) quoted in Khubchandani (1992), identifies this variation as areas of continuity (more than 75 per cent of the *adivasis* retaining their heritage language), the process of transition (between 25 and 75 per cent retention), and language shift (less than 25 per cent retention of the heritage languages). According to Khubchandani, 'average bilingualism claims among tribals run much higher than those of the dominant groups'.

Although the variationist picture is well established, it also refers to the communities in which language shift and language loss are becoming prominent.

> . . . many tribal groups in India, in the past have completely forsaken their languages. These are Bhil, Baiga, Bhuyan, Bhumji, and several branches of Malpharia, Lodha, and many others. (Mahapatra 1979)

> . . . a sizable number of Kuruxs (that is 565,526 out of a total, 1,600,345) have abandoned the Kurux language. There has been total lack of organised efforts for the maintenance of the Kurux language. There have been some efforts of the few educated Kuruxs who understand the value of maintaining their languages. (Ekka 1979)

Mohanty (1981) discusses the consequences of the Kui-speaking Konds majority tribal group in the Phulbani district of Orissa coming in contact with the Oriya-speaking Indo-Aryans. He suggests that in the North-East region tribals demonstrate a case of complete shift in favour of Oriya monolingualism, whereas in the areas south-west of Phulbani town the Kond tribals show an emerging stable form of Kui-Oriya bilingualism. However, Mohanty does not conclude that the language shift in one part of the population could be a precursor of language endangerment, which might slowly trigger complete language shift in the Kond community.

Annamalai (1990) too confirms this tendency of language shift among some tribal communities and of unstable bilingualism among others. He quotes Itagi *et al.* (1966), and says that 43 per cent of the tribals have reported a non-tribal language as their mother tongue:

> While the tribes number 29.9 millions people in 1961, there are only 12.8 million tribal mother tongue speakers (51.6 million and 19.3 millions respectively in 1981). This means that nearly half of the tribals have shifted their mother tongue.

Annamalai warns indirectly that this shift could lead to *language death* although interestingly he does not use this metaphor.

A recent analysis of the 1991 Census confirms the consequences of this threat. 'Due to linguistic and social pressures, some communities like Johar in Uttar Pradesh, along with Andro and Chairel of Manipur, have lost their mother tongues' (*Limca Book of Records* 1996). Although Article 350A of the Constitution has provided the right to education in the mother tongue at the primary stage for linguistic minority groups, in reality the majority privileged group has lacked the vision and socio-economic and political will to implement this provision.

> In Bihar textbooks are prepared in Santali, Kurukh, Mundari, Ho, Kharia but the state authorities have not shown great enthusiasm as far as its implementation is concerned. Madhya Pradesh Tribal Research Bureau also initiated a few textbooks in Gondi, Bhili, Korku, Halabi, but the implementation in school education is somewhat staggered. (Khubchandani 1992)

> The majority communities want to impose their own dominant languages for the region (e.g., Hindi in Bihar, Oriya in Orissa etc.), and in this attempt at detribalization expect the Santhals to give up their tribal traits. (Sridhar 1996)

A wide variety of sociolinguistic research in many parts of the world has highlighted the problems associated with majority-minority relationship. Laver and Roukens (1996) discussing the situation in Europe concluded:

> . . . the survival of smaller languages, with their associated cultures, depends on a complex of factors amongst which the relationship with larger, competitor languages is primary.

In *adivasi* areas where the missionaries have had the opportunity to introduce or impose English the mother tongue-English bilingualism has not had long-term stability. As Pattanayak (1992) remarks:

> To attempt to impose an ex-colonial language in place of a variety of mother tongues or regional languages is another way of declaring those mother tongues or languages irrelevant. For example, when English is imposed in Nagaland to meet the problems arising out of the twenty two mutually unintelligible Naga languages spoken in the state, all the Naga languages are marginalised and move towards decay. . . . In India, besides languages listed in the Eighth Schedule, languages of newly formed states such as Manipuri, Khasi and Konkani and languages recognised by the Sahitya Akademi, all the other languages are disabled.

Irrespective of whether it is English or a dominant state language, the pressure to assimilate to the language of power and jobs is evident in many tribal speech communities. Ekka (1986) remarks that

> the political status and functional value of the majority language in the states

> have exerted enormous socio-psychological pressure on the tribal communities to be proficient in the majority language to gain occupational mobility and educational advancement.

Let us now turn our attention to the sociolinguistics of the mother tongue of the transplanted Indian speech communities whose ancestors had to leave their homeland and their larger speech community more than a century ago. The case of the Romani people who travelled to and settled in various parts of Europe in the fifteenth and sixteenth centuries is very interesting. We shall discuss here the case of the British Romanis who have maintained their distinct life-style as travelling nomads, staying largely outside the mainstream of society. The questions often asked are:

- Have the descendants of these Roma people lost their mother tongue, that is, is it a case of language death and shift to English monolingualism?
- Have these Roma people successfully resisted the death of their heritage mother tongue, but succumbed to language change as a result of contact with a dominant language or languages, and become native speakers of English also?

Hancock (1991) has pointed out that this ethnic group has been religiously protecting its identity by insulating itself from the cultural impact of the dominant cultural group, by preserving and transmitting their beliefs and rituals across generations. Due to contact with other Romas in Europe, their ancestors-inflected Romani language gradually fell into disuse, but they did not shift to English monolingualism although English did become their first language. 'It is English which is the language learnt first in life, and which is the native language of the population' (Hancock 1991).

This shift to English did not however result in the death of Romani as such. Romani changed and evolved, and the old ethnic language was replaced by a new ethnic language, referred to as Angloromani. Angloromani is not the first language acquired. It is acquired by nine- or ten-year-old children, particularly the boys when they begin to work alongside their parents. It is used in limited domains, and is more part of the repertoire of the travelling Romas than of the settled population. The specific domains in which the use of Angloromani is more popular are weddings, funerals and horse-fairs. The linguistic structure of Angloromani is characterised more by a small set of specialist lexical items of Romani origin than by grammatical features. Thomason and Kaufman (1988) observed:

> Angloromani is a mixed speech form; the group's original language was not ultimately passed on as a coherent set of interrelated, lexical and grammatical structures. Currently, Angloromani is the product of two entirely distinct historical processes; inherited vocabulary, borrowed grammar.

Thomason and Kaufman (1988) point out that what distinguishes Angloromani from a case of language death is that unlike others in language contact situations, it is not grammatically impoverished. They ask a fundamental question and try to answer it:

> Why did Angloromani speakers replace the vanishing Romani structures with English ones, while speakers of other threatened languages replaced their vanishing grammars with nothing, so that what was left of their original language was no longer stylistically and grammatically rich enough to be used for most purposes? The answer seems clear: Angloromani continued to serve important communicative functions, and for those functions it needed adequate structural resources. This answer does not, of course, explain the differences; it merely shifts the forms of the puzzle.

Most sociolinguistic research in the area of the speech of the terminal speakers of a language, and in speech events in all the cases of language death has demonstrated that heritage language mother-tongue speakers of a dying language threatened by an economically and politically more powerful language do not display uniform patterns of language behaviour. In her research into the Gaelic semi-speakers' linguistic competence, Dorian (1981) found an asymmetrical relationship between their productive and passive competence in the Gaelic language. Tsitsipis (1989), on the other hand, found the Aranitika terminal speakers exhibiting a greater symmetry than the semi-speakers of Gaelic. Le Page and Tabouret-Keller (1985) in their extensive research into Creole contact languages also concluded:

> . . . no theory should blind us to the fact that all linguistic performance is mediated by socially and psychologically constrained choices by which possible forms are selected to be matched with possible meanings in actual contexts; and that we can never predict with certainty, even in the most homogeneous society, what systems will emerge in the process.

It will be interesting to look at two texts representing two situations in which transplanted South Asian languages have developed their own ethnic identity by creating and improvising new speech acts, and thus forestalling language death.

Following is an Angloromani text quoted in Hancock (1991):

(1) Mandi rokers to the diri *Devel* in Romanis, because I *jin* that Lesti jins duva *jib*. Foki akai vader at mandi like mandi's divia when they *shun* mandi roker. There is only one gera akai that jins it. Tuti, bicher mandi a lil when you sas the cherus, mandi is leling *sutious* and it is late in the *rati*. This buti that mandi is *kering* makes mandi to lel sutious during the *dives*. [italics mine]

In this short text the Indo-Aryan cognates have retained their appropriate use and meaning. *Divia* and *Dev, Devtaa* 'God'; *jin* and *jaannaa* 'to know'; *jnaan* 'knowledge'; *jib* and *jiib, jiibh* 'tongue'; *shun* and *sunnaa* 'to listen to, to hear'; *tuti* and *tuu, tum* 'you'; *suti(ous)* and *sunnaa* 'to sleep'; *ker(ing)* and *karnaa* 'to do'; *dives* and *divas* 'day' are the shared lexical items. This text has enough inherited heritage vocabulary to make it totally incomprehensible to a monolingual English speaker, who would, however, recognise the grammatical structure, and to monolingual Punjabi and Hindi speakers, who would recognise the heritage vocabulary. Bickerton (1988, quoted in Hancock 1991) observes:

> So far, the only attested cases of relexification, the Media Lingua and Angloromani, have occurred when the speakers concerned already had a language which linguistically, if not socially, was perfectly adequate for this communicative purpose (Quechua, Romani). There thus seem to be good sociolinguistic grounds for assuming that relexification . . . only occurs when a new language is invented for social-boundary marking or similar purposes.

In the Roma case Angloromani serves as an ethnic, secret language which has certain advantages. Wurm (1991) reports that some 'doomed' Australian aboriginal languages had similar functions as secret languages:

> This ability to derive advantages from being able to speak a language which their oppressors do not understand, serves also as a strong booster of the self-esteem of peoples who find themselves otherwise in an inferior position. Welsh and Gaelic have been used in Britain in similar roles, as have many other languages of people who find themselves in a losing cultural battle threatening their languages with extinction.

In language contact between languages belonging to two different families (Kannada/Dravidian and Marathi/Indo-Aryan) the bilinguals' strategy is to operate in these two languages with a single grammar. It reflects an emerging new identity, and is perhaps their strategy to combat language endangerment, assimilation and death. In most such situations new codes, new dialects and varieties continue to evolve for the projection of minority identity.

The second text consists of short extracts from Agnihotri's (1987) study of the speech acts of the transplanted Sikh community settled in Leeds:

(2)

panj	*pra:*	*te*	*tu:*	sister	*te*	mother
five	brothers	and	two	sisters	and	mother

de	*du:*	*cakkar*	round	*da*	*bi:d*
they	do	rounds	round	the	holy book

sa:re	*jane*	*otthe*	*olukan*	*si:iz*	red
all	people	there	all you can	see is	red

waef-nu	*leke*	*te*	*jelo*	*pags*	*paidija:*
wife-ACC	having taken	and	yellow	turbans	wear

Commenting on this sample of the young Sikh children's discourse in the 'mixed code' within the family and the community, Agnihotri (1987) observes:

> The mixed code is a kind of instant pidgin which reflects the linguistic creativity and dynamism of these children as much as their social and linguistic experience and environment. This is the speech of children who are creating their norms and roles of behaviour out of a state flux.

Both Angloromani and the 'mixed code' are strategies of insulating themselves from the dominant linguistic community and of projecting their ethnic identity. Occasionally this could be a strategy adopted by the older generation to exclude children and outsiders. As Mesthrie (1988) reports: in the South African Indian community of Awadhi-Bhojpuri (AB) descent a switch may be motivated by the 'desire to conceal information from non-AB speaking outsiders or from children'. But these could also be illustrative of the characteristic of a threatened or dying language.

In the transplanted communities whose ancestors were indentured largely from the Hindi-speaking states in India to the West Indies, Fiji, and the Mauritius islands the heritage mother tongues of the third and younger generations have been in a state of flux. They have been undergoing change, decline, shift, and revival in an environment of Creole, English and/or French, Bhojpuri and Hindi in constant conflict and rivalry. Bhatia (1997), researching into language and ethnicity in Trinidad, said,

> TH stands at a critical juncture. It is clear that TH as spoken by the first generation is a dying dialect. This gap is quickly being filled by an indigenous variety of SH. Modern media, particularly Hindi films, have stimulated and continue to stimulate the process of dialect/language shift. [TH stands for Trinidad Hindi and SH stands for Standard Hindi.]

A long period of extraordinary attempt at colonial social and linguistic engineering of people from the Indian subcontinent by transplanting them in an alien milieu where they, as slaves and indentured labourers, were forbidden from speaking their mother tongues has resulted in linguistic creativity on the one hand and decay and death of heritage languages on the other. Contemporary attempts in the post-colonial periods to revitalise and resuscitate the language of heritage and identity is also taking place in an environment of political and economic conflicts and rivalry aided by the globalisation of English and other dominant European languages. The prognosis for the future of these Indian languages is far from optimistic. Barz (1988) in his assessment of the viability of overseas Hindi (OH) said, '. . . it can not be predicted with confidence that any of the six varieties of OH will still be spoken a hundred years from now'.

To conclude, the 'minor' and 'minority' languages of India are at the crossroads, both at home and abroad. The institutional hierarchisation and discrimination, the economic disadvantages and the satellite and cable cultural neo-colonisation via English at home is beginning to weaken Pandit's (1978) characterisation of the Indian sociolinguistic scene as one where multilingualism was the norm, monolingualism an exception. The choice of a language other than the mother tongue for initial and academic literacy is also likely to have a long-term disempowering and disabling influence on the minority mother tongues. Pattanayak (1992) said:

> In India, besides languages listed in the Eighth Schedule, languages of newly formed states such as Manipuri, Khasi and Konkani and languages recognised by the Sahitya Akademi, all the other languages are disabled. With the demand for universal literacy, most of the spoken languages face extinction. Universal literacy means offering literacy in the scripts of literate languages and by extension in literate languages themselves.

This issue of endangerment is also carried across the world where transplanted Indian speech communities are struggling to preserve or revive their heritage languages in a climate of monolingualism or multilingualism. This climate excludes these languages because they are not *bhumi bhashas*, they are the mother tongues of the first-generation immigrants, who were not *bhumi putras* of the Western world or other ex-colonies. The current Western interest in the 'dying' languages of the *adivasis* of the ex-colonised nations of the world, and in bio-diversity does not include the transplanted languages on their agenda. The debate about what some of the sociolinguists in the Western world mean by language endangerment and what it means to the transplanted communities themselves is a real one, and one that should be addressed with the same vigorous research as any other.

Language and communities are inseparable, and as a consequence language death and community death have in the past been the common victim of colonial or neo-colonial policies. This fact is well attested by the experiences of the native Americans and the native Australians. At a meeting of the Indian Conference of Indigenous and Tribal People held in Calcutta it was reported that 'more than 10 small tribes in West Bengal, Bihar and Orissa face extinction with their population decreasing at an alarming rate' (*Asian Age* 21 March 1997). According to the Anthropological Survey of India's The People of India Project on the Andaman and Nicobar Islands, 'the Great Andamanese, Shompen and Onge of the Andaman and Nicobar islands are the most endangered communities today' (*Limca Book of Records* 1996).

A language that loses its speakers is virtually orphaned, and the efforts of linguists in recent years to record the speech of the last speakers for research, however important it may be, is of no comfort to the disappearing community. As Wurm (1991) remarks:

> For linguists of some common persuasions holding sway in the latter part of the twentieth century, the main subject of interest has been either the purely structural side of a language, or a language as one of the many surface forms of an underlying deep structure of human language as a whole. For them, the death of a particular language is not of the same importance: they are less concerned with the function of language as the means of expression of the world-view, philosophy and system of thought of its speakers and of a speech community, and with questions of the roles and the setting of a language within the culture and society of its speakers.

The role and responsibility of the linguist in the Indian context is becoming ever more important in the context of the imminent impact of the neo-colonial voices from the sky on the speech and culture not only of the poor, uneducated and marginalised but even of the young generation from the aspiring and ambitious middle classes. Satellite television broadcast is already contributing to the increase in Macaulay's (1835) numerous urban progeny who monopolise the computer-driven, hi-tech job market. Even a decade earlier than the arrival of the cable and the satellite dish in India, Mohan (1984) quite appropriately remarked:

> The story repeats itself, sadly. Hindi, Bengali, Tamil, the menials in the real contest, literary languages but not languages of science and technology, with the ultimate aggressor, English, cosily settled among us with its tiny, tiny share of the action: the hearts and minds of the Indian ruling class, and almost all of science, technology, and the higher levels of administration. The rest of India is safe, but marginalised in the process.

REFERENCES

AGNIHOTRI, R.K.

1987 *Crisis of identity: The Sikhs in England.* New Delhi: Bahri.

ANNAMALAI, E.

1990 Linguistic dominance and cultural dominance: A study of tribal bilingualism in India. In *Multilingualism in India. Multilingual Matters.* Clevedon.

ASIAN AGE

1997 21 March.

BARZ, R.

1988 Language maintenance and literary use: The case of Mauritian Bhojpuri, Sarnami and Fiji Hindi. In R. Barz & J. Siegel (eds.), *Language transplanted: The development of overseas Hindi.* Wiesbaden, Otto Harrassowitz.

BHATIA, T.K.

1997 Language and ethnicity in Trinidad: Linguistic attitudes and attrition. Paper read at the XVIII SALA Round Table, 1997. New Delhi: Jawaharlal Nehru University.

BICKERTON, D.

1988 Relexification. *The Journal of Pidgin and Creole Languages* 3.2.

CHATTERJEE, S.K.

1963 *Language and literature of India.* Calcutta: Bengali Publishers Pvt. Ltd.

DORIAN, NANCY

1981 *Language death: The life cycle of a Scottish Gaelic dialect.* Philadelphia: University of Pennsylvania Press.

DUA, H.

1986 Language planning and linguistic minorities. In Annamalai, *et al.* (eds.), *Language planning: Proceedings of an institute.* Mysore: Central Institute of Indian Languages.

EDWARDS, J.

1994 *Multilingualism.* London: Routledge.

EKKA, F.

1979 Language loyalty and maintenance among the Kuruxs. In Annamalai (ed.), 1990.

1986 Tribal languages and problems in Hindi translation. In M.G. Chaturvedi & K.K. Goswami (eds.), *Anuvad: Vividh Aayaam.* Agra: Central Hindi Institute.

EMENEAU, M.B.

1962 Bilingualism and structural borrowings. In *Proceedings of the American Philosophical Society.* 106 (5).

GUPTA, R.S. and A. ABBI

1995 Introduction. In Gupta *et al.* (eds.), *Language and the state.* New Delhi: Creative Books.

HANCOCK, I.

1991 The Romani speech community. In S. Alladina & V. Edwards (eds.), *Multilingualism in the British Isles.* London: Longman.

ISHTIAQUE

1985 Language shift among the tribal communities: A case study of Santals, Mundas and Oraons in Bihar. *The Geographer,* vol. 32. 69–78.

ITAGI, N.H. *et al.* (eds.)

1966 *Communication potential in the tribal population of Assam and Madhya Pradesh.* Mysore: Central Institute of Indian Languages.

JHA, S.N.

1994 *Language maintenance and bilingualism in Darbhanga.* Unpublished D.Phil. thesis. York: University of York.

KHUBCHANDANI, L.

1983 *Plural languages, plural cultures: Communication, identity and sociopolitical change in contemporary India.* University of Hawaii Press.

1992 *Tribal identity.* Shimla: Indian Institute of Advanced Study.

LAL, S.M.

1986 *Convergence and language shift in linguistic minorities.* Mysore: Central Institute of Indian Languages.

LAVER, J. and J. ROUKENS

1996 The global information society and Europe's linguistic and cultural heritage. In C. Hoffmann (ed.), *Language, culture and communication in contemporary Europe. Multilingual Matters.* Clevedon.

LE PAGE and A. TABOURET-KELLER

1985 *Acts of identity.* Cambridge: Cambridge University Press.

LIMCA BOOK OF RECORDS

1996

MACAULAY, T.B.

1835 *Minutes on Indian education in prose and poetry.* Selected by G.M. Young. Cambridge, Mass.: Harvard University Press. 1967.

MAHAPATRA, B.P.

1979 Santali language movement in the context of many dominant languages. In Annamalai (ed.), *Language movements in India.* Mysore: Central Institute of Indian Languages.

1991 An appraisal of Indian languages. In R.H. Robins & E.M. Uhlenbeck (eds.), *Endangered languages.* Oxford: BERG.

MESTHRIE, R.

1988 Toward a lexicon of South African Indian English. *World Englishes.* Vol. 7. 5–14.

MITRA, A.

1964 *Census of India 1961.* Vol. 1.

MOHAN, P.

1984 Two faces of a language. *India International Centre Quarterly*, 11.2. 133–44.

MOHANTY, A.K.

1981 Psychological consequences of mother tongue maintenance and multilingualism in India. In D.P. Pattanayak (ed.), *Multilingualism in India.* New Delhi: Oxford University Press.

MUKHERJEE, A.

1980 *Language maintenance and shift among Punjabis and Bengalis in Delhi:*
1981 *A sociolinguistic perspective.* Ph.D. thesis, University of Delhi.

PANDIT, P.B.

1978 Language and identity: The Punjabi language in Delhi. *IJSL* 16.

PATTANAYAK, D.P.

1981 *Multilingualism and mother-tongue education.* New Delhi: Oxford University Press.

1992 Decay and destruction of Indian languages. *Bhartiya Samajik Chintan,* vol. XV, no. 1–4, March–December.

SATYANATH, T.S.
1982 *Kannadigas in Delhi: A sociolinguistic study*. Unpublished M.Phil. thesis, University of Delhi.

SIMON, B.L.
1986 *Bilingualism and language maintenance in Banaras*. Ph.D. dissertation, University of Wisconsin-Madison.

SRIDHAR, KAMAL K.
1996 Language in education: Minorities and multilingualism in India. *International Review of Education*, vol. 42. 4.

THOMASON, S.G. and T. KAUFMAN
1988 *Language contact, creolization and genetic linguistics*. Berkeley: California University Press.

TSITSIPIS
1989 Skewed performance and full performance in language obsolescence: The case of an Albanian variety. In N. Dorian (ed.), *Investigating obsolescence*. Cambridge: Cambridge University Press.

WASEEM, M.
1995 Language and the state. In R.S. Gupta *et al.* (eds.), *Language and the state*. New Delhi: Creative Books.

WURM
1991 Language death and disappearance. In R.H. Robins & E.M. Uhlenbeck (eds.), *Endangered languages*. Oxford: BERG.

2

Dravidian languages in Fiji: Survival and maintenance

FRANCE MUGLER
University of the South Pacific

About a quarter of the indentured labourers recruited in India between 1879 and 1916 to work on plantations in Fiji came from South India. Most were speakers of Tamil, Telugu or Malayalam, and these languages are still spoken today, albeit by small numbers of Indo-Fijians. Dravidian languages in Fiji have been under great stress from the very beginning; South Indians only started arriving about 25 years after their fellow immigrants from North India, and they have always been a minority among Fiji Indians. On plantations a variety of Hindi soon became the lingua franca, and this 'Fiji Hindi' was well estab-

My thanks go to the informants, who gave generously of their time, to the interviewers, my colleague Veena Khan and students Urmila Chandra, Nirwani Devi, Rukeshma Lata, Vasu Deo Maharaj, Mohammed Taufil Omar, Anita Prasad, Geeta Prasad, Ruven Prasad, Chandra Rao and Estha Sami, to my colleague Jan Tent, and my collaborators in India, Sam Mohan Lal, V. Saratchandran Nair and G. Vijayasarathi. Data gathering for the survey and recorded language samples was made possible by two research grants from the University of the South Pacific (USP), and the analysis of recorded data was carried out from September to December 1994 while I was on study leave from USP and affiliated to the Central Institute of Indian Languages (CIIL) in Mysore, India. I gratefully acknowledge the support of both institutions. Thanks also to Rekha Sharma, Sudhir Mathur, O.N. Kaul, N. Nadaraja Pillai, Uma Rani for their comments and interest, and Rajeshwari IIS for computer assistance. I am particularly grateful to L. Annamalai, the then Director of CIIL, for his comments and his support.

lished by the time South Indians started arriving. It is likely, then, that language shift started early, and today nearly all descendants of South Indians have Fiji Hindi as their first language. Even among the older generation who may have retained the language of their ancestors, competence in Fiji Hindi is almost invariably higher than in that Dravidian language.

This paper reports on the results of a 1993 survey of language use and attitudes among descendants of South Indians in Fiji which documents the continuing erosion of all three Dravidian languages. It also examines efforts at language maintenance, essentially conducted by one South Indian organisation and centring on the teaching of Dravidian languages as subjects in Sangam schools. An evaluation of the effectiveness of these maintenance efforts by their own advocates is reported, and the chances of survival of Dravidian languages in Fiji are assessed. The results of the survey and an analysis of current maintenance efforts indicate that, if sociolinguistic conditions and maintenance measures remain the same, Malayalam and Telugu are in danger of disappearing from Fiji in the next generation or two, while Tamil, which has more speakers, is also threatened in the medium term.

DRAVIDIAN LANGUAGES IN FIJI: HISTORICAL BACKGROUND

According to current estimates of the 1996 Census, approximately 335,000 out of a total population of a little over 770,000 or 43.6 per cent of the population of Fiji are of Indian descent (*Statistical News 1997*: 2–3). Nearly all Indo-Fijians are descendants of some 60,000 labourers brought by the British colonial administration between 1879 and 1916 under the indenture system to work, mostly, on sugarcane plantations.[1] During the first 24 years of indenture, *grimitiyas*[2] were recruited from North India through the port of Calcutta, but in 1903 the colonial government started to recruit in the South as well, through Madras. Overall, South Indians accounted for nearly a quarter of all indentured labourers brought to Fiji (Gillion 1962: 209; Siegel 1987: 135).[3]

In the beginning: indenture

Most of the South Indian labourers who came to Fiji between 1903 and 1916 spoke one of the four major Dravidian languages: Tamil, Telugu, Malayalam or Kannada, although there were also some speakers of Marathi and Hindustani (Gillion 1962: 51; 1977: 110). According to Gillion (1962: 51, 204) most were recruited in the districts of North Arcot, Madras, Thanjavur, Coimbatore (in what is now Tamil Nadu), Krishna, Godavari, Visakhapatnam (Andhra Pradesh), and Malabar (Kerala). Most of those recruited in Madras district came from neighbouring districts, especially North Arcot and Chengleput, and the two districts of North Arcot and Madras contributed more than half the emigrants every year from 1903 to 1916, except for 1911 to 1913 (Gillion 1962: 51, 204). Unfortunately, the language of the indentured labourers was indicated only for the first year of recruitment from Madras, 1903 (see Table 1).

TABLE 1 *Languages of the 589 Madras-embarked emigrants, 1903*

LANGUAGE	NUMBER	PERCENTAGE
Telugu	318	54.0
Tamil	164	27.8
Kannada	32	5.4
Malayalam	17	2.9
Marathi	33	5.6
Hindustani	25	4.2

SOURCE: Siegel 1987: 145.

Siegel (1987: 146) cautions that the statistics for 1903 are not representative of the entire period of South Indian migration to Fiji, since more Tamil than Telugu speakers were recruited later on. He also points out that the migrants' district of origin is not a reliable guide to their language: North Arcot contributed not only speakers of Tamil but also of Telugu and Hindustani, while Bellary (in what is now Karnataka) contributed more speakers of Marathi than of Kannada. It also appears that only one language was recorded on the registration pass, while some migrants may well have known several languages. Tamil speakers were in the majority (Gillion 1962: 51).

By the time South Indians arrived – nearly a quarter of a century after their northern counterparts – a koinê based on Hindi (now known as *Fiji baat* or Fiji Hindi) had become well established as the lingua franca on plantations (Gillion 1962: 128). Although some arrangements were made to have Tamil and Telugu speaking *sardars* and interpreters, there was a tacit policy of favouring Fiji Hindi at the expense of Dravidian languages (Siegel 1987: 160–2). Another important factor is that South Indians were a minority among Indians from the start and it is likely that Dravidian languages suffered an immediate and drastic shrinking of domains and soon became reduced to what Pillai calls 'domestic languages' (1971: 3).

The 1956 and 1966 Censuses

If the historical record of indenture leaves questions unanswered about the precise geographical origins of South Indian labourers and their languages, more recent documents have similar limitations. Fiji censuses, conducted at ten-year intervals (from 1881 to 1921 and again since 1936), contain no information about language, with the exception of the 1956 and 1966 Censuses. Neither do censuses provide a breakdown of Indo-Fijians according to their ancestors' regional origin in India, so that even estimates of individuals of South Indian descent are not available (Mayer 1973: 145). The information on language in the 1956 and 1966 Censuses has been analysed by Siegel (1973: 7; 1975: 128). Table 2 displays the figures for Dravidian languages.

TABLE 2 *Home languages of Indo-Fijians 1956 and 1966 (number of households)*

LANGUAGE	1956	1966	%AGE OF CHANGE
Tamil	1,498	999	–33.3
Telugu	797	301	–62.2
Malayalam	134	47	–64.9
TOTAL	2,429	1,347	–44.5

SOURCE: Adapted from Siegel 1975: 128.

A comparison of the figures from the two censuses clearly indicates a serious loss for each of the three Dravidian languages listed in Table 2. But a number of questions arise. In both censuses, the question asked was: 'What language do the members of this household speak amongst themselves?' Nine alternatives were listed: eight names of Indian languages, and a category labelled 'Other' (*Report on the census of the population* 1958: 52; 1968: 91). Kannada, spoken by some of the original indentured labourers, does not appear in the tabulated results. It is possible that by 1956 there were already no longer any speakers of Kannada in Fiji. However, the census results cannot be interpreted as proof of this demise, since Kannada was not among the nine alternatives in the census schedule and any Kannada-speaking household would therefore have been classified under 'Other'.

Another problem is that only the most commonly used language was supposed to be recorded by enumerators. Many 1956 schedules were returned with more than one alternative marked, but in such cases only the first was recorded (*Report on the census of the population* 1958: 52).[4] If a household included speakers of more than one (Dravidian/Indian) language, this was not taken into account, so that the use of Dravidian languages is likely to have been under-reported. Curiously, for 183 households in 1956 and 3 in 1966, the answer to the question was recorded as 'not stated'.

Finally, it is difficult to deduce the number of individual speakers of a given Dravidian language from the census figures, as these are based on households where the language is spoken. As Mayer (1973: 145) observes, the 1956 figures indicate a proportion of households where a Dravidian language is spoken as only about 10 per cent of the total of Indo-Fijian households, while the proportion of South Indians and descendants of South Indians would presumably still have been around 25 per cent, as it was at the end of indenture. Mayer concludes that it is 'by no means certain that Southern languages were spoken in all households of the Southern cultural group'. In spite of the limited data available and the difficulties of interpretation, the erosion of Dravidian languages in Fiji is clear.

Geographical distribution

Indian labourers in Fiji worked, then settled, mostly in what is called the sugarcane belt, along the western side of the main island of Viti Levu and in the north of the second largest island, Vanua Levu, in and around the town of Labasa. The sugarcane belt has continued to have the highest concentrations of Indo-Fijians, including of descendants of South Indians. The geographical location of households that reported a Dravidian language in the 1966 Census is reproduced province-wise in Table 3.

DRAVIDIAN LANGUAGES IN FIJI TODAY

The 1993 survey

In 1993 a survey of language use and attitude of nearly 500 descendants of South Indians was conducted by the author in the sugarcane belt, on the Western side of Viti Levu and in and around Labasa, on Vanua Levu. Interviewers administered questionnaires to a sample of the population stratified by geographical region (with equal numbers of respondents from Viti Levu and from Vanua Levu), area of residence (with one-third urban dwellers and two-third rural dwellers, which reflects national proportions), sex (with equal numbers of men and women) and age (with three groups: 15–25 years old, 30–45 and +50).

The questionnaires were administered by a team of ten linguistics students and one lecturer from the University of the South Pacific. The interviewers were themselves descendants of South Indians or had close relatives who were South Indians. They worked in their home area, so that they belonged to some of the same social networks as the respondents. With interviewers and interviewees as members of the same community, the initial approach was natural, the consent of respondents was facilitated, and the reliability of the responses was probably enhanced. Initial contact was made in Fiji Hindi and, once they agreed to be interviewed, respondents were given the choice of answering the questionnaire, verbally, in Fiji Hindi or in English.

TABLE 3 *Dravidian language-reporting households by province, 1966*

PROVINCE	TAMIL	TELUGU	MALAYALAM	TOTAL
Ba	573	148	24	745
Ra	149	102	5	256
Nadroga/ Navosa	181	21	7	209
Suva City	42	8	6	56
Macuata	20	15		35
Cakaudrove	11	6	1	18
Naitasiri	10		4	14
Tailevu	7		7	
Lomaiviti	3	1	4	
Serua	2		2	
Rewa (excl. Suva City)	1	1		
TOTAL	999	301	47	1,347

NOTE: No Dravidian-language-reporting households were recorded in Kadavu, Lau, Namosi or Rotuma.

SOURCE: Based on *Report on the census of the population 1966* (1968: 240).

The questionnaire, whose main goal was to document any language shift away from Dravidian languages, included over 200 questions on language use and attitudes. Results dealing with three broad areas are presented here: the extent of the respondents' knowledge of Dravidian languages, the extent of use in different domains, and attitudes towards Dravidian languages.

KNOWLEDGE OF DRAVIDIAN LANGUAGES

In the first series of questions each respondent was asked 'Do you speak [Tamil/Telugu/Malayalam/Kannada]?' Overall, 40 per cent of the 480 respondents surveyed report speaking one Dravidian language, and 8 per cent more than one. For each language, the proportions of positive responses are: about 33 per cent for Tamil, a little over 10 per cent for Telugu, and around 5 per cent for Malayalam.[5] But the figures for the next series of questions: 'Is [Tamil, etc.] spoken in your house?' are lower for each of the three languages

(Table 4). This means that there are a number of people who, although they can speak, say Malayalam, do not use it at home, probably because no one else in the household speaks it. This presence of speakers who are merely latent, or potential, is one sign of language attrition.

Respondents were asked to rate their own competence in speaking and understanding the Dravidian language of their ancestors along a five-point scale. The questions were 'How good are you at speaking [____]?' and 'How good are you at understanding [____]?', with what they had previously identified as the particular Dravidian language of their ancestors in the bracket slot. The five alternatives were *'very good', 'good', 'fair', 'poor'* and *'not able to'*.

TABLE 4 *Do you speak ____? versus Is ____ spoken in your house?*

LANGUAGE	ABILITY TO SPEAK	SPOKEN AT HOME
Tamil	34	32.4
Telugu	11.4	7.9
Malayalam	4.6	2.5

First, these figures indicate a higher percentage of speakers than do the results in the first set of questions, in which respondents could only answer 'Yes [I do speak ____]' or 'No'. So some of the respondents who answered negatively to 'Do you speak Telugu?' (for instance) went on to 'admit' that they spoke the language, albeit poorly – rather than not at all. The different results are explained, then, by the different phrasing of each set of questions. Overall, more than half the respondents (51.4 per cent) report 'not able to' speak the Dravidian language of their ancestors, while more than a third (35.8 per cent) cannot even understand it. The difference between these two figures is also an indication of attrition, since it means that a number of respondents have only a passive knowledge of the language, and are thus able neither to use it themselves nor to pass it on to their children. Answers to these two questions are coded in such a way that a high score reflects a high self-evaluation of competence:

VERY GOOD 4 GOOD 3 FAIR 2 POOR 1 NOT ABLE TO 0

The correlation between the responses to these two questions and the respondents' age is highly significant and an unmistakable sign of continuing attrition: the older the respondents, the higher their self-evaluation of competence in speaking a Dravidian language (Table 5) or in understanding it (Table 6).

The most striking evidence of continuing loss of speakers by all three Dravidian languages can be seen in a trinomial regression based on figures for reported knowledge of a Dravidian language for four age cohorts (which cannot be reproduced here because of constraints on reproduction): the three age groups interviewed, and the parents of the older group (+50), since all respondents were also asked whether their parents (and grandparents) spoke their ancestral language. From responses relating to the knowledge of Dravidian languages among descendants of South India, we turn to their answers to questions about their actual use of these languages.

TABLE 5 *Self-evaluation of competence and age: speaking*

AGE GROUP	NO. OF CASES	MEAN RANK
15–25	163	162.2
30–45	154	223.0
+50	163	335.3

(Kruskal-Wallis: H corrected for ties: 152.3, DF = 2, p =0.0001)

TABLE 6 *Self-evaluation of competence and age: understanding*

AGE GROUP	NO. OF CASES	MEAN RANK
15–25	163	158.7
30–45	154	224.5
+50	163	338.0

(Kruskal-Wallis: H corrected for ties: 152.3, DF =2, p = 0.0001)

LANGUAGE USE

The questionnaire included many questions about language use in different domains, with different interlocutors, and about different topics. Given the historical background of Dravidian languages in Fiji and the continuing attrition demonstrated in the previous section, one would expect the highest reported incidence of use of these languages to be at home, the most private of all domains. Percentages of language use at home with different interlocutors are displayed in Table 7.

Figures of use of Dravidian languages are very low, varying from less than 3 per cent to about 15 per cent, depending on the interlocutor. The importance of age is again manifest, with the respondent more likely to use a Dravidian language with parents, then spouse and siblings, than with children. Friends, of course, may not all be descendants of South Indians – or Indo-Fijians at all, for that matter – so that the low use of Dravidian languages in that category is understandable. It is striking, though, that it is only marginally lower than their use to children. Fiji Hindi overwhelmingly predominates, and it is clear from these figures that the Dravidian languages' loss has been Fiji Hindi's gain. In fact, the figures for Dravidian languages and Fiji Hindi are a mirror image of each other, and the use of English is negligible.

TABLE 7 *Language use at home with different interlocutors*

LANGUAGE	PARENTS	SPOUSE	SIBLINGS	RELATIVES	CHILDREN	FRIENDS
Dravidian	15.2	10.9	7.9	5.6	2.9	2.7
Fiji Hindi	83.9	88.3	90.8	93.8	94.5	95.8
English	0.9	0.8	1.3	0.6	2.6	1.5

NOTE: Columns are ranked in order of percentage of usage of a Dravidian language.

The history of Dravidian languages in Fiji shows that Fiji Hindi started to exert pressure on South Indian indentured labourers as soon as they arrived, and Fiji Hindi has now become the dominant language of all Indo-Fijians, including descendants of South Indians whose ancestral tongue was a Dravidian language. Even in the most private domain, the home, Fiji Hindi has not only displaced but also nearly replaced Dravidian languages. The home is, nonetheless, the last bastion of Dravidian languages and, low as they are, figures on use at home are much higher than those in other domains, such as work, school, or tertiary institutions. Figures on use at work never go beyond 3 per cent, for instance, regardless of the type of interlocutor addressed or the topic discussed.

If we turn from the use of the spoken language to questions on language use in reading or writing, the range of figures for Dravidian languages is even lower, from less than 1 per cent to just over 5 per cent (Table 8). The figures for writing are all lower than those for reading, again reflecting the fact that a number of respondents have receptive but not productive skills in the language.

TABLE 8 *Use of a Dravidian language in reading and writing*

	READING		WRITING A LETTER		
	RELIGIOUS LITERATURE	LITERATURE	RELATIVE	FRIEND	BUSINESS
Count	25	19	15	12	4
%	5.2	4	3.1	2.5	0.8

NOTE: Columns are ranked in order of percentage of usage of a Dravidian language.

LANGUAGE ATTITUDES

Respondents were asked a number of questions intended to probe their attitudes towards the Dravidian language of their ancestors as well as other languages they might know. They were asked, for instance, to identify the most pleasing language, the most useful language, to evaluate the importance of having competence in their ancestral language, and whether they supported current maintenance efforts. Although Fiji Hindi is the winner of the popularity contest, identified by over 45 per cent of respondents as the most pleasing language, the relatively high percentage of respondents selecting their ancestral Dravidian language – over 20 per cent (Table 9) is very significant as well.

TABLE 9 *Most pleasing language*

FIJI HINDI	DRAVIDIAN LANGUAGE	ENGLISH	SHUDH HINDI
45.6	20.8	17.3	16

If we interpret these figures in the light of those on language use, what is striking is the discrepancy, with figures for Dravidian languages much higher for this question than the figures on use. If 20 per cent of the respondents name their ancestral Dravidian language as the most pleasing, but only 1 per cent to 15 per cent (depending on circumstances) use it, this means that a significant number of the respondents who use a Dravidian language little or not at all nonetheless name this language as the most pleasing. Conversely, although 85 per cent to 95 per cent of respondents report using Fiji Hindi at home (to take but one example), only 45 per cent name it as the most pleasing language. Thus, while Fiji Hindi has become the dominant language of nearly all descendants of South Indians, their ancestral Dravidian language evidently retains a powerful sentimental value for many. Although most of the respondents have low or no competence in the Dravidian language of their ancestors, this relatively high rating indicates a strong attachment to languages which, in spite of their very restricted use, are still considered by many a badge of group identity.

The relatively high percentage for English is understandable given the high profile of English in Fiji as the main de facto official language. It is the sole official medium of instruction beyond the first three years of primary school and therefore the key to education and white-collar jobs. Its overwhelming presence in the media, and its role as lingua franca among population groups with different first languages also contribute to its high profile.[6]

As for figures for Shudh Hindi (equivalent to Standard Hindi as used in mainland India), their interest lies in comparing them to those obtained for a general sample of Indo-Fijians (which contained very few descendants of South Indians), as was done in a parallel survey conducted in Suva (Mugler and Tent 1995). Only 16 per cent of descendants of South Indians named Shudh Hindi as the most pleasing language, against nearly 46 per cent of Suva's Indo-Fijians. Conversely, nearly 46 per cent of descendants of South Indians named Fiji Hindi, against only 29 per cent of Suva's Indo-Fijians. This reflects the prestige of Shudh Hindi and the corresponding lack of prestige of Fiji Hindi among the Indo-Fijian population as a whole, which is in inverse relation to the actual use of the two languages, with Fiji Hindi overwhelmingly the most commonly language used, and Shudh Hindi used extremely seldom.

South Indians – whose ancestral languages after all belong to a different family from that of Hindi – seem to share neither this awe for Shudh Hindi nor this low esteem for Fiji Hindi. That descendants of South Indians have such different attitudes from other Indo-Fijians towards both varieties of Hindi, together with their attitudes towards their ancestral Dravidian languages, confirms that they have a distinct identity within the Indo-Fijian community. All results to questions about attitudes show a highly significant correlation with age and education level. Dravidian languages are rated most highly by older respondents (Table 10), a rating in large part due to the fact that more of the older group know Dravidian languages, while very few of the young do.

The correlation between responses and level of education is also highly significant. The rating of Dravidian languages decreases with the level of education of respondents while that of English, conversely, increases – although the difference between the secondary- and tertiary-educated is not significant (Table 11).

This correlation is not surprising since English is the official – and sole – medium of instruction beyond the first three years of primary school. Some informants, particularly older rural residents, reported having no formal education, and would have had limited exposure to and competence in English.

We note that the figures for Fiji Hindi are similar across education levels, however. So are those for Shudh Hindi, except that it is named by significantly fewer respondents who have had no formal education at all, perhaps understandably since the major locus of exposure to Shudh Hindi is the school.

TABLE 10 *Most pleasing language by age group*

AGE GROUP	SHUDH HINDI	FIJI HINDI	DRAVIDIAN LANGUAGE	ENGLISH
15–25	14.2	44.4	4.9	36.4
30–45	20.7	56.8	13.6	9.0
50+	13.5	36.2	43.6	6.1

Chi-square = 126.70, df = p = 0.0001

NOTE: One informant in the +50 group (0.61 per cent) named Urdu.

TABLE 11 *Most pleasing language by education level*

EDUCATION LEVEL	SHUDH HINDI	FIJI HINDI	DRAVIDIAN LANGUAGE	ENGLISH
None	5.3	45.7	46.8	2.1
Primary	15.7	48.8	25.3	9.6
Secondary	21.2	43.0	5.7	30.0
Tertiary	18.5	44.4	11.1	25.9

Chi-square = 102.54, df = 9, p = 0.0001

NOTE: Urdu was named by one primary-educated informant (0.61 per cent).

A powerful contrast appears when we compare these figures with the results for the question on the most useful language. It is to be expected that English should get a high rating, since it is widely seen as the key to education and a 'good' (white-collar) job. Indeed about two-thirds of respondents name English as the most useful language, while the dominant language of the community, Fiji Hindi, is rated second (Table 12). The very low percentage of respondents naming a Dravidian language, less than 6 per cent, seems realistic. Indeed, if we keep in mind the figures on language use, this percentage is, if anything, optimistic. Nonetheless, what is striking is the difference between this very low percentage naming Dravidian languages as the most useful and the relatively high percentage naming them as the most pleasing (20 per cent). Thus, while descendants of South Indians acknowledge that the usefulness of the Dravidian language of their ancestors has become extremely circumscribed, their attachment to that language nonetheless remains high.

TABLE 12 *Most useful language*

ENGLISH	FIJI HINDI	DRAVIDIAN LANGUAGE	SHUDH HINDI
63.7	27.3	5.8	2.9

The figures for Shudh Hindi are the lowest of all, and this evaluation also is realistic and would not normally require much comment. Their interest here lies in the fact that they are much lower than those for the Suva Survey of Indo-Fijians, reflecting as do the results for the previous question, the difference in attitudes between descendants of South Indians and other Indo-Fijians (Mugler and Tent 1995: 26–9).

For this question also, the correlations with age and with education level are highly significant. Dravidian languages are rated increasingly more highly: the older the respondents the higher they rate Fiji Hindi, while the younger the respondents, the more highly they rate English (Table 13). As for education level, respondents with at most a primary education tend to see some usefulness in Dravidian languages, while those who are better educated tend not to (Table 14).

TABLE 13 *Most useful language by age group*

AGE GROUP	SHUDH HINDI	FIJI HINDI	DRAVIDIAN LANGUAGE	ENGLISH
15–25	3.1	19.6	1.2	76.1
30–45	3.9	23.4	3.9	68.8
50+	1.9	38.9	12.4	46.3

Chi-square = 44.47, df = 6, p = 0.0001

TABLE 14 *Most useful language by education level*

EDUCATION LEVEL	SHUDH HINDI	FIJI HINDI	DRAVIDIAN LANGUAGE	ENGLISH
None	2.2	50.5	10.8	36.6
Primary	1.2	32.1	18.5	57.6
Secondary	4.7	15.5	2.1	77.7
Tertiary	3.6	3.6	0	92.9

Chi-square = 72.61, df = 9, p = 0.0001

Respondents were asked 'How important is it to be good in [the Dravidian language of your ancestors]?' The results are displayed in Table 15.

TABLE 15 *How important is it to be good in [a Dravidian language]?*

Very important	30.7
Important	49.3
Not important	20

These figures are quite high, with positive answers ('important' or 'very important') given by 80 per cent of the respondents. But the figures for all the other languages listed are even higher: 94 per cent for Fiji Hindi, 98 per cent for English, and even 85 per cent for the nearly unused Shudh Hindi.

One could interpret these high figures as reflecting the belief that, in an ideal world, it would be good to know all these languages. Most crucially, these results remind us again of the gap between stated attitudes and actual behaviour. The figures relating to language use demonstrate that the majority of those who claim here that being good in a Dravidian language is important or very important either do not know that language at all, or have limited competence in it and rarely use it or do not use it at all.

Another question which elicited similar responses was 'Should South Indian languages be promoted more in Sangam schools?' (Table 16). The same observation about the difference between stated attitudes and actual behaviour is valid here.

TABLE 16 *Should South Indian languages be promoted more in Sangam schools?*

Yes	94.4	*No*	5.6

The evidence of language loss – only sketchily documented before the 1993 survey – seems incontrovertible. In spite of overall positive attitudes towards Dravidian languages, the extremely low figures on language use, the self-evaluation of competence of speakers, the existence of informants with only a passive knowledge of a Dravidian language, the gap between reported knowledge of the language and reported use at home all point again to a significant correlation between age and answers to questions on both language use and attitudes.

Structural attrition

In the aftermath of the 1993 survey, background interviews were conducted with a number of descendants of South Indians who still knew a Dravidian language, mainly among the older group participating in the survey. Samples of conversation (or, when this was not possible, monologues) in that language were also recorded. In all, 40 samples were collected (at least a dozen for each of the three languages) from informants mostly over 50 years of age, but overall ranging from 10 to 78 years old.

The language samples, representing about 6 hours of recorded data and ranging from 5 to over 30 minutes each, were analysed from September to December 1994 in Mysore, in collaboration with three linguists from the Central Institute of Indian Languages: Sam Mohan Lal (for Tamil), V. Saratchandran Nair (Malayalam), and G. Vijayasarathi (Telugu). The aim of the study was to ascertain the characteristics of the three varieties of Dravidian languages spoken in Fiji, and in particular to find out whether any structural features could be attributed to attrition, parallel to the considerable language shift these varieties have undergone.

While results are tentative due to the relatively small amount of data, several facts emerge which will be very briefly sketched here (for details, see Mugler 1995).[7] The Tamil, Telugu, and Malayalam of Fiji are clearly identifiable as diasporic varieties. They contain both archaisms as well as dialectal features which often lead to an unambiguous identification of the geographical origins of individual informants' ancestors. They also bear the signs of the influence of Fiji Hindi, not only at the lexical level but also in their phonology, syntax, and semantics.

This is not surprising given that Fiji Hindi has 'become the first language of most descendants of South Indians and, for those for whom it is not chronologically the first language, it is at least the language they use most frequently and in which they have the greatest competence. But the Fiji varieties of Tamil, Telugu, and Malayalam also display signs of language attrition, with simplification and loss of marking, particularly in morphology, such as case endings and concord markers, and complex syntax, like relative participles and causatives. If these signs of structural attrition are confirmed, they are another warning sign of the precarious state of Dravidian languages in Fiji.[8]

MAINTENANCE EFFORTS

We have seen that nearly all the descendants of South Indians surveyed (95 per cent) support Dravidian language maintenance efforts – regardless of whether they know or use a Dravidian language themselves. Maintenance activities centre on the teaching of Tamil and Telugu in the schools run by the Then India Sanmarga Ikya (TISI) Sangam, a cultural and educational organisation established in Fiji in the 1920s.

As early as the late 1910s, South Indians started informal schools where Tamil and Telugu were taught and organised maintenance efforts have been led by the Sangam since the 1920s. One of the incentives was the record of the colonial government with respect to the education of the children of indentured labourers.

The 1911 Census figures for literacy in any language are 86.5 per cent for 'Europeans', 52.8 per cent for Fijians and 9.4 per cent for Indians (Gillion 1962: 160). To this evident neglect was added the unofficial encouragement of the disuse of Dravidian languages already mentioned. In a memorandum to the Colonial Secretary (CSO 4780/1927), the Director of Education, A.A. Wright, wrote: 'We should avoid a tendency towards a multiplication of languages and without actually opposing Tamil and other Indian languages to foster a general adoption of Hindustani' (Siegel 1987: 204).

The TISI Sangam, founded in 1926 (Pillai 1971: 17), undertook social and educational work, and established schools managed by local committees where Dravidian languages were taught. Most of these schools were founded in the 1930s. The teaching of Dravidian languages seems to have hit a low ebb and nearly disappeared in the 1950s, but there was a renewed push in the 1980s. Table 17 shows the number of primary school children taking Tamil and Telugu language classes in recent years.

TABLE 17 *Primary school pupils enrolled in Tamil and Telugu classes, 1988–95*

YEAR	TAMIL	TELUGU
1988	1,962	979
1990	2,199	985
1992	2,393	886
1993	1,689	676
1994	1,645	573
1995	1,800	670

SOURCE: Based on Sangam Annual Convention magazines.

These figures are modest, and also somewhat misleading. Sangam schools are open to all children, not just those of South Indian background, so that classes can include also children of North Indian, Fijian, 'European', and mixed ancestry. And children of South Indian background are not necessarily studying the language of their ancestors since pupils are sometimes arbitrarily assigned to a Tamil or a Telugu class. In 1995 Tamil was taught in 17 schools, Telugu in 7, and the last time Malayalam was taught was in

1991 (in one school in Rakiraki). The languages are not taught in high school and are not examinable – this in a country where the school system is highly exam-driven.

Some of the problems with the teaching of Dravidian languages are identified by Sangam officials themselves. According to the *Annual Convention Magazine*, 'Constraints remain due to lack of trained language teachers aggravated by low wages paid to existing language teachers and general lack of interest among Sangam public' (1996: 19). Other areas of concern mentioned by Sangam officials include the scarcity of materials in general and suitable materials in particular (in spite of assistance from various universities and other institutions in India), the limited number of teachers, the level of proficiency of both teachers and students, the lack of understanding by parents, and the lack of support from the government.

I would add to this list the very significant distance between tne 'high' varieties taught in school and the home varieties, an issue which remains either unrecognised or at least unaddressed. This means that even if a child is exposed to Tamil, say, at home, he or she is faced in school with an entirely different variety of language. Thus, children are essentially asked to learn a foreign language. The teaching, a few hours a week, of varieties of Dravidian languages so distinct from the home varieties that a few of the pupils may be exposed to at home, together with the constraints mentioned above, is unlikely to have any significant impact on patterns of use and transmission in the home. If anything, the teaching of what is perceived as 'good' Tamil or Telugu may well lull parents into a false sense of security and away from making sure that they transmit their authentic ancestral mother tongue to their children. In recent years, the Sangam's appeals to parents have sounded increasingly desperate, such as this extended quote from G.S. Naidu reveals (*Sangam Annual Convention Magazine* 1995: unnumbered page):

> Let me conclude by very humbly pleading with you all at this convention to give your very serious, calm and collected thought and consideration to the facts put to you so that we can preserve like others our rich heritage and culture, and save ourselves from the stigma of being branded as those responsible for the total loss and doom of our languages and culture by the future generations as it is already being done by the present lot.

In recent conversations with several Sangam officials, I think I detect an increasing recognition of the importance of intergenerational transmission in the home. It is unclear, however, whether any steps are being taken or even planned in that direction.

CONCLUSION

The signs of continuing, massive language shift are incontrovertible while the extent of structural attrition needs to be further explored. It is also clear that current maintenance efforts, while laudable, are insufficient. The only general conclusion that can be drawn is that, if all remains as it is, both Malayalam and Telugu are threatened in the short term, and Tamil in the medium term. One must not be lulled by the generally positive attitudes that emerge from the results of the 1993 survey. The gap between stated attitudes and actual behaviour, on the part of older speakers in particular, does not augur well for the transmission of Dravidian languages to the young. On the other hand, the highly significant correlation between age and both language use and attitudes means that, increasingly, younger generations not only do not know or use these languages any more, but do not care as much about them. It is doubtful that any language can survive under these conditions.

NOTES

1. The other important migration from India has consisted mainly of Gujarati coming to Fiji to work in the commercial sector, particularly in the 1930s.
2. The term *girmitiya*, meaning 'indentured labourer', is derived from Fiji Hindi *grimit*, from English 'agreement'. *Girmit*, originally meaning 'the labourers' contract', came to refer to the experience and the historical period of indenture.
3. Some South Indians did come to Fiji before 1903, but in very small numbers. Gillion (1962: 68–9) mentions 69 labourers previously indentured in Reunion who came at the beginning of indenture in Fiji, but they do not seem to have stayed. In his study of Calcutta emigration passes, Lal (1983: 50–1) found that 0.2 per cent of labourers recruited in North India came from Madras (76 individuals). Some of the labourers previously indentured in other colonies must have been South Indians, particularly among those who had worked in Natal and Mauritius, where the proportion of South Indians was fairly high (Lal 1983: 44). A number of free migrants also came to Fiji, and some may have been from South India. Nonetheless, the total number of immigrants of South Indian origin who came to Fiji before the opening of the Madras depot in 1903 must have been very small – a few hundred at the most.
4. Although the report on the 1966 Census does not mention multiple answers, it is likely that they did occur again, since the format of both question and alternative answers was the same as for 1956, and the same recording procedure was followed.
5. Not a single respondent reported knowing Kannada. Two reported that at least one parent knew it and seven, at least one grandparent.
6. The role of English as a lingua franca tends to be overstated in the literature, as many Fijians and Indo-Fijians use Fijian or Fiji Hindi – rather than English – to

communicate, particularly outside urban areas (Mugler and Tent 1995: 37).

7. For details on each language variety, see Mugler and Lal 1995 (on Tamil), Mugler and Nair 1995 (Malayalam), and Mugler and Vijayasarathi 1996 (Telugu).
8. Research on the structure of the Fiji varieties of Tamil, Telugu and Malayalam continues. The current phase involves collecting recorded language samples (and background interviews) from a larger and more representative sample of the population, particularly in terms of age. To date about 25 such language samples (out of a planned total of 40) have been collected, but it has proved extremely difficult to locate middle-aged and young speakers of all three languages, and speakers of Malayalam and Telugu (of any age) in particular. Date collection continues and it is hoped that all new samples collected will be analysed, again in collaboration with CHI, in 1997–98.

REFERENCES

GILLION, K.L.

1962 *Fiji's Indian migrants*. Melbourne: Oxford University Press.

1977 *The Fiji Indians: Challenge to European dominance, 1920–1946*. Canberra: Australian National University Press.

LAL, BRIJ

1983 Girmitiyas: The origins of Fiji Indians. *Journal of Pacific History*. Canberra.

MAYER, ADRIAN C.

1973 *Peasants in the Pacific. A study of Fijian Indian rural society*. London: Routledge and Kegan Paul.

MUGLER, FRANCE

1995 South Indian languages in Fiji: Language contact and attrition. Paper presented to the Second International Conference on Oceanic Linguistics, The University of the South Pacific, Suva, Fiji. To appear in Proceedings of SICOI, 1997.

MUGLER, FRANCE and SAM MOHAN LAL

1995 Fiji Tamil: The structure of a language under threat. *International Journal of Dravidian Linguistics*, 24.2. 118–33.

MUGLER, FRANCE and V. SARATCHANDRAN NAIR

1995 Notes on Fiji Malayalam. Paper presented to the Twenty-Third All-India Conference, Trivandrum, India.

MUGLER, FRANCE and JAN TENT

1995 Some aspects of language use and attitudes in Fiji. Paper presented to the Second International Conference on Oceanic Linguistics, The University of the South Pacific, Suva, Fiji. To appear in *Proceedings of SICOI*, 1997.

MUGLER, FRANCE and G. VIJAYASARATHI

1996 Telugu in Fiji. Paper presented to the Twenty-Fourth All-India Conference, Kuppam, India.

PILLAI, RAYMOND C.

1971 The emergence and decline of the TISI Sangam. Unpublished ms, Pacific Collection, University of the South Pacific, Suva, Fiji.

REPORT ON THE CENSUS OF THE POPULATION, 1956

1958 *Government of Fiji Legislative Council Paper no. 8*. Suva: Government Press.

REPORT ON THE CENSUS OF THE POPULATION, 1966

1968 *Government of Fiji Legislative Council Paper no. 8*. Suva: Government Press.

SANGAM ANNUAL CONVENTION MAGAZINE

1989, 1991–1996 issues. Nadi, Fiji: TISI Sangam.

SIEGEL, JEFF

1973 A survey of language use in the Indian speech community in Fiji. Unpublished field study project for the Culture Learning Institute. Honolulu, Hawaii: East-West Center.

1975 Fiji Hindustani. *Working Papers in Linguistics,* 7.3. University of Hawaii. 127–44.

1987 *Language contact in a plantation environment: A sociolinguistic history of Fiji.* Cambridge: Cambridge University Press.

STATISTICAL NEWS 8. REPUBLIC OF FIJI

1997 Suva: Bureau of Statistics.

3
Participialisation in Sambalpuri: A case for convergence

B.P. SRIDEVI and RESHMA N. CHOUDHURY
Jawaharlal Nehru University

This paper explores the use of participialisation as a strategy of noun modification in Sambalpuri, an Indo-Aryan language spoken in Orissa. We argue that the pattern of participialisation in Sambalpuri provides a good example of

- the Theory of Chain of Contact, that is, convergence of the two major language families of India – Indo-Aryan (IA) and Dravidian, without any actual language contact between the two, and
- the Cline theory of distribution of features.

Relativisation and participialisation are strategies of noun modification which are traditionally associated with IA and Dravidian language families, respectively. This 'straitjacketing' of strategies, we hold to be essentially faulty. It is futile trying to pit relativisation against participialisation with reference to convergence. Our argumentation builds on the premise that participialisation as a strategy is available in both the language families.[1] However, there are important differences as to the type of participialisation and the grammatical categories available for participialisation. The convergence in Sambalpuri that we report relates to the mixing of the characteristics of IA and Dravidian types of participialisation.

The fact that there is participialisation in Sambalpuri, we hold, is not itself an indication of convergence. What needs to be looked at is the type and extent of participialisation, which would give us an insight into the nature of convergence. IA Hindi-Urdu and Dravidian Telugu represent the two extremes of the spectrum that participialisation covers in Indian languages. Sambalpuri represents languages that occupy the middle range of the continuum. It would be futile to argue for a unidirectional path of convergence. The aim of this paper is not to claim the Dravidianisation of an IA language; instead we posit a cline with all languages sharing the abstract qualities of participialisation, but in different manifestations. Thus, while Indo-Aryan languages have limited participialisation, Dravidian languages may have more extensive participialisation. Sambalpuri is a language of the middle range.

Languages like Sambalpuri may not be languages in transition as is usually assumed. We posit that they have evolved a mixture of strategies due to convergence but there is no need to assume that they will have to move to either extreme. They may simply remain as languages of the middle range. To argue this point in the paper, we apply various tests relating to the categories available for participialisation in order to gauge the extent to which this strategy of noun modification is used in the language. We note the features in Sambalpuri that set it apart from other IA languages and bring it closer to the Dravidian languages. Finally, we chalk up the score of IA and Dravidian features and confirm Sambalpuri as a language of the middle range.

DISTINCTIVE FEATURES OF PARTICIPIALISATION

Participialisation is defined as a device of noun modification, wherein the embedded clause occurs to the left of the head noun, and a verbal participle is used instead of the finite verb that occurs in relativised structures. Further, the noun in the main clause is retained while that of the subordinate clause is deleted and not replaced with a coreferent. These facts are demonstrated by the Telugu example in (1).

(1) *occina* *pilloDu-na* *tammuDu* TELUGU
come-VP boy I-GEN brother (younger)
'The boy who has come is my brother.'

Though participialisation occurs as a strategy of noun modification in both the IA and Dravidian language families there are important differences marking them as typical of either language family as Table 1 shows. We propose to analyse participialisation in Sambalpuri on the basis of this matrix. Sambalpuri, as the data following Table 1 will show, does not have typically IA features. Rather it shows a mix of both IA and Dravidian features.

TABLE 1

INDO-ARYAN	DRAVIDIAN
1. Tense distinction disallowed in the verbal participle	1. Tense distinction allowed in the verbal participle.
2. Embedded subject is genitivised.	2. Embedded subject is degenitivised.
3. Restrictions on the occurrence of the negative participle.	3. No restrictions on the occurrence of the negative participle.
4. Restrictions on the verbal participle in the progressive aspect.	4. No restrictions on the verbal participle in the progressive aspect.
5. 'VALA' constructions allowed.	5. No 'VALA' constructions.
6. Restrictions on the categories available for participialisation.	6. No restrictions on the categories available for participialisation.

Feature 1

Tense distinction is disallowed in Sambalpuri in the verbal participle as in other IA languages exemplified by Hindi-Urdu, as (2) shows:

(2) a. *Sita bOhi rakhithibar tebul-be nayi ciO* SAMBALPURI
Sita book VP-keep table-ACC NEG touch
'Do not touch the table on which Sita has kept the book.'

b. *sita-ki paRhi hui kitab-ko mat chuo* HINDI-URDU
Sita-GEN VP-read book-ACC NEG touch
'Do not touch the book which Sita has read.'

Feature 2

(2) also shows that the embedded subject in Sambalpuri is degenitivised, a phenomenon that is not allowed in Hindi-Urdu. Sambalpuri shares this feature with other Dravidian languages as (3) shows:

(3) *sita caduvina pustakam tebul-payina peTTundi* TELUGU
Sita VP-read book table-on kept-BE
'The book that Sita read is kept on the table.'

Feature 3

As (4) shows, IA does not allow the negation of the verbal participle. However, Sambalpuri allows it, as do the Dravidian languages.

(4) a. *nayi a:sithibar lok-ke ka:Na kOhebo* SAMBALPURI
NEG VP-come man-ACC INTERR say
'What do you say to the man who has not come?'

b. *rani manisini emi ama:la* TELUGU
NEG-VP-come man-ACC INTERR say
'What do you say to the man who has not come?'

c. **nahi a:ya hua a:dmi-ko kya kehna* HINDI-URDU
NEG VP-come man-ACC INTERR say
'What do you say to the man who hasn't come?'

Feature 4
There are no restrictions on the use of the verbal participle in the progressive aspect in Sambalpuri, a pattern not shared by other IA languages such as Hindi-Urdu.

(5) a. *apON kOhuthibar jaga se nayi dekhi* SAMBALPURI
2SG HON. VP-say-PROG place he NEG see
'He did not see the place you are talking about.'

b. *miru ceppe sta:nam atanu cuDaledu* TELUGU
2SG HON VP-say-PROG place he see-NEG
'He did not see the place you are talking about.'

c. **a:p keh rahe jagah usne nahi dekhi* HINDI-URDU
2SG HON say PROG place he NEG see
'He did not see the place you are talking about.'

Feature 5
Just like Dravidian languages, Sambalpuri does not have the VALA construction. VALA constructions, indicating habituality, are typical of IA languages, as the Hindi-Urdu (6a) shows. (6a) would translate into Sambalpuri as (6b).

(6) a. *ro:z a:ne-vale vyakti ka nam kya hE* HINDI-URDU
daily come-VALA man-GEN name INTERR AUX-BE
'What is the name of the man who comes everyday?'

b. *a:s ja:s kOruthiba:r lok-rO NakaNa* SAMBALPURI
come-go VP-do man-GEN name INTERR
'What is the name of the man who comes everyday?'

The progressive marker /u/ is used to indicate habituality due to the absence of the VALA constructions.

Feature 6

The Keenan–Comrie Accessibility Hierarchy of 1977 says that universally noun phrases on the upper end of the Accessibility Hierarchy (AH) are more easily accessible for various functions including relativisation. We have extended the functions to include participialisation as well. The AH reads as follows:

SUBJECT > DIRECT OBJECT > INDIRECT OBJECT > OBLIQUE > GENITIVE

Some languages have participialisation strategies which apply only to subjects. Others have ones that apply to both subject and direct object, others have ones applicable to the top three categories, and so on. In Sambalpuri, as in Dravidian, all categories in the AH are available for participialisation [(cf. (7)–(14)]. The genitive however fluctuates. (In IA only the first three categories are available for participialisation.)

(7) SUBJECT
se *ga:thi* *rOhuthibar* *pila-Ta* *mor* *sa*
that village VP-live boy-CLASS my friend
'The boy who lives in that village is my friend.'

(8) DIRECT OBJECT
mor *kael* *dekhithibar* *sa:Rhi-Ta* *ba:har* *kOri* *kOri* *diy*
ISG-GEN yesterday VP-see saree-CLASS out do give
'Show me the saree I saw yesterday.'

(9) INDIRECT OBJECT
muni *ra:m-ke* *deithiba:r* *bOhi* *se* *bikidela*
I Ram-ACC VP-give book he sell-PST
'Ram sold the book I gave him.'

(10) INSTRUMENTAL
daku *ra:m-ke* *ma:rithiba:r* *chOku-thi* *mohan-ke* *bi* *marla*
dacoit Ram-ACC VP-kill knife-INSTR Mohan-ACC also kill-PST
'The dacoit killed Mohan with the same knife with which he killed Ram.'

(11) DATIVE
mui *sa:Rhi* *deithiba:r* *tukel* *biha* *heigola*
I saree VP-give girl-GEN marriage go-PST
'The girl whom I gave the saree to has got married.'

(12) LOCATIVE
mui *kael* *khaithiba:r* *hotel-re* *pher* *khaili*
I yesterday VP-eat hotel-LOC again eat-PST
'I ate in the same hotel where I ate yesterday.'

(13) ABLATIVE

sita	*paen*	*anithiba:r*	*kuanu*	*bOhut*	*ga:Dh*	*E*
sita	water	VP-bring	well	very	deep	AUX-PRES

'The well from which Sita draws water is very deep.'

(14) GENITIVE

kael	*lenj*	*kOTithiba:r*	*bileir-Ta*	*mor*	*E*
yesterday	tail	VP-cut	cat-CLASS	ISG-GEN	AUX-PRES

'The cat whose tail got cut yesterday is mine.'

Chalking up the score of features, we may say that Sambalpuri behaves like Dravidian with respect to five features. Like IA, however, it does not have tense distinction and prefers relativisation as the strategy for noun modification. Besides, the genitivisation of the subject is not constant.

(15)

mui/mor	*pusithiba:r*	*kukur*	*poleigola*
ISG/ISG-GEN	VP-nurtured	dog	ran away

'The dog I looked after ran away.'

CONCLUSION

The results show the process of assimilation at work at the syntactic level across language boundaries which can be explained by the theory of convergence. However, what is of interest in the present instance is that convergence in Sambalpuri has not taken place due to actual language contact – Sambalpuri and Telugu do not border each other. Convergence here has been carried by Oriya, which is in actual contact with Telugu. We shall thus posit a chain of contact which involves Oriya as the via media. Oriya, then, acts as a host language disseminating Dravidian patterns into Sambalpuri. Sambalpuri thus can be seen as adopting the Oriya pattern of participialisation, which is itself the result of convergence with Telugu.

The sociolinguistic situation in Sambalpur promotes such a phenomenon since a diglossic situation exists where Oriya is the High variety. Oriya is seen as the language of education and opportunity. There is thus a striving towards Oriya patterns of language, consciously or otherwise. The dividing line thus, becomes very blurred. Participialisation as a strategy is itself held to be Oriya and not Sambalpuri. Oriya and Sambalpuri share a similar pattern of participialisation regarding the type and categories available for participialisation. We maintain that there has been an infusion of Dravidian patterns due to convergence, but do not believe this represents a Dravidianisation of either language. Instead a cline theory would be more beneficial which shows a grading as well as slow merging of features from either end. There is no evidence that either Oriya or Sambalpuri will cross over the border.

NOTE

1. There is no doubt that participialisation as a strategy of noun modification is used with greater frequency in Dravidian languages – hence its identification with the Dravidian language family. However, it is not exclusive to this language family, just as relativisation is not patented to the IA family.

REFERENCE

KEENAN, E.L. and B. COMRIE
1977 Noun phrase accessibility and universal grammar. *Linguistic Inquiry*, Vol. 8. 63–100.

4
Portuguese influence on Konkani syntax

ROCKY V. MIRANDA
University of Minnesota

This paper will examine the nature of syntactic modification in the Goan Christian dialect of Konkani due to the influence of Portuguese. Such modification was observed only in the written variety of the dialect and in formal speech such as sermons. This phenomenon appears to have been noticed first by V.P. Chavan (1924) who complained that, in this dialect of Konkani, 'the construction of sentences awkwardly follows the Portuguese style of sentences'.[1] He selected a few sentences of such modified Konkani from a couple of Goan Christian Konkani periodicals: *O Aviso* ('Notice' in Portuguese) and *The Goa Mail*. It is worth noting that neither of these Konkani periodicals has a Konkani title: the first one has a Portuguese title and the second one an English title as it was published in Bombay. Chavan then proceeds to give the same sentences as they would be constructed in a Hindu Konkani dialect which shows no Portuguese syntactic or lexical influence.

Two of the sentences from Chavan's specimens were reproduced by Katre (1942) in *The Formation of Konkani*. These sentences, which are from *The Goa Mail*, 8 July 1923, are presented here along with comments on their structure.[2]

(1)	*vortouta*	*tumcho*	*chodd*	*gorgecho*	*anim*	*bari*	*caido*
	is	your	very	essential	and	important	obligation

I wish to thank Peter Hook, University of Michigan, for going over an earlier version of this paper and making helpful comments.

diuncheak	*bori*	*dek*	*tumcheam*	*burgueanc*
to give	good	example	your	children-to
astanam	*tim*	*lanam*		
being	they	little		

'It is your very essential and important obligation to give a good example to your children while they are small.'

The sentence in (1) shows the Portuguese sentence structure NP Copula[3] NP, with the sentential subject NP extraposed also as in Portuguese. In normal Konkani, its structure should be NP NP Copula where the sentential subject NP cannot be extraposed but the Copula is to be deleted. In the main clause of the sentence contained in the subject NP *diuncheak bori dek tumchea burgueanc*, the direct object *bori dek* and the indirect object *tumcheam burgeanc* follow the verb *di* as in Portuguese and the verb is in the infinitive form *diuncheak* also as in Portuguese. According to normal Konkani structure, the direct and the indirect objects should precede the verb and the verb should be in the participle/gerund form *diuncho, diunchi,* or *diunchem.* The dependent clause of the sentence contained in the subject NP *astanam tim lanam* follows the main clause as in Portuguese. It also shows the Portuguese word order Copula NP Adjective, as compared to the normal Konkani word order NP Adjective Copula that precedes the main clause.

(2)	*avoi bapui*	*sabar*	*pauttim*	*khens cortat*	*aplim*	*burguim*
	parents	many	times	complain	one's own	kids
	aiconant vo	*bexearmi cortat*		*munn*	*aplea*	*sangnneanc*
	listen-not and	ignore		thus	one's own	instructions-to

'Parents often complain that their children disregard and ignore their instructions.'

In this second sentence, the complement clause occurs after the main clause as in Portuguese. In the complement clause, the direct object *aplea sangnneanc* occurs after the verbs *aiconant vo bexearmi cortat* and even after the complementiser *munn*. In normal Konkani structure, the complement occurs usually before the main clause with the complementiser placed at the end of the complement. Also, the object precedes the verb. These sentences, in an informal version of the same Goan Christian dialect, which can be expected to be free from Portuguese syntactic influence, are as follows.[4]

(3)	*tumchim*	*burguim*	*lanam*	*astanam*	*tankam*	*bori*	*dek*
	your	children	little	being	them-to	good	example
	diuncho	*tumcho*	*chodd*	*gorgecho*	*anim*	*bari*	*ka ydo*
	giving	your	very	essential	and	important	obligation

(4)

aplim	*burguim*	*aplea*	*sangnneanc*	*aiconant*	*vo*
one's own	kids	one's own	instructions-to	listen-not	and

bexearmi cortat	*munn*	*avoi bapui*	*sabar*	*pauttim*	*khens cortat*
ignore	thus	parents	many	times	complain

In sentences (3) and (4) we have seen instances of the direct object and the indirect object occurring after the verb, the predicate adjective or noun phrase occurring after the copula, and the dependent clause occurring after the main clause. There are also instances of extraposition of a sentential subject NP, the infinitivisation of the verb in the sentential NP, and non-deletion of the copula where it is normally deleted.

The Goan Christian literature I have examined also shows other instances of Portuguese syntactic influence such as the occurrence of the adjective, the genitive noun phrase, and the relative clause after the head noun and the occurrence of adverbial phrases after the verb. In the comparative construction, the standard appears after the adjective although the comparison marker still occurs after the standard. There is, however, not a single instance of the occurrence of an adposition before the noun. This is not surprising since the Konkani postpositions have affix-like characteristics. In the case of the comparative construction, since an adposition is used as the comparison marker, its occurrence after the standard is in keeping with the general behaviour of the adpositions in this dialect. It should be pointed out that all these syntactic innovations inspired by Portuguese have only an optional status in this dialect. They are confined only to the formal register, and even there, these innovations have by no means displaced their older counterparts.

PORTUGUESE INFLUENCE IN OLD KONKANI

The earliest Konkani literature that is extant is from the sixteenth and seventeenth centuries. Most of it is Christian religious literature produced by the Catholic missionaries who came from Portugal (such as works on Christian doctrine, lives of saints, etc.). It also includes several Konkani dictionaries (Konkani-Portuguese as well as Portuguese-Konkani), grammars, and a lone manuscript containing stories from the *Ramayana* and the *Mahabharata*. Some of this literature was published, but a number of works are available only in manuscript form. All the works are in Roman script. The stories from the *Ramayana* and the *Mahabharata* are entirely free from Portuguese linguistic influence.

On the other hand, the Christian religious literature shows some Portuguese influence. Works on Christian doctrine show the most Portuguese influence. They contain a number of Portuguese lexical items but these are almost all religious terms: for example, *agoa benta* 'holy water', *altara* 'altar', *anjo* 'angel', *Ave Maria* 'Hail Mary!' (name of a prayer), *bautismo* 'baptism', *bispo* 'bishop', *calix* 'chalice', *Christaõ* 'Christian', *comungar* 'to take communion', *comunhaõ* 'communion', *confessar* 'to confess', *confissaõ* 'confession', *consagraçaõ* 'consecration', *consagrar* 'to consecrate', *Coresma* 'lent', *Credo* 'I believe' (name of a prayer), *doutrina* 'doctrine', *fe* 'faith', *hosti* 'host', *matrimonio* 'matrimony', *missa* 'mass', *misterio* 'mystery', *Nossa Senhora da Piedade* 'Our Lady of Mercy', *oraçao* 'prayer', *padre* 'priest', *Padre Nosso* 'Our Father' (name of a prayer), *peccado original* 'original sin', *piedade* 'mercy', *profetu* 'prophet', *purgatorio* 'purgatory', *resurreiçaõ* 'resurrection', *rezar* 'prayer', *sacerdote* 'priest', *Salue Regina* 'Hail Queen!' (name of a prayer), *Santa Cruz* 'Holy Cross', *Santa Madre Igreja* 'Holy Mother Church', *Santissimo Sacramento* 'the Holiest Sacrament', *Santissima Trindade* 'the Holiest Trinity', *Spirito Santo* 'Holy Ghost', *vigairo* 'vicar', *Uirge* 'virgin', etc.

Even in the context of religious terminology, the missionaries have occasionally adapted native terms mostly associated with Hindu religious concepts (for example, *crupâ* for 'grace', *yamakundda* for 'hell', *vaicunttha* for 'paradise', *sumurti* for 'religion', etc.) instead of simply borrowing Portuguese terms. Portuguese syntactic influence on the Konkani of these works is quite limited. Occasionally, in the case of certain set Catholic prayers, the influence of Portuguese syntactic patterns may be observed. Take, for example, the following part of the prayer 'Hail Mary':

(5)	*sadaiua*	*phalla*	*tuzie*	*cussiche*
	blessed	fruit	thy	wombs

'Blessed is the fruit of the womb.'

Here, the genitive phrase follows the head noun as in Portuguese. The normal Konkani word order is *sadaiua tuzie cussiche phalla* or *tuzie cussiche phalla sadaiua*. In another set prayer, we have the following:

(6)	*soddai*	*âmacâ*	*paramesparâ*		*âmcheâ*	*drusttântule*
	Deliver	us	O Lord!		our	enemies-from
	bâpâche	*nâui*	*âni*	*putrâchie*	*âni*	*spiritâ sântâchie*
	father's	name-in	and	the sons	and	the Holy Ghosts

'Deliver us, O Lord, from our enemies, in the name of the Father, and of the Son, and of the Holy Ghost.'

In sentence (6), the object *âmacâ* and the postpositional phrase *âmcheâ drusttäntule* follow the verb *soddai* as in Portuguese, whereas they should precede the verb according to normal Konkani word order. Also, the element *nâui*[1] is deleted here except in the first instance as in Portuguese. According to normal Konkani structure, it should be deleted except in the last instance: *bâpâche âni putrâchie, âni spiritâ sântâchie nâui*[1]. None of these Portuguese patterns can be considered productive in Old Konkani.

Katre (1942) implies in his observations regarding the Portuguese influence on Konkani syntax that the Portuguese missionaries were responsible for it.[5] We can safely conclude from our examination of Old Konkani literature that at least the early Portuguese missionaries were not responsible for the wholesale Lusitanisation of Konkani syntax which we examined in the introductory section. We do not know what the role of the later missionaries was in this matter although one expects it not to have been significantly different. It is more likely that native Goans who were admirers of the Portuguese language and were well-versed in it, consciously introduced Portuguese syntactic patterns into Konkani at some point. That the clergy played a principal role in this is obvious as much modern Goan Christian literature is religious literature composed by the clergy.

Old Konkani literature goes back to the sixteenth and seventeenth centuries.[6] It is during this period that a large number of Konkani speakers migrated outside Goa, especially to coastal Karnataka. Also, it is during this period that the Konkani community came to be divided into Hindus and Christians. However, it is likely that appreciable differences between the Konkani of Hindus and Christians and between the Konkani of Goa and the Konkani of coastal Karnataka developed only later.

PORTUGUESE INFLUENCE IN MODERN KONKANI

Modern Konkani writings appear only in a small subset of the numerous dialects into which this language is fragmented according to region, religion, and caste. A substantial number of writings are available in only three dialects: Goa Hindu, Goa (Bardes) Christian, and South Kanara Christian. A few writings are available also in North Kanara Hindu and South Kanara Hindu dialects. Three different scripts are used in the literature of these five dialects: the Roman script in the Goa Christian literature, the Nagari script in Goa Hindu and North Kanara Hindu literature, and the Kannada script in the South Kanara Christian and South Kanara Hindu literature.

The literature in the various modern Konkani dialects goes back only to the later decades of the nineteenth century. In 1963, Ravindra Kelekar, a prominent Konkani writer and publisher in Goa, published a bibliography of Konkani literature (Kelekar 1963). The writings from the Goa Christian dialect listed in Kelekar (1963) number over 1000.[7] It is clearly ahead of the other dialects in the number of writings.[8] A large number of the writings in this dialect were produced for the propagation of religion by the Catholic clergy. Popular fiction was also abundant.

Consider now the extent of Portuguese influence on the principal modern Konkani dialects. In the South Kanara Christian dialect, 350–400 Portuguese lexical items are found. More than half of them have to do with religious terminology. The influence of Portuguese syntax is found only in some set phrases and prayers which have come down from the Old Konkani times. The situation in this dialect is quite comparable with that in Old Konkani. The only difference is that Old Konkani hardly shows any influence of Portuguese in its non-religious vocabulary, whereas in the South Kanara Christian dialect the number of non-religious Portuguese lexical items is considerable although not as large as that of religious terms.

There are hardly any Portuguese loans in North Kanara Hindu or South Kanara Hindu Konkani. This is not surprising since the Hindu Konkani speakers of North and South Kanara are believed to have fled Goa soon after the advent of the Portuguese in the sixteenth century because of religious persecution, whereas the Christian Konkani speakers of South Kanara are believed to have left Goa considerably later, probably in the eighteenth century.

Dalgado (1913) has a list of about 1800 Portuguese words borrowed into Goan Christian Konkani, many of which exhibit pervasive and productive Portuguese syntactic patterns. Portuguese syntactic influence can be seen not only in the Christian religious literature but also in the secular literature of this dialect. Among the approximately 1000 Goan Christian Konkani works listed in Kelekar (1963), about 175 (about 17 per cent) show influence of Portuguese word order in their very titles![9] Typically, the title consists of a head noun followed by a (reduced) relative clause. The most common Portuguese syntactic pattern is the placement of the genitive NP after the head noun (about 125 out of 175 cases):

(7) *Noven* *Perpet Socor* *Saibinnichem*
Novena Perpetual Succor Lady-s
'Novena to Our Lady of Perpetual Succor'

(8) *Dog* *voiz* *pidda-pestinche:* *St. Sebastiao* *ani* *St. Roque*
Two doctors diseases-of St. Sebastian and St. Roque
'Two Healers of Diseases: St. Sebastian and St. Roque'

(9) *Noven* *San* *Francisco* *Xavierachem*
Novena Saint Francis Xavier-of
'Novena to St. Francis Xavier'

(10) *Preparaçao Communhavachem*
Preparation Communion-of
'Preparation for Communion'

(11) *Leonild Bai Aldonchem*
Leonilda Lady Aldona-of
'Lady Leonilda of Aldona'

(12) *Istor Cuncolechi*
History Cuncole-of
'The History of Cuncole'

(13) *Educassaum amchea ostreanchem*
Education Our Women-of
'The Education of Our Women'

(14) *Estrela do Oriente vo Neketr Udentichem*
Star of Orient or Star Orient-of
'The Star of the Orient'

(15) *Icravo Mandament Povachea Upegacho*
Eleventh Commandment People-of Use-of
'The Eleventh Commandment of Use to the People'

(16) *Porzoll Goa Xaracho*
Brilliance Goa City-of
'The Brilliance of the City of Goa'

(17) *Povitr Vangel Jesus Kristacho, S. Lucasan boroila*
Holy Gospel Jesus Christ-of St. Luke Written
tea pormannem
That According
'The Holy Gospel of Jesus Christ According to What St. Luke has Written'

(18) *Martir Golgotacho*
Martyr Golgotha-of
'The Martyr of Golgotha'

(19) *Judi Ojeapanchi*
Coat Miracles-of
'The Miraculous Coat'

(20) *Contha Concani Bhaxechi*
Story Konkani Language-of
'The Story of the Konkani Language'

In other titles, the postnominal modifying noun phrase is dative or locative:

(21) *Pustok* *Randitoleac*
Book Cook-for
'The Book for the Cook'

(22) *Otmo* *Deucharac*
Soul Devil-to
'Soul to the Devil'

(23) *Nimanni* *Rat* *Tujea* *Gopant*
Final Night Your Embrace-in
'The Final Night in Your Embrace'

(24) *Nimanno* *Adeus* *Hospitalant*
Final Good-bye Hospital-in
'The Final Good-bye in the Hospital'

In some titles, the modifier is a simple adjective, and in others, a whole clause, relative or adverbial.

(25) *Deu* *Curpevont*
God Merciful
'The Merciful God'

(26) *Catecizm* *Concanim*
Catechism Konkani
'A Konkani Catechism'

(27) *Magnni* *Pap Saiban* *Mhunnunc* *Formailelim*
Prayers Pope To say Ordered
'Prayers Which the Pope has Ordered to be Said'

(28) *Magnni* *Dispotto* *Saib* *Ghetana*
Prayers Daily Lord Receive-while
'Prayers While Receiving Daily Communion'

There are also a few instances of the direct or indirect object or an adverbial element occurring after the verb or a predicate noun occurring after the copula.

(29) *Di* *Maca* *Tujem* *Utor*
Give Me Your Word
'Give Me Your Word'

(30) *Callzam* *Bettoumia* *Devac*
Hearts Dedicate God-to
'Let's Dedicate Our Hearts to God'

(31) *Sodtam* *Novro* *Firngui,* *Nociban* *Meulo* *Kharvi*
Looking for Bridegroom White luck-by got Fisherman
'Looking for a White Bridegroom, I got by Luck a Fisherman'

(32) *Conn* *Pussit* *Mozim* *Ducam*
Who Wipe My Tears
'Who will Wipe away my Tears?'

(33) *Tem* *Rautalem* *Foras Road*
She lived Foras Road
'She Lived on Foras Road'

(34) *Roddtoloi* *Tum* *Eka* *Dissa*
Cry (2ND SG, FUT) You One Day
'You will Cry One Day'

(35) *Tem* *Zalem* *Randd*
She Became Widow
'She became a Widow'

(36) *Bail* *Vortouta* *Buniad* *Dadosponnachi*
Wife is Foundation Happiness-of
'The Wife is the Foundation of Happiness'

Of course, variations from the normal Konkani word order can be due not only to Portuguese syntactic influence but also because of discourse or stylistic considerations.[10] Thus, for example, it is possible that in a case like (37), the object is placed after the verb for the sake of contrast or rhyme or both and Portuguese influence is not involved.

(37) *Sodtam* *Novro* *Firngui,* *Nociban* *Meulo* *Kharvi*
Looking-for Bridegroom White luck-by got Fisherman

In this connection, it is worth examining the word order in the titles of Konkani works in the other Konkani dialects. It is reasonable to assume that the effect of discourse or stylistic considerations should be about the same in the titles from the different dialects.

Kelekar (1963) has over 500 titles from other Konkani dialects. However, only seven of these (that is, under 2 per cent) show any deviation from the usual Konkani word order (as opposed to 17 per cent of the titles from the Goa Christian dialect). Among the titles from other Konkani dialects in Kelekar (1963), 131 are under *A Bibliography of Konkani Literature in Devanagari Characters*. The works in the Devanagari script are mostly from the Goa Hindu dialect but this list includes also a few works from the Goa Christian and the North Kanara Hindu dialect.

Among the works from the Goa Hindu and the North Kanara Hindu dialects, only three were found which deviated from the usual Konkani word order:[11]

(38)	*Yevjilem*	*Ek*	*ani*	*Zalem*	*Ek*
	(Someone) thought	one (thing)	and	happened	one (thing)

'(Someone) Anticipated Something and Something Else Happened'

(39)	*Aiz*	*re*	*Dholar*	*Poll'lli*	*Boddi*
	today	address PART.	drum-on	fell	(drum)stick

'Today, the (Drum) Stick Hit the Drum'

(40)	*Andhllo*	*Magta*	*Ek*	*Dollo*
	The blind man	is asking for	an	eye

'The Blind Man is Asking for an Eye'

Although the deviation in the word order in these titles is compatible with the Portuguese word order, the word order seems to be altered here for stylistic or other such considerations. For example, contrast is involved in the first title and the title of the second work is taken from the body of this poetical work where *boddi* must be placed last for the sake of rhyme.

Kelekar (1963) also has 403 titles under *A Bibliography of Konkani Literature in Kannada Characters.* The works in the Kannada script are mostly from the South Kanara Christian dialect but there are a few works there from the South Kanara Hindu dialect as well. In the list of Konkani works in the Kannada script, only four titles were found which deviated from the normal Konkani word order and the deviation in the word order is compatible with the Portuguese word order:

(41)	*Bara*	*Khambe*	*Igorz*	*Mateche*
	Twelve	Pillars	Church	Mother-of

'Twelve Pillars of the Church'

(42)	*Khambe*	*Igorz*	*Mateche*
	Pillars	Church	Mother-of

'Pillars of the Church'

(43)	*Tum*	*Zaun assai*	*Khoddap*
	Thou	Art	Rock

'Thou Art Rock (Peter)'

(44)	*Noman*	*Tuka,*	*Raya*
	Hail to	Thee	O King

'Hail to Thee, O King'

These are all religious works from South Kanara Christian Konkani which often involve translation. It has been pointed out before that Portuguese syntactic influence is occasionally found in this dialect in the translation of set phrases and prayers. For this reason, it is possible that these are also cases of Portuguese syntactic influence. In that case, the number of titles which deviate from the usual Konkani word order because of stylistic or discourse considerations among the works from the other Konkani dialects is even smaller (under 1 per cent).

Kelekar (1963) does not include Konkani periodicals and Portuguese syntactic influence appears to be most conspicuous in Goan Christian Konkani periodicals although not all periodicals are equally affected by Portuguese syntactic patterns. It is conspicuous in the earliest Konkani periodicals such as *O Concani* (founded in 1893) as well as in the recent issues of some Konkani periodicals, although after the departure of the Portuguese from Goa in the 1960s, more and more periodicals have abandoned the Portuguese syntactic patterns.

Here is information regarding the relative frequency of some Portuguese word order patterns in an article titled *Suru Zalem?* 'Has it Started?' from *The Goa Times* (Saturday, 25 November 1967). Only Object Verb versus Verb Object, Adverb Verb versus Verb Adverb, Genitive Noun versus Noun Genitive, Adjective Noun versus Noun Adjective constructions were checked.

Object Verb: 24	Adverb Verb: 8	Genitive Noun: 23	Adjective Noun: 11
Verb Object: 13	Verb Adverb: 11	Noun Genitive: 9	Noun Adjective: 0

In the examined materials, the Verb Adverb pattern is slightly more frequent than the Adverb Verb pattern. However, the Verb Object, Noun Genitive, and Noun Adjective patterns are considerably less frequent than the Object Verb, Genitive Noun, and Adjective Noun patterns, respectively. In fact, there isn't a single instance of Noun Adjective in the examined material. However, it is found elsewhere in this dialect although it does appear to be a lot less common than the Adjective Noun pattern. The only purpose of presenting this information here is to illustrate the extent of Portuguese influence that one might find in a random sample of Goan Christian literature. It is impossible to say how typical these figures are without a similar examination of a variety of materials.

CONCLUSION

The nature of syntactic modification in the Goan Christian dialect of Konkani due to the influence of Portuguese was examined in this paper. Such syntactic modification was found only in the written variety of this dialect and in formal speech and it had an optional status. This phenomenon was first observed by Chavan (1924). Old Konkani shows only limited Portuguese influence and Portuguese syntactic patterns are not productive there. However, in modern Goan Christian Konkani these syntactic patterns have become quite productive. The earliest specimens of such modified Konkani go back to the late decades of the nineteenth century. After the departure of the Portuguese, there has been a movement to purge this dialect of excessive Portuguese influence as a result of which more and more writers are abandoning the practice of introducing Portuguese syntactic patterns in Goan Christian Konkani.

The syntactic patterns adopted from Portuguese include mostly word order patterns, such as the placement of the direct and the indirect object and of the adverb after the verb, the placement of the predicate noun phrase after the copula, and the placement of the relative or reduced relative clause after the head noun. There are, however, some transformations as well among these patterns. It has been argued here that such Lusitanisation of Konkani syntax was not brought about by the early Portuguese missionaries and that, in all likelihood, the native Goans who were well-versed in Portuguese and were admirers of this language were responsible for it.

NOTES

1. Chavan (1924) further complains after presenting his specimen sentences:

   It will be seen from the . . . instances that the oriental way of subject, predicate, and object and qualifying sentences is given up and the Portuguese grammatical method is adopted. To a lover of Konkani, this method acts as a repellent. This sort of style, with good many Portuguese words preponderating, deprives the dialect of its natural sweetness.

2. Neither Chavan (1924) nor Katre (1942) have analysed the structure of these sentences. Some of the Roman characters used in Konkani writings have special phonetic values: *tt, dd, nn,* and *ll* indicate the retroflex consonants [ṭ], [ḍ], [ṇ], and [ḷ], respectively. *nh* stands for [ñ]. Word-finally, *m* usually indicates that the preceding vowel is nasalised. In Old Konkani, a variant of the tilde that looks like ˈ is also commonly used to indicate nasalisation. In Old Konkani, [ə] and [a] are represented respectively by a and *a* in print and by *a* and *â* in manuscripts. In modern Goan Christian Konkani, [ə] has changed into [o] and, therefore, *a* just represents [a]. As in Portuguese, *c* is [k] in Konkani before back vowels and in the final position, ç stands for [s]. *ch* is pronounced as [č] before front vowels, but as [ts] elsewhere. Similarly, *z* is pronounced as [ǰ] before front vowels, but

elsewhere it is [dz] word-initially and [z] in other environments. *s* is [š] before front vowels. [š] is sometimes also written as *x* as in Portuguese. *g* represents [ǰ] before front vowels and *gu* occasionally represents just [g] before front vowels.

3. Also, the form of the Copula used is not the native element as (from Middle Indo-Aryan *acch-*) but *vərtə-*, evidently a borrowing from Sanskrit.
4. Chavan and Katre have given a version of the Konkani sentences in Hindu Konkani which differs from this dialect not only with respect to Portuguese influence but also with respect to other grammatical and lexical characteristics.
5. Katre says:

   It is a clear indication of the manner in which the [Goan Christian] literature has come into existence under the guidance of Portuguese missionaries who evidently introduced this translation method as the best way of building up a new ecclesiastical literature.

6. There is hardly any Konkani literature available from the eighteenth century and the first half of the nineteenth century.
7. Kelekar (1963) does not have a separate list of modern Goan Christian Konkani works as such. What it really contains is three separate lists of Konkani writings:
   a. A bibliography of Konkani literature in Devanagari characters.
   b. A bibliography of Konkani literature in Roman characters.
   c. A bibliography of Konkani literature in Kannada characters.

   The second list contains not only modern Goan Christian Konkani works but also Old Konkani works which were always written in the Roman script and a few modern Goan Hindu and South Kanara Christian works which happen to be written in the Roman script. However, the Old Konkani and modern Goan Hindu as well as South Kanara Christian works included here are not many, and when these are excluded, the remaining works are still over 1000.
8. About 400 items listed in the bibliography are from the South Kanara Christian dialect. The number of writings in the Goa Hindu dialect included in the bibliography is only about 80.
9. Also, about 80 of the Konkani works have wholly Portuguese titles, 20 have English titles, and three have Latin titles. This is not unreasonable when the work happens to be a bilingual work such as a dictionary. However, only seventeen of the works with a Portuguese title and two of the works with an English title are bilingual works.
10. Also, it is possible that normal word order is altered in titles of works or headings of chapters for stylistic or other considerations. For instance, in Hindi literature of an earlier period, we often find the genitive noun phrase placed after the head noun on titles of chapters, etc. Although it might be due to Persian influence, it must be considered a stylistic feature.
11. A bibliography of Konkani literature in Devanagari characters in Kelekar (1963) includes fifteen titles of Goan Christian Konkani which happen to be in the Devanagari script. Interestingly, four of them deviate from the usual Konkani word order. In all cases, the genitive noun phrase is placed after the head noun.

REFERENCES

CHAVAN, V.P.

1924 The Konkan and the Konkani language. *Journal of the Anthropological Society of Bombay*, vol. XII, no. 7. 853–917.

DALGADO, S.R.

1913 *Influência do Vocabulário Português em Línguas Asiáticas*. Coimbra: University Press.

KATRE, S.M.

1942 Reprinted, 1966. *The formation of Konkani*. Poona: Deccan College.

KELEKAR, R.

1963 *A bibliography of Konkani literature in Devanagari, Roman, and Kannada characters*. Goa: Gomant Bharati Publications.

5
Multilingualism

D.P. PATTANAYAK
Plenary Lecture

India has been a multilingual, multiethnic and a multicultural country ever since its known history. The last census to give mother tongue information is the 1961 census. It gives a list of 1652 mother tongue names. If one counts mother tongue names beginning from the first-ever census in India, one comes across approximately 3000 mother tongues. They approximate to 200–700 languages (some claiming 200, some 700 and the Peoples of India Project 324) depending on how one counts. All these belong to four language families, maybe five if Nahali is counted as the fifth.

Those who consider many languages a problem are desperate when they confront large numbers. They do not stop by to note that 471 of these mother tongues are spoken by five or less persons; 652 are spoken by at least 10,000 speakers each; and out of these 33 are spoken by 10,00,000 speakers each. Add to this the fact that speakers belonging to an area outside the language zone they are interviewed in, such as Pardeshi, Bahargaon, as well as speakers speaking the language of a specific area such as Bilaspuria are reported. It appears that one can without fear of contradiction say that the 1652 mother tongues reported by the census are not language names. They are identity tokens, which need analysis and clarification.

How political interference changes the language map can be seen from the 1981 census. A political decision was taken to merge languages spoken by 10,000 speakers and less with dominant languages of the area. According to the 1981 census, 221 languages are spoken by 10,000 speakers. Within this

90 languages exceed 10,000 speakers out of which 49 are spoken by speakers between one and ten lakhs. It is the change in the measuring rod which is responsible for this havoc. The concern to reduce the number of languages and to inflate the number of speakers of Hindi and other dominant languages is at the root of such devastating consequences.

A different perspective of the multilingual status of India can be seen from the following. Although eighteen languages are recognised by the Eighth Schedule of the Constitution of India, the Sahitya Academy has given recognition to 22 languages and has recognised fifteen minor languages for development. In India, newspapers and periodicals are published in 35 languages, 67 languages are used for primary education, and the National Literacy Mission imparts literacy in 80 languages and the All India Radio broadcasts in 104 languages. Under these circumstances to speak of reducing the number of languages and move towards dominant monolingualism is against the spirit of multilingualism.

Multiculturalism finds expression in the 330 millions of gods and goddesses of the Hindus. Even the Muslims and Christians who have come to this country have become so diversified that there are 100 Muslim groups and 70 Christian groups in the country. There are 46,000 species of plants, 65,000 animal varieties, 4000 castes and communities and an approximately equal number of faiths and beliefs. At one end there is the assertion *Ekoham bahussam* ('one becomes many') and at the other end *Tasmai devaaya havisaa vidhema* ('To which gods shall I offer ghee sacrifice'). The kind and complexity of diversity present in India is not to be found anywhere else in the world.

The divergence is neither a barrier to admixture nor is it a barrier to communication. Apart from bi-/multilingualism, two other processes have contributed to cultural unity. One is the creation of pidgins. Nagamese, Sadri and Desia are the three pidgins that bind mutually unintelligible disparate languages together. Nagamese is spoken in North-Eastern India, Sadri on the borders of Assam, Bengali, Hindi and Oriya and Desia on the Andhra-Orissa border. The second is different languages operating with a single grammar. The study of Kupwar, a village on the Maharashtra-Karnataka border, initiated by John Gumperz, shows that three languages, Kannada, Marathi and Urdu belonging to two language families, operate with a single grammar. It is no wonder that travellers to India in their travel records recognise it as a single linguistic, sociolinguistic, and semantic area.

Dominant monolingualism and multilingualism divide the world in the same way as rich and poor, information-rich and information-poor, and developed and developing. The imbalance is so great that 10 per cent of the people belonging to the rich, information-rich and the developed consume 90 per cent of the world energy, control and consume 90 per cent of the world's information resources and manipulate 90 per cent of the world's wealth in order to maintain their life-style.

The world is multilingual with 5000 languages. Instead of building theories on the basis of multilingualism, the developed countries have built theories from the vantage point of their dominant monolingual experience. This is of importance as the bulk of research funding is utilised in the developed countries. Paul Neergaard, former Director of the Danish Institute of Seed Pathology, has pointed out that in 1973, 97 per cent of the research funding in the world was spent in the First and the Second World. Only 3 per cent was spent in the developing world. There is little difference between then and now. Therefore, whether it is multilingualism or multimodal state, about multicropping or pluriculturalism, theories were constructed in the First and the Second World with a view to universalising their experience. This permanently handicapped the developing world and made them permanent parasites on the colonial world.

The mindset of the western-educated Indian leadership, whether left or right, was naturally in conformity with European thinking. They were far away from Gandhi who was called the Father of the Nation. Gandhi said that India lives in its 50,000 villages. Karl Marx considered the villages as an impediment to development. Ambedkar, the chief architect of the Indian Constitution, in his speech in the Constituent Assembly on 4 November 1948 said,

> No doubt the village communities have lasted where nothing else lasts . . . but mere survival has no value. . . . What is a village but a stink of localism, a den of ignorance, narrow-mindedness and communalism? (VII, CAD 38–39)

Jawaharlal Nehru was also part of the same mindset. In his letter of 9 October 1945 to Gandhi he wrote, 'A village is backward intellectually and culturally and no progress can be made from a backward environment. Narrow minded people are much more likely to be untruthful and violent.' It is a wonder that Gandhi's Gram Swaraj 'autonomous village' and Lohia's Four-Pillar State were not considered as alternatives by our nationalists who wanted to fashion the Indian state in the image of their colonial masters.

The developed countries talk about post-modern and post-colonial discourse. When they do not recognise the Third World as modern, to talk about post-modern and post-colonial discourse is meaningless. This is meant to divert attention from the fact that we are still the victims of colonial exploitation. The difference between the colonial and the post-colonial perspective is that colonial countries like Britain, France, Portugal, and Spain imposed colonialism by force and through deception, whereas at the present time the Third World elite, having been co-opted into the vested interest fold, welcome colonialism.

Colonialism is an ongoing process. Those who talk about post-colonialism forget the rationalisation of the newer garbs in which it enters into the developing world. The first rationalisation is that colonialism came to civilise the natives. The Second Coming is to develop the underdeveloped. The justification of the Third Coming is to protect the ecology and the environment. Whether the motive be to civilise, to develop or to protect, the net result is exploitation. Exploitation is stabilised by putting the indigenous languages in adversary postures with the colonial language and by robbing the mother tongues of the indigenous people.

The developed countries appropriated the First and Second World status, lumped the countries of Asia, Africa, and Latin America and christened them the Third World. The First and the Second World, otherwise called the Developed World, are monomodal societies, whereas the Third World is multilingual, multi-ethnic, and pluricultural. The developed countries are colonial whereas the developing countries are colonised.

The relationship between the one, the two and the many, monolingualism, bilingualism and multilingualism is very complex. It can be seen as parallel to singular, dual, and plural. The dual is a historic relic in languages like Sanskrit. So is bilingualism, a rare category between monolingualism and multilingualism. The variations within a single language, dialects, sociolects, styles and registers, were hardly recognised by dominant monolingual states, though literary styles received some attention. French is an example where many deputies insisted that French had no dialects. UK, USA and the developed European countries are examples of the denial of the existence of mother tongues and native speakers, both of which concepts were attributed to minor and minority languages.

In English, some nouns have different meanings in singular and plural. For example, 'air' refers to 'the air we breathe' or 'the atmosphere'; 'airs' means 'pretentiousness'. Some nouns have two meanings in the singular, but one in the plural. For example, 'light' means 'radiance' or 'lamp-like things that emit light' such as torchlight, candle-light, etc. But in its plural form it refers to its second meaning. Some nouns have one meaning in the singular, but two in the plural. For example, 'spectacle' means 'a sight'; 'spectacles' mean 'sights' as well as 'eye glasses'. Similarly, monolingualism refers to the use of one language or the dominant use of a language. Multilingualism refers to the use of two or more languages. Multilingualism may refer to the conglomeration of different single language speakers in a locality or may refer to many languages shared by a community.

Most of the theories emanating from the developed world perceive different as deficient and assume that structures built around unitary symbols are superior to those built around multiple symbols. Bilingualism was considered inferior, subtractive and less in intelligent quotient than monolingualism. Development was made contingent on monolingualism. Unilingual and monocultural states were considered superior to bilingual and multilingual states. Canada, a bilingual state, came to the verge of secession, as both English and French are perceived to be in adversary relation. Switzerland, which had three languages and with the introduction of English became a four-language state received grudging recognition from theory-builders. It was theorised that states having more than three or four languages are muddle-headed. Once bilingualism received recognition, the theory builders accepted bilingualism and multiculturalism. They are unwilling to accept multilingualism as a carrier of multiculturalism.

Theories of state idealised the nation state built around unitary symbols. One language, one religion, one culture and in its extreme manifestation one party and one leader defined the nation state. The Third World countries, when decolonised, built their states in the model of their colonial masters. From unitary to federal, the state was considered a quantum jump in the same way as monolingualism progressed into bilingualism.

The word 'development' has been used in diverse ways in social science literature. Language development is detached from (economic) development and has not found place in any developmental study. It is not appreciated by theory-builders that adequacy/inadequacy is not to be sought in the language but in the individual user. Vitality is not to be sought in the language structure, but in the user. It is a well-known maxim in sociolinguistics that the maintenance of a language depends on the loyalty of its speakers. As development presupposes under development, according to the theory-builders, language development must presuppose language underdevelopment. The development theorists brand all Third World languages as underdeveloped. The minor and minority languages in the developed world are referred to as the Fourth World. In Canada and in Australia the itinerants and the tribals are referred to as the First Nations or the Fourth World in seize.

Multiple scripts have raised controversies in India. Those who plead for a single script forget that languages in India belong to four language families, while scripts other than Roman and Perso-Arabic belong to a single family. All of them go back to a single source, Brahmi. The Peoples of India Project speaks of 25 scripts. But if one takes into consideration revealed and invented scripts and the new scripts created to replace existing scripts the number will be four times as much. Professor S.K. Chatterjee pleaded for Roman, but he refused to set an example by writing in Roman instead of Bengali. Reduction of scripts as well as languages are pressures exerted by monomodal logic. The controversy overlooks two factors. One is that the current claim of 50 per cent literacy will come down to 2 per cent once one script replaces the many in use. Secondly, there is bound to be a major break between tradition and modernity as transmission of traditional culture through the literacy mode is ruptured.

There are many points of departure to distinguish between monolingualism and multilingualism. One of the points is idiolect, which is the ensemble of language resources of an individual. So far it is taken for granted that the idiolect refers to a single language. So far to my knowledge no scholar has spoken about multilingual idiolect and what the many languages do in an idiolect. When an English teacher was asked how he handled the classroom where different children came with diverse English resources, he said, that he idealised his variety of English and told the class that he was the last word in the classroom. Even Chomsky's statement about the language of the ideal speaker-hearer is the result of his monolingual inheritance.

Another factor is the measurement of language competence of a monolingual and a multilingual learner. Until recently the competence of the multilingual was measured against that of a monolingual and the multilingual was found wanting. It was not taken into consideration that the monolingual manages his entire universe of discourse with a single language whereas the multilingual handles his with a number of languages. Take for example my own case. I use Oriya for intimate communication. I use English for most professional communication and elite communication. I use Hindi as well as broken Kannada for proximate communication. I read Bengali for entertainment as well as enrichment and pray in Sanskrit. I use French for research.

The domains of language use have evolved over years. Any change in language use is bound to create ludicrous situations. Therefore, it is unfair to compare my English competence with that of a dominantly monolingual English speaker and declare me incompetent. Similarly, it is unfair to compare the language competence of a first-generation learner with one who has education for generations at home. There is very little definitive research about it in the Third World countries.

A new category of people has emerged as a result of import of cheap labour, indentured labour or skilled labour in the developed countries. They are not considered citizens of the host countries. Their languages are called transplanted languages. Terms such as obliteration of transplanted languages, language endangerment, incipient language death are created and their import is debated by linguists. It is forgotten that language death takes place not because of loss of rules, but because of apathy of speakers and planners. In India, Marathis in Thanjavur, Bengalis in Varanasi, Telugus in Orissa have settled for generations without the fear of being assimilated. It is only now, because of aggressive regionalism, that the minority groups feel threatened. The more we talk about national integration and joining the mainstream, the more their hollowness is revealed. This is mere camouflage for assimilation. For the last few decades, I have been trying to identify the mainstream. I am yet to find it.

Before I close I must narrate an episode. In Uppsala I was presenting a paper on mother-tongue education. To my great surprise, a gentleman from the audience stood up and pointing his finger towards me shouted, 'You, people from the Third World countries, you make unsubstantiated generalisations. Can you give me a single example to explain the kinds of difference you are trying to make between monolingualism and multilingualism?' I was taken completely by surprise, as this was the first statement of the kind I had encountered in an academic meeting. I composed myself and told him that I would give two examples as he had asked for one. I told him that in the Western countries one language is the norm, two languages are a quantum jump, hundred per cent achievement over one, three languages are fairly tolerable and many languages are absurd.

For us, people of the Third World countries, many languages are a fact of life. Any restriction on the choice of language use is oppressive, three languages are a strategy for language acquisition, two languages are tolerable and one language is absurd. I asked him to keep on standing as I had yet to give my second example. I told him that Professor Brian Weinstein, looking at the American system, formulated a question, 'How much diversity can this culture tolerate?' I said, 'If someone formulates such a question in my country, he would not be worth his salt as a social scientist. He must formulate the question, how much uniformity can this culture tolerate?' Needless to say that my answer was well received.

On another occasion I pointed out that the kind of theory building pursued by the American scholars was unsuitable for the Third World. The Americans first of all formulated the Melting Pot theory. The assumption was that people from diverse ethnicities would melt and fuse their identities and assume a single American identity. After 200 years of experimentation they awoke to the reality that the pot had melted leaving the identities in tact. Then they formulated the Salad Bowl theory. Unfortunately, this is a metaphor of eating. Whether one eats them singly or severally, the consequence will be the same. The smaller languages and cultures were gobbled up by the larger ones. The same approach can be adopted to analyse the theory of distant strangers. The thinly plastered English education on the Indian system has made the neighbour a stranger and the distant vaguely familiar.

There is no dearth of mono-model logicians in India. The first time I came to Delhi after assuming charge of the Central Institute of Indian Languages, someone accosted me in the corridors of the Ministry of Education and asked me, which according to me was the national language of India. I told him that all languages spoken in India are national languages of the country. Not one is anti-national.

I would like to quote Gandhi in conclusion. Gandhi is the only politician who understood the pulse of the country. A policy is needed to spell out the use of different languages for designated purposes. Gandhi was the only person who seems to have had a clear understanding of the problems and prospects facing India. Gandhi was against intolerance. He was aware that a pluricultural country cannot be sustained through intolerance, whether the intolerance is from the majorities to the minorities or vice versa. A multilingual country cannot be isolationist. Gandhi said,

> I do not want my house to be walled in all sides and my windows stuffed. I want the cultures of all lands to be blown about my house as freely as possible. But I refuse to be blown off my feet by any. (*Gandhi's thoughts,* Govt. of Goa 1984)

A multicultural state can only thrive on respect for the different. Intolerance cannot coexist with respect for the different.

REFERENCES

CONSTITUENT ASSEMBLY DEBATES
1950 Government of India, Ministry of Law. CAD VII.
GOVERNMENT OF GOA
1984 *Gandhi's thoughts.*

II

PHONETICS, PHONOLOGY AND MORPHOLOGY

6
Assessing the role of Punjabi phonological skills in English literacy development in Punjabi/English bilingual children

JANE STUART-SMITH and DEIRDRE MARTIN
University of Glasgow *University of Birmingham*

This paper presents the interim research findings on bilingual Punjabi/English children developing English literacy in England. We focus on the relationship between oracy in both languages and the development of English literacy. The particular aspect of oracy is phonological processing and the aspect of literacy is single word processing. The purpose of the research is to enable us to understand better how bilingual children develop literacy by throwing more light on the relationship between phonological processing and literacy. Originally, we wished to look at this relationship across both phonologies and both literacies. This was not possible because most of the children participating in the study were not yet literate in Gurmukhi, the script of Punjabi-speaking Sikhs. The Punjabi classes did not start teaching literacy fully until the children were about ten years old and the children in the study were only seven years old, and many did not attend Punjabi class. (Only two of the children were able to attempt the Punjabi literacy tasks; their results do not appear to be

We are grateful for the assistance of Kuldip Kaur Dhesi as bilingual co-worker in this research. This study is part of a one-year ESRC funded research project held at the School of Education, University of Birmingham, grant no. R000221501 (principal investigator: D. Martin). Jane Stuart-Smith is grateful to the Humanities Research Board of the British Academy for a grant enabling her to attend the *18th South Asian Language Analysis Roundtable*, 6-8 January 1997, New Delhi, at which a version of this paper was presented.

any different from those of the other children, and have therefore been included.)

The paper addresses three questions. Firstly, how can we assess phonological processing skills across both languages? Are there constraints arising from the nature of the different phonologies and are we able to identify them? Secondly, what is the profile of phonological processing across both languages? Are there differences and how may we explain them? Thirdly, are there specific links between Punjabi phonological processing and the development of literacy in English? We would hypothesise that Punjabi phonological processing does not detract from English literacy development and that there are no grounds for a 'deficit' theory. Assuming that the children are using common cognitive meta-linguistic knowledge to carry out the tasks, we would hope to show that children are able to process phonological information similarly across both languages. However, we would look for differences in processing which we might attribute in part to different features of the two phonologies and also to the effects of literacy instruction in English.

PHONOLOGICAL PROCESSING SKILLS AND LITERACY DEVELOPMENT IN CHILDREN

In the wealth of research on the development of literacy some recent research has focused on the role of phonological processing skills and, in particular, on phonological awareness in children (for reviews, see Wagner and Torgesen 1987; Goswami and Bryant 1990; Snowling and Stackhouse 1996).

Phonological awareness is our ability to store, access and retrieve the sound structure of spoken language, in particular, of words and syllables. The stored knowledge of the sound structure of the word is called phonological representation. Phonological processing entails an ability to manipulate the phonological representation. There are different forms of knowledge, or phonological awareness, that we have about sequences of sound structures, namely, syllabic, phonemic and intra-syllabic. Syllabic awareness in sound sequences is the awareness of the rhythmic segmentation of the sequence. So, for example, English *cat* has one beat, *hap-py* two beats, *but-ter-fly* three beats and *cau-li-flo-wer* four beats. Examples in Punjabi are /ʃer/ 'lion' with one beat, /ke-la/ 'banana' with two beats, and /hɔ-thɔ-ɽa/ 'hammer' with three beats. Phonemic awareness is the knowledge of the separate sounds (phonemes) in a word, which can be demonstrated, for example, by segmenting the sounds of English *cat* into /k-a-t/, or Punjabi /bol/ 'speak' into /b-o-l/. Awareness of intra-syllabic units is shown by knowledge of the onset/rime structure of the syllable; in English *cat*, /k/ is the onset and /at/ is the rime, while in Punjabi /bol/, /b/ is the onset and /ol/ is the rime. Onset and rime awareness are usually assessed through tasks of alliteration (same onset) and rhyme (same rime).

In the literature about phonological awareness, the syllable is taken as the processing unit, with an assumed hierarchical structure of onset and rime, where the rime contains a nucleus (usually the vowel), and the coda. We would argue that this approach is appropriate for investigating phonological processing. Psycholinguistic research has shown that storage, access and retrieval processes seem to be best explained by assuming a hierarchical syllable structure in phonological processing (for example, Treiman 1983). However, we are not unaware that the phonological awareness of sound structures as described above is largely based on English phonology. Furthermore, we suspected that our results from Punjabi, a language with a phonology quite different from English, could challenge some of the accepted ways of segmenting and manipulating sound structures used in phonological awareness tasks (see Stuart-Smith and Martin, in press).

There may be links between awareness of syllables and early progress in literacy, in young children (for example, four-year olds; see Liberman *et al.* 1974). However, there are stronger indications that awareness of phonemes and intra-syllabic units play a greater role in the successful acquisition of literacy (for example, Bradley and Bryant 1983). Furthermore, it seems likely that there is a reciprocal relationship between phonemic awareness and literacy development. The importance of this for our study is that our participants are older – aged seven years – than those in many studies, and they have had at least two years of literacy instruction in English. In addition, most of the studies have been done either with monolingual children, or in only one language of the bilingual children (for example, Campbell and Sais 1995; or Durgunoglu *et al.* 1993, who investigate transfer across two literacies). In reporting our findings on children's processing for different forms of phonological awareness across both languages and the effect on the development of one literacy, we hope to extend the monolingual paradigm to include bilingual processing.

METHODOLOGY

We took a quasi-experimental approach, where we asked a cohort of children to respond individually to twelve sets of phonological awareness tasks in Punjabi and English and to two literacy tasks in English. We checked that their non-verbal performance skills were not giving concern, using the WISC/R, which did not involve items with obvious culture bias and has been used in other phonological awareness studies (Bradley and Bryant 1983). We ran some preliminary statistical analyses on the numerical data from the tasks using the Wilcoxon test and Spearman's correlation given the observed distribution of the scores; these are reported later in the results.

The results from 30 children are presented here although the main study had a cohort of 65 children. Since these are interim findings we appreciate that later analysis may present a different picture. The thirty children, comprised fifteen boys and girls (x = 7.3 years), who spoke fluent Punjabi and English. All the children came from a similar socio-economic background from three primary schools in west Birmingham, UK. They were developing literacy in English only, except two children who were biliterate.

ASSESSMENT PROCEDURES

The procedures used to investigate the children's ability to access, retrieve and manipulate their phonological representations were similar to those used in other phonological awareness studies (Stahl and Murray 1994). The procedures are given in full in the Appendix. The tasks investigated phonemic and syllabic awareness by phonemic and syllabic segmentation tasks, through tapping out the sounds (phonemic) and through clapping out the syllables. Knowledge of the intra-syllabic forms of the phonological representation were assessed by alliteration and rhyming tasks.

All these tasks investigated knowledge at the receptive level, that is the children's ability to access, and at the expressive level, that is their ability to access and retrieve. The children were asked to match or detect the correct or incorrect item from a short selection. They were also asked to generate the skill, such as tapping the phonemes or generating rhymes. A further set of tasks required manipulation of the phonological representation, through isolating and deleting the sounds of words. The children were asked to isolate the onset or the coda of the word. They were also asked to delete the onset or coda, and say what remained. The (English) literacy tasks comprised reading and spelling single words.

The tasks were drawn up in both languages. It is important to note that sensitivity to the phonology of each language is required both for the development of the task stimuli and for the analysis of the results of each task (Stuart-Smith and Martin, in press). For example, investigating phonemic segmentation (tapping) in English involves offering stimuli, which contain both single consonants and consonant clusters in onsets and codas, which may have implications for phonological processing in terms of linguistic complexity. In contrast, Punjabi, and particularly the variety (from the rural area around Jalandhar) spoken by the children and our co-worker, has fewer consonant clusters, and the stimuli we used for the phonemic segmentation task had no consonant clusters. In developing the stimuli and analysing the results of the data, we were aware of the need to be sensitive to the implications of the two different phonologies across all the tasks.

TASK RESULTS

Phonological processing skills

Before looking for specific links between Punjabi phonological processing skills and English literacy, we first considered the profile of the children's phonological awareness across both languages. We had assumed that the children would show similar ability in the phonological processing tasks in both languages, on the grounds that they would draw on the same cognitive metalinguistic knowledge to perform them. In general, the children did seem to perform similarly across both languages; where they did not, the reasons seem to lie in the different phonologies of Punjabi and English, and in the effects of literacy instruction in English.

In both languages children were significantly better at tasks which involved manipulating or recognising sounds in words, rather than syllables. That the children were performing relatively well in phonemic tasks could be consistent with their accumulated experience of (English) literacy instruction, which emphasises the relationship between sounds and letters; the children in this study have already had three years of literacy training. What is interesting is the apparent drop in syllabic awareness in this group of children. Other studies, and notably that of Liberman *et al.* (1974), have shown that syllabic awareness is basic for younger children. Perhaps the shift from syllabic to phonemic awareness is partly a developmental phenomenon, which is exacerbated by literacy instruction.

We also notice the tendency (not significant in these interim results) that children found phonemic segmentation easier in Punjabi than in English. This difference could be due to differences in the nature of the task stimuli, resulting from the phonologies of the two languages. We mentioned earlier that English stimuli for phonemic segmentation contained consonant clusters as these occur regularly in English words, while in Punjabi consonant clusters are far less frequent, and were not present in our task stimuli. Children have been observed to find manipulating consonant clusters difficult (Bruck and Treiman 1990). It seems likely that the Punjabi stimuli were easier for the children to segment because they did not contain consonant clusters.

We did not find any difference between ability at alliteration and rhyming tasks, except that children could alliterate better in English than in Punjabi. This may be due to the active literacy training that the children have received in English, but not in Punjabi. In English many methods of teaching children to read and write focus on the first sound of a word, thus promoting awareness of onsets.

As well as investigating children's knowledge of aspects of the phonological representation, our tasks also assessed their ability to access, retrieve and manipulate elements of the stored sound structures of words. We had assumed that deletion tasks would involve a more complex set of operations than isolation tasks, and so we expected that the children would find deleting sounds more difficult than isolating them. However only in Punjabi did we find that the isolation tasks were easier than the deletion tasks; in English there was no significant difference between the two mean scores. Moreover, we found that children could isolate sounds better in Punjabi than in English.

The reason for these different results in English and Punjabi may again lie in the phonologies of the two languages. The isolation tasks require the children to give the onset or coda of a given word. In English each task contained a number of words with consonant clusters at the beginning of the word (complex onset, for example, ***swop***, ***flame***) or at the end of the word (complex coda, for example, ***vest***, ***hand***). The children found isolating the cluster as a whole difficult, and often just gave one sound; difficulty with initial consonant clusters in English was found by Bruck and Treiman (1990). Difficulties were also encountered in the deletion tasks, where we required children to delete an entire onset or coda, but often only one sound of a cluster was deleted. The phonology of English led to a set of stimuli, which were potentially ambiguous for the children, and thus may have obscured any overall difference between ability in isolation and deletion. The Punjabi stimuli, on the other hand, had no consonant clusters. The children were able to isolate onset and coda with few problems, but deletion was much more difficult, as expected. This also explains why the children could isolate sounds so much better in Punjabi than in English.

We had also assumed that the tasks grouped together under 'generation' involve more complex processing (access and retrieval) than those under 'detection' (access and mapping). In line with this assumption, the children found detection tasks much easier than generation tasks in both languages. The finding across both languages suggests that this form of phonological processing is not language-specific. We found that the children were much better at the reading task than the spelling task ($p < 0$).

PUNJABI PHONOLOGICAL PROCESSING SKILLS AND ENGLISH LITERACY

Once we had obtained a profile of the children's phonological processing skills in both languages, and had the results to the simple English literacy tasks, we were in a position to try and identify which aspects of phonological awareness in each language might be linked to English literacy. We carried out a preliminary correlational analysis on the scores using Spearman's correlation. The results are given in Table 1. (Significant correlations are in bold and starred according to the degree of statistical significance.)

TABLE 1 *Spearman's ranked correlation coefficients for phonological tasks and English literacy tasks (N = 30)*

TASKS	READING	WRITING
English phonemic tasks	**0.34**	**0.56**
Punjabi phonemic tasks	n/a	n/a
English syllabic tasks	**0.32**	**0.28**
Punjabi syllabic tasks	0.21	0.37
English alliteration	**0.37**	**0.33**
Punjabi alliteration	0.18	0.17
English rhyme	0.10	0.23
Punjabi rhyme	0.14	0.20
English isolation	-0.26	-0.00
Punjabi isolation	0.00	0.07
English deletion	**0.49**	**0.38**
Punjabi deletion	n/a	n/a
English detection	**0.31**	**0.27**
Punjabi detection	n/a	n/a
English generation	**0.43**	**0.58**
Punjabi generation	0.10	0.30

$p < 0.05$, *$p < 0.01$

NOTE: n/a indicates instances where correlations could not be found because of missing values.

In general, strong positive correlations emerged between ability in English phonological processing and English literacy. While we did not find evidence for positive correlations between good Punjabi phonological awareness and English literacy, at the same time there was no instance of a negative correlation. In other words, our results show no support for a 'deficit' hypothesis that speaking Punjabi could detract from developing English literacy successfully.

If we consider the relationship between English literacy and tasks which investigated knowledge about elements of phonological representations (phonemic/syllabic tasks; alliteration/rhyming), we found that strong correlations exist with English phonological tasks, but not with Punjabi tasks. (There is one exception, between Punjabi syllabic awareness and English word-spelling which is difficult to explain.) This makes sense if we assume that reading and writing in English requires knowledge of the structure of the phonological representations of *English* (and not Punjabi).

There is a strong correlation between good phonemic awareness in English and English reading, and an even stronger relationship with English word-spelling. The picture for the links between syllabic awareness and literacy is less clear. The link between ability in English phonemic tasks and successful literacy has been frequently demonstrated (Liberman *et al.* 1974; more recently, Muter 1994). We can only speculate about the causal nature of the correlation; but it seems reasonable to assume that there is a reciprocal relationship between phonemic awareness and literacy achievement, and that during literacy acquisition phonemic awareness is promoted by literacy training (Cataldo and Ellis 1988; Campbell and Sais 1995).

High scores in English literacy also correlate strongly with English alliteration tasks. This seems to be in line with the earlier result that children were particularly proficient in alliteration tasks in English. Both results, together with the lack of correlation between Punjabi alliteration tasks and literacy scores, suggest that literacy instruction in English promotes awareness of onsets in English words (or at the very least, that there is a reciprocal relationship between English onset awareness and developing English literacy). Interestingly, we do not appear to find evidence of 'cross-language transfer', (Durgunoglu *et al.* 1993); the correlation only exists with the English tasks, but not the Punjabi tasks. Our finding would suggest that some forms of phonological awareness (about phonological representations) relevant to literacy achievement are language-specific. This is not in itself surprising; again, why should we expect that knowledge of the sound structure of Punjabi words could help a child learning to read and write in *English*?

Unlike other studies (for example, Bradley and Bryant 1983; Frederickson 1995), we did not find a link between ability in rhyming tasks and literacy (in either language). This result is not as unusual as it might seem. Muter's longitudinal study (1994) shows that rhyming does not necessarily play a role at all stages of literacy development. It is also possible that our literacy tasks were too brief for any connections to emerge; for example, the use of analogical strategies, linked with rhyming by Goswami (Goswami and Bryant 1992) could not have been demonstrated.

The second group of phonological awareness tasks (isolation/deletion; detection/generation) assessed the children's ability to access, retrieve and manipulate the phonological representation. We assumed that deletion and generation tasks involved more complex sets of operations on the phonological representation, and this was reflected in the results, as the children found these tasks more difficult. The decoding of text required in reading and the access and retrieval of sounds needed for spelling also require relatively complex phonological processing. We would expect positive correlations between ability in deletion and generation and good literacy scores (cf. the results from the PhAB alliteration and rhyme fluency (= generation) tasks in Frederickson (1995). We also recall that, overall, the children showed a similar performance across both languages, suggesting that these tasks do not involve language-specific processing. Thus, we expected not only strong correlations between deletion and generation tasks and literacy scores, but also that the correlations would hold across both languages.

Strong correlations were found between deletion and generation tasks and English literacy, but only for the English phonological processing tasks. While we could not find the correlation coefficient for Punjabi deletion tasks due to missing values, the values of the (positive) correlations for Punjabi generation tasks and literacy were not significant. However, a finer-grained analysis of the individual scores making up the correlations suggests that outliers may perhaps skew the correlation between the Punjabi generation tasks and English spelling scores. We can identify two types of outliers:

- a group of three children who are good at Punjabi generation but poor at English spelling. Assuming that good processing would underlie better spelling ability, we would expect these children to show better spelling scores; presumably other factors, either linguistic, or extra-linguistic, contribute to their relatively poor scores.
- one child who is poor at Punjabi generation but good at English spelling. This case is more unusual, since we might assume that relatively good literacy might presume proficiency in processing skills. Perhaps this child has developed visual strategies for acquiring spellings, thus compensating for poorer phonological processing. This may also explain how the same child achieved a reasonable score in the English generation tasks.

This closer analysis of the apparent contradiction between the correlations for English spelling scores and generation tasks in *both* languages raises some interesting points. A child's performance in English generation tasks may be mediated by visual strategies derived from their experience with English literacy. Their performance in Punjabi generation tasks, on the other hand, may not be influenced by contact with Punjabi literacy acquisition, and thus may show more clearly the child's processing skills. Examination of the correlation between the *Punjabi* generation tasks and spelling gives us a better insight into the child's possible literacy strategies.

Clearly for us to gain a better understanding of the developing literacy in this group of bilingual children, it was crucial that we assessed the children's phonological awareness skills in both English and in Punjabi.

CONCLUSION

There are three main conclusions we wish to draw from this study in response to the three questions we posed at the beginning of the paper. It seems that it is possible to investigate phonological processing across both languages, Punjabi and English, using existing procedures, provided we take into account the phonological constraints of the two languages both when developing the stimuli and when analysing the data.

Bilingual children perform similarly across both languages in phonological processing, which seems to support the notion that a common metalinguistic knowledge is operating across both phonological representations. Where there are exceptions, these can be explained by particular constraints of the two different phonologies of Punjabi and English, or by the effects of literacy instruction in English.

Finally, the study did not find specific links between Punjabi phonological processing and English literacy development. There is no evidence from our results to support a 'deficit' hypothesis, that speaking one language detracts from speaking and becoming literate in another language. Moreover, close analysis of the correlations between the Punjabi phonological processing tasks and the English literacy scores demonstrates the importance of investigating the pre-literacy skills of bilingual children in *both* languages.

APPENDIX

Assessment procedures given to the children, giving the English instructions and stimuli, followed by the Punjabi stimuli in phonemic transcription

ASSESSMENT PROCEDURES

(1) PHONEMIC JUDGEMENT (DETECTION)
Now I'm going to say a word all stretched out. I want you to tell me what the word is. Like this: I shall say ***s-u-n****, and you say* ***sun****.*

PRACTICE WORDS: sheep, pram.

TASK WORDS: cup, seat, nut, flame, spot, desk, sand, belt

PUNJABI PRACTICE WORDS: /rat/ /ʃer/ /sɪŋg/

PUNJABI TASK WORDS: /pɛr/ /vak/ /gol/ /ʃʊndʒ/ /khəɳɖ/ /tʃɪɽi/ /kela/ /kɪtab/

(2) PHONEMIC SEGMENTATION (GENERATION)
*Now I want you to tap out the sounds in a word. I can tap these words as they sound. Listen (*tap out sounds in ***cat, glass, hand****). This time you tap out the words when I point to them. Here are some new pictures. Tap the one I am pointing to.*

TASK WORDS: leg, cup, seat; plug, slide; wind, belt, vest.

PUNJABI PRACTICE WORDS: /gol/ /ʃer/ /hathi/

PUNJABI TASK WORDS: /val/ /pər/ /pɛr/; /səp:/, /həth:/; /tʃaku/ /məʈər/ /topi/

(3) SYLLABIC JUDGEMENT (DETECTION)
In this game I am going to clap out words. I can clap these words as they sound. Listen (clap out syllables in ***tree, lion, telephone, motorcycle****). Now I will clap them again and you point to the one I am clapping. Now here are some new pictures. Point to the one I am clapping.*

TASK WORDS: drum, umbrella, postman, cauliflower; television, flower, envelope, chair; elephant, helicopter, bag, rabbit

PUNJABI PRACTICE WORDS: /seb/ /kʊɽi/ /həthɔɽa/

PUNJABI TASK WORDS: /əkh:/ /lʊfafa/ /kə̀ɽi/; /məʈər/ /gʊbara/ /həth:/; /pɔɽiã/ /pər/ /tʃaku/

(4) SYLLABIC SEGMENTATION (GENERATION)
This time you are going to clap out the words when I point to them. Like this (child claps out **tree, lion, telephone, motorcycle***). Here are some new pictures. Clap the one I am pointing to.*

TASK WORDS: drum, umbrella, postman, cauliflower; television, flower, envelope, chair; elephant, helicopter, bag, rabbit [words were presented in a different order from task 3]

PUNJABI PRACTICE WORDS: /seb/ /kʊɽi/ /həthɔɽa/

PUNJABI TASK WORDS: /əkh:/ /lʊfafa/ kə̀ʈi/; /məʈər/ /gʊbara/ /həth:/; /pɔʈiã/ /pər/ /tʃaku/

(5) JUDGING ALLITERATION (DETECTION)
In this game we are going to match words that have the same firs sound, like ***cat, call, kite, king****, or* ***fish, fall, foot, feel****. Listen for the first sound in the first word I say, and tell me which of the other words I say starts with that sound. Like this* (say the words in bold first):

TARGET		ALLITERATION	SEMANTIC DISTRACTOR
look	/	**lip**	sight
rat	/	rock	**mouse**
sun	/	**soap**	moon
		TASK WORDS	
man	/	**meal**	girl
pen	/	pin	**write**
tall	/	**tin**	long
sail	/	**sign**	boat
bowl	/	bike	**dish**
chip	/	chin	**sauce**

PUNJABI PRACTICE WORDS

/nətʃ/ dance	/nal/ with	/tʃəl/ walk
/həth:/ hand	/hor/ more	/lət:/ leg

PUNJABI TASK WORDS

/səp:/ snake	/sɪŋg/ horn	/rɪtʃ:/ bear
/dIn/ day	/dekh/ look	/sal/ year
/kən:/ ear	/kol/ with	/sɪr/ head
/lɪkh:/ write	/lal/ red	/pəʈ/ read
/nək:/ nose	/nəl/ tape	/kən:/ ear
/pɛr/ foot	/pʊl/ bridge	/lət:/ leg

(6) GENERATING ALLITERATION (GENERATION)
This time you must say words that have the same first sound as the word I say,

like: **cat, call, kite, king,** *or* ***fish, fall, foot, feel****. Say some words with the same first sound as* ***cat*** (accept TWO words). (If child cannot, then prompt: **can, case.)**

PRACTICE WORDS: bun, safe

TASK WORDS: pen, man, chin, tap, fork, spin, climb, pram

PUNJABI PRACTICE WORDS: /səp:/ /tɪn:/

PUNJABI TASK WORDS: /nək:/ /kən:/ /rat/ /pɛr/ /kal/ /həth:/

(7) JUDGING RHYME (DETECTION)

This game is about rhymes. A rhyme is like **mat, cat, bat**; *or* **chair, hair, bear;** *or* **tan, man, lan**. *I am going to say a word. Then you have to find the word that rhymes with it from the next two words I say. Like this:* (say the words in **bold** first)

TARGET	RHYME	SEMANTIC DISTRACTOR
egg	**leg**	hen
star	car	**moon**
tin	**pin**	can
	TASK WORDS	
pan	**man**	pot
boat	coat	**sea**
dog	log	**cat**
tea	**key**	cup
game	name	**play**
sick	pick	**ill**
	PUNJABI PRACTICE WORDS	
/val/ hair	/dal/ lentils	/sɪr/ head
/mor/ peacock	/hor/ more	/kã/ crow
/bəs/ bus	/dəs/ ten	/kar/ car
	PUNJABI TASK WORDS	
/bol/ speak	/gol/ round	/tʃʊp:/ (be) silent
/har/ necklace	/kar/ car	/tə̀ɳ/ neck
/ʃer/ lion	/der/ late	/rɪtʃ:/ bear

contd. . .

TARGET	RHYME	SEMANTIC DISTRACTOR
/dɪl/ heart	/bɪl/ hole	/ʈɪɖ:/ stomach/tummy
/sur/ pig	/bur/ mould	/pèɖ/ sheep
/pɛr/ foot	/ser/ walk	/lət:/ leg

(8) GENERATING RHYME (GENERATION)
This time you must make up the rhymes yourself. I will say a word and you must say some words that rhyme with it. You can make up words if you like. Like this: say some words that rhyme with ***cat****.* (If child cannot, prompt with **bat**, **pat**)

PRACTICE WORDS: can, safe

TASK WORDS: cap, rain, hill, hoot, west, mend, tents, desks

PUNJABI PRACTICE WORDS: /gol/ /hor/ /pɛr/

PUNJABI TASK WORDS: /hɪl/ /mən/ /lal/ /der/ /git/ /gã/

(9) ISOLATING THE ONSET
This time I want you to listen to just one sound in the word. Tell me the first sound you hear in the word after each word I say. Like this: when I say ***fix****, you say '****f****'.*

PRACTICE WORDS: nut, shop

TASK WORDS: look, save, purse, mat, chip

Now I want you to listen to the first sounds you hear in the word after each word I say, like this: when I say ***spin****, you say '****sp****'.*

PRACTICE WORD: frog

TASK WORDS: swop, break, flame

PUNJABI PRACTICE WORDS: /lal/ /har/ /sɪr/

PUNJABI TASK WORDS: /ʃer/ /git/ /dʊ́d:/ /nal/ /pʊl/ /luɳ/

(10) ISOLATING THE CODA
Now I want you to listen to the sound at the very end of each word I say. Like this: when I say ***watch****, you say '****ch****'.*

PRACTICE WORD: time

TASK WORDS: knife, lot, mash, comb

Now I want you to listen to the sounds at the very end of the word, like this: when I say ***jump****, you say '****mp****'.*

PRACTICE WORD: test

TASK WORDS: crisp, box, bank, belt

PUNJABI PRACTICE WORDS: /bol/ /rat/ /vak/

PUNJABI TASK WORDS: /pɛr/ /luɳ/ /kɪs/ /git/ /gʊʈ/ /nal/

(11) DELETING THE ONSET
*I wonder if you could take a sound away from a word and say what is left of the word. Like this: when I say **let** you say it but don't say 'l' (-et)*

PRACTICE WORDS: bell, stop

TASK WORDS: cat, bike, sand, note, pick, skin, glass, train

PUNJABI PRACTICE WORDS: /pʊl/ /rat/ /ʃer/

PUNJABI TASK WORDS: /sɪr/ /hor/ /val/ /git/ /dəs/ /pɛr/

(12) DELETING THE CODA
*This time listen for the sound at the end of the word. Like this: I say **dog**, and you say it but you don't say 'g' (do-).*

PRACTICE WORDS: bush, box

TASK WORDS: loop, case, knife, beat, necks, vest, hand, belt

PUNJABI PRACTICE WORDS: /seb/ /val/ /git/

PUNJABI TASK WORDS: /pʊl/ /har/ /luɳ/ /bol/ /rat/ /ʃer/

REFERENCES

BRADLEY, L. and P. BRYANT
1983 Categorizing sounds and learning to read – A causal connection. *Nature*, 301.419–21.

BRUCK, M. and R. TREIMAN
1990 Phonological awareness in normal children and dyslexics: The case of initial consonant clusters. *Journal of Experimental Child Psychology*, 50. 156–78.

CAMPBELL, R. and E. SAIS
1995 Accelerated metalinguistic (phonological) awareness in bilingual children. *British Journal of Developmental Psychology*, 13. 61–8.

CATALDO, S. and N. ELLIS
1988 Interactions in the development of spelling, reading, and phonological skills. *Journal of Research in Reading*, 11(2). 86–109.

DURGUNOGLU, A., W. NAGY and B. HANCIN-BHATT
1993 Cross-language transfer of phonological awareness. *Journal of Educational Psychology*, 85. 453–65.

FREDERICKSON, N.
1995 *Phonological assessment battery*. University College London, research edition.

GOSWAMI, U. and P. BRYANT
1990 *Phonological skills and learning to read*. London: Lawrence Erlbaum.
1992 Rhyme, analogy and children's reading. In P.B. Gough, L.C. Ehri & R. Treiman (eds.), *Reading acquisition*. Hillsdale NJ: Lawrence Erlbaum. 49–63.

LIBERMAN, I., D. SHANKWEILER, F. FISCHER and B. CARTER

1974 Explicit syllable and phoneme segmentation in the young child. *Journal of Experimental Child Psychology,* 18. 201–12.

MUTER, V.

1994 Influence of phonological awareness and letter knowledge on beginning reading and spelling development. In C. Hulme & M. Snowling (eds.), *Reading development and dyslexia.* London: Whurr. 45–62.

SNOWLING, M. and J. STACKHOUSE

1996 *Dyslexia, speech and language: A practitioner's handbook.* London: Whurr.

STAHL, S. and B. MURRAY

1994 Defining phonological awareness and its relationship to early reading. *Journal of Educational Psychology,* 86. 221–34.

STUART-SMITH, J. and D. MARTIN

(in press) Developing assessment procedures for phonological awareness for use with Punjabi/English bilingual children.

TREIMAN, R.

1983 The structure of spoken syllables: Evidence from novel word games. *Cognition,* 15. 49–74

WAGNER, R. and J. TORGESEN

1987 The nature of phonological processing and its causal role in the acquisition of reading skills. *Psychological Bulletin* 101. 192–212.

7

Perceptual influence of vowel on vowel: Data from English, Italian and Punjabi

M. GRAZIA BUSA' and JOHN J. OHALA
Universita' di Bologna *University of California*

Assimilation processes are common across languages. They arise when speech sounds are modified under the influence of adjacent sounds. Vowel-to-vowel assimilations have been discovered in a number of languages and probably occur in most languages to some degree. A phonological constraint, which can be viewed as the fossilised or phonologised result of phonetic between vowel assimilations, is Vowel Harmony. Vowel harmony determines the co-occurrence of vowels within a certain domain, usually the word, so that all the vowels occurring within the domain agree in some of their parameters, for example, in the front/back or in the height parameter.

Typically, vowel harmony is manifested in morphological or morphophonemic processes. In Hungarian, for example, the vowel of the plural suffix varies according to the vowels in the stem, for example, /*astal*/ 'table' ~ /*astalok*/ 'tables'; /*ember*/ 'man' ~ /*emberek*/ 'men'. Although we have a general, intuitive understanding of vowel harmony there is still much in the details that is not understood (Ohala 1994). In a few cases an explanation has been provided grounded in phonetic factors. In palatal harmony, for example, it has been shown what type of intervocalic consonant may inhibit

We wish to thank Prof. Atamjit Singh, of the Department of South and Southeast Asian Studies at the University of California, Berkeley for his assistance in finding the Punjabi speakers.

the harmonic process. This happens in the case of consonants with low F2 (for example, labials and back velars) contrasting with the high F2 necessary for palatalisation (Anderson 1979). More often no phonetic explanation has been provided to account for common aspects of vowel harmony.

Among the things that are not yet explained is why harmony applies only on certain features of vowels but not on others, which phonetic segments favour or inhibit the process, and why some vowels seem to be neutral to harmony. The possibility of studying these and other issues arises if one accepts that vowel harmony and any other common cross-phonological process is the phonologisation (or fossilisation) of phonetic effects (Ohala 1993).

Phonetic studies on V-to-V processes have shown that the formant patterns of V1 in V1CV2 sequences are variable and affected by the quality of the postconsonantal vowel (Öhman 1966), such that, for example, V1 shows higher F2 when V2 is [i]. This is due to the coarticulation of segments, which is one of the main sources of acoustic variation in speech. It has also been shown that listeners are highly sensitive to the acoustic effects of coarticulation and that speech sounds are identified in respect to their phonetic context (Ladefoged and Broadbent, 1957).

In a study investigating the coarticulatory and perceptual effects of vowels spanning a consonant, Fowler (1981) looked at the F1 and F2 shifts on a medial central vowel /ʌ/ by initial and final flanking vowels /i, a, u/ and found that stressed vowels have in fact coarticulatory effects on a preceding or following unstressed transconsonantal vowel, and that the perception of unstressed vowels depends on the acoustic properties of their stressed vocalic context. In normal speaker-to-listener interaction, however, listeners can generally accommodate acoustic variability by reverting to their linguistic experience and thus correctly parse the influence of contextual effects on speech segments (Ohala and Feder 1994). When this for some reason does not happen, there is a potential for sound change.

In the experiment reported in this paper we aim to discover how listeners deal with the contextual variation of vowels in the context of other vowels. Our purpose is to demonstrate that the origins of some aspects of (palatal) vowel harmony can be found in the perceptual domain and studied via lab-based perception studies. We believe that before phonological variation can develop, it must have phonetic 'seeds'; and that it should be possible to study the seeds of phonological patterns in the lab. Listeners apparently 'adjust' their criteria for front-back differentiation as a function of adjacent V frontness. This is due to the fact that listeners normalise or correct for the predictable distortion of an adjacent palatal vowel, thus accepting as a back vowel a vowel that is more front than usual.

We are seeking the seeds of palatal vowel harmony in listeners' perceptual correction of vowel backness in the environment of an adjacent palatal vowel. The subsequent stage – failure to correct for this contextual distortion – has not been formally demonstrated but is a quite plausible occurrence. Our strategy is similar to looking for evidence of an infectious disease by trying to find not the infectious organism itself but antibodies to it (we hasten to add that this is just an analogy, an imperfect one, perhaps; we do not regard phonetic variation as a defect of language).

The following hypotheses were tested. In a V1CV2 sequence where V2 is [i], V2 will cause the vowel in the preceding syllable to be perceived as less fronted, due to listeners' perceptual correction of vowel backness in the environment of an adjacent palatal vowel. Vowel harmony, the phonologisation of the phonetic vowel fronting, would occur when listeners for some reason fail to implement this correction. A shorter intervocalic interval will have a greater effect than a longer one. This perceptual process will be independent of the listeners' native language.

The reactions to the perceptual influence of vowel on vowel of English, Italian and Punjabi native speakers were compared. These three languages were chosen because they present relevant differences with regard to stress assignment, vowel inventory size and vowel and consonant contrasts. In particular, English presents no vowel or consonant contrasts depending solely on duration; Italian has fewer vowels than both English and Punjabi, has consonant but not vowel contrasts depending solely on duration; Punjabi has a large vowel inventory and consonant but not vowel contrasts depending on duration. None of the three languages chosen has vowel harmony in its current phonological processes. It is appropriate to seek the universal *phonetic* basis of a common cross-language sound pattern in languages which do not at present show the *phonologisation* of the given pattern (Ohala 1993).

METHOD

Stimuli

Six continua were prepared for the experiment: an isolated 100 ms short vowel [i]–[u] continuum, an isolated 150 ms long vowel [i]–[u] continuum, and four [ibi]–[ubi] continua (V1bi) with the following combinations of V1 and b:

- short vowel and short consonant;
- short vowel and long consonant;
- long vowel and short consonant; and
- long vowel and long consonant.

The two isolated vowel continua served as control continua, while the four [ibi]–[ubi] continua were designed to test the effect of various combinations of intervocalic interval length on V1 perception.

The continua were created using LPC synthesis (with the CSL-ASL speech analysis and synthesis software) of a natural [i'bi] utterance. The isolated vowel continua were constructed by deleting the /bi/ parts of the V1bi continua. In all the continua, V1 consisted of 19-step stimuli of steady state transitionless 100 ms or 150 ms vowels between and including [i] and [u]. In the four test conditions the intervocalic consonant selected was a voiced labial stop to ensure a context of low F2, as well as a consonantal context that listeners might expect would interfere least with V1 to V2 assimilation. The short and long consonants in the continua were respectively 60 ms or 90 ms long. The durations of the vowels and consonants were chosen between possible values of American English and Italian vowels and consonants and adjusted until a natural sounding combination of the segments was obtained.

The V1 continuum formant frequency endpoints were modelled on the averaged values of the American English and Italian [i] and [u] vowels, as found in the literature and judged for quality by the two authors. The F1, F2 and F3 frequency values for [i] were: 300, 2258, 2960 Hz, respectively; for [u], they were 300, 860, 2260 Hz, respectively. In the continua F2 was decreased by steps of 45 to 50 Hz up to 1700 Hz and then by steps of 140 Hz; F3 was decreased by steps of 20 to 25 Hz up to 2680 Hz (corresponding to the point where F2 was 1700 Hz) and of 70 Hz afterwards. This particular variation in F2 and F3 was made nonlinear to get the crossover between vowel categories closer to the middle of the continuum. A pilot experiment had showed that without this adjustment the categories saturated to /u/ for almost the entire continuum.

Perceptual test

The perceptual test was divided in two parts. The first part consisted of the randomisation of the four continua with the vowels in context, each token repeated twice, for a total of 19 x 4 x 2 = 152 trials. The second part consisted of the two continua with the isolated vowels, each presented twice and randomised, for a total of 19 x 2 x 2 = 76 trials. In each part, the stimuli were presented to the subjects through headphones over a computer.

The subjects were instructed that they would be hearing 'ibi' and 'ubi' sequences in the first part of the experiment, and single vowels in the second, and that they were to identify, by clicking on an [i] or an [u] box on the computer screen, which (first) vowel they were hearing. They were also told that some of the vowels might have a not very distinctive quality as these had been modified to make the listeners' task harder. The total perception task lasted ten minutes.

Subjects
The subjects of the experiment were native speakers of English (20 speakers), Italian (20 speakers), and Punjabi (six speakers), all non-paid volunteers. The smaller number of Punjabi speakers, compared to the other two language groups, is due to the fact that of the Punjabi subjects (recruited at the University of California, Berkeley where the experiment was run) only six met the requirements for monolingual native speakers.

RESULTS

Figures 1–6 present the results of the data (in the form of probability of 'u' judgements). In all the figures a smooth curve calculated with Probit analysis is superimposed on the raw data. For the Italian and American speakers, each data point represents 40 judgements (20 subjects x 2 token repetitions). For the Punjabi speakers, each data point represents 12 judgements (6 subjects x 2 token repetitions). In the figures, the numbers on the x-axis correspond to the stimulus number, so that 1 and 19 represent the first and last endpoint stimuli, that is, [i] and [ʉ] respectively; the values on the y-axis indicate the probability of 'u' judgements, from 0 to 1. The statistical analyses (ANOVA's), both between and within group, were performed on the raw data.

Figures 1–3 show the results for the isolated vowels for the three groups of speakers. All language groups show saturated judgements at 0 and 1 endpoints, which indicates that the subjects in the three language groups had no trouble identifying the endpoint vowels [i] and [u]. The language groups show no relevant differences in the perception of short versus long isolated vowels. Such differences are non-significant for all language groups. The three groups differ, however, in where they have the crossover between [i] and [u]. For the Americans it is around token 9. The Italians identify a lower percentage of tokens as 'u' and for them the crossover is between tokens 7 and 8. The Punjabi speakers are not very different from the Americans, and their crossover is between tokens 8 and 9.

Figures 4–6 show the results of the tests for the vowels in context. Here too, the saturation at both points of the continua for all groups indicates that the subjects were able to identify correctly the endpoint target vowels [i] and [u]. Compared to the data of the vowels in isolation, these data show that, for all language groups, there is a clear shift in the probability of 'u' iden-

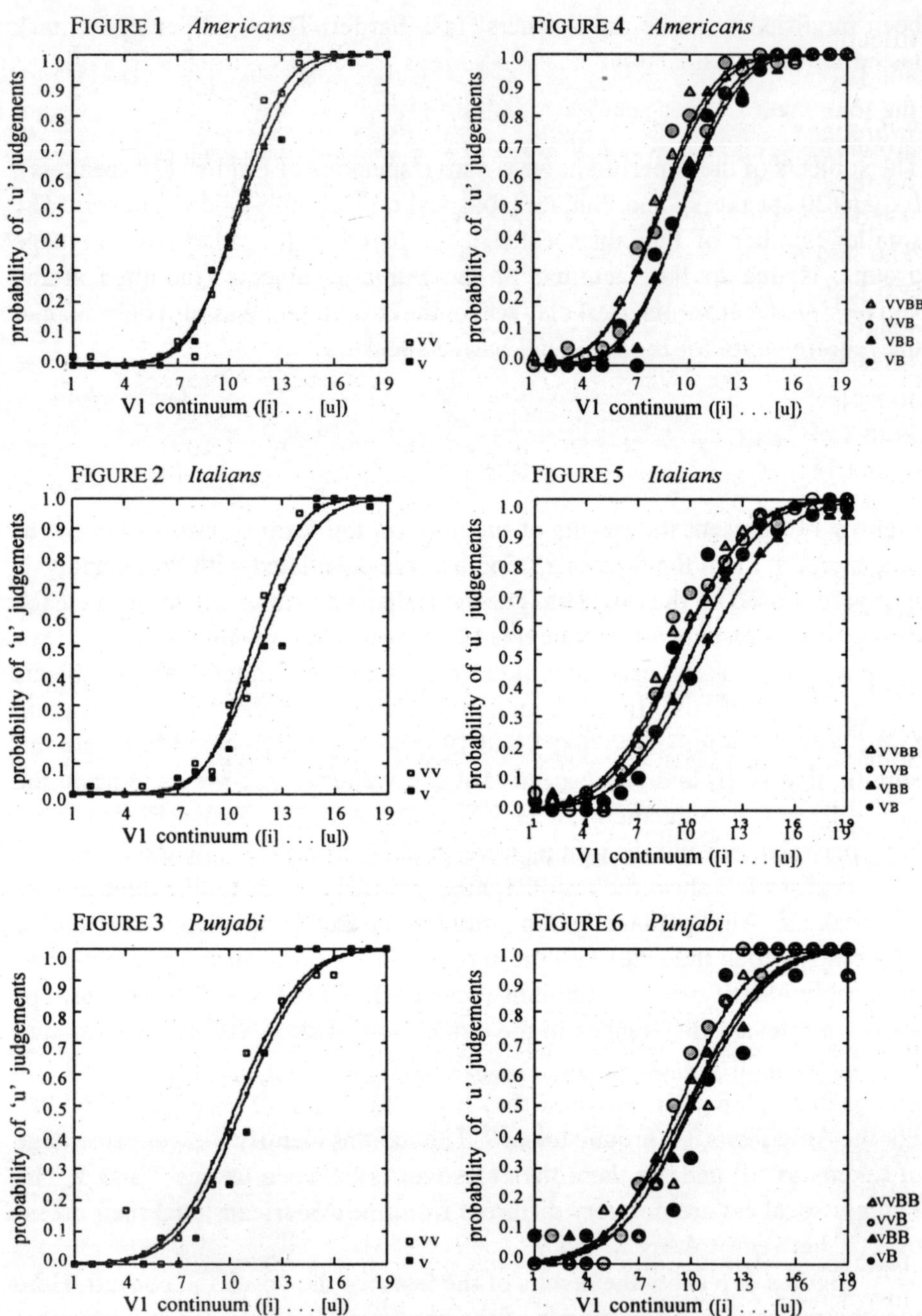

FIGURES 1–3 *Listeners' judgements of the stimuli from the isolated [i] . . . [u] vowel continuum*

FIGURES 4–6 *Listeners' judgements of the stimuli from the [i] . . . [u] vowel continuum in the bi context*

tification due to the context. For the Americans, the crossover between [i] and [u] has shifted to token 10 for the short V1 continua and to token 11 for the long V1 continua. For the Italians, the crossovers between [i] and [u] are around token 9 and 10 for the short vowel continua and around 10 and 11 for the long ones. For the Punjabi speakers, the crossovers are around token 9 and 10 for the short vowel continua and 9 and 10 for the long vowel continua. The language as well as the context effect are significant (for L, $F(2, 273) = 5.837$, $p < 0.003$; for C, $F(5, 270) = 13.540$, $p < 0.000$). Unexpectedly, a longer vowel-to-vowel interval appears to cause a greater shift in identification threshold than the short vowel continua. The differences in perception due to isolated vowels, and short versus long V1 in the continua were significant both for the language and the context factors (for L, $F(2, 267) = 7.263$, $p < 0.001$; for C, $F(2, 267) = 19.808$, $p < 0.000$). This pattern is clearer in the American and the Italian data, while it is less marked in the Punjabi data.

The data also show that the three language groups differ in the way in which the four context conditions affect the degree of shift in percept. The Americans show two distinct trends, one for the two continua with short V1 and the other for the two continua with long V1 (the context factor is significant, $F(3, 76) = 5.399$, $p < 0.002$). The Italian data too show a greater effect of the two long V1 continua, though they show evidence of a sensitivity to the long-short consonant distinction – a short vowel followed by a short consonant has a greater effect than when it is followed by a long consonant (but the differences due to context do not reach significance). Finally, for the Punjabi speakers the contexts having a greater effect in relation to the probability of 'u' judgements are again those where V1 is long, though it is harder to identify a clear pattern, probably due to the scarcity of data for this language group (the differences are not significant).

CONCLUSION

As predicted, there is strong evidence of a vowel-to-vowel perceptual effect affecting V1. For all the language groups, the probability of 'u' judgements for V1 increases when the stimuli are in the environment of an [i] in the following syllable, that is, when they occur in the V1bi context as compared to when they are found in isolation.

This finding is consistent with past such data and is explained on the basis of listeners' perceptual mechanisms, which lead listeners to normalise and correct for speech segmental distortions. Listeners compensate for the effect of the neighbouring vowel by accepting as a back vowel /u/ some vowels that previously had been identified as an /i/. This shows that listeners have learnt to expect that a high back vowel followed by a high front vowel becomes fronted and that this phonetic effect (back vowel fronting) occurs in their language. We believe that this perceptual mechanism can explain how palatal vowel harmony arises. There is a potential for vowel harmony every time listeners fail to normalise this effect, by mistakenly interpreting the speaker's intended speech sound. The magnitude of the effect, as well as the way in which the four contextual conditions affect the shift in perception, varies for different language of listeners. This suggests that universal as well as language-specific factors may be involved. Unexpectedly, a longer vowel-to-vowel interval seems to have a greater effect than a shorter one. More experiments need to be done to explain this aspect of our results, as well as other poorly understood aspects of vowel harmony.

REFERENCES

ANDERSON, LLOYD B.

1979 Using asymmetrical and gradient data in the study of vowel harmony. In Robert M. Vado (ed.), *Issues in vowel harmony*. Amsterdam: Benjamins. 271–340.

FOWLER, CAROL

1981 Production and perception of coarticulation among stressed and unstressed vowels. *Journal of Speech and Hearing Research*, 46. 127–39.

LADEFOGED, PETER and DONALD E. BROADBENT

1957 Information conveyed by vowels. *Journal of the Acoustical Society of America*, 29. 98–104.

OHALA, JOHN J.

1993 The phonetics of sound change. In Charles Jones (ed.), *Historical linguistics: Problems and perspectives*. London: Longman. 237–38.

1994 Towards a universal, phonetically based theory of vowel harmony. Proceeding of the International Conference on Spoken Language Processing, 94, 2. 491–4.

OHALA, JOHN J. and DEBORAH FEDER

1994 Listeners' normalization of vowel quality is influenced by 'restored' consonantal context. *Phonetica*, 51. 111–118.

ÖHMAN, SVEN E.G.

1966 Coarticulation in VCV utterances: Spectographic measurements. *Journal of the Acoustical Society of America*, 39. 151–68.

8
Syllable phonotactics as prosodic alignment

K.G. VIJAYAKRISHNAN
Central Institute of English and Foreign Languages

One of the current assumptions regarding syllable phonotactics is that syllable codas are a subset/proper subset of syllable onsets. It is maintained that, universally, the set of segments in the coda are equal to or less than that of the segments in the onset and that this fact can be derived from the assumption that the coda is only a secondary licensor (Goldsmith 1990) and, in Optimality Theoretic terms, the fact that whereas the constraint Onset (henceforth Ons.) is a positive requirement, the constraint –No Coda is a negative constraint, and the two may not be directly rankable with respect to one another in the constraint hierarchy (Prince and Smolensky 1993). In this paper, this particular claim regarding the universal superiority of the onset over the coda is falsified with data from Mizo, Malto (Section 1) and other languages (Section 2). It is argued that syllable licensing should be seen as part of prosodic alignment requirements (in Optimality Theoretic terms) specified in terms of the prosodic hierarchy in (1).

(1)	m	Morpheme/word
	|	
	F	Foot
	|	
	e	Syllable
	|	
	μ	Mora
	|	
	x	Melody

Section 2 demonstrates, with data from Indian languages, the need for positive and negative alignment requirements with respect to the highest node 'm' morpheme/word at both the edges. Section 3 discusses the foot as a licensor (specifically the head of the foot).

1. ELEMENTS IN THE RHYME NOT LICENSED BY THE ONSET: THE CASE OF MIZO

Mizo, a Tibeto-Burman tone language spoken in the state of Mizoram in North-eastern India, has an interesting segmental inventory shown in (2). The Mizo data cited is from Fanai (1992) and Fanai and Vijayakrishnan (1995).

(2) MIZO CONSONANTS AND THEIR DISTRIBUTION

	ONLY AS ONSET	AS ONSET OR CODA	ONLY AS CODA
i.	p^h, b (coronal and velar sets with /g/ missing)	p	?
ii.	f, v, s, z, h		
iii.	t^L, $t^{L\,h}$ (laterally released)		
iv.	t^R, $t^{R\,h}$ (trilled)		
v.	t^s, $t^{s\,h}$ (affricated)		
vi.		m, n, ŋ	
vii.	m^h, n^h, $ŋ^h$		
viii.		l, r	
ix.	l^h, r^h		
x			y, w

Whereas fricatives and marked segments are possible only in the onset, the glottal stop and the glides /y and w/ are possible only in the 'rhyme' part of the syllable. Contrary to Kenstowicz (1994) and the literature cited there, the glottal stop in Mizo cannot be analysed as a glide but must be taken to be a placeless stop as it can occur after glides as well as liquids in the coda, for example, */keu?/* 'to throw down from the shoulder or back' (Fanai 1992: 42), */Dai?/* 'to throw away' (Fanai 1992: 42), */r^hal?/* 'to sell' (Fanai 1992: 113), and */D^hor?/* 'to take off' (Fanai 1992: 114).[1] And it must be stressed that Mizo does not allow sonority plateaus (there are no geminates in the language inter- or intra-syllabic) or sonority reversals in the coda.

Turning to the glides, apart from occurring as coda after any dissimilar vowel, that is, Mizo has the diphthongs, ei, ai, oi, ui, iu, eu, au and ou, they occur in the pre-vocalic position before the vowel /a/. A couple of arguments are advanced in Fanai and Vijayakrishnan (1995) to prove that prevocalic glides in Mizo must be parsed with the rhyme or moraic constituent rather than the onset.[2]

Firstly, Mizo onsets are non-branching and the rhyme can dominate a maximum of three segments. The sequences /ia/ and /ua/ can be followed by not more than one consonant, for example, whereas /.VG?/ and /.VL?/ are possible, */.iaG?/ and */.iaL?/ are not. Furthermore, if the sequence /.ia{G.L}?/ occurs as a result of /?/ insertion in verb conversion – a process of lexical verb allomorphy – then the sequence /.GV./ is simplified to a short vowel as illustrated in (3).

(3) SIMPLIFICATION OF THE PREVOCALIC GLIDE-VOWEL SEQUENCE

H H		L		
nuar ~ /*nuar* + ?/	→	/*nor?*/	'to sulk'	(Fanai 1992: 111)
FORM I		FORM II		

As Fanai and Vijayakrishnan (1995: 55) observe: 'It is clear that the simplification of the sequence "GV" to a "V" in the course of the derivation is to satisfy the rhyme condition – no more than three positions in the rhyme.'

Secondly, the distribution of the tonal melodies 'HL' and 'LH' in Mizo is difficult to explain if prevocalic glides are taken to be part of the onset. Though the high and low tones are free to occur singly or as rising and falling tones in Mizo, dynamic tones are found only in rhymes with at least two positions linked to sonorants [see (4i)–(4iv)], that is, many-to-one linking of tones to a sonorant is prohibited in Mizo. (4v) and (4vi) demonstrate the inability of onset sonorants to link to tones. The fact that prevocalic glide-vowel sequences can be linked to dynamic tones in (4vii) and (4viii) argue for the parsing of the prevocalic glides with the rhyme rather than the onset.

(4) THE DISTRIBUTION OF HL AND LH IN MIZO (Fanai 1992: 72)

i.	LH	u:	'to howl'
ii.	HL	a:t	'to cut'
iii.	LH	Sam	'hair'
iv.	HL	huN	'to fence'
v.	HL	*mas	

vi.	LH	*guk	
vii.	HL	Dʰ iat	'to sweep'
viii.	LH	hua	'to hate'

I would now like to offer another example of segments licensed only in the coda. Consider the language Malto, a Dravidian tribal language spoken near the Rajmahal Hills in the Santal Parganas in Bihar. The high nasal (ŋ / ɲ) is reported to occur only in the coda in Malto according to Das (1973). He asserts that whereas /ɲ/ occurs only when followed by palatals or finally in monosyllables (5i–ii). /ŋ/ occurs elsewhere in the coda (5iii–iv). It can be observed that the high (velar) nasal is distinctive from the coronal nasal in this environment (5v–viii).[3] And Das (1973: 16) notes: '/ŋ/ does not occur intervocalically: it contrasts with /m, n/ in the final position and in medial clusters.'

(5) THE DISTRIBUTION OF /ɲ/ AND /ŋ/ IN MALTO (Das 1973)

i.	gosaɲvi	'god'	(p. 15)
ii.	hoɲ	'also'	(p. 15)
iii.	aŋli	'finger'	(p. 15)
iv.	paṭraŋg	'the wooden slab'	(p. 15)
v.	ange	'to seize tightly'	(p. 16)
vi.	aŋga	'shirt'	(p. 16)
vii.	iamga	'a string to hang clothes'	(p. 16)
viii.	jaŋga	'part of woman's clothes'	(p. 16)
ix.	tam	'they'	(p. 15)
x.	ni:n	'you'	(p. 37)

Finally, in Palayachi, which belongs to the Burmese group of languages. Jones (1961: 76) notes: 'In syllable final position only /?/ and /g/ occur, and /g/ occurs only in that position. Both phonemes are glottal stops; but /g/ is lenis, does not affect preceding vowels, and may be released with slight aspiration.'

In this section, we saw that there are instances of certain segments, which occur exclusively in the coda, and these segments do not belong to a natural class either in terms of sonority strength or featural specification. For instance, in Mizo, whereas /?/ belongs to the least end of the sonority scale, /w, y/ belong to the other end of the scale. In fact, the occurrence of fricatives exclusively in the onset and the glides in the rhyme must be stated as a conditional statement:

If [+CONTINUANT], then [+CONSONANTAL] in the onset
and [+SONORANT] in the rhyme

Such a statement does not disguise the fact that the selection of segments for the various prosodic constituents is basically arbitrary in languages and that individual grammars may have to specify the licensing of segments either singly or in sets to specific prosodic constituents. This claim is further reinforced in the case of Malto where the [+high] nasals (/ŋ ~ ɲ/) are excluded from onsets.

Assuming that the only sub-syllabic constituent is the mora, in line with the mosaic theory of the syllable (Hayes 1989), and that while the onset requires linking to the syllable node, rhymal elements are linked to the mora, we can account for the parsing requirements of glides in Mizo as follows. Assume that the Peak and the Margin Harmonies of Prince and Smolensky (1993) which rank the relative harmony of parsing a segment as Peak/Margin with respect to the other segments in the inventory of the language are reformulated as a family of Link to Syllable/Mora constraints which are mutually rankable. Then the phonotactic statements of Mizo in (6a) can be stated as the ranked Link Constraints in (6b).

(6) LINK TO SYLLABLE/MORA CONSTRAINTS IN MIZO

a. i. It is better to parse [–consonantal] as a rhyme than as an onset.

ii. It is better to have an onsetless syllable than to parse [–consonantal] as an onset.

b. CONSTRAINT HIERARCHY

i. Link [i . . . a] to Mora

\>>

ii. Ons.

\>>

iii. Link [i, u] to syllable

Given the constraint hierarchy in (6b), sequences like CGVC and GVC will be optimally parsed as in (7).

(7) THE PARSING OF PREVOCALIC GLIDES IN MIZO

a. CGVC

```
      e
     /|\
   /  μμ
  C   | | \
      G V  C
```

b. GVC

```
   e
   |\
   μ μ
   | | \
   G V  C
```

In (7b), linking G to e would have satisfied the onset requirement but at the cost of the higher ranked Link [i . . . a] to mora. That explains why, given the Constraint Hierarchy (CH), the parsing in (7b) is optimal. An argument in favour of the low ranking of Ons. in Mizo is the fact that syllable-final consonants never re-syllabify with the following vowel even when a vowel-initial suffix follows (Fanai, personal communication). It must be noted that Link to Mora cannot be equated with the earlier Peak Prominence since it must account for codas as well. Take the case of /ʔ/, for instance. In the deverbal adjective $[[l^{h}au?]_{V.\ II}\ om]_{Adj}$ 'fearful / scary / dangerous'. /ʔ/ is not re-syllabified with the following vowel. In this case, the higher ranking Link /ʔ/ to Mora >> Ons. prevents the re-syllabification of /ʔ/ with the suffixal syllable.[4]

Thus, we see that Link to *e*/*μ* can account for the slightly unusual distribution of segments in the discussed codas. However, if we take the Mizo case, where we have a fairly detailed phonological description in Fanai 1992, we see that the parsing requirements, however unusual, do not upset the sonority sequencing principle if the entire syllable is taken as a unit for computing the sonority curve. We could assume that the Harmonicity requirement 'x is more harmonious than y in the context a-b' reflecting a Universal Sonority Hierarchy (yet to be established) computed on the entire syllable is ranked fairly high (is perhaps inviolable) and that is why languages do not exhibit crazy onset-coda requirements in spite of the presence of arbitrary ranking between 'Link x to *μ*' and 'Link x to *e*' in individual grammars.

2. MORPHEMIC/WORD LICENSING AT THE RIGHT AND LEFT EDGES

In this section, the licensing requirements at the right and left edges of morphemes/words in languages are taken up with a view to establishing the need for stating them as alignment requirements at the highest level of the prosodic tree in (1). Taking up the case of the right-edge requirement first, it must be noted that this phenomenon has been reported sporadically in the literature. For instance, Yiddish allows obstruent voicing in codas only word-finally, and Kenstowicz (1994: 496) notes:

> . . . word-final [voiced] in obstruents must then be licensed by another statement. This situation is reminiscent of syllable phonotactics, where word-final clusters are often more complex than word-medial ones. How to state this connection precisely requires further research.

I would like to show, in this section, that at the right edge, it is not just a matter of clusters being more complex, but the selection of segments itself being fairly arbitrary. Consider the following cases of right-edge requirements of different languages.

(8) THE RIGHT-EDGE REQUIREMENTS OF WORDS

CASE 1: Irula, a Dravidian, tribal language spoken in the Nilgiri region and the surrounding districts of Tamil Nadu, Kerala and Karnataka (Perialwar 1979)

Final segment — No non-syllabic

Non-final coda
a. All consonants occur as geminates.
b. In C_1 C_2 where C_1 can be (ʈ, c, k, m, n, l, r, y) but not (p, t, ɲ, ʋ)

CASE 2: Tamil (the literary variety)

Final coda — All sonorants (vowels and m, n, ɲ, l, ɭ, r, ʐ, y)

Non-final coda
a. All consonants occur as geminates except (r, ʐ)
b. In C_1, C_2C_1 can be a sonorant or (t, ʈ)[5]

CASE 3: Gondi (Adilabad dialect), a Dravidian, tribal language spoken in the Adilabad district of Andhra Pradesh (Subrahmanyam 1968)

Final coda
Only (p, t, d, k, g, c, j, s, ṛ, r, l, m, n, ŋ, ʋ, y)
Excluded (aspirates, b, ʈ, ɖ, h)

Non-final coda
a. As geminates only (p, b, d, ʈ, ɖ, k, g, c, j, l, m, n, ŋ, g, ʋ, y)
Excluded (aspirates, s, ṛ, r, h)
b. In C_1, C_2C_1 can be (p, t, d, ʈ, k, g, c, j, s, ṛ, r, l, m, ŋ, n, g, ʋ, y, h)
Excluded (aspirates, b, ɖ)

CASE 4: Lotha Naga of the central group of Naga languages (Tibeto-Burman) is spoken mainly in the Wokha district of Nagaland (Acharya 1983)

Final coda
Only (p, k, v, s, h[6], m, n, ŋ, l, r, y)
Excluded (aspirates [plosives, affricates, nasals, liquids], t, pf, pv, ts, c, f, z, š, ž, ɲ, w)

Non-final coda
a. No geminates
b. In C_1, C_2C_1 can be (p, k, f[7], v, m, n, ŋ, l, r, y)
Excluded (aspirates, t, pf, pv, ts, c, s, z, š, ž, h, ɲ, w)

A couple of observations are in order. Firstly, the segments which are licensed as non-final coda across languages are fairly arbitrary, for example, while Tamil allows sonorants and (t (alveolar), ṭ), Lotha disallows /t/ (dental), allows /y/ but not /w/. Secondly, final codas are not necessarily segments added on to the non-final set. Whereas in Irula and Tamil the final coda is a (much smaller) proper subset of the non-final coda, in Lotha, /h/ and /s/ are possible finally, but excluded non-finally. It is quite clear that the licensing requirements of the right edge of words are distinct from that of the right edge of the syllable, that is, the coda.

Take the case of Lotha Naga. As mentioned earlier, /s/ does not occur as a non-final coda, but does occur finally in words like 'box', 'paper', Hindi */ka:gaz/* and 'blouse' which are listed as */pákós/*, */kákós/* and */plós/*, respectively (Acharya 1983: 42). This cannot be explained in terms of the constraint –No Coda.

In other words, whereas the non-occurrence of /s/ as a coda can be explained as a consequence of the ranking –No Coda >> Parse /s/, some other explanation is required for instances of final /s/. The only possibility is to recognise the need for a constraint, which requires the right edge of words to be aligned, which is superior to –No Coda. I propose the constraint family 'Align Right: (Word, Feature Complex)' (Align W; M, F, C) which can take care of the specific featural complexes allowed at the right edge as a higher ranked constraint in violation of –No Coda. The feature complex, which is thus required to be aligned at the right edge, is (+consonantal, –sonorant, +continuant, +coronal, –voice).[8] Since Align W; M, F, C is higher ranked than –No Coda, /s/ will be parsed as a coda at the right edge in violation of –No Coda. Notice, however, that the voicing of */z/* in */ka:gaz/* (among other features) is not parsed in Lotha. The only non-controversial assumption necessary at this stage is that features other than the ones licensed by the Align constraint are not parsed: in this case the feature [voiced].[9]

Having established the need for Align R at the morphological level, let us now look at the data pertaining to the left-edge requirement in morphemes/words. Since cases of left-edge requirements have not been discussed in the literature we will consider the data in some detail.

(9) LEFT-EDGE REQUIREMENTS IN MORPHEMES/WORDS

A. *Only at the left edge*

CASE 1

Gondi (Adilabad dialect) (Subrahmanyam 1968): Gondi has voiceless and voiced aspirates at the labial, dental, retroflex and velar places. However, aspirates occur only stem-initially, for example, */b^h a:ve:y/* second month of the Gond year (p. 220) and */bur̥ bʰ a:ve:y/* third month of the Gond year (p. 219).

The Hooghli dialect of Bangla also has a rule of de-aspiration, which applies selectively to non-initial aspirates and, as in Gondi, aspirates in the initial position of left as well as right stems in compounds are exempt from de-aspiration (Rajat Ghosh, personal communication). */ci ṭʰ i/* standard Bangla ~ */ci ṭi/* 'letter'; but */dʰupdʰuno/* 'incense stick'.

Perhaps these are instances of a feature gradually being phased out of the language. If that is so, the best way to account for the data would be to invoke a constraint which is the converse of Parse F–*Parse F, that is, a negative requirement on the parsing of a feature. The constraint, in this case, is *Parse [+spread glottis]. The fact that aspiration survives only at the left edge can now be attributed to the higher ranked Align Left (Stem, *e*) (Align L; S, *e*)[10] which forces the parsing of the feature [+spread glottis] which is a part of the onset of the first syllable. .

CASE 2

/h/ in English is present in unstressed syllables only when stem-initial, for example, 'heˈredity ~ heˈreditary', 'Hoˈratio', 'hoˈrrendous', 'hoˈrizon' (optional, Jones 1988), 'huˈrray'. Notice that these are words where the initial syllable was never accented at all. The CH, in this case, is Align L:S, *e* >> *P /h/.

CASE 3

In the Adilabad dialect of Gondi, the distribution of length is very interesting, Subrahmanyam (1968: 10–11) observes that:

> Short vowels occur mostly only in the initial syllable and therefore the contrast between long and short vowels is found only in the initial syllable . . . double consonants mostly occur only after a short vowel of the initial syllable. Single consonants do not occur in this environment i.e., after a short vowel of the initial syllable.

It is generally agreed that length is to be attributed to the multiple linking of melodies with prosodic positions. These facts imply that the first syllable has either a long vowel or a long consonant after a short vowel. In other words, the first syllable licenses only one multiple link. Since length is represented underlyingly as linking to mora, in the mosaic framework as in a. or b.,

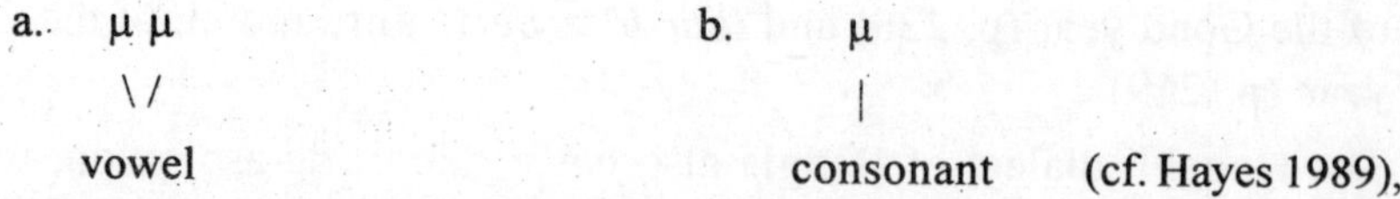

we can capture this distribution of length in Gondi as an Align Left (Stem, *e*) requirement where the syllable is deemed to be properly aligned if and only if the input elements it dominates (melodies and the mora linked to the geminate consonant) are linked properly. Two other constraints in the CH of the language which are required are syllable bimoraicity which places an upper limit on moras in a syllable, and multiple link of vowel to mora which ensures that vowel length, which is entirely predictable (with the single exception of the first and second person future-tense markers in the second syllable in monosyllabic verbs ending in the consonants /k/ or /g/), is always long in all non-initial syllables. Since vowel length is predictable, length need not be indicated in the input representation but derived with the help of the constraint multiple link of vowel to mora. The CH required for explaining segmental length in Gondi is the following:

GONDI CONSTRAINT HIERARCHY FOR
ACCOUNTING FOR SEGMENTAL LENGTH

i. Syllable Bimoraicity, Align Left (Stem, *e*), (Parse Mora)
>>
ii. Multiple Link of Vowel to Mora

The three constraints in i. are mutually unranked with respect to each other, they are all undominated and hence inviolable. It is thus ensured that all syllables are bimoraic, the left syllable is properly aligned and if a mora is associated with the first consonant it is parsed in the optimal output.

We have looked at left-edge requirements which are positive in nature, which permit certain features/constituents only stem-initially, namely the presence of the feature [+spread glottis] in Gondi and the Hoogli dialect of Bangla or the feature complex for the segment /h/ in English or the mora linked to the consonant in Gondi. We now turn to negative requirements at the left edge of stems.

B. *Not at the left edge*

CASE 4

In the hyper-literary variety of Tamil, words cannot begin with any segment from the set (l, r, ṭ, ḍ, ɲ, ẓ). Words borrowed from Sanskrit which begin with /l, r/ are suitably modified. For instance, words like */ra:m/* and */lakṣmaɳ/* proper names are pronounced [*ira:man*] and [*ilakkumaɳan*], respectively. An epenthetic vowel is inserted at the left edge to overcome the prohibition on words beginning with the segments /l.r/.[11]

It is logical that the negative requirement be formalised as a negative alignment requirement, namely *Align Left (Word, r, l). The repair strategy of epenthesising a vowel on the left can be accounted for by ranking the constraint Fill Nucleus (which incurs a violation every time a vowel is epenthesised) lower than *Align L; W, Feature Complex which in turn is higher than Ons.

INITIAL EPENTHESIS IN TAMIL

Constraints → Output Rep.↓	*Align L(W, r, l)	>>Fill Nuc. → >> →	Ons.
i. *[(*ra:m..*	*!	✓	✓
ii. ☞ (V[*ra:m..*	✓	*	*
iii. *V (V[*ra:m..*	✓	* !*	*,*

In this case, alignment is a mapping between phonological and morphological structures and since epenthetic elements have no morphological status by the principle of 'Containment' which ensures that the input is properly contained in every output representation (cf. McCarthy and Prince 1993), the epenthesised vowel is shown outside the morphological bracketing '['. The first candidate violates *Align which is fatal. The third candidate has two gratuitous Fill and Ons. violations and is hence sub-optimal. Therefore, the second candidate emerges as the optimal output representation.

Before we turn to the next case, it is necessary to explicate a couple of major differences between the positive left-edge requirements we had looked at earlier (Cases 1–3) and the negative left-edge requirement we just now examined. Firstly, the positive constraints do not require the specific features to be mentioned as Align L: (S, *e*) would require all the features present in the input to be parsed. Secondly, it may not be an accident that all the positive align-left requirements were stated on stems but this negative align-left requirement is defined on words. That *Align L in Tamil is stated on words is proved by prefixed forms and compounds where the stems begin with the prohibited segments, for example, /*lakṣya*/ objective is [*ilaṭciyam*] but /a + *lakṣya*/ 'indifference' is [*alaṭciyam*] and /*ra:m*/ is [*ira:man*] but /*sita:* + *ra:m*/ is [*si:ta:ra:man*]. Whether this distinction between Align and *Align is systematic cannot unfortunately be tested, as Cases 5 and 6 do not provide adequate data for different reasons.

CASE 5

In many languages retroflex consonants (either the entire set or members of the set/ sometimes the velar nasal and /ʔ/ are prohibited in the word-initial position. An incomplete list of languages with the segments prohibited in the word initial position is given below:

i.	Irula (Dravidian)	*ɳ, *ɭ, *r, *y, *ŋ	(Perialwar 1979)
ii.	Kuvi (Dravidian)	*ɳ, *y, *ʔ	
iii.	Gondi (Dravidian (A))	*ṛ, *ŋ	(Subrahmanyam 1968)
iv.	Kodagu (Dravidian)	*ɳ, *ɭ, *ṣ, *ŋ	(Balakrishnan 1976)
v.	Kasaba (Dravidian)	*ɳ, *ɭ	(Pillai 1976)
vi.	Ka:ŋgari: (Himachal dialect)	*ṣ, *ɭ, *r	(Sharma 1974)
vii.	Karbi (Tibeto-Burman)	*ʔ	(Jeyapaul 1987)
viii.	Pattani (Himalayan group)	*ɳ	(Sharma 1989)
ix.	Tinani (Himalayan Group)	*ɳ	(Sharma 1989)
x.	Gahri (Himalayan Group)	*ɳ	(Sharma 1989)

The prohibited segments listed here can be analysed along the lines of Tamil. However, since detailed generative phonological descriptions are not available for these languages, the question whether *Align L should be stated on stems or words cannot be resolved. But if the ban on retroflex segments in Tamil is comparable to these cases, a few observations are in order. In Tamil, the ban was total on all native morphemes, and consequently, one cannot find any violation either in stems or in words. However, if recent borrowings from English are any indication, English /t/ and /d/ are generally pronounced /ṭ/ and /ḍ/, respectively. Therefore, words like 'tumbler' and 'driver' do begin with retroflex sounds. Perhaps, the ban on retroflex stops has been lifted in Tamil. But as for /ɳ/ and /ɭ/, one cannot still find any word violating the ban, and therefore, perhaps the ban is still in force: but more as a means of lexical optimisation rather than an active phonological constraint. The cases listed above could however be located anywhere between these extreme positions in Tamil, namely an active constraint requiring a repair strategy as in the case of /r, l/, a constraint which is no longer active with respect to current vocabulary as in the case of /ʈ, ɖ/ and a constraint which optimises lexical entries as in the case of /ɳ, ɭ/.

CASE 6

The last case to be discussed is that of voiceless obstruent weakening in the Naokhali dialect of Bangla (Das, in press). In this dialect, initial /p/, /pʰ/ and /ʃ/ (the only fricative in the underlying inventory of the language) of the cognates in Standard Bangla are weakened to /h/ as the following data indicate. Das reports that this process is exceptionless and is extended to recent loans as well.

NAOKHALI BANGLA VOICELESS OBSTRUENT WEAKENING

	Standard		*Naokhali form*	*Gloss*
i.	*pagOl*	~	*hagOl*	'mad'
ii.	*pʰ ul*	~	*hul*	'flower'
iii.	*ʃuta*	~	*huta*	'thread'
iv.	professor	~	*hofesor*	'professor'

Das explains that this process cannot be treated as a change from /p, pʰ, ʃ/ to /h/ as /h/ is no longer a part of the underlying segmental inventory of Naokhali Bangla. The /h/ of the cognates of the standard are deleted in the dialect everywhere obligatorily, for example, */holud/* ~ [*olud*] 'yellow'; */mahut/* ~ [*maut*] 'mahut'. Therefore, this weakening must be treated as a deletion of all features other than the root features [+consonantal] and [–sonorant] and later on specified as /h/, perhaps in the phonetic implementation module. Given this background information, the data can be explained in terms of the inviolable constraint *Align Left; W/S(?), Feature Complexes ([Labial], [–Voice]) and ±continuant (if dominated by [+consonantal]). The morphological specification is deliberately left indeterminate since crucial data that will fix it one way or the other is not available at present.

In this section we looked at the left and right-edge requirements at the morphological level in diverse languages and established the following generalisations:

- Right-edge requirements are stated on the word and they are statable as positive Align R constraints with respect to an arbitrary set of segments.
- Left-edge requirements are stated on stems in case of positive Align L constraints.
- Left-edge requirements which are statable only as negative constraints, namely *Align Left, may perhaps be stated on words rather than stems. However, this conclusion is only tentative and subject to further research.
- Whereas the positive left-edge-align requirements were all stated as requirements on the syllable to be aligned, the negative-align requirements have to be stated with respect to specific feature complexes.

3. LICENSING AS ALIGNMENT TO FOOT

In this section I consider cases of segment licensing in the head of the foot. Some of these cases are well known. For instance, rules of vowel reduction in unstressed syllables as in English and Spanish (Harris 1983) can be subsumed under foot licensing. Only the head of the foot licenses the entire gamut of featural distinctions. In alignment terms, certain vowel height features have to be aligned to the head of the foot (which in turn is dominated by Ons.). This explains the expanded inventory in the head of foot position. The two cases we will examine are /h/ in English and the mid vowels in Tamil.

CASE 1: ENGLISH /H/

In addition to the stem-initial position discussed in the previous section, /h/ is obligatory in stressed syllables. See data in (10).

(10) DISTRIBUTION OF /H/ IN ENGLISH

i.	'vehicle	[*m*]	~	ve'hicular	[h]
ii.	inhi'bition	(*m*)[12]	~	in'hibit	[h]
iii.	inha'lation	(*m*)	~	in'hale	[h]
iv.	prohi'bition	(*m*)	~	pro'hibit	[h]
v.	'vehement	[*m*]			
vi.	ˌreha'bilitate	(m)			

The data in the right-hand column of (10) clearly proves the point regarding the licensing of /h/ in the foot-initial position in English. Therefore, in addition to stem-initial position (see Section 2), /h/ is licensed in stress-initial position. An explanation along similar lines is possible here also with the already inducted *Parse /h/ >> Ons. The constraints in question are Align Left; (Foot, *e*) and the one proposed earlier, that is, (Align L; W, *e*). The CH required to explain the entire set of data (in Section 2 and 10) is:

Align L; W, *e*. Align L; Foot, *e* >> *Parse /h/ >> Ons.

Surely, the facts that /h/ is licensed foot-initially and that voiceless stops are aspirated in the same environment are not purely coincidental. Perhaps they should be analysed as the licensing of the feature [+spread glottis] by the foot. However the details of such a comprehensive analysis are yet to be worked out.

CASE 2: THE DISTRIBUTION OF MID VOWELS IN TAMIL

The mid vowels have a restricted distribution in the native vocabulary of Tamil (cf. Vijayakrishnan 1984). They occur only in the initial syllable of morphemes when the following syllable does not have a long vowel. Before we examine the data pertaining to the distribution of mid vowels. let us establish the foot typology of Tamil. Vijayakrishnan (1978) has shown that prominence in Tamil is assigned to the second vowel in case the first vowel is short and the second vowel is long, for example, */pa'laa/* 'jackfruit' and */pa'laakkaṉam/* 'funeral dirge'; in all other cases it is on the first vowel – even when the first syllable is an open syllable and the second syllable is not, for example, */'marɨndɨ/* 'medicine'. Tamil prominence can be explained in terms of a trochaic foot at the left edge where only vowel quantity is taken into consideration. Now consider the data in (11).

(11) THE DISTRIBUTION OF MID VOWELS IN TAMIL

i.	*ceḍi*	'plant'	ii.	*koḍi*	'creeper'
iii.	*cehadi*	'slush'	iv.	*koḍimai*	'cruelty'
v.	**ceha:di*		vi.	**koḍa:mi*[13]	
vii.	*pe:ḍi*	'coward'	viii.	*to:ḍi*	'name of a raga'
ix.	*me:dini*	'earth'	x.	*mo:diram*	'ring'
xi.	**me:da:ni*		xii.	**mo:da:ram*	

The distributional facts of mid vowels ought to be explained in terms of alignment to the foot and not the stem because of the restriction on short vowels in the following syllable. Thus, the required constraint is Align L; (Foot, *e*) and the required CH is: Align L; (Foot, *e*) >> *Parse mid vowel.

It is possible that the Gondi facts are also amenable to an analysis invoking the foot as all syllables are uniformly bimoraic, and, perhaps, prominence is fixed at the left edge. However, since Subrahmanyam does not discuss prominence, this issue cannot be pursued further now.

The two cases discussed here of Alignment to Foot are fairly clear cases involving the foot and not cases which may be subsumed purely under Alignment to a morphological category. Both the cases are of trochaic feet and alignment to the left edge. It would be reasonable to assume that the edge of the foot that may be aligned need not be fixed independently, that is, trochaic feet will permit only the left edge to be aligned and iambic feet the right edge. This hypothesis is, of course, subject to verification.

CONCLUSION

In this paper, I have shown that codas are not necessarily (proper) subsets of onsets and that the choice of coda consonants can be fairly arbitrary both in including and excluding segments from any part of the segment inventory arranged according to the sonority scale. Further, I have shown that final codas may be selected from the inventory fairly randomly, sometimes not even from the non-final coda set. However, universally, marked segment types seem to be excluded in both final and non-final codas. Before we launch into a theory of segment markedness and syllable phonotactics, a word of caution is necessary. As far as the exclusion of complex segments and aspirates from codas are concerned. We may be correct in invoking segmental markedness. But the exclusion of /ʔ/ and retroflex sounds from initial onsets cannot be explained along similar lines. It is also suggested that, in spite of codas selecting segments fairly arbitrarily, the fact that one does not encounter 'crazy' coda-onset asymmetries must be attributed to the undominated constraint enforcing the 'Sonority Sequencing Principle' on the syllable as a unit.

Since onsets and codas are specified arbitrarily, I have suggested that they should be accounted for as instances of Align e/μ to feature complexes. Stronger evidence for treating licensing as prosodic alignment comes from the left and right-edge requirements of stems/words and the foot. Thus, we see that the alignment requirements range from the lowest prosodic constituent –μ to the highest – the morphological stem/word which is invoked in the morphology-phonology interface. Unlike the M category where we have evidence for left and right alignment, when it came to the foot, there is evidence only for trochaic foot and the left edge. However, I hypothesise that, at the level of the foot, only one edge is accessible for alignment, the left edge for trochaic foot and, perhaps, the right edge for iambic foot – the edge where the head is located.

NOTES

1. Also notice that /h/ patterns with the fricatives in occurring only in the onset.
2. Mizo is by no means unique in parsing the prevocalic glide as part of the rhyme as Spanish (Harris 1985) and Korean (Kim and Kim 1991) have similar parsing requirements.
3. The distinctive nature of /n/ and /ɲ/ is however not quite evident in Das's transcription of Malto data, though words like */ni:n/* 'you' and */e:n/* 'I' (1973: 37) as opposed to */hoɲ/* 'also' lead us to believe that the coronal ~ 'high' (palatal) distinction could indeed be phonemic.
4. However, it must be pointed out that this argument is not very strong since none of the coda consonants apparently resyllabify under suffixation (Fanai, personal communication). Perhaps a higher ranked Align R (M, *e*) ought to be invoked in all these cases which ensures the alignment of syllables and morphemes at the right edge.
5. /t/ is alveolar in this case.
6. Final /h/ is reported only in one lexical item */cʰ-ekméh/* 'wild bee' (the bigger variety) (Acharya 1983: 44).
7. Only in Vf.VV as in */efvi/* 'thief' (tone not indicated) (Acharya 1983: 40).
8. The details of the other segments licensed at the right edge can be spelt out along similar lines.
9. Notice that Lotha Naga is unusual in not having voicing contrast in stops but only in fricatives, that is, /s, z, š, ž/. Perhaps one cannot invoke a general rule of devoicing in codas as Acharya (1983) notes the occurrence of /v/ in codas. However, it is quite possible that what is transcribed as /v/ is the glide /ʋ/ since it patterns with /y/ in occurring after a plosive initially, for example, /ky./ and /kv./ (Acharya 1983: 63).
10. There is some evidence for claiming Align L; S, *e* to be distinct from Align L; Foot, *e* at least in Bangla where compounds seem to have a foot constructed only on the left stem (see Ghosh, in press).
11. The epenthetic vowel is /u/ when the first vowel is either /u/ or /o/, for example, */lo:k/* ~ [*ulo:gam*] 'universe'. However, a word like */raŋgna:dan/* 'a proper name' is [*araŋgana:dam*] not *[*iraŋgana:dan*] probably for consideration of homophony as [*iraŋgɨ*] is a verb meaning descend.
12. ( ) indicates optionality.
13. A word like */pora:mai/* 'jealousy' looks like a counter-example at first blush. However, the morphological make-up of the word is

    /por + a: + mai/
    wait(v) neg. nom.

REFERENCES

ACHARYA, K.P.
1983 *Lotha grammar*. Mysore: CIIL.

BALAKRISHNAN, R.
1976 *Phonology of Kodagu*. Annamalai Nagar: Annamalai University.

DAS, A.S.K.
1973 *The structure of Malto*. Annamalai Nagar: Annamalai University.

DAS, S.
(in press) Consonant deletion rules in the Naokhali dialect of Bangla: Their lexical status and mode of application. In M. Hari Prasad *et al.* (eds.), *Phases and interfaces of morphology*. Hyderabad: CIEFL.

FANAI, L.T.
1992 *Some aspects of the lexical phonology of Mizo and English: An autosegmental approach*. Unpublished Ph.D. Dissertation. Hyderabad: CIEFL.

FANAI, L.T. and K.G. VIJAYAKRISHNAN
1995 Mizo rhyme structure. *CIEFL Occasional Papers in Linguistics* 5. 53–64.

GHOSH, T.
(in press) Word formation and vowel quantity: A lexical phonological account. In M. Hari Prasad *et al.* (eds.), *Phases and interfaces of morphology*. Hyderabad: CIEFL.

GOLDSMITH, J.
1990 *Autosegmental and metrical ohonology*. Oxford: Blackwell.

HARRIS, J.
1983 *Syllable structure and stress in Spanish: A non-linear approach*. Cambridge, Mass.: MIT Press.
1985 Spanish diphthongs and stress: A paradox resolved. *Phonology yearbook* 2. 31–45.

HAYES, B.
1989 Compensatory lengthening in mosaic phonology. *Linguistic Inquiry* 20. 253–306.

JEYAPAUL, V.Y.
1987 *Karbi grammar*. Mysore: CIIL.

JONES, D.
1988 *The English pronouncing dictionary*. London: J.M. Dwent and Sons.

JONES, R.B.
1961 *Karen linguistic studies*. Berkeley and California: University of California.

KENSTOWICZ
1994 *Phonology in generative grammar*. Cambridge. Mass: Blackwell.

KIM, C.W. and H.Y. KIM.
1991 The character of Korean glides. In C.W. Kim *et al.* (eds.), *Studies in linguistic sciences*. Urbana: University of Illinois.

MCCARTHY, J. and A. PRINCE
1993 Prosodic morphology I: Constraint interaction and satisfaction. Ms, University of Massachusetts, Amherst and Rutgers University, New Brunswick.

PERIALWAR, R.
1979 *Phonology of Irula with vocabulary*. Annamalai University: Annamalai Nagar.

PILLAI, V.C.
1976 *The grammar of the Kasaba language*. Annamalai University: Annamalai Nagar.

PRINCE, A. and P. SMOLENSKY
1993 Optimality theory: Constraint interaction in generative grammar. Ms, Rutgers University, New Brunswick.

SHARMA, D.D.
1989 *Tribal languages of Himachal Pradesh* Part I. New Delhi: Mittal Publications.

SHARMA, S.
1974 *Kangari: A descriptive study of the Kangra valley dialect of Himachal Pradesh*. Hoshiarpur: Punjab University.

SUBRAHMANYAM, P.S.
1968 *A descriptive grammar of Gondi*. Annamalai Nagar: Annamalai University.

VIJAYAKRISHNAN, K.G.
1978 Stress in Tamilian English. Unpublished M.Litt. Dissertation, CIEFL, Hyderabad.
1984 Morpheme structure constraints on vowels and the prosodic foot in Tamil. *CIEFL Working Papers in Linguistics* 1. 1.

9
Consonant geminates in Sinhala nouns

NIMAL PARAWAHERA
University of Kelaniya

In Modern Sinhala, nouns are marked for singular or plural number by means of a suffix. There are two singular and three plural suffixes namely respectively [a, ∂] and [o, u, ø]. In addition to suffixation, there are other changes that follow in the process of number marking in nouns. Following is an example that shows nominals in four groups as they will appear in their surface forms at the end of suffixation. (For clarity of illustration, morpheme boundaries are marked.)

(1)

		SINGULAR	SUFFIX	PLURAL	SUFFIX
i.	'fox'	*nari-*	y- a	*nari-*	y- o
	'lad'	*kolu-*	w- a	*kolu-*	w- o
ii.	'crane'	*kok-*	a	*kok-*	k- u
	'ox'	*gon-*	a	*gon-*	n- u
iii.	'lad'	*kol-*	ɭ- a	*kol-*	ɭ- o
	'tortoise'	*ib-*	b- a	*ib-*	b- o
iv.	'branch'	*at-*	t- ∂	*atu-*	ø
	'bag'	*mal-*	ɭ- ∂	*malu-*	ø

Firstly, according to the examples in (1), the choice of the suffix depends on the following morphophonemic factors.

(2) a. The difference between animate and inanimate nouns is observed.

All inanimate nouns take [ə] in singular and [ø] in plural.

b. Among animate nouns, those that end in a consonant in the underlying form take the suffix [u] in the plural.

c. For the rest, all animate nouns have [a] suffix in singular and [o] suffix in plural.

Secondly, suffixation is followed by the following phonological changes:

(3) a. Between the nominal stem and the suffix, a semi-vowel is inserted. This is predictable by the quality of the vowel that appears at the end of the nominal stem, that is, front vowels attracting 'y' and back vowel 'w'. This is a kind of hiatus formation naturally found in many languages with similar phonological context.

b. The final consonant of the nominal stem is lengthened as observed for nouns in singular form in groups (1iii) and (1iv) and for nouns in plural seen in groups (1ii) and (1iii).

Morphophonemic factors mentioned in (2) are predictable. The division of nouns into animate and inanimate is based on semantics while the morpheme structure is responsible for point (2b), which is the choice between the two plural suffixes o/u. This is further summarised as follows:

(4)

NOUN	+	SUFFIX	NOUN	+	SUFFIX
+animate +singular	=	a	–animate +singular	=	ə
+animate –singular	=	o/u	–animate –singular	=	ø

Thus, it turns out that any discussion about number marking in Modern Sinhala nouns is incomplete without an adequate explanation as to the phonological behaviour that leads to the phonetic representation of nouns. As mentioned earlier, the insertion of semi-vowels is predictable. However, the lengthening of the final consonant of nominal stems is not as clear cut as it may seem to be. In this regard, the following points are being observed.

(5) a. Consonant lengthening is not predictable morphologically; this can be noticed both in singular and plural.

b. Nor is it lexically predictable as there are no words that have double consonants word-finally. And the underlying forms of the noun stems under discussion are as follows.

(6) i. *nari* *kolu* (CVCV)

ii. *kok* *gon* (CVC)

iii. *kolu* *ibi* ((C)VCV)
iv. *atu* *malu* (C)VCV)

Underlying forms further reveal that it could be either a vowel-final or a consonant-final form that would undergo consonant gemination. In (6i), the final vowel remains unchanged and there is an insertion of either one of the two semi-vowels between the stem and the suffix. However, in (6iii), the final vowel is lost and it is the suffixed vowel that syllabifies with the noun stem. During this process, the stem with final consonant is lengthened. Therefore, it could be easily explained that consonant lengthening in this context is triggered by the loss of a segment. Nevertheless, in the case of stems of the type in (6ii), the triggering factor for consonant gemination remains unclear as there is no such segmental loss and yet the lengthening takes place.

This paper argues that in both cases of final consonant lengthening of nouns, it is the concept of 'quantity dimension' that operates underlyingly. Further, it is discussed that this is adequately explained through a non-linear analysis of the phonological system of Sinhala.

In the literature of Modern Sinhala linguistics, this issue of consonant gemination of nouns has been noticed by De Silva (1963), Dissanayake (1969), and Parawahera (1990). Both De Silva and Dissanayake presented a structural description based on methods of taxonomic linguistics. According to this explanation made by looking at the structural distribution of the stems, it is not clear whether their suggestions meant that these nominal stems had a long consonant in the underlying form or whether it was a morphophonemic variation of (CVC): (CVCC) that had to be treated in the lexicon. However, in the discussion it was concluded that some nouns had two stem forms, that is, one with two consonants and the other with a single consonant word-finally. Dissanayake, who made this suggestion, argued that it was necessary because those nouns that show double consonants in number marking will have a single consonant when they take part in compound formation. See the following examples.

(7) NUMBER MARKING COMPOUNDING
[*gonnu*] 'oxen' [*gon haⁿdə*] 'sound of the ox'

The weakness of this kind of analysis is that it has left the discussion without a theoretical explanation about the gemination process. The current approach is expected to bring about a systematic explanation about the phonological behaviour in the derivational morphology of Modern Sinhala nouns.

Quantity dimension is a regular occurrence in languages. It is constantly maintained in the phonological system of a language either in keeping up with a diachronic process which may exist as an abstract phenomenon in the synchronic phonology or can be available as a new rule in the synchronic phonology of the language.

There is enough evidence from historical linguistics to show that the concept of quantity dimension is a vital issue in phonological processes. For example, it is this same concept that has influenced the phonological process, which produced the Modern English word 'night' [nayt] from the Old English word 'nixt'. In the current phonetic form, we find that the 'x' of the old system is lost and the vowel has received a diphthonal quality. If just the velar fricative 'x' was lost in the word 'nixt', we would see a word like 'nit' in Modern English.

But, the diphthonal vowel in the modern pronunciation reveals that there was a long 'i' sound in the old system, which was later affected by the historical Vowel Shift. There are two possible explanations to argue for a historical long vowel in the modern word 'night'. According to one explanation which is based on the segmental analysis of sounds, two phonological rules are in order: one that lengthens 'i' before 'x' and the other to delete 'x'. However, there is no historical evidence to show that there was a stage where there was a lengthening of the vowel before velar fricative.

The second explanation which this paper adopts is based on the non-linear analysis of the phonological structure. Accordingly, it is obvious that there is a connection between the loss of 'x' and lengthening of the 'i'. The loss of one segment has created a vacuum which is filled by 'i' which expands by lengthening to be 'i:'. It is a similar kind of compensatory lengthening that is taking place in the case of double consonants in Sinhala nouns. Thus, when a segment is lost the neighbouring segment expands to fill the gap. This shows a universal phenomenon that 'the quantity dimension of a phonological string is in principle capable of remaining stable while the phonetic-quantity dimension is in a state of flux' (Harris 1994).

Through a non-linear analysis, it is possible to separate the quantitative information from the rest of the representation in a sound unit. The following illustration shows how the final consonant 'b' is lengthened after the loss of the final vowel in [[ibi] [a]].

(8)	(a) DELINKING			(b) SPREADING
SKELETAL TIER	X X X X		X X X X	X X X X
ASSOCIATION LINES	| | | |	→	| | | | →	| | / |
MELODIC TIER	i b i a		i b a	i b a

Illustration (8) shows how a single melodic unit is linked to two skeletal points. Since each skeletal unit represents a timing unit, a multiply-linked melodic unit takes up more timing space than a singly-linked one. In this example, [b] is further linked with the now vacant timing slot. Hence the lengthening of the final consonant in this context.

However, this explanation does not seem to give an answer to forms such as '*kok* + k + u' which is the plural form of '*kok* + a' mentioned in (1ii). As explained in (9), there is no accountable vacant timing slot that the melodic tier can spread out for association.

```
(9)  SKELETAL TIER        X X X X
     ASSOCIATION LINES    | | | |
     MELODIC TIER         k o k u
```

To derive '*kok* + k + u' from the underlying form /*kok*/, it is then necessary to assume some kind of melodically empty timing slot which is later associated by the neighbouring melodic unit. Thus, the representation looks as follows:

```
(10) SKELETAL TIER        X X X X X     X X X X X
     ASSOCIATION LINES    | | | | |  →  |  | | / |
     MELODIC TIER         k o k   u     k o k x u
```

Illustration (10) holds ground only if there is an explanation to justify the presence of an empty timing slot which allows the spreading of the melodic unit.

The Old Sinhala grammar explains that the plural suffix of a noun such as /*minissu*/ meaning 'people' is /*minis* + *hu*/. In fact, this 'hu' plural suffix can be seen with nouns in the Old Sinhala literature. For example, this plural suffix is used with a singular noun to indicate respect for the person identified by the noun. Thus, an Old Sinhala expression for the Buddha is /*bud* + *hu*/. It is, therefore, evidently arguable that the old suffix 'hu' has lost its segment while still retaining the timing unit. According to this explanation, it is then argued that the plural suffix 'u' has two timing slots in its underlying representation and this is only evident phonetically by the lengthening of the neighbouring segment.

This situation is reminiscent of what Chomsky and Halle (1968) pointed out for pairs such as [divine] and [divinity]. According to them, the underlying form of the two variants is /divIn/ – the capital 'I' representing a long 'i'. This is actually the form that this word had prior to the Great Vowel Shift. It is this historical long vowel which is accountable for the two phonological processes namely Great Vowel Shift and Trisyllabic Shortening. However, this long 'I' is an abstract phoneme which never surfaces in modern pronunciation.

Similarly, in Modern Sinhala the 'h' in the suffix has received the status of an abstract phonological segment. Within non-linear analysis, this abstract phonological unit is realised not as a segment but as a timing unit, which remained intact with the morpheme even when its segment, which represented the melodic unit, was lost. This abstract empty timing slot is available for a melodic unit to get associated within a suitable phonological form. This should then justify the assumption presented in depicting illustration (10) for consonant lengthening.

Next, in the case of hiatus formation in forms such as '*nari* + y + a', '*kolu* + w + a' the phonological process is quite obvious as it depends on the quality of the final vowel in the stem. However, in line with the theoretical approach adopted in this paper, it is necessary to show the association of this additional melodic unit with a timing slot. This paper recognises that the consonant lengthening and the hiatus formation are two different phonological processes. Therefore, following theoretical explanation put forward in lexical phonology (Mohanan 1986), this paper argues that the consonant gemination is a lexical process whereas the hiatus formation is post-lexical. As explained in lexical phonology, post-lexical rules do not have to be executed necessarily in the phonetic representation of a speaker. Thus, one can hear instances where the word */nariya/* is also pronounced */naria/*. But never is it heard */koku/* or */kolo/* for the words */kokku/* and */kollo/*, respectively. This then explains the fact that the consonant lengthening necessarily takes place in a module within the lexicon and the timing slots are underlyingly available for the melodic spreading which results in lengthening of the segment.

As for inanimate nouns the plural suffix is zero which means that it is lexically as well as spatially void. Therefore, the plural forms in inanimate nouns are unmarked. Finally it should also be pointed out that the argument to support to have level ordering in the Modern Sinhala lexicon (see Parawahera 1990) is further supported by yet another point that arises out of this discussion. That is it was seen that in a situation where there are two adjacent vocalic segments, one was lost. In [[*ibi*] + [a]], the final vowel of [*ibi*] was lost. Even though this vowel loss is a phonological process, it is not practised throughout the lexicon as we have forms such as [[*ibi*] [*oluwə*]] 'head of tortoise'. In the surface forms, we see [*ibba*] and [*ibioluwə*]. This situation shows that the derivation and compounding in the Modern Sinhala lexicon take place lexically in separate modules. Therefore, the phonological process available at one level is not observed in the other.

In summary, it was argued in this paper that the consonant lengthening in Sinhala nominals takes place in keeping up with the universal phenomenon of quantity dimension of the phonological system. Further, it was pointed out, that it was possible sometimes that the historical information about words can still determine the way phonological processes operate synchronically. Non-linear analysis is better suited in explaining the phenomena seen in the Modern Sinhala lexicon. Moreover, the necessity to recognise level ordering in the lexicon – which in turn allows for lexical and post-lexical phonological applications – was pointed out.

REFERENCES

CHOMSKY, NOAM and MORRIS HALLE
1968 *The sound pattern of English*. New York: Harper & Row.

DE SILVA, SUGATHAPALA
1963 *Vigrhatmaka Vagvidyava*. Colombo, Sri Lanka: Educational Publications Department.

DISSANAYAKE, J.B.
1969 *Bhashavaka Rata Samudaya*. Colombo, Sri Lanka: Lake House Investments Co.

HARRIS, JOHN
1994 *English sound structure*. Oxford, UK: Blackwell.

MOHANAN, K.P.
1986 *The theory of lexical phonology*. Dordrecht, Holland: D. Reidel Publishing Company.

PARAWAHERA, N.
1990 Phonology and morphology of Modern Sinhala. Unpublished Ph.D. dissertation, University of Victoria, Canada.

10
Acoustic correlates of lexical stress in Hindi

RAMI NAIR
Northwestern University

Although a majority of linguists writing about stress in Hindi assume its existence and in fact describe the rules of lexical stress in Hindi (Hayes 1991, 1995; Pandey 1989; Mehrotra 1970; Kelkar 1968) only Ohala (1977, 1986, 1991) has actually tried to determine its acoustic correlates. The work of the former group of authors relies mainly on intuition (Pandey 1989; Kelkar 1968; Mehrotra 1970), on evidence from poetic meter (Hayes 1991 based on Fairbanks' analysis) and on non-acoustic analysis of speech data (Pandey 1989). The pioneering work of Ohala (1977, 1986, 1991), on the other hand, is based on the acoustic analyses of Hindi words. Ohala's results, however, are at times ambiguous, which reflect the intricacies in the issue of Hindi stress. Ohala's two strongest claims in favour of stress in Hindi are that

- stress may be a privileged location in a word for placing a pitch contour, and
- renditions of some words where the 'wrong' syllable is stressed are judged by the native speakers of Hindi as unacceptable, and these judgements vary depending on whether the word is embedded in a sentence or is rendered in isolation.

I would like to thank Michael Broe, Manjari Ohala, Janet Pierrehumbert and Yi Xu for their valuable comments on the previous drafts of this paper. I would also like to thank Sarmad Hussain and Biju Nair for their help with computer programs that made the task of processing the data much easier and much more accurate. The errors are, of course, solely mine.

This research was supported by NSF Grant No. BNS-9022484 to Northwestern University.

Lack of consistent results supporting these claims leads the author to believe that perhaps Hindi has pragmatic stress instead of lexical stress. The aim of this paper is to show that there exists substantial acoustic evidence for lexical stress in Hindi, namely, syllable duration and, to a lesser extent, formant structure of the vowel.

Stress is usually defined in acoustic terms as an increase in duration, amplitude (intensity), and pitch (Fry 1955; Lehiste and Peterson 1959). For example, in the English minimal pair *object* versus *object*, /o/ in *object* is longer and more intense than in *object*, while /ɛ/ in *object* has a longer duration and a higher amplitude than in *object*. Studies of other languages show that formant structure of vowels can play an important role in determining stress as well. Van Bergem (1993) showed for Dutch that the less a word or syllable was stressed, the more its vowel resembled /ə/. In other words, stress tended to expand the vowel space of a speaker, perhaps in an effort to make the vowel (and the syllable) more distinct and clear for the listener.

Ohala (1977, 1986) looked at CVCV pairs like */gʌla/* 'throat' and */gʌla/* 'melt, SING. IMP.', which have been claimed by some authors to be minimal in Hindi. A native speaker was recorded producing these words in natural sounding sentences, controlling for prosodic position. The words were then spliced out of their carrier sentences and played back to the same native speaker, who had to judge which word (or rather which meaning) they heard. The informant was unable to differentiate the two meanings. Hence, as in some other dialects of Hindi (see also Pierrehumbert and Nair 1996), the informant and the experimenter found these pairs to be homophonous. The specific intonation pattern of the imperative seemed to be a factor that distinguished the two */gʌla/* meanings from each other.

Ohala (1986) also reports other production experiments, as well as a perception experiment on Hindi stress. For the production experiment, 36 test words were chosen, with stress placed according to Kelkar's (1968) algorithm. The duration of the stressed vowel and the stressed coda was then analysed. Neither the vowel nor the coda duration was found to be significantly different from its unstressed counterpart. In fact, some codas of the unstressed syllables were found to be longer than those of the stressed ones. In another experiment in the same study, Ohala (1986) analysed the pitch contour of the stressed syllable and found that it could usually be identified as a syllable with a rising pitch followed by a fall in pitch in the following syllable. However, there were many exceptions where the pitch on the stressed syllable was falling, or was higher than all other syllables, or had an ambiguous pitch contour. For the perception experiment, Ohala (1986) read words embedded in two carrier sentences to the subjects, varying the stress each time. The subjects judged which of the words that they heard were the preferred forms. There was some general agreement among the informants as to which type of lexical stress placement the native speakers found acceptable and which they found unacceptable.

Ohala (1991) conducted further experimentation on pitch as the possible acoustic correlate of stress in Hindi. Synthesised speech with two different pitch contours (rise, and rise and fall) on each of the syllables of disyllabic words like /*gobər*/ was used. Twenty-two native of speakers of Hindi judged 24 synthesised tokens on a scale of 1–5 for acceptability. The results did not show any preference for a particular pitch. Also, the results for words-in-isolation and words-in-sentence were different: more variations in pitch contour were judged as acceptable for the sentence condition, leading the author to hypothesise that perhaps Hindi has pragmatic stress instead of lexical stress.

One of the possible explanations for Ohala's (1986) ambiguity of the vowel/coda duration for Hindi may partly involve Pandey's (1989) consonant gemination rule. According to that rule, a consonant C_1 followed by a sonorant consonant C_2 (especially /j/, /W/ or /r/) in a C_1C_2 consonant cluster is subject to gemination. This seems to be precisely the context where Ohala (1986) reports results opposite to what is predicted if stress affected the duration of segments in a syllable: duration of /t/ in /*mʌtlab*/ versus /*prʌtjek*/ is 125 ms versus 177 ms. According to Pandey's rule, /t/ is more prone to get geminated when followed by a /j/ rather than by an /l/, and perhaps that is why the /t/ in /*prʌtjek*/ is longer than in /*mʌtlab*/. Also, one of the reasons why the vowel-duration measurements for the stressed and unstressed vowels might not be yielding a significant result for Ohala, which the author also acknowledges, seems to be because the syllables compared have onsets that do not always match in their complexity, as in the /*mʌtlab*/ – /*prʌtjek*/ example.

Some authors may argue that a language has lexical stress only if there are minimal pairs based on stress (like the English 'con*trast*' – '*con*trast' example). In the light of the non-contrastiveness of the /*gʌla*/ ~ /*gʌla*/ pair in Hindi, it can be argued that Hindi does not have stress. The argument against considering pairs like /*tʃʊna*/ 'chose' and /*tʃuna*/ 'lime' is that the contrast in this pair can be reduced to the length of the first vowel (even though there is also a considerable difference in the length of the second vowel). However, Hindi does have another set of minimal pairs. The words in these minimal pairs have a CVCCV structure. They are verb forms, one of which usually is a singular masculine past participle (or an adjective), while the other is a singular causative imperative form, for example, /*sʌmdʒʱa*/ 'understood' and /*sʌmdʒʱa*/ 'make somebody understand'. The past participle or adjectival form bears trochaic stress, while the imperative form always bears iambic stress.

A pilot experiment involving */sʌmdʒ^{h}al/* type minimal pairs was conducted. Two subjects read the target words embedded in natural sounding sentences, and controlled for the prosodic position. Acoustic analysis of these sentences showed (as in Ohala [1986] for the */gʌla/* ~ */gʌla/* pairs) that the pitch for the target words varied considerably (HL for the participles and LHL for the imperatives), making it impossible to compare their pitch tracks for stressed and unstressed vowels (the assumption here was that the pitch would rise or fall earlier in the word for trochees than for iambs). From the */tʃuna/* ~ */tʃuna/* analogy, one can argue that as in the */gʌla/* ~ */gʌla/* pairs, the difference between the */sʌmdʒ^{h}al/* type of pairs lies only in the sort of intonation that each requires. Measurement of the syllable duration showed that the vowel in the stressed syllable was considerably longer than the vowel in the corresponding unstressed syllable (/a/ in */sʌmdʒ^{h}al/* was shorter than in */sʌmdʒ^{h}al/*).

However, the */sʌmdʒ^{h}al/* – */sʌmdʒ^{h}al/* contrast should not be reduced merely to the difference in the intonation pattern. Had stress played no role in the differentiation of the two members of this pair, one would have expected everything to be equally emphasised or de-emphasised. So, either both the syllables of */sʌmdʒ^{h}al/* for either case would be lengthened, or both would be shortened, or nothing would happen. However, for the imperative form, only the second syllable is lengthened. This is an indication of stress, that is, the magnification of the weak and the strong syllables.

Since the experiment involving pairs of the */sʌmdʒ^{h}al/* type has the flaw that the intonation cannot be totally teased apart from the duration, it was necessary to design another experiment. The following experiment controls for the syllable structure under investigation and for its prosodic position.

THE EXPERIMENT

In his 1993 paper, van Bergem looked at the factors that affected stress in Dutch. His experiment looked at the effects of sentential and lexical stress, and at the effects of being a function word versus a content word (word frequency effects). He found that stress affected not only the duration of the vowel in question (stressed vowels being longer than the unstressed ones) but also its quality. He found that the vowels in unstressed and frequently occurring words tended to become schwa-like, that is, the vowel space narrowed down for them. This paper looks at Hindi and see if the duration of the vowel and the value of its formants were affected by stress.

Ninety-six Hindi words (24 trisyllables, 40 disyllables and 32 monosyllables) or 32 triplets matching the first syllable for stressed, unstressed and isolated conditions were chosen (see Appendix 1). All ten non-nasal vowels were included, though not every vowel was equally represented because of the limitations of real speech. However, the number of vowels was roughly matched for front (36), back (39) and central (21). All the syllables that were investigated here were of the CV structure (except for the monosyllabic words where it was impossible to find all CV words only), so that the length of the vowel was not affected by the differences in the syllable onset and by the syllable coda. Except for the trisyllabic words which contain the lax vowels /ɪ/, /ʊ/ and /ʌ/, there is general agreement in the literature on where stress falls in these words.

This experimental design does not have the */tʃʊna/* ~ */tʃuna/* dilemma as the syllables that are compared here have the exact CV structure and differ only in where the stress falls. It may be argued that it is inappropriate to talk about lexical stress here since the pairs contrasted do not form lexically minimal pairs. However, it would not be out of place to talk about 'word accent'. 'Word accent' is 'lexical stress' that is not phonemic, but which is, nevertheless, present in a language. In other words, there is a pattern according to which syllables are emphasised in a language. Emphasis of syllables that do not follow this pattern, or failure to emphasise any syllable sounds strange to the native speakers of that language. Thus, even though French and Polish have no 'lexical stress', that is, there are no words in these languages that are distinguished solely by how the stress is placed, it is generally agreed that French has a 'word accent' on the last syllable, for example, */kõpaʀɛsõ)/* 'comparison', while Polish has it on the penultimate syllable, for example, */karuzela/* 'merry-go-round'. Placing the stress or accent on a different syllable than that specified here does not sound right to the native speakers of these languages.

The test words were embedded in two carrier sentences */kʌha ___ apne/* 'said ___ you' and */bola ___ apne/* 'told ___ you'. The two carrier sentences were chosen to counteract any effects of stress priming by the first word of the carrier sentence (*/kʌha/* is stressed on the second syllable while */bola/* is stressed on the first syllable).

The sentences were then randomised and read by three native speakers of Hindi[1] : three times in each carrier sentence giving a total of six renditions of each word by each speaker. Monosyllables were chosen only for providing a standard comparison. Nasals, rhotics, semi-vowels and aspirated plosives were avoided because they are either difficult to measure or they tend to obscure the formant structure of vowels. However, due to paucity of natural lexical pairs, I had to revert to using some of the nasals, although I completely avoided words that had a nasal on each side of the vowel under investigation.

The subjects were told to read the test sentences at a normal pace, preferably without changing their intonation.[2] Their speech was digitally recorded (in a sound-proof booth for the first subject and at home on a Sony TCD-7 DAT recorder for other two subjects) and then transferred onto the hard disk of a Sun UNIX Station where it was analysed with the help of speech software from Entropics Laboratories. For the syllables under investigation (first syllable or the only syllable of the word), the following measurements were made:

- length of the onset consonant,
- length of the vowel,
- value of the first formant of the vowel, and
- value of the second formant of the vowel.

PROCEDURE

Part A

For the first part of the experiment, the duration of vowels and syllables was measured as follows. The time at the beginning of the consonant, the beginning of the vowel (= end of the consonant) and the end of the vowel was marked by looking at the waveform and the spectrogram, the value of which was recorded automatically in an output file with the help of a computer shell script. This data was then imported into Microsoft Excel and unrandomised.

The duration of the vowel was measured by subtracting the time value for the beginning of the vowel from that of the end of the vowel, while for the syllable duration, the time value for the beginning of the consonant was subtracted from that of the end of the vowel. During the measurement of the vowel and the syllable duration, it was found that data for all test words starting with a vowel had to be eliminated. This was necessary either because there was a great deal of glottalisation that obscured the beginning of the target vowel, or because the final vowel from the first word of the carrier sentence (/a/ from /*kʌha̱*/ or /*bɑla̱*/) would be merged with the following target vowel, again obscuring the onset of the target vowel.

Part B

In the second part of the experiment, first and second formant values of the test vowels were measured. For the measurement of formants, another shell script was used that marked the frequency values at a given point in time. For all vowels, the formants were measured in the exact middle of the vowel.

These frequencies were then imported into Excel and unrandomised. Next, they were transformed into the mel scale, which is more in accord with how we perceive speech. The following formula (taken from Makhoul and Cosell 1976, cited in van Bergem 1993) was used for the mel transformation of formant frequencies:

mel = 2595 log (1 + f/700) (where f is the formant frequency in hertz)

Euclidean distances were measured for each vowel from an 'average schwa', that was computed for each subject separately, based on the average formant values of all test /ʌ/s that the informants produced. The formula used was:

$$\text{Euclidean distance} = \sqrt{(\text{Avg. } f_1 - f_1)^2 + (\text{Avg. } f_2 - f_2)^2}$$

(where f is the mel converted formant frequency of a vowel in hertz)

Calculation of the Euclidean distances of the vowels to the 'average schwa' was the best way of way of determining if the vowel space was affected by stress. It also facilitated comparison of the Hindi data herein to the Dutch data in van Bergem (1993). Van Bergem (1993) found that the vowel spaced narrowed (vowels became more schwa-like) as the stress condition changed from ISOLATION[3] → STRESSED → UNSTRESSED.

RESULTS AND DISCUSSION

The results are reported for each subject as it is impossible to pool the formant data from male and female subjects. Also, the data from all three subjects differs in how each of them chooses to emphasise strong syllables and de-emphasise the weak ones.

1. *Mean vowel and syllable duration*

SUBJECT 1: The mean duration of the vowel for this subject was found to be longest for the isolated syllables despite the fact that most of these syllables contained a coda. Next in length came vowels that were stressed. The unstressed vowels were the shortest. The results for mean syllable duration are similar to those of mean vowel duration and can be found in Appendix 2.

Interestingly, the tendency ISOLATION < STRESSED < UNSTRESSED holds for all vowels except for /ʌ/, where the unstressed version of the vowel is not significantly longer than the stressed counterpart. Note that apart from /a/, /ɔ/ and /æ/ have the longest mean duration in isolation and in unstressed position. A possible explanation for this might be that underlyingly these vowels are diphthongs and the mid-lax monophthongs are their allophones (/ʌʊ/ ⇔ ɔ/, /ʌɪ/ ⇔ /æ/). Table 1 shows vowel-by-vowel results of paired *t*-tests calculated for the STRESSED-UNSTRESSED vowel and syllable pairs. These *t*-tests were based on the entire data for the speaker.

TABLE 1 *Probability values for paired t-tests comparing the duration of the stressed and unstressed vowels and syllables (Subject 1)*

VOWEL	P-VALUE ASSOCIATED WITH T-TEST	SYLLABLE	P-VALUE ASSOCIATED WITH T-TEST
/a/	0.0006	/a/	0.0003
/ʌ/	0.2	/ʌ/	0.2
/i/	0.003	/i/	0.009
/ɪ/	0.03	/ɪ/	0.00005
/u/	0.000007	/u/	0.0005
/ʊ/	0.004	/ʊ/	0.0001
/o/	0.0000001	/o/	0.00001
/ɔ/	0.00000002	/ɔ/	0.0000005
/e/	0.002	/e/	0.0004
/æ/	0.0000007	/æ/	0.00000006

Thus, except for /ʌ/, all vowels show a duration difference significant at $p < 0.05$ between the stressed and unstressed conditions, the stressed vowels being significantly longer than the unstressed ones. The measurement of the duration of the entire syllable showed difference between the stressed and the unstressed syllable (again except for /ʌ/) at even higher p values. This implies that for this subject, stress affects not only the length of the vowel, but the length of the entire syllable.

There is a possible explanation as to why /ʌ/ is anomalous in the data in Table 1. A reanalysis of 'stressed' /ʌ/s for Subject 1 showed that they were actually not stressed. The speaker spoke a dialect of Hindi where the LLH words containing /ʌ/ in the first syllable were stressed on the second syllable rather than the first one, as assumed by the experimenter. This implies that what was calculated to be the stressed vowel/syllable was indeed an unstressed one, hence the lack of a significant difference between the two conditions.

SUBJECT 2: For this subject, the duration of syllables in the three different stress situations bore more significance than pure vowel duration. This can be seen by comparing the numbers in Appendix 2, and by looking up the *p*-values for *t*-tests of STRESSED versus UNSTRESSED duration of each vowel and syllable type (shown in Table 2).

The short lax vowels /ʌ/, /ɪ/ and /ʊ/ for this subject are either equal or longer (even insignificantly longer) in the UNSTRESSED versus STRESSED condition. However, when we take the entire syllable into consideration, these differences reverse and the stressed syllable is found to be significantly longer than its unstressed counterpart at $p < 0.05$. The results of the paired t-test calculated for the STRESSED-UNSTRESSED conditions for vowels and syllables have been shown in Table 2.

TABLE 2 *Results of paired t-tests for the duration of stressed and unstressed vowels and syllables for Subject 2*

VOWEL	P-VALUE ASSOCIATED WITH T-TEST	SYLLABLE	P-VALUE ASSOCIATED WITH T-TEST
/a/	0.094	/a/	0.04
/ʌ/	0.224	/ʌ/	0.027
/i/	0.266	/ɪ/	0.035
/ɪ/	0.385	/ɪ/	0.066
/U/	0.119	/U/	0.012
/ʊ/	0.468	/ʊ/	0.016
/e/	0.11	/e/	0.005
/æ/	0.00005	/æ/	0.0002
/o/	0.062	/o/	0.031
/ɔ/	0.04	/ɔ/	0.053

SUBJECT 3: For this subject, the comparison of vowel versus syllable length for the three stress conditions shows effects on basically four vowels: /ɪ/, /u/, /ʊ/ and /æ/. Stressed /ɪ/ is significantly longer than its unstressed counterpart in the vowel-only condition, but at the syllable level, the unstressed /ɪ/ is insignificantly longer.

On the other hand, the remaining three vowels /u/, /ʊ/ and /æ/ are significantly longer when stressed rather than unstressed when the entire syllable is taken into consideration. There is no significant difference between stressed and unstressed /ʌ/ in either the vowel-only or the syllable condition. The results of the paired *t*-tests (at $p < 0.05$) for STRESSED-UNSTRESSED vowels and syllables are reported in Table 3.

A possible explanation for the lack of significance for the stressed-unstressed conditions for /ʌ/ resembles that given for Subject 1. The difference lies in that this subject stressed the second syllable of a LLH word beginning with a syllable containing a /ʌ/ for the word /sʌvɪta/ but stressed the first syllable of the word /kʌvɪta/. This means that what has been reported as the duration of the stressed /ʌ/ is in fact an average of stressed and unstressed /ʌ/. I have no good explanation as to why /ɪ/ remains anomalous for this subject. However, the data does indicate that Subject 3 shows a tendency towards the preference of syllable duration over simply vowel duration, as the indicator of stress in Hindi.

TABLE 3 *Probability values for paired t-tests comparing the duration of the stressed and unstressed vowels and syllables (Subject 3)*

VOWEL	P-VALUE ASSOCIATED WITH T-TEST	SYLLABLE	P-VALUE ASSOCIATED WITH T-TEST
/a/	0.021	/a/	0.018
/ʌ/	0.124	/ʌ/	0.48
/i/	0.038	/i/	0.044
/ɪ/	0.048	/ɪ/	0.311
/U/	0.054	/U/	0.004
/ʊ/	0.059	/ʊ/	0.001
/o/	0.0002	/o/	0.008
/ɔ/	0.00000002	/ɔ/	0.00000006
/e/	0.00000009	/e/	0.0000001
/æ/	0.076	/æ/	0.045

2. *First and second formant values and Euclidean distances*

As mentioned earlier, the purpose of the second part of the experiment was to investigate if formant values of Hindi were affected by stress. The hypothesis, following the findings of van Bergem (1993) for Dutch was that the vowel space would narrow as stress is reduced. Vowels in isolation are then predicted to be furthest away from the average schwa, while the unstressed vowels are predicted to be the closest. Following are subject-by-subject results involving the formant values.

SUBJECT 1: The mean values for the first and the second formants in mel for each of the ten non-nasal vowels are shown in Table 4. Table 5 presents this information in terms of the Euclidean distances.

As in van Bergem (1993) we see some tendency for the unstressed vowels to be more centred than the stressed ones, and the stressed ones to be more centred than the isolated ones (the centre here is an average schwa: f1 = 748.724, f2 = 1243.637). This is true for seven vowels: /i/, /ʊ/, /o/, /ɔ/, /e/, /æ/ and /ʌ/. For /a/, /ɪ/ and /u/, the unstressed vowels are more centred than the unstressed ones, but the isolated forms are not the furthest ones away from the centre as in van Bergem. For vowels /a/ and /u/ the isolated form is more centred than the stressed one, although it is still less centred than the unstressed one, while in the case of /ɪ/, on the other hand, the isolated vowel is the most centred one, which does not tally with the results in van Bergem (1993) at all. Paired *t*-tests that compared the first and the second formant of the stressed and the unstressed vowels do not have an impressive result. For f1, the test was significant at $p \leq 0.05$ for /a/, /ʌ/, /i/, /u/, /ʊ/, /o/and /ɔ/. *P*-values for /ɪ/, /e/ and /æ/ did not reach the significance level for either of the formants. For f2, only /ʌ/, /ɔ/, /u/ and /o/ reached significance at the $p \leq 0.05$ level.

TABLE 4 *Mean values of first and second formants of Hindi vowels in mel under various stress conditions (Subject 1)*

VOWEL	F1	F2	VOWEL	F1	F2
/a/ ISOLATION	874.857	1178.817	/ʌ/ ISOLATION	813.453	1236.449
STRESSED	866.812	1230.8	STRESSED	690.283	1285.988
UNSTRESSED	841.469	1199.301	UNSTRESSED	742.435	1208.473
/i/ ISOLATION	552.105	1750.192	/ɪ/ ISOLATION	548.44	1600.246
STRESSED	569.382	1743.931	STRESSED	538.967	1627.637
UNSTRESSED	591.297	1749.846	UNSTRESSED	545.6	1620.591
/u/ ISOLATION	567.136	852.426	/ʊ/ ISOLATION	546.533	965.835
STRESSED	520.353	839.626	STRESSED	574.065	1023.012
UNSTRESSED	563.118	903.56	UNSTRESSED	590.376	1023.676
/o/ ISOLATION	544.327	893.793	/ɔ/ ISOLATION	760.356	978.185
STRESSED	579.597	931.635	STRESSED	748.085	1029.275
UNSTRESSED	600.749	979.781	UNSTRESSED	729.265	1044.68
/e/ ISOLATION	584.134	1638.418	/æ/ ISOLATION	728.607	1563.779
STRESSED	608.293	1623.544	STRESSED	745.554	1498.417
UNSTRESSED	593.815	1616.218	UNSTRESSED	748.784	1511.577

Paired *t*-tests that compared the Euclidean distances of the stressed and the unstressed vowels from the 'average schwa' were also calculated. The results have been presented in Table 6. Euclidean distances for only three vowels – /a/, /u/ and /o/ – showed a result significant at $p < 0.05$ for the STRESSED-UNSTRESSED condition.

Although Table 6 shows that formant values are statistically not as important a cue for marking stress in Hindi as they are for Dutch, it is not possible to totally ignore them. At least the raw data indicates that there is some tendency for the unstressed vowels to be more centred than the stressed ones. Part of the reason why Hindi does not fully utilise formant values as stress markers (as Dutch does) could be because that would force the long (tense) vowels to reduce to short (lax) ones which, in Hindi, are in phonemic contrast (compare /un/ 'wool' ~ /ʊn/ 'those, OBL.' /ab/ 'water' ~ /ʌb/ 'now'). Keeping vowels distinct by their quality (formants) and differentiating a stressed version of vowel /x/ from its unstressed version with the aid of duration seems, therefore, to be a better option for languages like Hindi, which have tense and lax vowels in phonemic contrast.

TABLE 5 *Average Euclidean distances of all the vowels under three stress conditions from an average schwa-like vowel*

VOWEL	ISOLATION	STRESSED	UNSTRESSED
/a/	153.004	168.29	112.732
/ʌ/	104.891	76.068	50.898
/i/	540.847	529.794	528.387
/ɪ/	406.931	437.01	427.728
/U/	439.672	460.715	384.376
/ʊ/	340.592	281.45	271.289
/O/	401.407	351.61	300.954
/ɔ/	276.674	216.415	201.214
/e/	427.372	402.793	400.149
/æ/	326.26	273.231	269.521

contd. . .

TABLE 6 *Probability values for the paired t-tests comparing formant values and Euclidean distances of stressed and unstressed vowels*

VOWEL	P-VALUE ASSOCIATED WITH T-TEST		
	F1	F2	EUCLIDEAN DISTANCE
/a/	0.015	0.245	0.018
/ə/	0.003	0.000000000000009	0.068
/i/	0.021	0.346	0.46
/ɪ/	0.30	0.106	0.103
/u/	0.006	0.00000002	0.00007
/ʊ/	0.028	0.483	0.228
/o/	0.01	0.0004	0.0002
/ɔ/	0.048	0.00000000000003	0.152
/e/	0.097	0.271	0.423
/æ/	0.367	0.267	0.324

SUBJECT 2: The mean values of the first and second formants for the three stress conditions are given in Table 7.

TABLE 7 *Average first and second formant values in mel for Subject 2 for three stress conditions*

VOWEL	F1	F2	VOWEL	F1	F2
/a/ ISOLATION	747.395	1113.752	/ʌ/ ISOLATION	690.815	1124.711
STRESSED	750.73	1181.94	STRESSED	676.92	1175.66
UNSTRESSED	743.40	1163.49	UNSTRESSED	651.82	1135.66
/i/ ISOLATION	408.938	1624.468	/ɪ/ ISOLATION	481.408	1500.552
STRESSED	420.89	1585.78	STRESSED	455.17	1515.81
UNSTRESSED	415.48	1621.19	UNSTRESSED	441.28	1521.11
/ʊ/ ISOLATION	381.742	727.504	/ʊ/ ISOLATION	526.85	1089.25
STRESSED	363.96	762.02	STRESSED	502.91	1054.78
UNSTRESSED	405.81	772.7	UNSTRESSED	460.34	1054.97
/o/ ISOLATION	483.722	863.339	/ɔ/ ISOLATION	609.587	960.729
STRESSED	496.01	887.56	STRESSED	611.09	932.86
UNSTRESSED	515.72	932.00	UNSTRESSED	607.32	968.62
/e/ ISOLATION	531.777	1482.071	/æ/ ISOLATION	639.34	1415.442
STRESSED	564.47	1447.39	STRESSED	616.65	1407.45
UNSTRESSED	572.83	1432.49	UNSTRESSED	678.83	1371.57

Tables 8 and 9 give the average Euclidean distances for the vowels from an average schwa (f1 = 592.3026, f2 = 1199.365) for this subject, as well as the *p*-values associated with paired *t*-tests that compared f1, f2 and Euclidean distances for the stressed and the unstressed conditions. As can be seen from this data, at least seven vowels show the van Bergem (1993) type of tendency where ISOLATED > STRESSED > UNSTRESSED in terms of Euclidean distances from a central point in the speaker's vowel space. These are /a/, /u/, /ʊ/, /e/, /æ/, /o/ and /ɔ/. For two of the remaining three vowels /ʌ/ and /i/, the stressed vowel is closer to the 'average schwa' than its unstressed counterpart, but the isolated form is still the furthest one. /ɪ/ is the only one that has the entire order reversed, that is, the isolated form is the closest to the centre, while the unstressed is the furthest one. As for Subject 1, only three out of ten vowels show that the difference between the STRESSED and UNSTRESSED forms is at a significance level of $p < 0.05$, although two more almost reach the significance level. Again, although we do not see a concrete statistical generalisation here, we do notice on the basis of raw data some kind of tendency for the subjects to centralise their vowels as they destress a syllable.

TABLE 8 *Average Euclidean distances of all the vowels under three stress conditions from an average schwa (Subject 2)*

VOWEL	ISOLATION	STRESSED	UNSTRESSED
/a/	179.34	176.29	156.57
/ʌ/	125.22	89.82	90.66
/i/	464.38	423.29	458.43
/ɪ/	321.61	345.83	356.25
/u/	518.45	493.93	466.56
/ʊ/	296.22	275.2	273.19
/e/	291.02	260.68	238.14
/æ/	226.52	217.35	195.6
/o/	389.82	327.68	280.91
/ɔ/	292.15	275.42	233.55

TABLE 9 *Probability values for the paired t-tests comparing formant values and Euclidean distances of stressed and unstressed vowels (Subject 2)*

VOWEL	P-VALUE ASSOCIATED WITH T-TEST		
	F1	F2	EUCLIDEAN DISTANCE
/ɑ/	0.061	0.163	0.067
/ʌ/	0.02	0.00005	0.461
/i/	0.384	0.002	0.001 (reverse relationship)
/ɪ/	0.004	0.168	0.057 (reverse relationship)
/U/	0.001	0.39	0.237
/ʊ/	0.118	0.499	0.479
/e/	0.346	0.15	0.056
/æ/	0.0003	0.001	0.023
/O/	0.003	0.012	0.01
/ɔ/	0.412	0.053	0.028

SUBJECT 3: This subject showed least influence of the vowel formant values on stress as shown in Table 10. In other words, more than the previous two subjects, this subject chose vowel and syllable duration as primary cues for marking stress.

The data in Tables 11 and 12 show the average Euclidean distances (from the 'average schwa' at f1[mel] = 615.955, f2[mel] = 1285.045) and probability results for paired *t*-tests between stressed and unstressed first and second formants (in mel) as well as stressed and unstressed Euclidean distances, respectively.

TABLE 10 *Average f1 and f2 values in mel for ten vowels under three stress conditions (Subject 3)*

VOWEL	F1	F2	VOWEL	F1	F2
/a/ ISOLATION	731.351	1308.309	/ʌ/ ISOLATION	632.017	1327.897
STRESSED	783.28	1331.526	STRESSED	566.505	1296.903
UNSTRESSED	786.465	1355.406	UNSTRESSED	649.344	1230.336
/ɪ/ ISOLATION	320.836	1863.189	/ɪ/ ISOLATION	442.266	1697.71
STRESSED	331.103	1845.432	STRESSED	426.675	1633.698
UNSTRESSED	323.085	1746.424	UNSTRESSED	416.858	1694.484
/ʊ/ ISOLATION	382.579	807.984	/ʊ/ ISOLATION	440.521	1032.323
STRESSED	370.446	860.179	STRESSED	417.403	1124.406
UNSTRESSED	388.963	897.785	UNSTRESSED	426.642	1092.455

contd. . .

VOWEL	F1	F2	VOWEL	F1	F2
/o/ ISOLATION	411.798	927.572	/ɔ/ ISOLATION	553.041	953.512
STRESSED	446.126	1031.465	STRESSED	552.908	1011.972
UNSTRESSED	470.354	1082.383	UNSTRESSED	568.085	1084.904
/e/ ISOLATION	418.598	1753.4	/æ/ ISOLATION	662.187	1614.915
STRESSED	454.866	1736.699	STRESSED	595.268	1587.624
UNSTRESSED	488.388	1690.555	UNSTRESSED	549.53	1588.819

TABLE 11 *Average Euclidean distances for the ten vowels under three stress conditions (Subject 3)*

VOWEL	ISOLATION	STRESSED	UNSTRESSED
/a/	226.563	204.515	118.567
/ʌ/	93.813	124.213	89.486
/i/	649.262	628.788	548.028
/ɪ/	451.015	399.723	461.92
/u/	534.125	492.37	450.062
/ʊ/	323.874	280.607	308.08
/e/	511.927	485.637	437.522
/æ/	350.443	326.666	342.772
/o/	413.967	322.736	301.333
/ɔ/	372.885	317.76	236.679

TABLE 12 *Probability values for the paired t-tests comparing formant values and Euclidean distances of stressed and unstressed vowels (Subject 3)*

VOWEL	P-VALUE ASSOCIATED WITH T-TEST		
	F1	F2	EUCLIDEAN DISTANCE
/ɑ/	0.451	0.003	0.186
/ʌ/	0.005	0.037	0.103
/i/	0.195	0.006	0.007
/ɪ/	0.314	0.005	0.004 (reverse relationship)
/u/	0.173	0.127	0.116
/ʊ/	0.272	0.218	0.095
/e/	0.21	0.044	0.072
/æ/	0.134	0.471	0.209
/o/	0.088	0.029	0.021
/ɔ/	0.348	0.048	0.002

CONCLUSION

Previous experimentation trying to find the acoustic correlates of Hindi stress was not very successful because it either did not look at lexical pairs that actually had contrastive lexical stress, or it compared stressed and unstressed syllables that were not fully matching in their segmental structure. While the experiments reported here do not investigate the role of pitch as an indicator of stress, which was the main object of interest in other experiments (see Ohala 1986, 1991), it does look at the syllable and vowel duration, and at the first and second formant structure. Further experimentation is required for a conclusive generalisation about which of these factors is/are an acoustic correlate of stress in Hindi.

In this experiment we looked at pairs of words that have equal number of syllables and that differ in where the stress falls: it falls on the first syllable for the first member of the word pair and the second syllable for the second member of the pair. In all cases we looked at an identical first syllable, in order to minimise any prosodic effects.

The experiment gives us preliminary results pertaining to the acoustic cues of stress in Hindi. In the same prosodic position but with the stress varied, the syllable in Hindi varies in length: the stressed one being significantly longer than the unstressed one. Vowel formant values do change with stress, but unlike in languages such as Dutch and English, they are found to be unreliable cues as compared to duration. And even though the Euclidean distances from a vowel to an average schwa do not reduce for the ISOLATED > STRESSED > UNSTRESSED conditions at a *p*-level of 0.05 or less, yet, a definite tendency can be seen towards the centralisation of vowels as the stress reduces. The lack of a more definitive result regarding the formant structure is perhaps caused by the fact that tense and lax vowels in Hindi are in phonemic contrast and the reduction of tense vowels would obscure the contrast between them and the lax vowels. Table 13 presents subject by subject results of paired *t*-tests for vowel duration, syllable duration and Euclidean distances for the STRESSED-UNSTRESSED condition, based on the entire data for that speaker.

TABLE 13 *Overall p-values for three subjects based on paired t-tests for ten vowels for the stressed versus unstressed conditions*

	SUBJECT 1	SUBJECT 2	SUBJECT 3
Vowel length	p < 0.0001	0.0002	p < 0.0001
Syllable length	p < 0.0001	p < 0.0001	p < 0.0001
Euclidean distance	0.042	0.045	0.223

Variations in vowel/syllable duration and formant values do indicate that Hindi has lexical stress, even though most of the time this stress is non-contrastive. Native speakers of Hindi are aware of the stress patterns in the language and express them phonetically as described earlier. It would, therefore, seem reasonable to conclude that as reported earlier by other authors, Hindi does have lexical stress (or accent, as some may prefer to call it) and it is expressed acoustically as syllable lengthening and, less significantly, as more extreme vowel formants.

APPENDICES

APPENDIX 1 *List of words used for the experiment*

VOWEL TYPE	STRESSED	UNSTRESSED	ISOLATION
/a/	tala	talab	tal
	dava	davat	dav
	kali	kalin	kal
	saka	sakar	sak
/i/	nila	nilam	nil
/e/	megʰa	megʰant	megʰ
	tʃela	tʃelal	tʃel
/u/	kuʈa	kuʈartʰ	kuʈ
	muli	mulanʃ	mul
/o/	godi	godam	god
	dʒota	dʒotant	dʒot
	gopi	gopal	gop
	doha	dohag	doʃ
/ɔ/	tɔla	tɔʃar	tɔl
	tɔba	tɔhin	tɔn
	kɔpi	kɔpin	kɔp
/æ/	mæda	mædan	mæl
	pæsa	pækar	pæɖ
	tæli	tænat	tæl
	pæda	pægam	pæn
/ʊ/	kʊʈɪja	kʊʈɔni	kʊʈ
	kʊtɪja	kʊtʌrna	kʊl
	sukʰɪja	sʊkʰana	sʊkʰ
	mʊkʰɪja	mʊkʰɔta	mʊkʰ

contd

VOWEL TYPE	STRESSED	UNSTRESSED	ISOLATION
/ɪ/	ɪSɪta	ɪSara	ɪSk
	tɪgʊna	tɪbara	tɪb
	tɪkʊra	tɪkani	tɪl
	sɪkʊʈa	sɪkɔli	sɪk^h
	nɪvɪda	nɪvedʌn	nɪb
/ə/	ʌdɪtɪ	ʌdalʌt	ʌdH
	sʌvɪta	sʌvari	sʌb
	kʌvɪta	kʌvela	kʌb

For the STRESSED vowels, the first syllable is accented, for the UNSTRESSED vowels, the second syllable is accented.

APPENDIX 2 Average vowel and syllable duration for each of the three subjects under three different stress conditions (in seconds)

	SUBJECT 1		SUBJECT 2		SUBJECT 3	
	V	CV	V	CV	V	CV
/a/ ISOLATION	0.228	0.29	0.21	0.27	0.199	0.253
STRESSED	0.152	0.167	0.14	0.192	0.128	0.18
UNSTRESSED	0.127	0.142	0.134	0.181	0.12	0.17
/ʌ/ ISOLATION	0.112	0.195	0.106	0.204	0.091	0.177
STRESSED	0.065	0.132	0.07	0.153	0.062	0.137
UNSTRESSED	0.065	0.128	0.073	0.145	0.066	0.141
/i/ ISOLATION	0.173	0.269	0.164	0.317	0.171	0.293
STRESSED	0.126	0.208	0.119	0.24	0.124	0.233
UNSTRESSED	0.107	0.186	0.115	0.217	0.096	0.192
/ɪ/ ISOLATION	0.087	0.68	0.084	0.171	0.08	0.166
STRESSED	0.057	0.118	0.061	0.129	0.048	0.121
UNSTRESSED	0.05	0.104	0.062	0.123	0.048	0.121
/u/ ISOLATION	0.175	0.253	0.163	0.25	0.163	0.251
STRESSED	0.109	0.182	0.112	0.19	0.103	0.181
UNSTRESSED	0.086	0.145	0.107	0.175	0.09	0.154
/ʊ/ ISOLATION	0.082	0.178	0.069	0.157	0.068	0.149
STRESSED	0.048	0.122	0.054	0.126	0.046	0.115
UNSTRESSED	0.044	0.105	0.054	0.118	0.041	0.105
/o/ ISOLATION	0.191	0.222	0.183	0.196	0.185	0.223
STRESSED	0.146	0.171	0.14	0.152	0.128	0.163
UNSTRESSED	0.111	0.134	0.134	0.143	0.1	0.131
/ɔ/ ISOLATION	0.227	0.249	0.203	0.227	0.194	0.227
STRESSED	0.144	0.161	0.135	0.157	0.133	0.165
UNSTRESSED	0.12	0.136	0.126	0.147	0.127	0.159

contd.

	SUBJECT 1		SUBJECT 2		SUBJECT 3	
	V	CV	V	CV	V	CV
/e/ ISOLATION	0.201	0.292	0.215	0.323	0.178	0.28
STRESSED	0.134	0.205	0.141	0.238	0.125	0.214
UNSTRESSED	0.105	0.166	0.13	0.211	0.099	0.189
/æ/ ISOLATION	0.222	0.255	0.2	0.241	0.196	0.244
STRESSED	0.144	0.173	0.143	0.18	0.136	0.179
UNSTRESSED	0.12	0.152	0.129	0.163	0.106	0.147

NOTES

1. Subjects 1 and 2 are males while Subject 3 is a female. Subjects 1 and 3 have been residing in the US for about five years, while Subject 2 has been in the USA for about ten years. All three subjects are fluent in Hindi and use the language on a daily basis at home with their spouses, friends and relatives. Subject 1 is originally from Delhi, while Subjects 2 and 3 are from Ghaziabad, Uttar Pradesh.
2. It was noted in previous (pilot) experimentation that after two or three repetitions the subjects got bored and tired, and as a result started altering their intonation. This made it impossible to compare one rendition of a test word with the next one.
3. The isolation condition is somewhat different in van Bergem (1993) than it is here. In van Bergem, the 'in-isolation' syllable-word was spoken without a context, while in this case it was embedded in the carrier sentence. I have, therefore, included the 'in-isolation' condition here just for a rough comparison. A more strictly controlled experiment is necessary to evaluate the 'in-isolation' condition with respect to the stressed and unstressed ones.

REFERENCES

FRY, D.B.

1955 Duration and intensity as physical correlates of linguistic stress. *JASA*, 27.4. 765–68.

HAYES, B.

1991 Metrical stress theory: Principles and case studies. ms. Los Angeles: University of California.

1995 *Metrical stress theory: Principles and case studies*. Chicago: University of Chicago Press.

KELKAR, A.R.

1968 *Studies in Hindi-Urdu*. Poona: Deccan College Postgraduate and Research Institute.

LEHISTE, I. and G.E. PETERSON

1959 Vowel amplitude and phonemic stress in American English. *JASA*, 31.4. 428–35.

MAKHOUL, J. and L. COSELL
1976 LPCW: An LPC vocoder with linear predictive spectral warping. *Proceedings of the International Conference on Acoustic Speech Signal Processing*. 466–69.

MEHROTRA, R.C.
1970 *hɪndi dʰwanɪkɪ ɔr dHwanɪmɪ*. Nayi Dilli: Munshiram Manoharlal.

OHALA, M.
1977 Stress in Hindi. In L.M. Hyman (ed.), *Studies in stress and accent, Occasional Papers in Linguistics* 4. Los Angeles: University of Southern California. 327–38.
1986 A search for the phonetic correlates of Hindi stress. In Bh. Krishnamurti (ed.), *South Asian languages: Structure convergence and diglossia*. New Delhi: Motilal Banarsidass. 81–92.
1991 Phonological areal features of some Indo-Aryan languages. *Language Sciences*, 13.2. 107–24.

PANDEY, P.K.
1989 Word accentuation in Hindi. *Lingua*, 77. 37–73.

PIERREHUMBERT, J. and R. NAIR
1996 Implications of Hindi prosodic structure. In J. Durand & B. Laks (eds.), *Current trends in phonology: Models and methods*. CNRS, Paris-X and University of Salford: University of Salford Press.

VAN BERGEM, D.R.
1993 Acoustic vowel reduction as a function of sentence accent, word stress, and word class. *Speech Communication*, 12. 1–23.

11
Vowel harmony in Bangla: An optimality account

TANMAY GHOSH
Central Institute of English and Foreign Languages

Though the process of vowel harmony is utilised extensively in Bangla, it has not been adequately focussed in the literature. No doubt, the existing literature on Bangla vowel harmony (Chatterjee 1926: 395–421; Dan 1992: 57–63) offers some insightful observations. Firstly, these studies analyse Bangla vowel harmony as vowel height assimilation or vertical vowel harmony and secondly, they do not present a comprehensive analysis of the phenomenon as it obtains in the language requiring distinct rule systems for different portions of the Bangla lexicon.

An attempt is made in this paper to investigate the phenomenon of Bangla vowel harmony in terms of constraint hierarchy and interaction in the framework of Optimality Theory (henceforth OT) as developed by Prince and Smolensky (1993), and McCarthy and Prince (1993). This analysis also heavily depends on the implications of OT for the treatment of vowel harmony systems as examined by Pulleyblank (unpublished ms) and Archangeli and Pulleyblank (in press; cited in Pulleyblank, unpublished ms). It is argued that the general pattern of vowel harmony in Bangla can be explained in terms of the interaction of three types of phonological constraints, namely, *faithfulness* constraints, *alignment* constraints, and the constraints governed by *grounded* conditions. The analysis is restricted to the patterns of vowel harmony in Bangla monosyllabic verbs of CVC structure. However, it is extended to a few non-verbal categories in the language.

Section 1 presents a brief sketch of OT and how it helps to account for vowel harmony systems. Section 2 presents the notion of *grounded* conditions (based on the discussion of Archangeli and Pulleyblank (in press; cited in Pulleyblank, unpublished ms). Section 3 establishes the high vowels /i/and /u/ as the least marked vowels in Bangla. Section 4 focuses on the underlying feature specification of Bangla vowels. Section 5 deals with the patterns of vowel harmony in Bangla verbs. Section 6 extends the analysis of vowel harmony in Bangla to non-verbal categories.

1. OPTIMALITY THEORY AND VOWEL HARMONY

OT is a non-derivational approach in which constraints are defined as output conditions which are part of the vocabulary of Universal Grammar (henceforth UG). The function of the grammar of a language is not to select or design constraints, but to impose a rank order on constraints. In OT, the morphological conditioning of phonological phenomena can be accounted for in terms of the mutual ranking of morphological and prosodic constraints. Instead of taking an output and modifying it deterministically in a step-by-step derivation, OT allows the Universal function Gen. to generate an infinite set of output for each input and the function Eval. to evaluate all the representations simultaneously in parallel and thus choose the optimal output candidate that best satisfies (or least violates) a set of conflicting wellformedness conditions among the infinite number of competing candidates generated by Gen.

The basic hypothesis behind the optimality theoretic account of vowel harmony systems is that formal patterns of harmony are derived by the alignment constraints of OT (Prince and Smolensky 1993; McCarthy and Prince 1993; Kirchner 1993) while substantive properties of harmony are derived by Grounding Theory (Archangeli and Pulleyblank, in press; cited in Pulleyblank, unpublished ms).

The incorporation of *grounded* conditions into OT helps to derive many surface harmonic patterns. The effects of *grounded* conditions on patterns of distribution and alternations are numerous. Since UG determines the class of constraints that govern candidate evaluation, the absolute exclusion of *ungrounded* conditions from grammars follows from their inadmissibility as UG constraints.

The function Gen. provides candidate outputs that include any degree of structure, both in terms of prosody and in terms of autosegmental features and associations. The important aspect about the relation between inputs and outputs is that they are bound by close proximity. This is subsumed under the notions of *containment* and *faithfulness* family of constraints. The latter family includes RECF, RECP and PARSE (Prince and Smolensky 1993; McCarthy and Prince 1993). However, the above constraints alone would yield a degree of indeterminacy in deriving optimal outputs. This problem is resolved by positing constraints on feature alignment into the grammar of harmony (Kirchner 1993).

2. GROUNDED CONDITIONS

Archangeli and Pulleyblank (in press; cited in Pulleyblank, unpublished ms: 8) argue that feature co-occurrence conditions of a restricted type play a central role in accounting for phonological patterns. Their claim is that implicational relations between features must be phonetically motivated, *grounded.* Such *grounded* conditions govern properties of segmental inventories, harmonic neutrality (opacity and transparency), rules of redundancy, conditions on the targets and triggers of phonological rules, and so on.

For the phonetically *grounded* conditions of [ATR], they argue that since the tongue is a single volume, raising of the dorsum [+high] will tend to co-occur with advancement of the tongue root ([+ATR]), not retraction ([–ATR]). In the same way but in the opposite direction lowering of the tongue body ([+low]) will tend to co-occur with retraction, not advancement, of the tongue root. And they formally express the phonetically *grounded* conditions of [ATR] in the following way:

(1) HI/ATR CONDITION: If [+high] then [+ATR], not [–ATR].

LO/ATR CONDITION: If [+low] then [–ATR], not [+ATR]

3. THE LEAST MARKED VOWELS IN BANGLA

In the seven-vowel system of Bangla, the high vowels /i/ and /u/ are the least marked vowels. The argument for positing /i/ and /u/ as the least marked of vowels comes from the following data where /i/ and /u/ get deleted in (2a–b) and (2c), respectively. Notice that in (2b) also the vowel /i/ is deleted obligatorily in the *Chalit* variety.

(2) a. SADHU	CHALIT	
i. *SoriSa*[1]	*SorSe*	'mustard seeds'
ii. *morica*	*morce*	'rust'

Notice that in (2b) also the vowel /i/ is deleted obligatorily in the *Chalit* variety.

b. Verb root: /bOl/ 'say'

	(habitual past)	
	SADHU	CHALIT
i. FIRST PERSON	*bolitam*	*boltam*
ii. SECOND PERSON (ORD.)	*bolite*	*bolte*

In (2c) the /u/ is subject to deletion in the *Chalit* variety.

c.

i.	*sobuj*	'green'	+e (DIM.)	> *sobje* * *sobuje*	'greenish"
ii.	*bamun*	'priest'	+i (FEM.)	> *bamni* * *bamuni*	'wife of a priest'

No other vowel is deleted in Bangla in the same environment, that is, a medial open syllable, for example,

(3)	i.	*hiSeb*	'accounts'	+i (ADJ)	> *hiSebi* * *hiSbi*	'economical'
	ii.	*golap*	'rose'	+i (ADJ)	> *golapi* * *golpi*	'rosy'
	iii.	*binOy*	'modesty'	+i (ADJ)	> *binOyi* * *binyi*	'modest'

4. UNDERLYING FEATURE SPECIFICATION OF VOWELS IN BANGLA

If [high] is the least marked among the Bangla vowels, we can posit the underlying feature inventory of vowels in a tabular form as in (4). (Parentheses indicate default specifications.)

(4)	i	e	E	u	o	O	a
High	(+)	–	–	(+)	–	–	–
Coronal	+	+	+				
Dorsal				+	+	+	(+)
Radical/round							(+)/–
ATR	(+)		–	(+)		–	(–)

In (4), [ATR] stands for Advanced Tongue Root. Regarding the choice between radical/round in the underlying feature inventory of Bangla, I leave the issue indeterminate in this paper. I only assume the feature [radical] to be unary and [round] to be binary and assume without any supporting argumentation that non-alternating /a/ is specified as [radical] underlyingly.

There are manifold implications behind the representations in (4).

Firstly, /i/ and /u/ are less marked in comparison to the other vowels, the descending order of specification being /i/, /u/ < /e/, /o/, /a/ < /E/, /O/.

Secondly, Bangla has a marking condition *[+high, –ATR] for its vowels, i.e. the high vowels /i/ and /u/ automatically get their [+ATR] value by default because the raising of the dorsum ([+high]) will tend to co-occur with advancement of the tongue root ([ATR]_), not retraction ([–ATR]).

Thirdly, [coronal] and [dorsal] are unary features, while [high] and [ATR] are binary features.

Fortunately, /a/ is underlyingly unmarked for [dorsal] and [ATR] and the non-alternating occurrences are specified as [radical]. Lastly, we can reduce the overall pattern of the seven-vowel system into two heights.

Again, taking into account the notion of *grounded* conditions as outlined in Section 2, the unmarked value for non-low vowel in Bangla is [+ATR], while /E/ and /O/ are marked as [–ATR]. As we will see in Section 5 the feature [ATR] is responsible for vowel alternations in Bangla.

5. VOWEL HARMONY IN BANGLA VERBS

To examine the pattern of vowel harmony in Bangla verbs, we will have to look at their morphological make-up. In Bangla, monosyllabic verb roots, depending on their different morphological configurations, show systematic alternations, for example, */ken/* ~ */kin/* 'buy', */dEKh/* ~ /dekh/ 'see', */Son/* ~ */Sun/* 'listen', */bol/* ~ */bol/* 'say', */Dak/* ~ */Dek/* 'call'. Bangla has two standard dialects: *Sadhu* and *Chalit*. *Sadhu* has now the status of hyperliterary form and *Chalit* is now the dominant one. Let us look at both the verbal paradigms of the verbal root */bOl/* in *Sadhu* (abbreviated as 'S') and *Chalit* (C) dialects. The reason for doing so will become clear after we look at the paradigms which are presented side by side.

(5) Root /bOl/ 'say'

FINITE VERBAL PARADIGM

a.

	SIMPLE PRESENT		PRESENT PROGRESSIVE		PRESENT PERFECT	
	S	C	S	C	S	C
i. 1p[2]	*boli*	*boli*	*bolitechi*	*bolchi*	*boliachi*	*bolechi*
ii. 2p(ORD.)	*bOlo*	*bOlo*	*bolitecho*	*bolcho*	*boliacho*	*bolecho*
iii. 2p(FAM.)	*boliS*	*boliS*	*bolitechiS*	*bolchiS*	*boliachiS*	*bolechiS*
iv. 3p(NON-HON.)	*bOle*	*bOle*	*boliteche*	*bolche*	*boliache*	*boleche*
v. 2p & 3p(HON.)[3]	*bOlen*	*bOlen*	*bolitechen*	*bolchen*	*boliachen*	*bolechen*

b.

	SIMPLE PAST		PAST PROGRESSIVE		PAST PERFECT		HABITUAL PAST	
	S	C	S	C	S	C	S	C
i.	*bolilam*	*bollam*	*bolitechilam*	*bolchilam*	*boliachilam*	*bolechilam*	*bolitam*	*boltam*
ii.	*bolile*	*bolle*	*bolitechile*	*bolchile*	*boliachile*	*bolechile*	*bolite*	*bolte*
iii.	*bolili*	*bolli*	*bolitechili*	*bolchili*	*boliachili*	*bolechili*	*bolitiS*	*boltiS*
iv.	*bolilo*	*bollo*	*bolitechilo*	*bolchili*	*boliachilo*	*bolechilo*	*bolito*	*bolto*
v.	*bolilen*	*bollen*	*boltechilen*	*bolchilen*	*boliachilen*	*bolechilen*	*boliten*	*bolten*

	c. FUTURE INDEFINITE		d. PRESENT IMPERATIVE		e. FUTURE IMPERATIVE	
	S	C	S	C	S	C
i.	*bolibo*	*bolbo*	–	–	–	–
ii.	*bolibe*	*bolbe*	*bOlo*	*bOlo*	*bolio*	*bolo*
iii.	*bolibi*	*bolbi*	*bOl*	*bOl*	*boliS*	*boliS*
iv.	*bolibe*	*bolbe*	*boluk*	*boluk*	–	–
v.	*boliben*	*bolben*	*bolun*	*bolun*	*boliben*	*bolben*

NON-FINITE VERBAL PARADIGM

f. PERFECT CONJUNCTIVE

S	C
bolia	*bole*

g. CONDITIONAL CONJUNCTIVE

S	C
bolile	*bolle*

h. INFINITIVE

S	C
bolite	*bolte*

i. DEVERBAL NOMINAL

S	C
bOla	*bOla*

From these verbal paradigms, we find that the present tense is unmarked in Bangla while the other two tenses – past and future – are marked. From a scrutiny of the paradigms we can isolate the following inflectional markers in the *Sadhu* variety.

(6) TENSE MARKERS

i. /.Ø/ Present

ii. /i/ Past Tense

iii. /it/ Habitual Past

iv. /ib/ Future

(7) ASPECT MARKERS

i. /iach/ Perfective

ii. /itech/ Progressive

(8) PERSON MARKERS (alter according to the tenses)

	First	*Second*	*Third*
i. PRESENT TENSE	/i/	/o/ (ORD.) /iS/ (FAM.) /en/ (HON.)	/e/ (NON-HON) /en/ (HON.)
ii. PAST TENSE	/am/	/e/ (ORD.) /i/ (FAM.) /en/ (HON.) /iS/ (FAM.HAB.PAST)	/o/ (NON-HON.) /en/ (HON.)
iii. FUTURE TENSE	/o/	/e/ (ORD.) /i/ (FAM.) /en/ (HON.)	/e/ (NON-HON.) /en/ (HON.)

(9) MOOD MARKERS

	Second person	*Third person*
i. PRESENT IMP.	/O/ (ORD.) /Ø/ (FAM.) /un/ (HON.)	/uk/ (NON-HON.) /un/ (HON.) /un/ (HON.)
ii. FUTURE IMP.	/O/ (ORD.) /is/ (FAM.) /en/ (HON.)	/uk/ (NON-HON.) /en/ (HON.)

(10) OTHER INFLECTIONAL MARKERS

i. /ia/ Perfect conjunctive

ii. /ile/ Conditional conjunctive

iii. /ite/ Infinitive

(11) DERIVATIONAL SUFFIX

/a/ Nominal suffix

From the foregoing analysis we notice that the structural configuration of Bangla verbal morphology is the following:

ROOT + ASPECT (PERFECTIVE/PROGRESSIVE) + TENSE + PERSON

A careful scrutiny of the verbal paradigms in both the dialects reveals that the inflectional suffixes are underlyingly derived from the *Sadhu* dialect. And this also accounts for the vowel alternation in the verbal paradigm[4] in a straightforward manner. In (5), we find that whenever the alternation O ~ o occurs, the following vowel is a [high] vowel, that is, the following suffixal [high] vowel induces the alternation of the preceding vowel and the same alternation is found in the *Chalit* dialect without the apparent presence of the high (for example, Ip Simple past), or with the presence of the high vowel (Ip simple present).

We also notice that the augments of *Sadhu* dialect in progressive (/-ite-/), simple past (/-i-/), habitual past (/-i-/), future indefinite (/-i/), future imperative second person (ord.) (/-i/), conditional conjunctive /-i/ and indefinite (/-i/) get deleted in *Chalit* dialect. The *Sadhu* augment /-ia-/ in perfective and perfect conjunctive is substituted by the contracted /-e/ in *Chalit* Bangla. In a rule-based derivational account one could assume that in these cases /i/ affects vowel alternation and then gets deleted or substituted. However, since ours is a non-derivational approach, I argue that these suffixal forms in the *Chalit* dialect have been restructured with the deletion of medial /i/ in open syllables but these forms retain the floating feature [+ATR] of the high vowel /i/ in the *Sadhu* variety while losing all the other underlying features. And I assume that tense, aspect, perfect conjunctive, conditional conjunctive, and infinitive suffixes differ in the *Chalit* variety. All the other inflectional markers remain the same in both *Sadhu* and *Chalit* dialects.

(12) TENSE MARKERS

	Sadhu	*Chalit*
i. PRESENT	–Ø]	–Ø]
ii. PAST	–il] | cor	$^{\pm ATR}$l]

iii.	HABITUAL PAST	–it] | cor	±ATRt]
iv.	FUTURE	–ib] | cor	±ATRb]

(13) ASPECT MARKERS

		Sadhu	*Chalit*
i.	PERFECTIVE	–iach] | cor	+ATR -high -ech]
ii.	PROGRESSIVE	–itech] | cor	±ATRch]

(14) OTHER INFLECTIONAL MARKERS

		Sadhu	*Chalit*
i.	PERFECT CONJUNCTIVE	–ia] | cor	+ATR -high -e]
ii.	CONDITIONAL CONJUNCTIVE	–ile] | cor	±ATRle]
iii.	INFINITIVE	–ite] | cor	±ATRte]

The other monosyllabic verbs with CVC pattern, containing the root vowel /e/, /E/ and /O/ show similar systematic alternations, for example, /ken/ ~ /kin/, /dEkh/ ~ /dekh/, /Son/ ~ /Sun/. In the case of all these alternations, the suffix immediately following the root contains the [+ATR] feature from the suffixal high vowel (derived underlyingly from the *Sadhu* dialect). Vowel harmony, exemplifying the pattern of morphophonemic alternation, can now be considered a conditioned phonological process, provided that the stem-forming affixes are assumed to have an underlying [+ATR] feature as a required condition for [ATR] harmony.

My proposal for the constraints in the grammar of Bangla that account for the vowel harmony processes in the language is as follows. Following Archangeli and Pulleyblank's (in press; cited in Pulleyblank, unpublished ms) arguments for *grounded* conditions, as the tongue is a single volume, raising the dorsum [+high] will tend to co-occur with advancement of the tongue root [+ATR], not retraction [–ATR].

(15) HI/ATR: If [+high] then [+ATR], not [–ATR].

(16) Parse is 'a family of constraints which require that a given element be dominated by an appropriate node in the prosodic tree, parsed' (McCarthy and Prince 1993: 14).

(17) PARSE +ATR: Parse a [+ATR] specification present in the input.

(18) PARSE –ATR: Parse a [cor] or [dor] present in the input.

The *faithfulness* conditions ensure that outputs involve only minimal deviations from inputs.

(19) REC F: If $[...\propto...]_{output}$ then $[...\propto...]_{input}$

An F-element (feature or node) ∝ that is present in an output form is also present in the input.

(20) REC P: If $[...(\propto, \beta)...]_{output}$ then $[...(\propto, \beta)...]_{input}$

For any path between an F-element ∝ and some anchor β, if ∝ is associated to β in the output then ∝ is associated to β in the input.

As pointed out earlier, constraints on feature alignment are posited into the grammar of harmony to get over the problem of indeterminacy yielded by the above constraint alone.

(21) ALIGN R +ATR
The feature [+ATR] aligns with the right edge of the nearest morpheme boundary.

(22) ALIGN R COR/DOR
The feature [cor] or [dor] aligns with the right edge of the nearest morpheme boundary.

(23) ALIGN L [+ATR]
The feature [+ATR] aligns with the left edge of the word domain.

(24) ALIGN L COR/DOR
The feature [cor] or [dor] aligns with the left edge of the word domain.

According to the *grounded* conditions as in (1), HI/ATR requires that high vowels be advanced. In other words, HI/ATR must be ranked above REC F because a candidate output with high vowels that are advanced will be more highly valued than a candidate whose high vowels are not advanced, even if such advancement is not faithful to the underlying input. Again, HI/ATR must be ranked higher than Parse + ATR, otherwise the later constraints will not get [+ATR] to link to a prosodic anchor. In the constraint hierarchy, constraints under Parse are not ranked with respect to each other in the evaluation of a candidate. Again, since only stem vowels undergo alternations and suffixal vowels are fully specified and, non-alternative, Align L must be ranked higher than Align R.

In the OT framework, I now propose the following constraint hierarchy in Bangla and illustrate how they make the correct predictions regarding the vowel harmony processes in the language.

(25) THE HIERARCHY OF CONSTRAINT RANKING

HI/ATR >> Parse + ATR, Parse cor/dor, Parse – ATR >> Align L + ATR, Align L cor/dor >> Align R+ ATR, Align R cor/dor >> REC F >> REC P.

The tableaux in (26) and (27) show how (25) enables us to make the correct predictions about the stem vowel alternations as in bOl + i > boli 'say-Simple Pres-IP', dEkh + i > dekhi 'see-Simple Pres-IP'. In each tableau, an asterisk mark (*) indicates violation and an exclamation mark (!) following an asterisk mark denotes a 'fatal' violation, which crucially causes a form to be rejected as monoptimal. The linear order of the constraints from left to right shows the ranking of the constraints. A dotted line between two constraints indicates that those two are not ranked with respect to each other. The optimal output candidate is marked by an arrow mark (→).

Among the competing candidates in (26) and (27), we find that (26i) and (27i) surface as non-optimal since the most dominant constraint, HI/ATR, is fatally violated in these forms. (26ii) and (27ii) incur the fatal violation of the higher constraint Parse + ATR, and therefore, they are sub-optimal. (26iii) and (27iii) fatally violate Align L constraints and thus, these are not optimal. (26iv) and (27iv) incur minimal violations, and therefore, these surface as optimal.

(26) INPUT REPRESENTATION : [[b Ol] i]
–high dor cor

OPTIMAL OUTPUT REPRESENTATION : +ATR
[[b O l] i]
–high dor cor

	HI/ATR	Parse +ATR	Parse cor/dor	Parse –ATR	AlignL +ATR	AlignL cor/dor	AlignR +ATR	AlignR cor/dor	RecF	RecP
i. *[[b Ol] i] -high dor cor	*!					*				
ii. +ATR *[[b Ol] i] -high dor cor		*!			*	*			*	
iii. +ATR *[[b Ol] i] -high dor cor					*!	*!			*	*
iv. +ATR *[[b Ol] i] -high dor cor						*			*	**

(27) INPUT REPRESENTATION : [[d Ekh] i]
–high dor cor

OPTIMAL OUTPUT REPRESENTATION : +ATR
[[d ekh] i]
–high dor cor

	HI/ATR	Parse +ATR	Parse cor/dor	Parse –ATR	AlignL +ATR	AlignL cor/dor	AlignR +ATR	AlignR cor/dor	RecF	RecP
i. *[[d Ekh] i] -high dor cor	*!					*				
ii. +ATR *[[d Ekh] i] -high dor cor		*!			*	*			*	
iii. +ATR *[[d Ekh] i] -high dor cor					*!	*!			*	*
iv. +ATR → *[[d Ekh] i] -high dor cor						*			*	**

As for the underlying specification in verbs, notice that underlying verbs do not have a high vowel. So we posit a five-vowel system for Bangla verbs. And, this five-vowel system has a separate system of marking underlying specifications (with only one level of height as opposed to the seven-vowel system, proposed in (4), with two levels of height) as in (28).

(28)	e	E	o	O	a
High			–	–	–
Cor	+	+			
Dorsal			+	+	
Radical/Round					(+)/-
ATR		–		–	

According to (28) in the vowel system in Bangla verbs, there are no [+high] vowels. In the e ~ i and o ~ u alternations, [ATR] spreads leftwards from the suffixal [high] vowels (because we have a seven-vowel system in the case of suffixes) or the remaining [+ATR] of the deleted high vowel to the root vowels /e/ and /o/ and we automatically get /i/ and /u/ (assuming that the default value of features get specified later in the phonetic implementation module).

However, the verbal paradigm of the root containing the vowel /a/, for example, in /Dak/ 'call' follows a different pattern. Here /a/ is changed to /e/ only in the perfective, perfect conjunctive and future imperative (2p [ord.]) in the *Chalit* dialect. The root vowel remains unaltered throughout the paradigm in the *Sadhu* dialect as in (29):

(29) ROOT: /Dak/ 'call'

a.	SIMPLE PRESENT		PRESENT PROGRESSIVE		PRESENT PERFECT	
	S	C	S	C	S	C
i.	*Daki*	*Daki*	*Dakitechi*	*Dakchi*	*Dakiachi*	*Dekechi*
ii.	*Dako*	*Dako*	*Dakitecho*	*Dakcho*	*Dakiacho*	*Dekecho*
iii.	*DakiS*	*Dako*	*DakitechiS*	*DakchiS*	*DakiachiS*	*Dekechi*
iv.	*Dake*	*Dake*	*Dakteche*	*Dakche*	*Dakiachen*	*Dekechen*
v.	*Daken*	*Daken*	*Dakitechen*	*Dakchen*		

b.

	SIMPLE PAST S	SIMPLE PAST C	PAST PROGRESSIVE S	PAST PROGRESSIVE C
i.	*Dakilam*	*Daklam*	*Dakitechilam*	*Dakchilam*
ii.	*Dakile*	*Dakle*	*Dakitechile*	*Dakchile*
iii.	*Dakili*	*Dakli*	*Dakitechili*	*Dakchili*
iv.	*Dakilo*	*Daklo*	*Dakitechilo*	*Dakchilo*
v.	*Dakilen*	*Daklen*	*Dakitechilen*	*Dakchilen*

PAST PERFECT S	PAST PERFECT C	HABITUAL PAST S	HABITUAL PAST C
Dakitechilam	*Dekechilam*	*Dakitam*	*Daktam*
Dakitechile	*Dekechile*	*Dakite*	*Dakte*
Dakitechili	*Dekechili*	*DakitiS*	*DaktiS*
Dakitachilo	*Dekechilo*	*Dakito*	*Dakto*
Dakiachilen	*Dekechilen*	*Dakiten*	*Dakten*

c. FUTURE INDEFINITE — d. PRESENT IMPERATIVE — e. FUTURE IMPERATIVE

	c. S	c. C	d. S	d. C	e. S	e. C
i.	*Dakibo*	*Dakboi*	–	–	–	–
ii.	*Dakibe*	*Dakbe*	*Dako*	*Dako*	*Dakio*	*Deko*
iii.	*Dakibi*	*Dakbi*	*Dak*	*Dak*	*DakiS*	*Dakis*
iv.	*Dakibe*	*Dakbe*	*Dakuk*	*Dakuk*	–	–
v.	*Dakiben*	*Dakben*	*Dakun*	*Dakun*	*Dakiben*	*Dakben*

f. PERFECT CONJUNCTIVE — g. CONDITIONAL CONJUNCTIVE

f. S	f. C	g. S	g. C
Dakia	*Dake*	*Dakile*	*Dakle*

h. INFINITIVE — i. DEVERBAL NOMINAL

h. S	h. C	i. S	i. C
Dakite	*Dakte*	*Daka*	*Daka*

In this paradigm, in the perfective and perfect conjunctive, the *Sadhu* augment /–ia/ is first substituted by /-e/ in the *Chalit* dialect and then this /–e/ induces the alternation a ~ e in these cases. Since the initial vowel of the suffix in these cases is /i/ in the *Sadhu* dialect, the forms in these cases in the *Sadhu* dialect remain unaltered. And I assume that the suffixal /-e/ is marked underlyingly as [+ATR, cor, –high] which aligns leftwards by Align L+ATR to trigger the alternation a ~ e in the root vowel and that the root /Dak/ is underlyingly specified as [–high] and [–round].

The a ~ e alternation in the root vowel in future imperative (2p [ord.]) can be accounted for along the same lines. In this instance, the *Sadhu* suffix /-io/ is first restructured as [-o] having the underlying specification [+ATR, –high, dor] and only [+ATR, –high] spread leftward and not [dor] because the root vowel /a/ is specified as [–round]. The explanation must be in terms of the fact that Bangla does not have any vowel with the configuration *[+ATR, –high, dor, –round]. Perhaps the vowel in [Dak] is underlyingly marked as [–round, –high]. Again, /i/ of the future imperative (*Sadhu*) suffix /–io/ cannot induce the a ~ e alternation in the root vowel in [Dak] since /i/ by the default gets the specification [+ATR, high] and [+ATR] can link only along with [–high] (since the root vowel in [Dak] is specified as [–high]). However, the perfective and perfect conjunctive suffix /–e/ in *Chalit* is specified as [+ATR, cor, –high] and hence it can spread its features to alter the root vowel. For example,

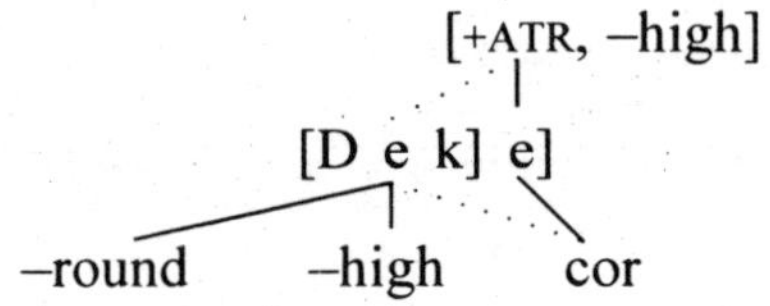

One thing to be noticed in the instances of perfective conjunctive and conditional conjunctive is that the suffixal vowel /-e/ in the former triggers harmony whereas in the latter it does not. This can be accounted for by the fact that the latter is unspecified for [+ATR] (it gets it by default in the phonetic implementation module), but the former has the input representation [+ATR, –high].

Let us look at the tableau in (30) to see how different constraints interact to yield the optimal output candidate (30iii).

In the tableau in (30), (i) surfaces as non-optimal by incurring the fatal violation of AlignL constraints. (ii) fatally violates AlignL cor constraint and hence it is suboptimal. (iii) is the optimal candidate since it incurs only two violations of the lowest constraint REC P.

(30) INPUT REPRESENTATION : [+ATR, –high] [[Dak] e] –round –high cor

OPTIMAL OUTPUT REPRESENTATION : [+ATR, –high] [[D ek] e] –round –high cor

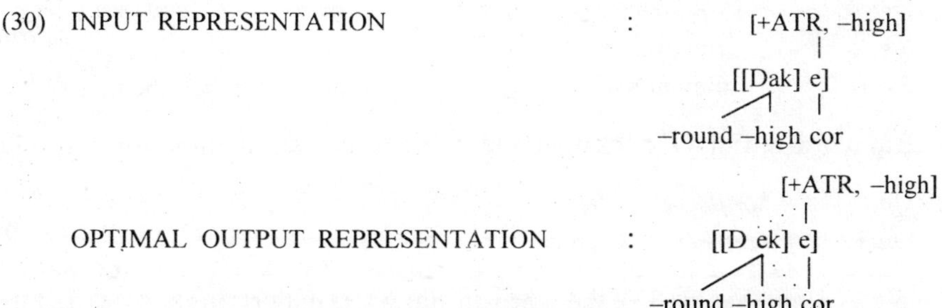

	HI/ATR	Parse +ATR	Parse cor/dor	Parse –ATR	AlignL +ATR	AlignL cor/dor	AlignR +ATR	AlignR cor/dor	RECF	RECP
i. [+ATR, –H] *[[Dak] e] -R –H cor					*!	*!				
ii. [+ATR, –H] *[[Dak] e] -R –H cor						*!				*
iii. [+ATR, –H] →*[[Dek] e] -R –H cor										**

NOTE: R and H here stand for round and high, respectively.

6. VOWEL HARMONY IN NON-VERBAL CATEGORIES IN BANGLA

Besides verbs, regressive vowel harmony also operates in Bangla at least in three other grammatical categories – nouns, pronouns, and adjectives (denominal) – where, like that of the verbal paradigm in (5), the same [ATR] harmony is at work. In the case of nouns, the following suffixal vowel /i/ which has the specification [+ATR], induces the alternations, E ~ e, 0 ~ o and o ~ u in the root vowel by spreading [+ATR] leftwards, as shown in (31).

(31) *pEMca* 'male owl' *PeMci* 'female owl'

In the case of pronouns too, the process of vowel harmony applies, (the o ~ u and e ~ i alternation is a consequence of a portion of the Bangla lexicon having a restricted inventory of vowels [see (28)], for example,

(32)	*tomra*	'you-ORD.-PL'	*tumi*	'you-ORD.-SG.'
	tora	'you-FAM.-PL'	*tui*	'you-FAM.-SG.'
	eMra	'they-HON.-PL'	*ini*	'(s)he-HON.-SG.'

But word-initial /O/ does not undergo harmonic alternation, for example,

(33)	*Onil*	**onil*	'air'
	Onik	**onik*	'army'

We assume that in (33), the word-initial /O/ is underlyingly specified for [–ATR], and consequently, it is not harmonised by the following [+ATR] high vowel /i/.

Similarly, in the following words, the word-initial /O/ acts as a prefix having a negative meaning which comes with [–ATR] specification, and hence the harmonising process (by the following high vowel of the root) is blocked.

(34)	*OSim*	[O[Sim]]	**oSim*	'endless'
	Otul	[O[tul]]	**otul*	'incomparable'
	Odhir	[O[dhir]]	**odhir*	'restless'

Turning to the process of vowel harmony in the derived words in (35), we find that these cases can be explained by the same constraint hierarchy proposed for verbs provided we assume that root vowels are unspecified for [ATR] and suffixal vowels are specified for the features. Let us look at the following examples.

(35)	a.	*jOl*	'water'	*jolo*	'watery'
		jOr	'fever'	*joro*	'feverish'
		pOT	'canvas for painting'	*poTo*	'painter of a pot'
		mOTh	'shrine'	*moTho*	'pertaining to a shrine'
		ghOr	'home'	*ghoro*	'domestic'
	b.	*bon*	'forest'	*buno*	'wild'
		goMph	'moustache'	*guMpho*	'moustached'
		Tol	'traditional school of scholastic Sanskrit learning'	*Tulo*	'pertaining to a *tol*'

(36)	a.	*jOT*	'knot'	*joTe*	'knotty'
		ghOr	'house'	*ghoro*	'belonging to a house'
	b.	*moT*	'goods'	*muTe*	'porter'
		koMdol	'quarrel'	*KuMdule*	'quarrelsome'

In the examples in (35a), the denominal adjectival suffix /o/ is lexically specified for [+ATR], but the root vowel /O/ is devoid of any lexical [ATR] specification. As a result, the feature [+ATR] from suffixal /o/ spreads leftwards, and the harmonic alternation O ~ o occurs. In (35b), since the root vowel /o/ has not any lexical [ATR] specification, it is linked to [+ATR] which is spread leftwards by the suffixal vowel /o/ and then the root vowel gets [+high] by default because according to *grounded* conditions when [+ATR] is linked, it gets [+high] by default (see Section 2 for details). Likewise, in (36), the suffixal vowel /e/ is underlyingly specified for [+ATR] so it gets [+ high] by default [see (20) for details]. In (36a) and (36b) the root vowels /O/ and /o/ are not underlyingly marked for [ATR]. So, /O/ and /o/ are altered to /o/ and /u/ respectively, triggered by the suffixal underlying [+ATR] vowel /e/.

Again the data in (37) follow the same pattern as that of the verbal paradigm in (29) as the root vowel /a/ is altered to /e/ by the suffixation of the adjectival suffix /e/, presumably marked [+ATR] in the lexicon.

(37)	*jal*	'fishing net'	*jele*	'fisherman'
	gaMT	'knot'	*geMT*	'knotty'

Besides regressive vowel harmony, discussed till now, progressive vowel harmony is also found in a few cases in Bangla. In (38a) and (38b), /a/ alternates with /e/ or /o/ because of the preceding /i/ or /u/ respectively.

(38)			SADHU	CHALIT	
	a.	i.	*iccha*	*icche*	'wish'
		ii.	*jira*	*jire*	'cumin seed'
			SADHU	CHALIT	
	b.	i.	*puja*	*pujo*	'worship'
		ii.	*udam*	*udam*	'bare'

We assume that in cases (38a) and (38b), /a/ alternates with /e/ or /o/ due to the preceding /i/ or /u/, /a/ is not specified for [ATR] and [dorsal] underlyingly unlike the cases in (39) where the non-alternating /a/ is specified as [–ATR] and perhaps, also [dorsal] and [radical].

(39)	i.	*biSal*	**biSel*	'big'
	ii.	*udaS*	**udoS*	'indifferent'

Moreover, in cases like (38a) and (38b) /i/ and /u/ are underlyingly specified as [cor] and [dor] respectively and the two high vowels get their default specification [+ATR] by *grounded* conditions as in (1). These features [+ATR], [cor] for /i/ and [+ATR, dor] for /u/ then align with the right edge of the morpheme by Align R + ATR and Align R cor/dor respectively and we get the desired a ~ e and a ~ o.

CONCLUSION

From the above account, we find that the phenomenon of vowel harmony in Bangla can be interpreted in a better way in terms of the framework of OT than a rule-based derivational approach. The main characteristics of Bangla vowel harmony are derived from the interaction of three kinds of phonological constraints.:

- *faithfulness* constraints, which parse features into prosodically well-formed structures with as little change as possible;
- *alignment* constraints, which align edges of featural domains with the edges of phonological domains; and
- the constraints governed by *grounded* conditions which cause the exclusion of phonetically marked combinatorial possibilities from grammars.

We have shown that Bangla has two vowel systems with separate underlying specifications for the stem vowels of lexical categories and for suffixal vowels – a five-vowel system for the former, and a seven-vowel system for the latter. As we have noticed, Bangla vowel harmony is mainly a case of [ATR] harmony. In some cases, in addition to [ATR] harmony, the harmony process also includes/incorporates [coronal] harmony, (for example, /*iccha*/ ~ /*icche*/) or [dorsal] harmony (for example, /*puja*/ ~ /*pujo*/), rather than vowel height assimilation or vertical vowel harmony (Dan 1992).

NOTES

1. In this paper the phonetic symbols of Ray, Hai and Ray (1966) have been used in transcribing the Bangla data. Some of the key symbols used are described as follows:

t: voiceless unaspirated dental stop	d: voiced unaspirated dental stop
T: voiceless unaspirated retroflex stop	D: voiced unaspirated retroflex stop
R: retroflex stop	N: velar nasal
S: voiceless palato-alveolar sibilant	M: nasalises the vowel preceding it
j: voiced unaspirated palato-alveolar affricate	y: front high semi-vowel
w: back high semi-vowel	E: front low-mid vowel
O: back low-mid vowel	e: front high-mid vowel
o: back high-mid vowel	

2. Number is not distinguished in Bangla for verbal forms, that is, singular and plural have the same forms in the language.
3. Although second and third person (HON.) are distinguished by personal pronouns (/*apni*/ [SG.] and /apnara/ [PL.] for second person; /*tini*/ [SG.] and /*taMra*/ [PL.] for third person), there is only one set of verbal suffixes for both.

4. Our analysis of vowel harmony in Bangla verbs is restricted only to the regular monosyllabic verbs with CVC pattern. The irregular verbs like */bOS/* 'sit' (which has the irregular (bare) imperative form */boS/* in Standard *Chalit* Bangla instead of the expected */bOS/*), and completely irregular verbs like */aS/* (VC) 'come', */ja/* (VC) 'go' are not being considered in this work because the latter may be considered cases of suppletion.

REFERENCES

ARCHANGELI, D. and D. PULLEYBLANK
(in press) *Grounded phonology.* Cambridge, MA: MIT press.

CHATTERJEE, S.K.
1926 *The origin and development of the Bengali Language.* London: George Allen & Unwin, 1971 reissue, 3 vols.

DAN, M.
1992 Some issues in metrical phonology of Bangla: The indigenous research tradition. Unpublished Ph.D. dissertation. Pune: Deccan College.

KIRCHNER, R.
1993 Turkish vowel harmony in optimality theory. Paper presented at the Rutgers Optimality Workshop # 1. Rutgers University.

MCCARTHY, J. and A. PRINCE
1993 Prosodic morphology 1: Constraint interaction and satisfaction. Unpublished ms. New Brunswick, NJ: University of Massachusetts, Amherst, and Rutgers University.

PRINCE, A. and P. SMOLENSKY
1993 *Optimality theory: Constraint interaction in generative grammar.* Unpublished ms. NJ: Rutgers University; Boulder: University of Colorado.

PULLEYBLANK, D.
Vowel harmony and optimality theory. Unpublished ms. University of British Columbia.

RAY, P.S., M.A. HAI and L. RAY
1966 *Bengali language handbook.* Washington DC: Center for Applied Linguistics.

12
On a vowel template asymmetry in Bangla verbs

PROBAL DASGUPTA
University of Hyderabad

This paper is about denominals (non-causative disyllabic verb stems) in Bangla (or Bengali). We note that back vowel denominals exhibit the templates /CuCo/ (/*phuro*/ 'get used up', /*bulo*/ 'stroke') and /CoCa/ (/*gonga*/ 'groan', /*bola*/ 'stroke'), while front vowel denominals display only /CiCo/ (/*cibo*/ 'chew', /*Dingo*/ 'step across'), never /CeCa/. This asymmetry is unexpected. Causative stems exhibit /CoCa/ (/*bojha*/ 'explain', /*ghora*/ 'turn, rotate') as well as /CeCa/ (/*Sekha*/ 'teach', /*meSa*/ 'mix') and are thus symmetrical. We seek to illuminate the asymmetry observed.

In this paper,

- read CVCV as denoting (C)V(CC)V; and
- the transcription system has E O for low vowels, Y W for mid semivowels, T D R for retroflexes, S for a palato-alveolar, and M for nasalisation.

I thank Rajendra Singh both for the specific stimulus he provided for this intervention and for what he has done for decades to make the present type of morphology possible. I also remember gratefully the help of Mark Aronoff, for whose morphology course in 1977 I first worked out some of the phenomena reported here in a term paper that used for its phonological execution the already obsolete SPE framework, much to his quite proper annoyance. It is a pity it took me this long to try to come up with a better idea than 'there just IS this asymmetry in the language, Mark'. And I thank Raghavachari Amritavalli for encouragement and discussion while the paper was being written. I await, with some trepidation, the verdict of the community of inquirers on the present proposals. The usual disclaimers apply.

Our inquiry takes us to a corresponding asymmetry in the shapes of adjectives, to some peculiarities of the conjunctive inflection of the verb, to the unusual denominal stem template /CeCo/, and to a family-theoretic perspective on morphology enabling us to weave these considerations into an account. The perspective rests on and extends the projection morphology approach due to Ford *et al.* (1996).

1. THE SYMMETRY OF THE CAUSATIVES

Pairs of simplex (s) and causative (c) verbs in Bangla look like this in the zero inflection or 'bare' form (in the second person antiformal imperative):

(1) s. *Sekh* 'learn'
c. *Sekha* 'teach'

(2) s. *bojh* 'understand'
c. *bojha* 'explain'

(3) s. *dEkh* 'see'
c. *dEkha* 'show'

(4) s. *pOR* 'read, study'
c. *pORa* 'teach'

(5) s. *nac* 'dance'
c. *naca* 'manipulate'

The simplex base is in each case a monosyllable. The vocalism we exemplify exhausts what one finds. Of Bangla's seven vowels, high /i/ and /u/ do not occur in bare simplexes or bare causatives (3). We cleave to bare forms in this statement. Some inflected forms have raised vowels and do exhibit /i/ and /u/. In what does occur, front /e/ and /E/ match back /o/ and /O/, symmetrically, with an umpire of an /a/.

We shall not consider the full range. The rest of this paper takes as a point of departure the initial fact that (1) and (2) are symmetrically matched. This we call the symmetry of the causatives.

2. ASYMMETRY IN DENOMINAL VERBS

We shall, considering only bare forms for this purpose, classify Bangla verbs into four subclasses:

(6) s. simplex monosyllabics: *Sekh, bojh*
c. causative disyllabics ending in /a/: *Sekha, bojha*
d. denominal disyllabics ending in /a/ or /o/: *khoMRa* 'limp', *paTha* 'send'
e. expressives: polysyllabics ending in /a/ or /o/: *kOnkOna* 'ache (s.o. a tooth)', *ghEnghEna* 'whine'

This grouping ignores the obvious fact that many 'denominals' on this reckoning have no real nominal congener. We are using the term Denominal for expository convenience in the sense of 'non-causative disyllabic'.

Consider first denominals with a nonlow back vowel in the first syllable. These denominals exhibit two templates, the causative-like /CoCa/ and the distinctively denominal /CuCo/:

(7) a. *gonga* 'groan'
b. *poa* 'bask in'
c. *khoMRa* 'limp'
d. *gocha* 'arrange'
e. *bola* 'stroke'
f. *opRa* 'uproot'
g. *Sodhra* 'correct'

(8) a. *kuRo* 'pick up'
b. *phuro* 'get used up'
c. *Suko* 'dry'
d. *gucho* '(7d)'
e. *bulo* '(7e)'
f. *upRo* '(7f)'
g. *Sudhro* '(7g)'

What about their front vowel counterparts? We do observe, as expected, a /CiCo/ template:

(9) a. *niko* 'scrub'
b. *Dingo* 'step across'
c. *cibo* 'chew'
d. *jiro* 'rest'

But the expected replicated of the causative /CeCa/ template in the denominal verb subclass does not take place. No denominal exhibits the /CeCa/ template. This fact lies at the heart of the asymmetry that this paper addresses. How does one go about seeking an explanation for this phenomenon?

3. SEEKING TO EXPLAIN THE ASYMMETRY

Our strategy, which readers are welcome to treat as no more than a point of departure, is to link this phenomenon to specific segments of other phenomena, one by one. We then offer this set of links as an explanation for our phenomenon.

There is more to this, of course, than just one case and its satisfactory solution. We are working out one problem in a way that one hopes carries over to others. The following proposals are to be considered, and criticised, with this generality in mind.

What we shall do is organised as follows. In section 4, we look at the general significance of the conjunctive participle for Bangla verbs as a frequently solitary head of the verb family. Then we turn, in section 5, to our verbs in particular. We note that conjunctives provide them with a natural alternation key that underwrites the back vowel template alternations seen at (7)/(8d–g). Once we have done this, we state the asymmetry in terms of specific mechanisms. Despite the facilitating role of the conjunctive in the set-up, then, Bangla still does not let any member of the set exemplified at (9) flow into the causative-like front vowel template /CeCa/. Or to put it differently, some factor stops the facilitation, which we must assume is in general available. Sections 4 and 5, then, link our problem to the analysis of the conjunctive and the claim that it plays a distinguished role in the verb family.

In section 6 we identify, as the factor responsible for blocking the expected alternations, a set of verbs whose bare form displays the anomalous template /CeCo/. This set is doubly anomalous. We observe, first, the absence of any /CoCo/, /CECo/, /COCo/, /CaCo/ to match it. Second, its conjunctive template comes out as /CeCie/ – anomalously identical to the conjunctive template for /CECa/, an anomaly in that no /CeCo-CECa/ alternations exist.

We argue that this anomalous /CeCo/ harbours a significant denominal /o/ – its significance related to the apparent anomaly – contrasting with the likewise significant causative /a/ in /CeCa/. Section 6 proposes an account of exactly how the secondary significance of the _o/a_ contrast in the environment /CeC_/ holds up the otherwise expected traffic, via the conjunctive, between /CiCo/ and /CeCa/. We go on to note some evidence that there is, though not via the usual conjunctive shunting point, some alternation-traffic between /CiCo/ and /CeCo/ instead.

Section 7 holds up for inspection some supportive material from adjectival shapes in the language. They too exhibit a kindred asymmetry. We put forward a view, open of course to challenge, on how this material might count as supportive of the view we have developed. But we agree with potential critics that a link from our verbs to these adjectives per se would be too tenuous to count as initiating an explanation. We suggest, however, that a link too weak to start something may yet be strong enough to continue a chain already initiated elsewhere. Finally, in section 8, we return to matters theoretical.

4. THE SINGULARITY OF THE CONJUNCTIVE

We wish to pick up here an old thread. It was suggested in Dasgupta 1977 – revised as Dasgupta 1989: chapter 6 – that the affiliation fields opened up for investigation there and other paradigmatic formal objects should be developed to balance the excessively syntagmatic approach to the study of patterns in language. This paradigmatic emphasis was renewed in Dasgupta 1995 on a new empirical basis.

In the present paper, we explore the family as a general paradigmatic notion – corresponding to the construction in the syntagmatic realm – and the notion of the nodal member of a family as a key actor through which paradigmatic forces flow. We work with Singh and Ford's projection morphology formalisation of some of these forces as Word Formation Strategies (WFS). An example will serve to make all this concrete. Consider conjunctive participle forms such as */dhore/* 'caught-and', set in an actual sentence in (10) to give some idea of how the form is used:

(10) *beRalTa* *iMdurTake* *dhore khelo*
cat-CLA mouse-CLA-DAT caught-and ate
'The cat caught and ate the mouse.'

This form figures in several WFSs, such as (11)–(15) – where, departing from our abbreviatory conventions, C in each case stands for zero or one consonant. Note that the */dhore/* of (10) participates in (12).

(11) $[CoC]_{V}$, bare ↔ $[CuCe]_{V}$, CJV

(12) $[COC]_{V}$, bare ↔ $[CoCe]_{V}$, CJV

(13) $[CeC]_{V}$, bare ↔ $[CiCe]_{V}$, CJV

(14) $[CEC]_{V}$, bare ↔ $[CeCe]_{V}$, CJV

(15) $[CaC]_{V}$, bare ↔ $[CeCo]_{V}$, CJV

As (14) and (15) show, the conjunctive is not a point of maximal differentiation and thus makes a poor citation form. The bare form beats it on that score. Why, then, should one bring it into focus? The language singles it out by giving a central role to the compound verb construction exemplified in */dhore phello/* in (16), described in Dasgupta (1977/1989) as a combination of a pole or main verb with one of a dozen vector or semi-auxiliary verbs:

(16)

beRalTa	*iMdurTake*	*dhore*	*phello*
cat-CLA	mouse-CLA-DAT	catch-and	VECTOR

'The cat finally caught the mouse.'

Now, some verbs appear only in the polar position of a compound verb (though of course they used to be more versatile in earlier periods of the language). Consequently these verbs occur in the conjunctive inflected form alone:

(17)

raka	*e*	*nie*	*naliS*	*kore*	*kore*	*_hedie_*	*gEche*
Raka	this	about	complain	do-and	do-and	bore-and	VECTOR

'Raka has complained and complained about this and gotten bored.'

(18)

khOborTa	*Sune*	*dipen*	*_Siure_*	*uThlo*
news-CLA	hear-and	Dipen	shudder-and	VECTOR

'On hearing the news, Dipen shuddered.'

(19)

ghOrer	*bhitorTa*	*_bhepSe_*	*uTheche*
room-GEN	inside-CLA	become-stuffy-and	VECTOR

'The inside of the room has become stuffy.'

(20)

baghTa	*_teRe_*	*elo,*	*lokTa*	*bhOYe*	*_SiMTie_*	*gElo*
tiger-CLA	charge-&	VECTOR,	man-CLA	fear-LOC	freeze-&	VECTOR

'The tiger charged at him, the man froze with fear.'

For these and other reasons worth recounting in detail in some context where serious interest in Bangla itself shapes the agenda, many verbs appear in the conjunctive to the exclusion of all other inflected forms. No other inflectional form of Bangla verbs has this property. Vijayakrishnan (1991) notes that an entire paradigm in Tamil undergoing change reduces to the conjunctive participial form as 'the sole survivor in Madras Brahmin Tamil', for example, */ka_t_t-/* from */kal/* 'learn' and */ee_t_t-/* from */eel/* 'accept'. This indicates that there may be areal generalisations here that need to be explored.

We may propose the initial language-specific generalisation that, if a verb in this language has a one-member family, that member bears the conjunctive inflection. Now, given a syntagmatic construction that sometimes comprises one member and alone and sometimes that member plus some companion, it is standard usage to call that privileged member the construction's syntagmatic head. When a family has a potentially solo member, then, let us agree to call it that family's paradigmatic 'head' or, to avoid giving the term Head a confusing melange of syntagmatic and paradigmatic work, its nodal member.

A conjunctive verb in Bangla, then, counts as nodal in the verb's lexemic family – the family of the inflected forms of that verb.

What is it exactly that distinguishes the nodal from the nonnodal members of a lexemic family? In trying to identify a nodal member, one does not seek maximal distinctiveness, as a lexicographer choosing a suitable citation form would. In the case of Bangla verb lexemes, the bare form used in this paper for expository convenience so far is not in general suitable as a citation form, for it exhibits crucial irregularities (for verbs like /*aSa*/ 'to come', bare form /*ae*/ and /*boSa*/ 'to sit', bare form /*boS*/). The gerund-participle form, glossed in this paper as 'to Verb', works better as a citation form. It is often so used in grammars and dictionaries. The gerund-participle has the advantage of being a point of maximal differentiation. If two verbs contrast in their vocalism for some inflected forms (for example, /*dEkho*/ 'you see' versus /*rakho*/ 'you keep') but not for other (/*dekho*/ 'you please see' versus /*rekho*/ 'you please keep'), then they consistently contrast at the gerund-participle (/*dEkha*/ 'to see' versus /*rakha*/ 'to keep').

Note that the conjunctive lacks this advantage. In the case given, for instance, the conjunctives are /*dekha*/ 'see-and' and /*rekhe*/ 'keep-and', with the same vocalism. But, if future work bears our proposal out, every conjunctive does count as the nodal of its verb's lexemic family. We must then distinguish, for a Bangla verb lexeme:

a. the minimally affixed or 'bare' second person antiformal imperative, and
b. the maximally differentiating gerund-participle, useful as a citation form, from
c. the conjunctive participle, the nodal member.

Of these three points at which a lexemic family comes to a head, no single point can be usefully identified as 'unmarked'. See Ford *et al.* (1996: 40–2) for a critique of naive notions of markedness in morphology.

5. THE CONJUNCTIVE CONNECTION

It remains, now, to connect the conjunctive to our specific line of inquiry. Bangla verb lexemic families break up into a citation vowel subfamily (CVS) that keeps the citation form vocalism intact and a raised vowel subfamily (RVS) that raises the stem vowel in the manner exemplified in (11)–(15). RVS size depends on verb subclass in the sense of (6). A simplex verb has a moderately large RVS. A nonsimplex (causative or denominal or expressive) has a tiny RVS consisting basically of the conjunctive; what also belongs there with it theoretically, but is for many verbs a never-used form in practice, is the second person neutral future imperative; for example, */bujhie/* and */bujhio/* constitute the RVS in the lexemic family identified by the citation form */bojhano/* 'to explain'.

RVS size has some bearing on whether a verb lexeme with the vocalism CV1CV2 can get into, or stay in, an alternation with a verb with the vocalism CV3CV4. When the conjunctive is alone (or basically alone because of the rarity of its future imperative companion) in a verb's RVS, that is, when the verb has a polysyllabic stem, we can envisage the following state of affairs:

(21)	Verb Lexeme Family V1V2	The	Verb Lexeme Family V3V4
	1/2a, 1/2b, 1/2c, . . .	Transition	3/4a, 3/4b, 3/4c, . . .
	1/2 conjunctive	=	3/4 conjunctive

For instance, let there be a family identified by the citation form /bulono/ 'stroke' (see [8e]). Place it in (21) as Family V1V2. Then the conjunctive /bulie/ 'stroke-and' serves as a transition from V1V2 to V3V4, in this case the lexeme family with the citation form /bolano/ (see [7e]):

(22)	*/bulono/*'s family	Transition	*/bolano/*'s family
	buloe, bulon, buloS . . .	*bulie*	*bolae, bolan, bolaS . . .*

How exactly does the conjunctive key pull this off? Working with the projection morphology model due to Ford, Singh and Martohardjono, we propose that Word Formation Strategy (23) links the typical denominal's gerund-participle to its conjunctive:

(23) $[\text{CuCie}]_{\text{d, CJV}} \leftrightarrow [\text{CuCono}]_{\text{d, g-p}}$

There is of course a WFS for the causatives as well, as (24c) demonstrates.

(24) c. $[\text{CuCie}]_{\text{c, CJV}} \leftrightarrow [\text{CoCano}]_{\text{c, g-p}}$

This version does not represent a template that the denominal /bulie/ can succumb to. But we do have a version of (24) for denominals:

d. $[\text{CuCie}]_{\text{d, CJV}} \leftrightarrow [\text{CoCano}]_{\text{d, g-p}}$

(24d) and (23) enable us to propose the following account. Family type CuCono/d and type CoCano/d meet at the shared conjunctive CuCie/d, where one passes into the other. Hence the actual alternations at (7)/(8)d–g.

Such an account shifts the asymmetry from the alternations to the independent existence of the non-alternating /CoCano/ denominals like (7a-c). Our story ends up saying that it is asymmetric of the causative WFS (25c) to be matched by no denominal (25d) (to put it differently, there are no denominal /CeCano/ verb shapes) when causative (24c) is matched by a denominal WFS (24d):

(25) c. $[\text{CiCie}]_{c, \text{CJV}}$ ↔ $[\text{CeCano}]_{c, \text{g-p}}$

d. *$[\text{CiCie}]_{d, \text{CJV}}$ ↔ $[\text{CeCano}]_{d, \text{g-p}}$

We need to go slow at this point. The simplex family types /CaCa/ (like /*Daka*/ 'to call', /*naca*/ 'to dance') and /CECa/ (/*phEla*/ 'to drop', /*dEkha*/ 'to see') also share a conjunctive template /CeCe/ (/*Deke*, *nece*, *phele*, *dekhe*/). Does our story compel us to expect /CaCa-CECa/ alternations based on the conjunctive connection? If so, we have a problem, as there are no such alternations.

My response is to argue that the conjunctive does not emerge as a transitional form in this case. Far too many nonconjunctive forms of /CECa/ verbs have a raised vowel /e/: /*pheli*, *pheliS*, *phello*, *phelbo*, *phelten*/ 'I drop, you drop, s/he dropped, I'll drop, s/he-formal used to drop', etc. share the vowel /e/ with the conjunctive /*phele*/. Given that /*phEla*/ ↔ /*phele*/ is not the only road to the raised vowel, the conjunctive does not stand out so sharply within both the families – but only within the /CaCa/ family, where /CaCa/ ↔ /CeCe/ is indeed practically the only road to the raised vowel. The conjunctive therefore does not emerge as an alternation-facilitating transition. Hence the failure of the shared conjunctive template to encourage alternations in this case. We see here the concrete effect of Raised Vowel Subfamily size on our phenomenon.

What does this section leave us with? We now think we know what type of mechanism facilitates the emergence of something like the /bulono-bolano/ alternation. And we think we know that what prevents this mechanism from producing any /CiCono-CeCano/ alternations is the fact that no denominal /CeCano/ verbs – which would have enabled the mechanism to do the trick – exist. Why don't they?

6. THE SECONDARY SIGNIFICANCE FACTOR

Because – we shall now argue – the language has so arranged things that the verbs that do exist in the /CeCano/ template family endow the post-/CeC/ vowel /a/ with secondary significance as a causative marker. Such a state of affairs sets up a resistance to the emergence of any /CeCano/ template denominals. This resistance has proved strong enough to impose a ban. The forces that facilitate the emergence of /CuCono-CoCano/-type alternations do not have a chance against the ban in the /i-e/ sector.

The secondary significance of the post-/CeC/ vowel /a/ may be understood as a side effect of the contrast between the causative template /CeCano/ (26c), and the so far unmentioned anomalous denominal template /CeCono/ (26d):

(26) C(AUSATIVE):
i. *nebano* 'to switch off, put out'
ii. *pherano* 'to send back, turn away'
iii. *Sekhano* 'to teach'
iv. *bhejano* 'to wet'

(CANONICAL CONJUNCTIVE /CiCie/: *nibie, phirie. . .*)

D(ENOMINAL):
vi. *egono* 'to move ahead'
vii. *pechono* 'to move back'
viii. *berono* 'to go out, come out'
ix. *perono* 'to cross'
x. *SeMdono* 'to sneak (into)'

(CANONICAL CONJUNCTIVE /CeCie/: *egie, pehcie . . .*)

Before going into the anomalous character of the denominal template (26d), we may quickly state the basic proposal. Speakers of Bangla know that the language has this anomalous verb pattern /CeCono/; that all these verbs are non-causative; that it minimally differs from a regular verb template /CeCano/; that that template comprises only causatives; and that every Bangla causative consists of some X plus /ano/, featuring the crucial vowel /a/. We submit that these items of knowledge lead the mind to wish to make sense of the direct contrast between post-/CeC/ low /a/, consistently present in causatives, and post-/CeC/ mid /o/, consistently present in denominals – given that in no other environment do these /a/ and /o/ contrast directly. (The templates 'always denominal /CuCono/' versus 'often causative /CoCano/' are a non-minimal pair because of the concomitant /u:o/ contrast.)

Consequently, the mind decides that, after /CeC/, /o/ shall signify 'denominal', and /a/, 'causative'. This is what we mean by secondary significance. By calling the significance secondary we intend to suggest that the relevant lexical items stipulate no specific association between the vowel and the meaning, and that there is no reality to such sub-word items as /o/ 'denominal' and /a/ 'causative' as such throughout the language. (Of course, formal tricks are always an option. If you postulate the sub-word items /o/ and /a/, and then compel them to occur exactly in the context /CeC_/, then we are stunned into silence, and gladly accept this notational variant. It is the point of such exercises that remains elusive, not whether they can be made to 'work'. Of course, they can.)

Why 'anomalous'? Because the /CeCono/ template dashes several hopes.

First, the WFSs [CeCano] ↔ [CiCie], [CoCano] ↔ [CuCie], [CECano] ↔ [CeCie], and [COCano] ↔ [CoCie] lead us to expect all conjunctives of the template /CV*Cie/ to have a V* one step higher than the corresponding V** in the gerund /CV**CVno/. But /CeCono/, as noted in (26), has the conjunctive template /CeCie/ instead of the expected /CiCie/.

Second, you would expect this anomaly to sort itself out with reference to the conjunctive /CeCie/ which the anomalous set /CeCono/ shares with the more regular-looking set /CECano/. The Raised Verb Subfamily size factor familiar from section 5 supports this expectation. But, alas, not a single verb exhibits a /CeCono-CECano/ alternation. And the /CECano/ template is evenly split between denominals like /*ERano*/ 'to avoid' or /*bhEngano*/ 'to mimic' and causatives such as /*deKhano*/ 'to show' or /*SEMkano*/ 'to get (someone) to roast, to get (something) roasted'. This subclass, then, does not even bear any global affinity or exact complementarity with the consistently denominal /CeCono/ subclass.

Third, the denominal /CeCono/ subclass verbs that do go in for an alternation do so in an unexpected direction:

(27) e. *pechono* 'to move back', CONJUNCTIVE: *pechie*
SeMdono 'to crawl (into)', CONJUNCTIVE: *SeMdie*

f. *pichono* 'to move back', CONJUNCTIVE: *pichie*
SiMdono 'to crawl (into)', CONJUNCTIVE: *SiMdie*

You would expect /CiCono/ subclass verbs to alternate with the /CeCano/ subclass and to share a conjunctive form with it. But we see /CiCono/ here alternating with the /CeCono/ template, not /CeCano/: and the conjunctives, being distinct, cannot be the alternation-enabling factor.

Fourth, the /CeCono/ template, along among all denominal templates, is unmatched by any */CeCCVno/.

This fourfold anomaly needs to be connected to other things one believes one understands. We take up that task in section 8. Meanwhile, we accept the anomaly as given. It underpins the secondary significance of the contrast between the post-/CeC/ vowels /o/ and /a/.

7. ADJECTIVES AND FAMILY SHAPE SUPPORT

We stop next at a set of phenomena that seem to tie in with the main facts: adjectival shapes as a family. The templates /CuC(C)o/ and /CoC(c)a/ are well represented, as are /CiC(C)e/ – and the anomalous /CeCo/ which, true to its character, has no /CeCCo/ instantiations:

(28) i. *buno* 'wild' ii. *kuMjo* 'stooping'
iii. *kuno* 'unwilling to go out' iv. *buRo* 'old'
v. *khuMto* 'faulty, blemished' vi. *Sukno* 'dry'
vii. *phulko* 'puffed up (s.o. a puri)'

(29) i. *Soja* 'straight' ii. *khola* 'open'
iii. *bhoMta* 'blunt' iv. *boka* 'stupid'
v. *roga* 'thin' vi. *totla* 'having a stammer'
vii. *koMkRa* 'curly'

(30) i. *bhije* 'wet' ii. *miThe* 'sweet'
iii. *Sidhe* 'straight' iv. *miche* 'false'
v. *phike* 'pale' vi. *chiMcke* 'petty'
vii. *micke* 'perverse'

(31) i. *DeMpo* 'uppity' ii. *keTho* 'wooden'
iii. *ghemo* 'sweety' iv. *khelo* 'tawdry'
v. *kejo* 'busy' vi. *Teko* 'bald'
vii. *beno* 'flood-related'

But there is no /CeCa/ pattern. One comes across an exceptional */Sera/* 'best', of Persian origin, which does not set up mutual support relations with other shapes. In contrast, (31) corresponds to /CaC/ nouns:

(32) i. *kaTh* 'wood' ii. *gham* 'sweat'
iii. *kaj* 'work' iv. *Tak* 'bald pate'
v. *ban* 'flood'

Likewise, (28) corresponds to */bon/* 'forest' at (i), to */KhuMt/* 'blemish' at (v), to */Sukono/* 'to dry' at (vi). (29) has the cognates */khola/* 'to open' for (ii), */totlano/* 'to stammer' for (vi), */koMkRano/* 'to curl up' for (vi). (30) has affinities with */bheja/* 'to get wet' at (i), to */miThai/* 'sweets' at (ii).

While these congeners give us no right to invent quasi-etymological abstract forms and derive the variants from them, one does find it striking that the one clear /CeCa/ adjective */Sera/* 'best' has nothing at all to do with any other word in the language, Persian-derived or otherwise. I propose to put */Sera/*'s isolation first. Its Persian origin only confirms one's hunch that it does not exemplify a true pattern of Bangla adjectival shape.

How do the shapes of adjectives matter in Bangla? They provide lateral support to the pattern of verbs, I would like to suggest. Not that the templates are identical. Adjectival /CiCe/ contrasts with verbal /CiCono/. The language has no /CiCo/ adjectives. But it does have some /CuCe/ adjectives like */Dure/* 'striped' (related to */Dora/* 'stripe'), */KuMRe/* 'lazy', etc. The overall patterns work out thus:

(33)

TEMPLATE	VERBS		ADJECTIVES
CiCo(-no)	Yes	><	No
CiCe(-no)	No	><	Yes
CuCo(-no)	Yes	=	Yes
CuCe(-no)	No	><	Yes

Only one out of four templates gets the same entry in the V and A columns. And yet one can speak of the adjectival shape pattern providing lateral support to the shape families concerned. Adjectival /CiCe/, unmatched by any adjectival /CiCo/, corresponds to the verbal /CiCono/ unmatched by any verbal /CiCeno/; while the /CuCo/ templates of V and A are helpfully identical.

One striking aspect of this lateral shape family support is the fact that adjectives exactly replicate the front-back asymmetry that this paper is about, as shown in chart (34), where we ignore final vowel quality at (i) (ii), (v), and (vi) to bring out sharply what is shared:

(34)

	TEMPLATE	DENOMINAL VERBS	ADJECTIVES
i.	CuCV	Yes	Yes
ii.	CuCCV	Yes	Yes
iii.	CoCa	Yes	Yes
iv.	CoCCa	Yes	Yes
v.	CiCV	Yes	Yes
vi.	CiCCV	Yes	Yes
vii.	CeCa	No	No
viii.	CeCCa	No	No
ix.	CeCo (*anomalous*)	Yes	Yes
x.	CeCCo	No	No

This goes to show that the pattern under investigation is not confined to a little corner, but represents a serious component of the way the language as a whole shapes its words.

I do not wish to claim that the type of factor discussed in this section can all by itself underwrite so robust an effect. In other words, it is not as if adjectives falling into certain patterns can be big enough, so to speak, to pull verbs into exactly similar grooves. But lateral support, though insufficient by itself, may be jointly sufficient to produce an effect if allied with other factors that are more potent.

8. THE NEIGHBOURHOOD OF THE ANOMALY

This section explores the consequences of placing the anomalous phenomena in the context of the following phonotactic facts:

(35) Nonsimplex Bangla verb words exhibit the following high-vowel-final diphthongs in the first syllable – an asymmetric set:

iu	[*uu]	versus	ui	[*ii]
eu	ou	versus	oi	!![*ẹi]
[*Eu]	[*Ou]	versus	[*Oi]	[*Ei]
au		versus	ai	

(36) Bangla verbs permit stem-internal /Vu/ diphthongs, /iu eu ou au/, but – asymmetrically – prohibit stem-internal /Vi/ diphthongs, not even /ui oi ai/, let alone /ei/. The /Vi/s of (35) arise when stem-final V meets suffix-initial /i/.

(37) No Bangla word of any class begins with /CeiCV/
(The Perso-Arabic-derived exceptions */beiman/* 'traitor' and */beijot/* 'humiliated' do not affect the generality of this.) In this context, suppose we tentatively put forward – on the same basis as my 1994 hypothesis that the Bangla velar nasal is phonotactically equivalent to /ng/ – the following Phonotactic Interpretation Strategy to begin to account for the apparent anomaly we face:

(38) /CeCVX/ ↔ /CeiCVX/

A word of the /CeCo/ adjectival type or the /CeCono/ verbal type, in other words, does phonotactic double duty – as itself with an /e/, and as an alter ego with an /ei/.

We may now tick off the ingredients of the anomaly. No /CoCono, CECono, CoCono, CaCono/ verbs to match /CeCono/? Of course not. The pre-/no/ vowel /o/ occurs only if the template has a high vowel in the pre-/o/ syllable to license that /o/. /CeCVX/ may lack such an /i/, but its alter ego steps into the breach, indirectly licensing the pre-/no/ vowel /o/ even in the /CeCono/ incarnation.

The /CeCono/ type's conjunctive /CeCie/ anomalously coincides with that of the /CECano/ template despite lack of /CeCo-CECa/ alternations? Only an apparent coincidence, we now see. Take */berie/* the conjunctive of */berono/* 'to go out'. These now turn out to have the alter egos */beirie, beirono/*. Thus, the single-bodied conjunctive */beRie/* of */bERano/* 'to travel, go around' does not really coincide with the double-bodied */berie-beirie/*.

To make this solution work, we cannot cleave to proposal (38), which must be revised as (39):

(39) /CeCNHX/ ↔ /CeiCNHX/, NH for 'non-high vowel'

This formulation plus the Word Formation Strategy family that mediates between nonsimplex verbs and their conjunctive participles ensures that */berono-beirono/* will have the conjunctive */berie-beirie/*. The oversimple formulation (38) permitted the conjunctive */beRie/* from the */bERano/* lexemic family also to slide, via (38), into the alter ego */beiRie/*, which would make us lose our account.

We now return to the point. That the /CeCono/ template keeps its /e/ intact in the conjunctive (as distinct from the /CeCano/ template which raises it to /i/: /CiCie/) was supposed to be the anomaly. But the comparison with /CeCano/ turns out to have been misplaced. The alter ego /CeiCono/'s real match /CouCono/ does keep its /o/ intact:

(40) i. *douRono* 'to run' : *douRe*
ii. *pouMchono* 'to arrive' : *pouMche*

Is it unexpected that there are no /CeCono-CECano/ alternations and that the /CeCono/ template verbs that do go in for an alternation choose partners from the unexpected /CiCono/ subclass despite the non-sharing of the conjunctive? Well, one does not really expect /CeiCono/ to alternate with /CECano/; and an /e/ in a pre-/i/ context often alternates with an /i/ variant, as in (40), although such alternation is not automatic, cf. */hiSebi/* 'calculating' associated with */hiSeb/* 'calculation':

(41) i. *deSi, disi,* 'indigenous', cf. *deS* 'country'
ii. *bileti, biliti* 'western', cf. *bilet* 'England etc.'
iii. *ingreji, ingriji* 'English', cf. *ingrej* 'Englishman'

So, the fact that one or two /CeiCono/ verbs do alternate with the /CiCono/ template may just mean that the /e/ in the pre-/i/ context here alternates with /i/, yielding a result which left unrepaired would come out as /CiiCono/, except that phonotactics intervenes to compel the word-internally-excluded /ii/ to give way to a simple /i/, hence /CiCono/.

Final point of the anomaly: 'The /CeCono/ template, alone among all denominal templates, is unmatched by any */CeCCVno/.' Unmysterious now.

We were in the wrong reference set. /CeiCono/ is certainly not alone among /CaoCano, CEoCano, CouCono/, which exactly like it insists that the second C site in the template (unlike the first one, which may be null) definitely be a single C, neither null nor double.

Once we pack all the apparent points of the anomaly into a single strategy (39), we begin to place the asymmetry in the adjectival shape family also in a broader context. There too /CeCa/ seems to be expected but anomalously absent. We now regard it as again a matter of the required alter ego /CeiCa/ encountering the language's perfectly general and fierce resistance to all /Xica/ forms, adjectival or verbal (again, with rare non-native exceptions, like the Sanskrit-borrowed adjective /*mittha*/ 'false'). This clears up some of the surrounding issues. But the account leaks at one crucial spot. Strategy (39), as it stands, forces us to reconstrue even straight causatives as follows:

(42) i. *Sekhano* 'to teach' = **Seikhano*
ii. *bhejano* 'to wet' = **bheijano*
iii. *meSano* 'to mix' = **meiSano*

This compulsion creates two hurdles for us. For one we get a class of counterexamples to the otherwise total rejection of /XiCa/: the bare forms of (42), now coupled with counterexemplary alter egos. For another, one cannot derive the secondarily significant contrast between /o/ and /a/ after /CeC/ from basic principles.

My solution, which preserves the results obtained so far, is to revert to the Singh and Ford notion of a morphological, rather than phonological, construal of such a morphonological phenomenon as the main factor underlying our vowel template asymmetry. Thus, I revise (39) to propose the final version (43):

(43) a. WORD EQUIVALENCE (MORPHOLOGY)

$[\mathrm{CeCo}]_{A,V} \leftrightarrow [\mathrm{CeiCo}]_{A,V}$

b. SOUND EQUIVALENCE (PHONOLOGY)

i. /CeiSYLL/ ↔ /CeSYLL/

ii. /CiiSYLL/ ↔ /CiSYLL/

It is clear to readers who have been following us that both sides of equivalence (43a) are operative. The left hand side gives rise to the secondary significance phenomenon. The right hand side runs all the other stories of interest via the fact that the high vowel /i/ licenses the next syllable's /o/. This fact belongs to the part of Bangla morphology that considers the shaping of possible words.

What may take longer is the realisation that (43b) also works in both directions. Here the left hand side takes up the phonotactic pattern space that would have gone to 'real' candidates with the extra /i/, had the language allowed them to occur. And the right hand side is in some sense more economical and blocks the left in actual output. The task before any full-fledged theory of phonological economy is to be able to specify quite generally what is going to upstage what at the level of phonological occurrence.

We may provisionally take a position compatible with whatever future elaborations of economy theory force us to add. For example, an item with multiple shapes occupies space at all the places that it touches in its body-multiplication. But an item surfaces, in the sense of being available at one of the interfaces between language and the other cognitive systems, only at the point co-determined by the economics relevant at that interface. Surfacing, or visibility or interpretability, as it is often called, is then a matter of one interface. Space occupation is a paradigmatic question, a matter that concerns more than one interface at a time. The appropriate subsystem for space occupation concerns is the set of lexical entries. For lexical shaping is a co-ordination of levels and impinges on several interfaces at once.

Our provisional position makes the spirit of non-derivational or representational thinking compatible with the flesh of derivational computations. An item involved in a derivation may be construed, then, as successively hooking up with a series of various types of neighbours. But the hook-ups may be viewed as simultaneous multiple affiliations, and it is okay to define the item itself as the set of those affinities. The succession of hook-ups and its presentation as a processual derivation may be regarded as an expository matter. But the locality relations between hook-ups may have some reality that does not reduce to this.

This type of speculative talk has a way of going on without fruit. Our task will be to pin it down empirically. There is a danger that an apparatus of equivalences and strategies may end up inheriting all the debates of the abstractness period. To avert this danger, consider a real case. We have determined that */berono/* 'to go out', say, is also */beirono/*. Do we therefore jump to the abstractionist conclusion that it is also */bEirono/* and also */bEirOno/*? That would already take us half-way to the derivation */bEirOno > bEirono > beirono > berono/* and plunge us into exactly the old abstractness debates. The question of whether all these alter egos must be postulated is one of how much unoccupied neighbouring territory must be grabbed for a shape to behave as a responsible sovereign grabber. This is too big a question for this sort of paper to do more than broach. But I would like to say off-hand that the 'also /O/' idea does some work, that of preventing */*berulo*/ instead of the real /*berolo*/ for 'went out' in the standard dialects. Presumably the dialects that actually use /*berulo*/, some of which were once standard, do not treat the relevant /o/ as also an /O/. In contrast, the 'also /Ei/' idea looks like an idle formal abstraction to me. I would suggest that a serious theory of economy across levels will be interested in whether a given formal gadget does real work or remain a pretty toy.

May these words work for peace between the representation-bound and the derivation-bound styles of work in our divided houses. Or, if such peace is difficult of attainment here as elsewhere, may these words serve to indicate that the differences between these styles may not lie exactly where we tend to think they do.

REFERENCES

DASGUPTA, P.

1977 The internal grammar of the Bangla compound verb. *Indian Linguistics*. Revised as Dasgupta 1989. chapter 6.

1989 *Projective syntax: Theory and applications*. Pune: Deccan College.

1994 No dhoni. *Baromas,* 15:2. 96–101.

FORD, A., R. SINGH, and A. MARTOHARDJONO

1996 *Morphology: A word-based approach*. New York: Peter Lang, forthcoming.

VIJAYAKRISHNAN, K.G.

1991 The role of the lexicon in language change. Paper presented at the DU seminar on Theoretical Approaches to Languages Variation.

III

LANGUAGE, SOCIETY AND COMMUNICATION

13

Language, knowledge and inequality

TARIQ RAHMAN
Quaid-i-Azam University

LITERACY AND INEQUALITY

Let us begin from fairly self-evident propositions and go on to those which are far less evident and hence more interesting. Among the first set is that the invention of writing not only created new grounds for inequality but made it more systematic, rationalised it, and finally erected it into a condition of human existence. Those who knew how to create signs on a surface and decode them had the key to permanence to an extended memory. This marginalised the whole world of oral tradition including the myths on which it was contingent and in this sense, quite paradoxically, de-emphasised memory (Ong 1982: 15). The figure of the storyteller, the poet, underwent a loss of status, and a bureaucracy with permanent records became possible. Perhaps the very philosophies of individualism, logic and thus modernity and science were created by the written word (Goody 1968). In the words of Walter J. Ong 'writing has transformed human consciousness' (1982: 78). It creates 'context-free' language, that is, it treats words as 'things', not as part of specific interactions in certain contexts. In short, literacy creates the possibility of using abstract language, impersonal logical processes, and being self-conscious. This is the road to modernity and science, which we are going to discuss later.

The gulf between the literate and the illiterate grew till the latter became synonymous with the obsolescent or the exploitable, and literacy became a badge of status and an identification for the middle class (Graff 1979: 316). The written word set about the creation of a hierarchical order that is posed to be just because its leading myth was egalitarian – everybody can learn to read and write. What remains unsaid is that not everybody can learn to read and write for various reasons and, what is more relevant, these skills are not the sole determiners of status (Graff 1979: 72). Above all, even under ideal conditions, the differences in the cognitive abilities of people bar them from having access to certain bodies of knowledge and the power and status that they confer. In Pakistan, for instance, out of the 36 per cent literate people, most are in subordinate positions. However, the stigma of being a *jahil*, or 'illiterate', which has the connotation of being benighted and inferior, is reserved only for the illiterate. Indeed, when Pakistanis talk about the 'rationality' or 'decency' of the educated (*paRhe likhe*), they are really privileging those who do not do manual labour. The privilege of the educated then is really the privilege of class.

EMPOWERMENT AND LITERACY

One aspect of writing is, as Kathleen Gough argues, that it is, 'an *enabling* factor, permitting large-scale organisation' (in Goody 1968: 84). It has the potential to enable individuals to rise in society. It is also an empowering factor, at least in the short run for a few people. Thus, in Latin American countries – such as Nicaragua, Honduras and Ecuador – literacy made people conscious of their rights and appeared to contribute to the creation of a just social order (Archer and Costello 1990). This has been emphasised less because it is offered as salvation for the whole world. That is an exaggeration but the fact remains that literacy breaks down the older, more rigid, forms of hierarchical systems such as castes, guilds and classes, and substitutes a new form – merit-based functional differentiation – in their place. That this is the basis of democracy, human rights and social flexibility cannot be denied. And because of it one supports literacy for all in Pakistan. This literacy should be in the indigenous languages but if these indigenous languages are not used in the domains of power – administration, judiciary, commerce, media, education, etc. – it will be merely ghettoising. So, along with literacy, one also supports the empowering of the common people by bringing their languages into the domains of power.

LITERACY AND POWER

It is a fact that literacy and numeracy extended control over human beings and then over nature. Because it rationalised intervention and created a vast machinery for it, rulers supported numeracy and literacy. That is why literacy became 'an instrument of power' and, in the case of English, 'once Offa established his own scriptorium, written English would take on a *form* that reflected the kings' vested interest in its *uses*' (Toon 1983: 214). Similar processes appear to have taken place elsewhere as in the case of the ancient Church which opposed written Latin, being the language of *Pax Romana* but later 'adopted the literacy of the empire that its founders had denounced and defeated' (Pattison 1982: 77).

While the rulers were interested in power over human beings, writing also made power over nature – at least the illusion of power – possible. As objective reality and accounts of it began to converge at some points, human beings found they could intervene more effectively in the processes of nature. Thus, they could prevent epidemics; likewise they could destroy life more easily. In short, they could colonise plants, animals and other human beings much more efficiently and completely than ever before. This power over nature through science is an aspect of modernity, which created all the enthusiasm about technology and development till the middle of the twentieth century. And because the other aspect of this power is the marginalisation of other knowledge-systems, the degradation of all but the 'modern' (and generally Western) man, the colonisation of the earth and the ecosystem there are those who call science violent (Nandy 1984, 1987; Banuri 1990: 55). It is, in a word, a creator and maintainer of inequality not only among human societies but also between parts of the ecosystem. This is a point to which I will return later when I relate language to the creation of power-differentiating knowledge systems.

THE STANDARD LANGUAGE AND POWER

So far, we have talked only of the written word, which is at a remove from the spoken word. The politics of the spoken word, which is language in the primary sense, is no less related to knowledge and inequality than writing. To begin with, although any arrangement of sounds can create a system of signification (*la langue* as Ferdinand de Saussure [1960] called it – see Culler 1976), we have power-related definitions of *la langue*. We have terms like language, standard language, dialect, and patois and so on for *la langue*. These are all mutually intelligible varieties of what can be called a language. But under a hierarchical definition, the label language is not used for the sum total of all varieties of it, it is used for the standardised variety.

What is ignored, or not realised, is that standardisation is a political act, involving selecting one variety because it is, in some sense, the language of the powerful. The very act of standardisation devalues other varieties: from competing equals they become degraded stigmata or oddities. Schooling and use in the domains of power make the standard languages elitist and elites view them as evidence of their superiority and privilege (Kroch 1978). Because they justify and create inequalities while appearing to be available to all it is in the interest of elites to promote' them 'as the single model of correctness' (Cooper 1989: 135). The 'ideology of standardisation', as Milroy and Milroy call it in their book on correctness in language (1985), serves to confer authority and legitimacy on elitist power, elitist institutions, and elite culture. They are seen as being intrinsically superior rather than being powerful.

Speakers of non-standard varieties have to acquire the standard variety in which knowledge – the kind of knowledge that leads to power and high status – is produced. That they find it challenging in ex-colonies like Pakistan and India where elitist discourse is in English is easy to understand. What requires attention is that even in countries where everyone officially speaks one language – say, English in England – language remains a major factor for maintaining inequality.

In this context, Basil Bernstein's work (1964) is very insightful. Although Bernstein has used different terminology over the years and his concept of class has been called 'inadequate' by critics (Rosen 1972: 13), his notion of 'elaborated' and 'restricted code' is useful for understanding how linguistic practices create and reinforce inequality in the school. Since middle-class children are more used to an 'elaborated code' even at home, and this is the one used in schools, they achieve better results than their working-class counterparts (Jeffcoate 1984). Bernstein's codes can be seen in the light of the orality-literacy dichotomy Ong has expatiated upon in such detail. He says that the 'restricted' code is 'oral-based' whereas the 'elaborated' one is 'text-based' because the former is formulaic, aggregative and context-based whereas the latter is not (Ong 1982: 106).

In Pakistan where most children, except upper middle class and upper class ones, come from oral-based backgrounds the transition from orality to 'textuality' must be a major obstacle. Moreover, they are confronted with another language, be it Urdu or English, which is another formidable obstacle. The linguistic hierarchy places English on top followed by Urdu and then the indigenous languages. In the Punjab, Punjabi has the lowest social status. In Sindh, the NWFP and Baluchistan there may be no culture shame as far as the use of Sindhi, Pashto and Balochi/Brahmi are concerned but for social and pragmatic reasons, English and Urdu still occupy high status among educated people – those whom Hamza Alavi calls the 'salariat' (Alavi 1992: 265).

So, as elsewhere in the world, the educational system sets up 'sociolinguistic barriers' of which 'the power of social attitudes to language' (Stubbs 1983: 21) is one. The pupils may feel such shame about pronouncing 'school' as *ischool* or *sachool* (see Rahman 1990: 31) that they become tongue tied. Moreover, since the language of formal knowledge is different from the language of home, it is difficult to acquire it (Wight 1983: 29). In Pakistan, of course, the greatest barrier is the fact that the English language remains the marker of elitist social status and it is costly to acquire (Rahman, forthcoming). Moreover, even costly elitist schooling is not enough to make a child fluent in English. Fluency is achieved not by being taught by teachers in a school alone but by being exposed to English in such informal domains as the playground and the family circle. This is impossible to attain for many families with money but without Westernised socialisation.

THE QUESTION OF REFERENTIALITY

I now come to the more philosophical, and possibly the more interesting, aspects of language and knowledge. The positivist as well as the common sense view of language is that it is referential, that it refers to things, concepts, phenomena, events, or states of being. Analytic linguists – notably Wittgenstein (1953) and Austin (1962) – pointed out that statements are not merely referential, they are constitutive, that is, they shape what we call 'reality'. Focusing on this aspect of language and referring to Husserl and Heidegger's theories of phenomenology and the notion of discursive practices – the assumptions, presuppositions and unspoken ideological bias we bring to our language – of Michel Foucault, the political philosopher, Shapiro (1981: 170) connects language with power:

> To the extent that one denies that language and speech constitute and shape experience as well as providing a transaction medium for sharing it, one will neglect the value that statements have in allocating power, authority, and control.

The point is that all discourses place us in certain roles. They reflect values, including our standards for elevating one over another, and reinforce them. For Sapir and Whorf this precluded a universal or culture-neutral body of knowledge. According to Whorf (1956: 214–15):

> The fact that languages dissect nature in many different ways becomes patent. The relativity of all conceptual systems, ours included, and their dependence upon language stand revealed.

In the same essay, Whorf claimed that the Hopi recognised psychological time but not mathematical, linear time. If the Hopis had created physics they would have used concepts like intensity to measure acceleration, velocity and chemical action in a beaker (Whorf 1956: 217–18). Elsewhere, Whorf tells us that the division of reality into noun and verb is often without any objective foundation. A flash of lightning or cloud is much more in motion and short-lived than the act of running but we interpret the world through our language and the categories provided to us by it. Words are meant to construct a simplified social reality. Take the words 'whore' and 'sage'. When a woman is defined as a 'whore' one responds to her sexual conduct to the exclusion of every other aspect of her being. Similarly the label 'sage' emphasises one aspect of perceived conduct. If the 'whore-like' conduct is less socially prestigious than the 'sage-like' conduct, words have given us a certain construction of reality that excludes, ignores and simplifies in a manner which creates and reinforces inequalities.

SOCIAL KNOWLEDGE AND AUTHORITY

Social knowledge, arbitrated through language, creates our awareness of and acquiescence in legitimate 'power' as Barnes and Arendt use the word. It refers to being empowered by a certain number of people to act in their name (Arendt 1969: 44). This means that it is that authority which is perceived as legitimate. This, according to Barnes (1988: 100), is dependent upon the distribution of knowledge in a society.

In Pakistan, two models of power-distribution are part of our world-view, which our languages reinforce. First is the indigenous feudal and tribal leadership model. The possession of land or merely lineage makes one a *sharif, chaudhry, malik, khan, nawab,* etc. Those who actually use the soil to produce wealth are the *kammis, haris,* etc., who are associated with being *kameen* (ignoble). The rationalisation in both cases is based upon ascribed myths liked blood, lineage, family background, etc. which are all assumed to be intrinsically ethically superior rather than being only powerful.

The other is the imported colonial 'officer' model, which legitimises its privileged position through the possession of Western knowledge written in English, and the use of Western cultural norms. This is cloaked under the concept of merit. Since people accept both ascriptive qualities as well as acquired ones, both these models of authority continue to dominate in our society. Our languages also reflect and reinforce our hierarchical conception of social interaction. Honorifics used before and after names (*sahib, sahiba, Mr,* etc.) and deferential forms of address (*aap, tusi, taso* rather than *tum, tu* or *ta*) adhere strictly to the power dynamics. Our languages also reflect and reinforce our androcentric bias. Respect can be given to women in some Pakistani languages (for example, Punjabi) only by using the verb agreement markers for masculine, rather than feminine, gender). Though in theory, seniority of age entitles one to polite linguistic forms, in practice it is power which claims them as a right.

This is challenged or ignored by some Westernised Pakistanis – generally in the private sector or international agencies – who use Western forms of address (the first name without honorifics) for most people. This, however, is done from a position of power and, insofar as it ignores indigenous norms of politeness (such as the use of polite forms for older people), it is as 'colonial' and impositionist as any other form of cultural domination. A change is needed but it can also take the egalitarian form of using honorifics and polite pronouns of address for all – irrespective of power differentials – rather than the Western form of linguistic egalitarianism (Rahman 1995a).

LANGUAGE AND VALUES

Of course, social knowledge is not dependent solely on language. Language and values seem to be in a circular relationship as Neitzche pointed out long ago (Strong 1976 in Shapiro 1984: 84). In essence, Chomsky, and many others before him, notably Plato, argue that thought comes before language. Plato argues in the *Meno* that knowledge is remembered from a previous existence and Chomsky asserts that the language-using capacity is innate (Chomsky 1988: 4). However, nothing written by Chomsky suggests that concepts that are expressed in units of meaning are not influenced by world-view which, in turn, is reinforced by language. This circularity, it seems to me, can be disrupted both by change in language and change in the world-view.

One example of a language change with no change in the world-view is the use of exalted words for people of low status in South Asia. In such cases, the words lose status. For instance, the words *jamadar* and *mehtar* lost status when they came to be used for sweepers in Urdu. But when in

English the feminist movement insisted on using *he/she* and *chairperson* for *chairman*, etc. – that is, the removal of androcentric and sexist language – they did succeed in problematising the fact that women are ignored and trivialised in male-dominated societies. There was a partial change in world-view that fed the language change and was reinforced by it. That male domination is still in place is undeniable but some change has occurred and this is related to linguistic changes among others (Cooper 1989: 20–21). Thus, it is not in a simplistic manner that social reality, expressed and maintained through language, may be said to be wholly 'constructed' by it.

BIAS IN WESTERN SCIENCE AND INEQUALITY

One aspect of the organisation of knowledge in science is the primacy of binary oppositions (the voiced/unvoiced of sounds in phonology). Marglin says,

> The problem with this view [binary opposition] begins with the binary opposition between man and the environment . . . man is the rational, active subject exercising control over a passive, objectified environment. (Marglin 1990: 23)

Binary opposition may contrast modern/backward or normal/abnormal in such a way as to privilege the former. Mental illness, as Foucault (1961) argues, is a case in point in the use of binary oppositions to disempower the patient.

In Pakistan, certain binary oppositions are reflective of certain ideological stances. There was, in Akbar Allahabadi's days (1846–1921), the *Mister/Mullah* dichotomy. Those who supported modernisation, like Sir Syed, were the misters while those who opposed them among Muslims were *mullahs*. The divide flourishes even now and the translation of 'secular' as *la-deen* (without religion) illustrates how the use of such language may bring about the excommunication and persecution of secular democrats under the impression that they are atheists. If that happens the *mullahs* would have won. As it is the misters look down upon the *mullahs* and have marginalised them at least in the apparatus of the state.

There can be, in theory, a system of knowledge based on other than binary oppositions. For instance, one may use a scale. Then fat would not have thin as an antonym but both would be on a scale from invisibility to infinity. As Whorf pointed out in the case of Hopi physics, such a system would not be any less scientific than the Western one. It would be coloured as much by the Hopi world-view, expressed and constantly reinforced by the Hopi language, as modern science is by Western ones. In the case of economics the writings of the post-modernists have made this evident. Thus, few would quarrel with Banuri's (1990: 89) statement that 'the assumption that the impersonal world-view is the only important and relevant one for understanding human behaviour is seriously flawed'.

In fact, anomie, alienation and loneliness – the consequences of impersonality – are too well known to require comment. It should also be obvious that impersonality is related to individualism and freedom, which are the bases of both empiricism and rationalism. But for the faith in the mind of the individual, there would have been only religious faith, not secular science. What is perhaps still controversial is that Western science, despite its claim to objectivity and universality, is culture-bound in so far as it uses human language. The problems it formulates and the way it approaches them is influenced, though not determined, by the world-view mediated by Western languages. This is, of course, truer of the social sciences than the natural ones. To understand our biases we have to become especially sensitive to the ideological load of our use of language.

Western systems of knowledge appear to me to have become potentially powerful over nature but have not looked critically at the ideological bias of language. This has made them even more formidable maintainers of inequality than pre-modern myths of inequality. Since pre-modern myths of inequality posited certain beliefs which ultimately rested on faith, unbelief made one a heretic. But unbelief in modern science makes one a 'backward', 'stupid' or 'cranky' sub-human other'. Those outside science have now been placed outside rationality as the insane were in classical perception of madness (Foucault 1961). In short, they are no longer *homo sapiens*. This kind of 'sub-speciation' (Stevens (1989), I argue, rationalises the use of force against most of humanity – the semi-literate working class in the West, the illiterate masses of the Third World, in fact all those who do not acquiesce to institutions based upon 'rationality', such as impersonal bureaucracy and modern science. In this sense then, language and knowledge have a deep connection with inequality.

CONCLUSION AND SUGGESTIONS

This paper has emphasised the dark side of language and knowledge, because it brings out how language, both written and spoken, creates discourses that give some human beings tremendous and unprecedented power over other human beings and the environment. In Pakistan, literacy divides the potentially powerful and affluent from those who are weak and potentially exploitable. The use of English and the non-use of the indigenous languages restrict access to powerful positions in Pakistan for those who are not Westernised, affluent, and urbanised. The linguistic source of this inequality can be eliminated, or its ill-effects reduced, by spreading literacy in the indigenous languages, which (using Switzerland as a model) could also be used in the domains of power leading to decentralisation and empowerment of non-Westernised people.

The philosophical issues I mentioned help us understand that our language has so far valorised 'development', possession of consumer goods, and becoming 'modern'. Implicit in the words we use is contempt for the pre-modern (backward), the rural (*pendu*) and the non-Western. If we were to become aware of such linguistic biases, we could change them. We could change our colonial epistemology, for instance, which makes us dismiss all indigenous forms of knowledge as 'backward' rubbish. This could not only contribute to the creation of new forms of knowledge – knowledge expressed in terms made in Pakistani languages and therefore possibly more indigenised and accessible for ordinary Pakistanis than knowledge in English (Rahman 1995b) – but make our psychiatrists, physicians, architects, economists, policy-makers, lawyers, and bureaucrats more sensitive to our own cultural realities reinforced by our own languages. In short, it could lead to a decolonisation of the mind which the categories of thought implicit in Western languages do not facilitate.

Likewise, we could also change the language we use for women, the working class and the illiterate. The way language reflects hierarchy and power – in the use of honorifics and polite forms of address – also needs democratisation, but of an indigenous not Western kind. Deliberate linguistic change from above is, however, bound to meet with partial success, and what is required is a linguistic change along with a change in the power structure. When people become empowered and governance changes to public service, then a new and more egalitarian social reality will be created which will be reinforced by a new and less hierarchy-sensitive language. Any meaningful concept of sustainable development must give the reduction of inequality a central place, otherwise we may 'develop' and we may 'sustain' our development but this process will merely sustain inequalities.

REFERENCES

ALAVI, HAMZA

1992 Politics of ethnicity in Pakistan. In S. Akbar Zaidi (ed.), *Regional imbalance and the national question in Pakistan*. Lahore: Vanguard. 201–78.

ARCHER, DAVID and PATRICK COSTELLO

1990 *Literacy and power: The Latin American battleground*. London: Earthscan Publications Ltd.

ARENDT, HANNAN
1969 *On violence*. New York: Harcourt, Brace & World Inc.

AUSTIN, JOHN
1962 *How to do things with words*. Cambridge, Mass.: Harvard University Press.

BANURI, TARIQ
1990 Development and the politics of knowledge: A critical interpretation of the social role of modernization theories in the development of the Third World. In F.A. Marglin & S.A. Marglin (eds.), *Dominating knowledge: Development, culture and resistance*. New York: Oxford University Press. 29–81.

BARNES, BARRY
1988 *The nature of power*. Urbana: University of Illinois Press.

BERNSTEIN, B.
1964 Elaborated and restricted codes: Social origins and some consequences. In Gumperz & Hymes (eds.), *The ethnography of communication*. American Anthropologist special publication. Vol. 66, no. 6. 2, 55–69.

CHOMSKY, NOAM
1988 *Language and problems of knowledge*. Cambridge, Mass: The MIT Press.

COOPER, ROBERT L.
1989 *Language planning and social change*. Cambridge: Cambridge University Press.

CULLER, JONATHAN
1976 *Saussure*. London: Fontana & Glasgow: Collins & Co.

FOUCAULT, MICHEL
1961 *Madness and civilization: A history of insanity in the age of reason*. Trans. by Richard Howard. London: Tavistock Publications, 1967.

GOODY, JACK (ed.)
1968 *Literacy in traditional societies*. Cambridge: Cambridge University Press.

GRAFF, HARVEY, J.
1979 *The literacy myth: Literacy and social structure in the nineteenth century city*. New York: Academic Press.

JEFFOCATE, R.
1984 *Ethnic minorities and education*. London: Harper & Row.

KROCH, ANTHONY
1978 Toward a theory of social dialect variation. *Language in Society* 7. 17–36.

MARGLIN, STEPHEN A.
1990 Towards the decolonisation of the mind. In Marglin & Marglin, 1990. 1–28.

MILROY, JAMES and LESLIE MILROY
1985 *Authority in language: Investigating language prescription and standardisation*. London: Routledge & Kegan Paul.

NANDY, ASHIS
1984 Culture, state and the rediscovery of Indian politics. *Economic and Political Weekly* (December), 8. 2078–83.
1987 Towards a third world utopia. In *Traditions, tyrannies, and utopias: Essays in the politics of awareness*. New Delhi: Oxford University Press.

ONG, WALTER J.

1982 *Orality and literacy: The technologizing of the word.* London & New York: Routledge, 1991.

PATTISON, ROBERT

1982 *On literacy: The politics of the word from Homer to the age of rock.* New York & Oxford: Oxford University Press.

RAHMAN, TARIQ

1990 *Pakistani English.* Islamabad: National Institute of Pakistan Studies, Quaid-i-Azam University.

1995a Cultural imperialism and the pragmatics of Urdu in Pakistan. *Journal of Central Asia.* Vol. XVIII, no. 1 (July). 16–44.

1995b *Language planning and politics in Pakistan.* Islamabad: Sustainable Development Policy Institute.

in press The English-Urdu controversy in Pakistan. *Modern Asian Studies.*

ROSEN, H.

1972 *Language and class: A critical look at the theories of Basil Bernstein.* London: Falling Wall Press.

SAUSSURE, FERDINAND DE

1960 *Course in general linguistics.* Trans. from the French by Wade Baskin. London: Peter Owen.

SHAPIRO, MICHAEL J.

1981 *Language and political understanding.* New Haven & London: Yale University Press.

1984 *Language and politics* (ed.). New York: New York University Press.

STEVENS, ANTHONY

1989 *The roots of war.* New York: Pergamon.

STRONG, TRACY B.

1976 Language and nihilism: Neitzche's critique of epistemology. In Michael Shapiro (ed.), 1984. 81–107.

STUBBS, M.

1983 *Language, schools and classrooms,* second edition. London: Methuen.

TOON, THOMAS

1983 *The politics of early old English sound change.* New York & London: Academic Press.

WHORF, BENJAMIN LEE

1956 In John B. Carroll (ed.), *Language, thought and reality.* Cambridge, Mass: MIT Press.

WIGHT, J.

1983 The space between. In M. Stubbs & J. Hillier (eds.), *Readings on language, schools and classrooms.* London: Methuen. 226–37.

WITTGENSTEIN, LUDWIG

1953 *Philosophical investigations.* New York: Macmillan.

14

Hindi-Urdu construct: Analyses of antagonism

ABDUL MATIN, P.K. MATHUR and IMTIAZ HASNAIN
Aligarh Muslim University

The British introduced both representative and democratic institutions first at the local level and then at the provincial level, as well as the principles of competition based on merit in the areas of education and jobs. These developments contributed to the creation of new power structures and new elites, primarily on the basis of religion. The Hindu elites developed first and the Muslim elites developed later due to specific historical exigencies.

The uneven development of Hindu and Muslim elites engendered a conflict of political and economic interests between them, which in turn led subsequently led to a strengthening of both religious identities. The elites used language to reinforce the religious identity in reconfigured power structure. The Hindu elites used Hindi and the Muslim elites used Urdu, and Hindi and Urdu were thus constructed as two antagonistic linguistic identities. This has been conceptualised in the framework of 'instrumentalist approach' of ethnicity in which language and religion are used by elites in their pursuit of power. This paper attempts to unravel the structural conditions and processes that generated antagonism between Hindi and Urdu as a means of reinforcing the identities of the Hindus and Muslims.

We are grateful to Professor Selma K. Sonntag, Humboldt State University, for providing a detailed comments and criticisms on the earlier version of this paper. In the light of these comments and criticisms, the paper has been revised. However, we are entirely responsible for analysis of data and any errors.

CONCEPTUAL FRAMEWORK FOR ANALYSIS OF ANTAGONISM

In order to seek plausible explanations for Hindi-Urdu construction leading towards antagonism, the conceptual framework of 'ethnicity' with specific reference to the 'instrumental approach' provides tremendous insights into the problem. Isajiw's definition of ethnicity may be considered as a minimal statement. According to him,

> Ethnicity refers to an involuntary group of people who share the same culture or to descendants of such people who identify themselves and/or are identified by others as belonging to the same involuntary group. (Isajiw 1980: 24)

Isajiw's definition emphasises that an ethnic group shares the same culture. But it does not indicate the subjective belief that distinguishes one ethnic group from another. Edwards (1985: 10) is critical of this definition. According to him,

> Ethnic identity is allegiance to a group – large or small, socially dominant or subordinate – with which one has ancestral links. There is no necessity for a continuation, over generations, of the same socialisation or cultural patterns, but some sense of a group boundary must persist. This can be sustained by shared objective characteristics (language, religion, etc.), or by more subjective contributions to a sense of groupness, or by some combination of both. Symbolic or subjective attachments must relate, at however, distant a remove, to an observably real past.

These definitions highlight only particular dimensions of ethnicity, the objective and the subjective, that is, ethnicity is based upon cultural characteristics such as religion or language of which the group is subjectively conscious. Paul Brass (1991: 19) incorporates all the dimensions in his following definition and at the same time focuses upon the evolution of ethnicity.

> Any group of people dissimilar from other peoples in terms of objective cultural criteria and containing within its membership either in principle or in practice, the elements for a complete division of labour and for reproduction forms an ethnic category. The objective cultural markers may be a language or dialect, distinctive dress or diet or customs, religion or race.

Thus, Brass defines an ethnic category which evolves into an ethnic community and then into a nationality. He raises a number of questions of which the following one is the most relevant for our purpose: 'What are the conditions under which ethnic groups become communities and under which ethnic demand, ethnic competition, and ethnic conflict take place?' (Brass 1991: 23). He further observes that:

> The process of creating communities from ethnic groups involves the selection of particular dialects or religious practices or styles of dress or historical symbols from a variety of available alternatives. It is always the case that particular social groups, leaders, or elites stand to benefit and others to lose from the choices that are made (Brass 1991: 25).

Brass (1991: 75) studied the process by which elites and counter-elites within ethnic groups select aspects of the group's culture, attach new value and meaning to them, and use them as symbols to mobilise the group, to defend its interest, and to compete with other groups. Several scholars of ethnicity and nationality have pointed out that development in large, multiethnic societies tends to proceed unevenly and often, if not always, benefit some ethnic groups or some regions of a country more than others. However, inequality between different ethnic groups or culturally distinct regions does not by itself spur the development of communal or national consciousness.

Ethnic self-consciousness, ethnically-based demands and ethnic conflict can occur only if there is some conflict either between indigenous and external elites and authorities or between indigenous elites. However, in external colonial situations where a multiplicity of ethnic groups are often in competition with each other, the native collaborationist aristocracy may itself manipulate ethnic symbols in order to mobilise group support for its hegemony over counter-elites from other ethnic groups.

For example, in north India, the Muslim aristocracy, whose leading figures collaborated with the British authorities, sought to protect their privileges against rising Hindu elites and manipulated the symbols of language and religion in order to do so. The result was that there were two elite groups in the Muslim community, the native aristocracy and the *ulema*, competing with each other and with the Hindus in the mobilisation of the Muslim masses on the basis of ethnic appeals (Brass 1991: 29–30). They addressed themselves to both the ethnic symbols, that is, religion and language. The Hindu elites revitalised Hindi and the Muslim elites revitalised Urdu as a means for reinforcing their ethnic identities. These identities evolved in the course of the elites' pursuit of power.[1] Buttressing this argument, King (1994: 18) has pointed out that the Hindi movement in the nineteenth century has followed the sequence of transformation from ethnic group to community to nationality.[2]

There were certain structural conditions conducive for the conflict of political and economic interests between Hindu and Muslim elites that were a creation of the British rule. Although India was invaded many times during the pre-British period, the consequences of the British rule were distinct and different.

THE IMPACT OF BRITISH RULE IN INDIA

India was invaded many times in its chequered history successively by the Aryans, Greeks, Shakas, Kushanas, Huns, Muslims and British. While all the others settled down in the country and made it their home, the British were different because they did not make it their home. They came as traders of Indian goods in order to fill the coffers at home, which was thousands of miles away. When they found that conquering Indian territory fostered this, they also sought to establish their rule. Thus all earlier conquests were merely political changes in which one set of rulers was replaced by another set of rulers without affecting familiar traditional patterns of economic, social and cultural life. British rule in India was not just a political change but also a change in the economic, administrative, legal and educational aspects of life. Therefore, Nehru (1961: 302) calls British rule 'entirely a new phenomenon' in India's history.

The economic changes introduced by the British were those of a colonial economy in which trade with India was intended to provide raw materials needed for the industries at home and to provide a market for their finished products (Desai 1976: 79). They also introduced measures for collecting land revenue in which revenue was fixed for a long period of time and was to be paid in cash by selling the produce to traders (Desai 1976: 37–41). This led to the development of a trading class in India. The administrative changes introduced by the British were the formation of a national bureaucracy recruited on the basis of achievement in a competitive examination and this led to the development of a class of administrators in India. The legal changes introduced by the British were a hierarchy of courts and a legal code which was rational and universalistic (Singh 1973: 96–99). This led to the development of a class of professionals who were lawyers. The British introduced a system of communications that included not only posts and telegraph but also the press (Singh 1973: 112), the latter leading to the development of a class of professional journalists.

The British introduced a system of education which was rational, scientific, universalist, and open in place of a traditional education which was religious, metaphysical, particularistic and closed (Singh 1973: 101–102). Earlier, Oriental subjects were taught through the medium of the classical languages but now Western Arts and Sciences were taught through the medium of English. The new system of education served the economic, administrative and political interests of the British by ensuring that those having an English education would also constitute a market for British products. Indians would be able to participate in the administration in subordinate positions. It would also ensure that Indians knew about the achievements of their rulers in order to get legitimacy for their rule (Desai 1976: 143). This led to the development of a new urban, English-educated, middle class in India, which grew with the expansion of trade, administration, courts, press, and education.

The British conquest of India was not a single simultaneous event but it took place in stages. Thus, the economic, administrative, legal and educational changes introduced by them were uneven in their impact. Therefore, the development of the trading, administrative, professional and educated middle class was also uneven. These classes developed first in those regions and among those communities that were drawn into the ambit of these changes first because they were strategically placed in relation to the British conquest (Desai 1976: 174; Dutta 1974: 142; Seal 1968: 26; Brass 1974: 34). The British conquest of India took place by sea from the west, south, and east so that the maritime regions of Bombay, Madras, and Calcutta were drawn into the ambit of the changes first. The trading, administrative, professional, and educated middle classes developed first in these regions among those communities that were strategically placed during the British rule. These classes developed first among Hindu community because the Muslim community was strategically at a disadvantageous position at an initial stage of the British rule.

The Muslim conquest of India took place by land from the north and so the regions where they were established as a ruling elite of Lahore, Delhi and Lucknow were the last to be affected by the changes introduced by the British. Therefore, traders, administrators, professionals, and the educated middle classes developed later among Muslims than among Hindus. The backwardness of the Muslims in trade, administration, professions, and education accounted for the Hindu-Muslim divide during British rule. The introduction of the representative institutions at the local and provincial levels further accelerated this process. This gave rise to antagonism between the Hindu and Muslim elites, which had important consequences for the Hindi-Urdu construct (Brass 1991: 83–86; Robinson 1975: 70).

BACKGROUND OF LINGUISTIC ANTAGONISM

For the purpose of grammatical description, linguists treat both Hindi and Urdu not as two separate languages, but as a single linguistic system. This is on account of the fact that grammatical markers, processes and productive rules of word formation are essentially identical in both these languages. However, structural and grammatical proximity does not necessarily entail socio-political and cultural congruence. Despite the structural and grammatical resemblance, the rational linguistic considerations have not been able to stem the politico-cultural rhetoric of the divide between Hindi and Urdu, particularly in the perception of the common man because of competition, conflict and struggle for power between the elites. Striking difference in the script, presence of extra sounds in the inventory of Urdu sound system, and use of certain literary and cultural lexicons and expressions have led to the belief that Hindi and Urdu are two distinct languages, mutually unintelligible to each other. These beliefs, that belie the common bases of Hindi and Urdu, have not only heightened and exaggerated the consciousness of language divide, but have also allowed the constructionists (elites) of the divide to look at Hindi-Urdu as an ideology of meaningful antagonism.

The British rule in India evinced keen interest in the Indian classical and vernacular languages primarily for the purpose of effective administration. This resulted in the revival/continuation of classical languages such as Sanskrit, Persian, and Arabic, and recognition of vernacular languages such as Urdu and Hindi. This had a bearing upon two great religions in India – Hinduism, and Islam. Sanskrit was the classical language of the Hindus and Arabic and Persian of the Muslims. Of the two vernacular languages, Urdu got identified with the Muslims and Hindi with the Hindus.

Historically, consciousness of the divide may be traced to the establishment of Fort William College (henceforth, referred as FWC). With its establishment, the process of divergence between Hindi and Urdu at the linguistic, socio-cultural, and literary levels assumed a new dimension. *Khadi boli* was communalised. Hindu and Muslim writers from far-flung places were called to write prose in two styles of *khadi boli* by using two different scripts: Devanagari and Perso-Arabic. While Lallu Lal and Sadal Mishra were hired for writing *khadi boli* prose in the Devanagari script by using words of Sanskrit origin, Meer Amman, Haidar Baksh Haidari, Sher Ali 'Afsos' were encouraged to write *khadi boli* prose in the Perso-Arabic script by using Perso-Arabic words. *Prem Sagar* ('The Ocean of Love') of Lallu Lall (which was begun in 1804 and completed in 1810) in Hindi and *Bagh-o-Bahar* (published in 1803) of Meer Amman are the most representative literary works of FWC.

Thus, the establishment of FWC brought about both the overt policy of divergence between Hindi and Urdu language, and the covert and subtle policy of divide between Hindus and Muslims. This seemingly innocuous literary venture did attribute Hindi to Hindus and Urdu to Muslims. What became significant in this literary venture was the conscious use of Devanagari script, which incited the minds of the Hindu revivalists. Hindi was considered as the most suitable language for the expression of their socio-cultural thought.

Consequently, the development of Hindi as the medium of modern education became a major concern of the Hindu revivalists. Both the literary heritage and political contingency contributed towards the revival of Hindi linguism. The entire devotional poetry of Braj, Awadhi, and Maithili was available in the script with Nagari character which was purely Indian, more accessible and easier to learn and adopt. Muslims in general and some mystic thinkers and saints in particular who had mastered the regional languages had shown no interest in the use of Devanagari script.

This had further led to the sharpening of the divide between Hindus and Muslims and deepened Hindi-Urdu differentiation. The political value of Hindi as a symbol of anti-colonialism combined with Hindi-Urdu differentiation. Hindi was perceived as the symbolic instrument for fighting colonialism and English. Urdu was considered to be an extension of Mughal imperialism and was perceived basically as an instrument for preserving Muslim self-identity. The decision made by the English administration to use Urdu as the court language had further reinforced the suspicion with regard to Urdu and even questioned its suitability for the anti-colonial struggle.

Between Hindi and Urdu there was more a question of self-identification, and issues pertaining to apparent linguistic similarities and differences became rather secondary. Self-identification basically involves issues like attitude towards the differences, the functional roles assigned to them, and the uses made of them. Two distinct scripts and deliberate use of Sanskritised Hindi and Persianised Urdu accentuated the question of self-identification and it subsequently gave rise to the Hindi movement. Agitation of the Hindus of North-Western provinces and Oudh between 1868 and 1900 over the replacement of Persian by Urdu finally culminated in the offensive against Urdu and its defence by the Muslims. All this linguistic antagonism led to the reinforcement of the communal divergence between Hindus and Muslims.

The late nineteenth and early twentieth century mark the period of exaggerated difference between Hindi and Urdu. Both these languages became the means as well as the symbol of community creation. It was during this period that Nagari Pracharini Sabha was formed (1893), Hindi Sahitya Sammelan was founded (1910), Anjuman Taraqqi-e-Urdu was established (1903), Arya Samaj's and Urdu campaign was initiated and the Anjuman-e-Islam of Lahore waged a counter-attack against the Hindi movement. The setting up of the Benaras Hindu University (BHU) in 1915 as a modern institution with a religio-cultural agenda and establishment of Hindi departments in universities and colleges strengthened the self-image of the Hindi literati and contributed immensely towards the success of their cultural agenda.

The early twentieth century also marked the deliberate creation and crystallisation of Hindi speakers' identity mediated through Hindi curriculum and texts. At this point, the contribution of Acharya Ramchandra Shukla, a teacher at the BHU, is worth mentioning. For, he not only shaped the format of the syllabi of Hindi but also 'defined the heritage of Hindi language and literature in a manner that few have dared to quarrel with' (Kumar 1990: 180). His book *Hindi Sahitya Ka Itihas* ('History of Hindi Literature'), first published in 1929, gave a distinct Hindu identity to the Hindi heritage:

> It is my opinion that Hindi and Urdu are two very different languages. The Hindus of this country speak Hindi, while Muslims and those Hindus who have studied Persian speak Urdu. Sanskrit words abound in Hindi as Arabic and Persian words abound in Urdu. There is no necessity to use Arabic and Persian words in speaking Hindi, nor do I call that language Hindi, which is filled with Persian and Arabic words. (Ramchandra Shukla, quoted in King 1994: 23)

The deliberate construction of Hindi-Hindu identity has been rightly highlighted by Kumar when he says:

> Shukla went well beyond the territory of the literary historian, and took a strong ideological position indicating the irrelevance of the Urdu-Persian tradition for the development of modern Hindi. He ignored major Urdu poets of the eighteenth and nineteenth centuries in his otherwise meticulous chronology. . . . In an autobiographical essay, Shukla had written that . . . he used to enjoy the mixing lines of Persian poetry with the lines written by Hindi poets. . . . By denying the literary works written in the mixed Hindi-Urdu tradition a valid place and status in Hindi's literary history, he performed a decisive symbolic act in shaping the cultural identity of college/educated men and women for generations. (Kumar 1990: 180)

This not only formalised the linguistic divisions but also strengthened the tendency to identify Urdu as the language of the Muslims and Hindi as the language of the Hindus. It is around the same period that these linguistic identities further merged with national identity. A new meaning of nationalism emerged and was publicised through the religio-nationalist and linguistic slogan of 'Hindi, Hindu, Hindustan', a three-fold assertion of the identity of language, religion and motherland, by the then Hindi stalwarts. Pandit Pratap Narayan Mishra's famous couplet is a testimony to this fact.

Japau nirantar ek zaban
Hindi, Hindu, Hindustan

The perception of Hindi as a symbol of anti-colonial struggle added a fillip to the rhetoric of nationalism. As a result of this conflict, the modernisation and development of Urdu was seriously affected and, in post-independence India, Urdu lagged behind Hindi in most of the spheres of language development.

CONCLUDING REMARKS

We have argued that the British rule in India was beneficial to only certain regions and communities. This uneven development and unequal benefits at various levels generated discontentment. It further resulted in the revitalisation of language identity. The Hindi-Urdu construct is one of the manifestations of discontentment and revitalisation movements. Thus, the language antagonism had a bearing upon ethnic revivalism, governed and articulated by various competing and conflicting elites.

NOTES

1. Leitin (1992) examines the issue of language in terms of conflict between the indigenous elite and the external elite in Africa. He has also drawn attention to language policy and political strategy in India. Hechter (1975) had addressed the issue of unequal development between ethnically/culturally distinct regions in Britain. Both the authors' writings have relevance for India for a proper understanding of its language identity as well as unequal development.
   Rahman (1997: 177–78) echoes these arguments for Pakistan. Observing that Urdu was an important part of the ideology that inspired Pakistan, he holds that, after partition, the Muslim League continued to project 'Urdu' as the unifying symbol for Pakistanis, who actually belonged to different linguistic and ethnic groups, like Bengali, Punjabi, and Sindhi. For him, in the 46 years of Pakistan's independence:

   > Urdu has been supported at the rhetorical levels by the ruling elites of Pakistan in order to counter ethno-nationalist sentiment and to increase the power base of the elite. . . . However, English continues to be the official language of Pakistan today, almost as it was at the birth of the country in 1947. (Rahman 1997: 203–204)

2. King (1994: 18) has observed that before the 1860s no Hindi movement existed, although there was a potential for differentiation between Hindi and Urdu. It was during the 1860s that statements identifying Hindi with Hindus and Urdu with Muslims started appearing. The process of developing an awareness of a common identity on the basis of language and religion crystallised into a movement by 1900 and won a major political victory.

REFERENCES

BRASS, PAUL

1974 *Language, religion and politics in North India.* Delhi: Vikas Publishing House.

1991 *Ethnicity and nationalism.* New Delhi: Sage Publications.

DESAI, A.R.

1976 *Social background of Indian nationalism.* Bombay: Popular Prakashan.

DUTTA, RATNA

1974 The process of modernisation: Some structural constraints. In Suren Navlakha (ed.), *Studies in Asian social development.* No. 2. Delhi: Vikas Publishing House.

EDWARDS, JOHN

1985 *Language, society and identity.* Oxford: Basil Blackwell Ltd.

HECHTER, MICHAEL

1975 *Internal colonialism.* Berkeley: University of California Press.

ISAJIW, W.

1980 Definitions of ethnicity. In J. Goldstein & R. Bienvenue (eds.), *Ethnicity and ethnic relations in Canada.* Toronto: Butterworth.

KING, CHRISTOPHER R.

1994 *One language two scripts: The Hindi movement in nineteenth century North India.* Bombay: Oxford University Press.

KUMAR, KRISHNA

1990 Hindu revivalism and education in North-Central India. *Social Scientist,* vol. 18, no. 10, October. 173–95.

LEITIN, DAVID

1992 *Language repertoires and state construction in Africa.* Cambridge: Cambridge University Press.

NEHRU, JAWAHARLAL

1961 *The discovery of India.* Bombay: Asia Publishing House.

RAHMAN, TARIQ

1997 The Urdu-English controversy in Pakistan. *Modern Asian Studies,* 31 (1). 177–207.

ROBINSON, FRANCIS

1975 *Separatism among Indian Muslims: The politics of U.P. Muslims.* London: Cambridge University Press.

SEAL, ANIL

1968 *Emergence of Indian nationalism: Competition and collaboration in the later nineteenth century.* London: Cambridge University Press.

SINGH, YOGENDRA

1973 *Modernisation of Indian tradition.* Delhi: Thomson Press.

15

The politics of linguistic sub-alternity in North India

SELMA K. SONNTAG
Humboldt State University

In the summer of 1993 in the state of Bihar in North India, the Chief Minister of the state suggested introducing the mandatory study of English into the school curriculum. Next door in Uttar Pradesh (UP), the Chief Minister had launched in 1989 an effort to implement a 'banish English' (*Angrezi hatao*) policy in the state administration.

Despite the overt divergence of these policies on the use of English espoused by recent heads of state governments in North India, there is a fundamental convergence underlying them, that of reappropriating vernaculars as part of an anti-elite project. This paper outlines the contours of this anti-elite project by examining the evolution and relation of dominant and subordinate discourses on language in post-colonial North India. My focus will be primarily on articulations regarding the English language and to a lesser extent Urdu, both in their relation to Hindi.

My argument is that although threads of an anti-elite alternative discourse on language have been articulated in North India since the anti-colonial movement earlier this century, these were co-opted or marginalised, through political (opportunistic) alliances, until very recently. The memory of these past alternative discourses inspires the current anti-elite project. The politics of change in North India has finally allowed this alternative discourse to emerge. The moment of linguistic sub-alternity may be upon us. But this alternative discourse itself contains many articulations to the language problem resulting in different overt language policies, such as the policy preferences of Laloo Prasad Yadav compared to those of Mulayam Singh Yadav.

THE ANTI-COLONIAL MOVEMENT

The English language was used by the stellar Indian nationalists in challenging British political power. It provided access to the discourse on liberalism and political democracy. These Western-educated urban professionals, through the Indian National Congress, initiated a dialogue with the British imperial rulers on the illegitimacy of colonial rule. As was the case throughout the colonial world, Western education provided the ideological tools to challenge colonialism within its own paradigm: 'The main lines of an urban middle and professional class critique of colonialism was to grow out of English education itself' (Raina 1991: 286).

But Indians were perhaps unique in that they never let English get 'under their skin' (Dasgupta 1993: 99). According to Chatterjee (1993), Indians maintained an 'inner domain' that was impenetrable by British cultural imperialism. This inner domain was the fountainhead for the cultural renaissance that provided the spiritual endurance for the anti-colonial struggle. The language(s) of this inner domain was/were indigenous common speech. In making this case for Bengal, Chatterjee (1993: 55) notes, '[W]here written prose marked a domain already surrendered to the coloniser, common speech thrived within its zealously guarded zone of autonomy and freedom.'

Chatterjee demonstrates the attraction of this common-speech discourse to the middle-class urban English-speaking professionals. Despite the gap between the poverty-stricken masses and themselves, their desire for affinity, their search for that affinity, through the 'discovery of India', was as important to them as was the anti-colonial agenda. It was Mohandas K. Gandhi who turned the desire into practice. Indeed, Gandhi blamed the gap on English language education: '. . . by reason of English being the medium of instruction. . . we have been isolated from the masses' (quoted in Raina 1991: 284). Gandhi questioned the role of English in challenging British political power: 'Of all the superstitions that affect India, none is so great as that a knowledge of the English language is necessary for imbibing ideas of liberty . . .' (quoted in Raina 1991: 279). In the 1920s Gandhi convinced Congress to organise along regional language lines (Austin 1966: 270–77).

Gandhi was, in essence, privileging an alternative discourse. But there was more than one alternative. While the text of spiritual leaders such as Ramakrishna contained a 'rustic colloquial idiom' (Chatterjee 1993: 51), the

Brahmo and Arya Samajists advocated Sanskritised Hindi as the alternative to English (Das Gupta 1970). Revivalist spiritual organisations (such as the Arya Samaj, Hindu Mahasabha, and RSS in the Hindi heartland) provided the increasingly westernised middle class with a theology that was Hindu yet reformist, furnishing them with their sense of self-hood and nationhood. The language policy of these organisations, the promotion of Hindi, was 'perceived as the symbolic instrument for fighting colonialism and English' (Kumar 1990: 1247). But it was not Gandhi's Hindi. It was a Sanskritised Hindi that was theologically validated by its association with the language (Sanskrit) of Hindu texts. It was class-appropriate as well with the Hindi literati arguing that the commonly spoken Hindi, advocated by Gandhi, was not appropriate for 'serious discourse, as in education and parliament' (Kumar 1990: 1253). It also had a strongly communal element as it sought to distance itself from the Persianised, Urdu-ised vocabulary of common speech. According to Kumar (1990: 1254), 'The struggle for Hindi . . . became a means for upper caste groups, some of whom had substantial landed interest, to establish political identity.' Many joined the Congress, committed to protecting their caste-privileged traditional elite status, perceiving themselves as a counterweight to the English-speaking Nehruvian wing of Congress (McLane 1988: 54, 56; Das Gupta, 1970: 118).

THE MOVEMENT OF INDEPENDENCE

On the eve of independence then, there were at least three positions on the English language: the Nehruvian, the Gandhian, and the revivalist/traditionalist. All three, frequently overlapping, positions were represented in the Congress party, which assumed power upon independence. Both the Gandhian and the revivalist positions perceived English as an impediment to Indian cultural identity and as a tool of British hegemony; indigenous language was a symbol of anti-colonialism. The two positions differed however on the nature of the indigenous language(s). This difference implied a difference in perception of the symbolism of language for class and communalism.

For Gandhi, English was a barrier to equality and the mass mobilisation necessary for the anti-colonial struggle; it reinforced class privilege and status hierarchy. Gandhi's position was 'essentially a revolt against the practices of the [communally] partisan literary elite and the political revivalists' (Das Gupta 1970: 111). In this he made common cause with Nehru, with both Gandhi and Nehru advocating spoken Hindi (Hindustani) over Sanskritised Hindi. For the traditional elite, Sanskritised Hindi was a bulwark against English but would also reinforce the existing status hierarchy, upheld through conservative politics.

With the anti-colonial struggle over, the debate on Hindustani versus Sanskritised Hindi, with its symbolism for class and communal issues, intensified at the political centre, leading to a close vote in the Constituent Assembly adopting Hindi over Hindustani (Austin 1966). In the end, 'Gandhi's pleas for Hindustani proved a straw in the wind' (Kumar 1990: 1253). Not only was Gandhi's alternative discourse on language marginalised at the moment of independence, but his politico-economic discourse was rejected by Nehru himself.

Nehru's advocacy of a modern, industrial society pitted him against Gandhi and the traditional elites. And it had linguistic overtones: 'The ideological tie-up between a secularising modernity and the use of English came to be established during the Nehruvian phase' (Raina 1991: 288). For Nehru, Hindustani was a tool for combating the backward, communally inspired traditional elite on their own terms (and Nehru had lost that battle), but the larger issue was the future of India as a modern, secular polity, and English was the tool to accomplish this. Indeed, he did not seriously join in the Hindi versus Hindustani debate until the battle lines were sharply drawn, and then only to have his irrelevance pointed out by the traditional elites when they mocked his dependence on English (Das Gupta 1970: 163; Austin 1966: 271–74). Nehru and other 'secular-minded political leaders had rather little genuine interest in' Hindi and the Hindutva revivalist symbolism it implied (Kumar 1991: 44). Indeed, Kumar suggests a 'foul contract' was implicitly agreed to by the Nehruvian and revivalist/traditional elites, marginalising the Gandhian alternative discourse in the process.

This 'contract' resulted in what Austin (1966) has called 'the half-hearted compromise': although Hindi (and not Hindustani) would become the official language it would not become the 'national' language and English would continue to have 'associate' official language status for at least fifteen years. Nehru in essence won the battle on English: English was deemed necessary for modernity, for science and technology in the promotion of industrialisation. While indigenous languages were necessary in the mass mobilisation phase of anti-colonialism, the assumption of power meant prioritising English as the language in which to construct a modern state, according to the Nehruvian vision (Kaviraj 1990: 68; Dasgupta 1993: 142; Annamalai 1991: 37).

For Nehru, English increasingly was needed for national unity as well. English was necessary for co-opting the South to participate in the new national project, as was clear from the South Indians' animosity to proposals to adopt

Hindi as the national language in the Constituent Assembly (Austin 1966). Nehru reassured the South Indians in 1960 that English would retain its status as associate official language as long as the South desired. The South's anxiety over the sincerity of this promise after Nehru's death led to the 1965 language riots in Tamil Nadu as the fifteen-year transition period for retaining English as associate official language drew near. For the youth in Tamil Nadu who led the riots, English was a ticket for coveted central government jobs, jobs geared towards building Nehru's modern, secular, industrialised, and English-speaking polity.

Nehru's perception of English as 'national cement' provided his fall-back position as he grew increasingly worried about the fissiparous tendencies that would be unleashed by a linguistic re-organisation of the states, a re-organisation that had been promised by the Congress since the 1920s (Geertz 1973: 255–56; Raina 1991: 287). Nehru 'suspect[ed] the Indian languages of harbouring populism and sentiment as their natural element' (Dasgupta 1993: 168); '[A]nybody who show[ed] greater familiarity or attraction to the vernacular [was] immediately suspected of things that would ultimately slide into secessionist tendencies of various types' (Kaviraj 1990: 69). Although the States Reorganisation Act of 1956 began the process of redrawing state boundaries along language lines, the rejection of an alternative discourse on language had been solidified among the Nehruvian elite.

THE LANGUAGE POLITICS OF RAMMANOHAR LOHIA

There was one politician who voiced an alternative discourse on language repeatedly in the late fifties through the mid-sixties. This was Rammanohar Lohia, leader of the socialist party in its various avatars during this period. Lohia wrote extensively on the language issue, calling for the banning of English. He viewed English as a barrier to class equality, to democratisation, to economic development for the poor. He called on socialists to organise committees and conferences on the *Angrezi hatao* (remove/banish English) issue, and to deface English signs in North India. But he was clear that 'the chief aim of our movement should be removal of English and not the establishment of Hindi' (Lohia 1966: 6–7). He complained that '[O]rthodox pundits with their high-flown Sanskritised Hindi and Bengali are doing a great harm to the cause of their languages. The Hindi of our newspapers is becoming more and more unintelligible' (Lohia 1966: 16). He himself 'had his own style of writing and speaking Hindi, which was very simple and direct' (Mishra and Pandey: 1992: 53).

Although Lohia was clearly for the use of the spoken variety of Hindi, that is, Hindustani, in government and schools in North India and opposed to the communal tendency of those advocating Sanskritised Hindi, he was obsessed with opposing Congress and Nehru in particular and hence prioritised banishing English over elevation of the language(s) of the have-nots. Lohia 'had dedicated himself, with an amazing singleness of purpose, to the task of destroying Congress rule' (Limaye 1988: 169, 139). This led him in the 1960s to seek electoral alliances and coalition partners with other non-Congress parties, including the Jana Sangh, a Hindu nationalist party with strong communalist overtones that had formed in the early 1950s as the traditionalists lost out to the Nehruvians within Congress (Graham 1993).

The Jana Sangh espoused Sanskritised Hindi as the national language. Just as the traditionalists and the Nehruvians had a 'foul contract' that marginalised an alternative discourse on language. Lohia contracted with the Jana Sanghis against the Nehruvian Congress, marginalising his own alternative discourse. The Lohia-Jana Sangh contract was temporary and for purely electoral purposes, compared to the deeper cultural implications of the Nehruvian-revivalist 'foul contract' that, according to Krishna Kumar, remain today.

Nevertheless, I would argue that even an ephemeral electoral alliance between Lohia-ties and the Jana Sanghis aided in the marginalisation of Lohia's alternative discourse on language. Exemplary of this loss of prominence of Lohia's alternative discourse were the language policies of the state government of Bihar in the late 1960s. This government, resulting from the 1967 election, which was the first to chip away at the dominance of the Congress, was a broad-based coalition, with socialists predominating but including the Jana Sanghis. The education minister and deputy chief minister of the government, Karpoori Thakur, a disciple of Lohia, banished compulsory English from the school curriculum. But when the government moved to recognise Urdu as a second official language in the state, second to (Sanskritised) Hindi, and thus implicitly to 're-appropriate' Hindi by legitimising Hindustani, communal riots, allegedly fomented by the Jana Sangh, erupted, resulting in the death of close to 200 people (Sonntag 1996: 4). The policy regarding Urdu was abandoned. By the end of the decade, Lohia had died, the non-Congress governments in the North Indian states had fallen, and Indira Gandhi was beginning to consolidate her power in the Congress and the country.

THE INDIRA-RAJIV DYNASTY

By the early 1970s, Indira Gandhi had adopted populist rhetoric and a centralising, authoritarian style of rule. The epitome of her ruling style was the Emergency she declared in June 1975, lasting until 1977. Her return to power in 1980 and the prime ministership of her son, Rajiv, from 1984 to 1989, continued the pattern of strong central control with chief ministers in states of the Union having no independent base for power or policy-making (including language policy) (Sonntag 1996: 4–5). Rajiv didn't quite have the touch of his mother and his attempt to copycat her strong centralisation resulted in floundering on policy initiatives. To compensate, he increasingly invoked the 'foul contract' of his grandfather and played the communal card, hoping to shore up Hindutva support. In urban areas, his communal rhetoric struck a chord with aspiring entrants into the burgeoning middle class. He changed his mother's populist rhetoric to yuppie rhetoric, appealing to young technocrats (as he was himself). And of course English was and is the symbol and language of this class (Sheth 1990). It was also the language of the Centre and centralisation; Rajiv 'condemned linguistic states as the greatest blunder of free India' (Puri 1990: 705).

Despite Indira Gandhi's authoritarian policies, alternative discourses didn't disappear, but indeed flourished in a blooming of new social movements in the early 1970s (Omvedt 1993). With experimentation and alternatives cut off in the political sphere, civil society picked up the slack. The epitome of this efflorescence was the JP (Jayaprakash) movement against Indira Gandhi's increasingly amoral and corrupt politics. The movement started in Gujarat and then was transported to Bihar by Jayaprakash Narayan himself, an old socialist and former colleague of Lohia. The success of this movement in mobilising students was viewed as a serious threat by Indira Gandhi and was one of the factors leading her to declare the Emergency. Although the JP movement and the other new social movements that Omvedt discusses did not have an explicit language component, it was in these movements that the regional politicians of the 1990s, who did speak an alternative discourse on language, got their feet wet.

The traditionalist/revivalist/Hindutva discourse on language was audible during all this as well, particularly in the late 1970s when the Janata party came to power at the Centre upon the defeat of Congress (Indira) in the elections at the end of the Emergency. The Janata party was made up of basically the same coalition that Lohia had helped forge in the North Indian states in the late 1960s – that is, socialists, Jana Sanghis, dissident Congress and representatives of the backward-caste middle peasantry of North India. The prime minister was Morarji Desai, a former Congressman in the mould of the traditionalists.

Again, because of the Jana Sangh component, the non-Congress government advocated Sanskritised Hindi; however, it had to contend with a powerful reaction from the South, something the coalition governments of the Northern states did not have to confront. Because of this and the intense in-fighting within the coalition, the rhetoric on language was never implemented by the Janata government (Sonntag 1995: 103–104). Indeed, once in power, the Janata ministers slipped into using the language of power, English (Limaye 1988: 184), although Atal Behari Vajpayee, who was foreign minister in the Janata government, is remembered for addressing the UN General Assembly in Hindi.

THE YADAV MOVEMENT IN UTTAR PRADESH AND BIHAR

By the end of the 1980s and Rajiv Gandhi's tenure as prime minister, the political dominance of the Congress had deeply eroded, particularly in North India. In late 1989, Rajiv's Congress lost in the general elections. His former finance and defence minister, V.P. Singh, as leader of a new party, the Janata Dal, became the new prime minister. Although V.P. Singh himself was an upper-caste Hindu royal scion and had been politically dependent on Indira Gandhi in the early 1980s (Sonntag 1996: 4–5), he now appealed to the lower-caste, middle peasantry who had been transformed into small-time (capitalist) farmers as a result of the Green Revolution and the land reforms in the 1950s and 1960s. These were the same constituents to whom Lohia had appealed, but by the 1980s their economic gains had translated into increasing political sophistication and a desire for political power. The largest among these 'backward castes' in Bihar and Uttar Pradesh is the Yadav caste. In 1989, Mulayam Singh Yadav became chief minister of Uttar Pradesh; in the spring of 1990 Laloo Prasad Yadav became chief minister of Bihar. Both were allied with the V.P. Singh government in New Delhi.

The V.P. Singh government lasted less than a year. There were two primary causes for the fall of his minority government, both of which clearly illustrate the nature of the changing politics on the Gangetic Plains, indicating a maturing of the constituency that Lohia had nurtured in the 1960s. The first was V.P. Singh's attempt in the summer of 1990 to dust off the Mandal Commission report. This report, written a decade earlier and then shelved, recommended extending the reservations policy beyond Scheduled Castes and Scheduled Tribes to include OBCs (Other Backward Classes), for example, Yadavs and other rural 'bullock capitalists' (as Rudolph and Hoeber 1987 call them). Upper-caste youths reacted violently and tragically to what they perceived as a policy allocating fewer university seats and government jobs for open competition, in which they were advantaged. Dozens of them engaged in self-immolation in protest. V.P. Singh backed off from implementing the Mandal Commission report.

The final straw that led to the fall of the V.P. Singh government was the withdrawal of support by the BJP (the successor to the Jana Sangh), support that was necessary for Singh's minority government. The BJP withdrew its support because V.P. Singh, through Laloo Prasad Yadav, had the leader of the BJP arrested. At the time of his arrest, the BJP leader, L.K. Advani, was in Bihar in his motorised van decorated to look like Lord Ram's mythical chariot on his way to the Babri Masjid (a sixteenth-century mosque) in Ayodhya, UP, the alleged birthplace of Lord Ram. This 'rath yatra' or chariot ride was infamously successful at rousing anti-Muslim fanaticism. V.P. Singh and Laloo Prasad Yadav decided to put a stop to it (although they succeeded in doing so only temporarily).

Although the V.P. Singh government at the Centre was short-lived, the Yadav chief ministers continued, uninterruptedly in Bihar and intermittently in UP. Like his counterpart in Bihar, the chief minister in UP, Mulayam Singh Yadav, enacted policies and conducted politics strongly indicating his anti-BJP, pro-backward caste sympathies. The 'Yadav movement' is as anti-communal as it is anti-upper caste. It also has a linguistic component:

> Social groups and formations that began to register a political and economic presence in the sixties (and emerged into leaderships – with the franchise of 1989) seem to retain in potent measure critical and conceptual links with [M.K.] Gandhi and Lohia. Such leaderships which speak for a new resurgent rural elite are beginning to critique, from all accounts along a secular politics, the linkages between a dominant English-knowing urban middle class and developmental hypotheses which have, over the last four decades, fattened the metropolitan sectors at the expense of the vast countryside. In that critique, once again, the English language and English education are perceived to be key determinants of a comprehensive historical oppression. Thus, in the strategic states of Uttar Pradesh and Bihar, Hindi protagonism seems to re-emerge not as a communal or entirely provincial phenomenon, but essentially as a second anti-colonial movement. (Raina 1991: 293)

While I agree with Raina that the politics of change in post-colonial North India suggest the moment of arrival for a more radical politics, a politics of sub-alternity or 'second anti-colonial movement', his analysis cannot explain why in Uttar Pradesh Lohia's banished English has been turned into a policy by Mulayam Singh Yadav (and supported by the BJP state government in between Mulayam Singh Yadav's two stints as chief minister), while Laloo Prasad Yadav has pushed for the re-introduction of compulsory English in the school curriculum in Bihar (albeit unsuccessfully so far). Elsewhere (Sonntag 1996) I have tried to explain this difference in political terms: while both Mulayam Singh Yadav and Laloo Prasad Yadav appeal to the same constituencies, that is, backward castes, particularly Yadavs, along with Muslims and Dalits, Laloo Prasad Yadav's consolidation of this support base and hence of political power is much further along than Mulayam Singh Yadav's. In other words, political competition in Uttar Pradesh has been much fiercer in recent years than it has in Bihar. Laloo Prasad Yadav can relax more and suggest non-populist policies, such as the re-introduction of English for school matriculation.

Yet this political explanation fails to suggest a commonality in the language politics agenda of Mulayam Singh Yadav and Laloo Prasad Yadav, a commonality that must exist if both are a part of a 'second anti-colonial movement'. This commonality is easy to miss if one defines the battle as pro-English versus anti-English. There are more than two sides, a point on which Lohia failed to follow through. The anti-Sanskritised Hindi (writ large, anti-communal) agenda is just as important to the politics of sub-alternity as the anti-English agenda. It is the inner domain that Partha Chatterjee describes which must talk the politics of sub-alternity, in the language of the Ramakrishnas, not the Arya Samajists. In other words, the language policies of Mulayam Singh Yadav and Laloo Prasad Yadav must be policies validating common speech, rather than being just anti-English, to be part of an anti-elite project – for 'post-1947 Hindi cannot be considered a "popular national language" versus the "elite national language" English. Rather they represent two different elites' (Orsini 1995: 58).

Laloo Prasad Yadav's image is one of a common man, a 'rustic buffoon' to some, who shows up at IMF headquarters in Washington, D.C. in a dhoti looking for a spittoon for his mouthful of *paan*. He speaks colloquially, lacing his Hindustani with Bhojpuri (his mother tongue, officially designated as a dialect of Hindi). This makes him popular, and demonstrates his political astuteness: he 'gave impetus to the backward class movement by his perfect use of the language of the poor, Dalits and slum-dwellers in his speeches' (Verma 1993). Why, then, would Laloo Prasad Yadav embrace English, the symbol of the upper class elite, puzzled his colleagues (Verma 1993)? He's not embracing English, he's hijacking it, suggests a young Indian sociolinguist:

> Like gunboat diplomacy, in the hands of a few English helps maintain a kind of balance that will be destroyed if the instrument passes over to those who have kept beyond its reach so far.
>
> By wanting to hand over the instrument to the backward castes or the local people, Laloo Prasad Yadav has in fact attempted piracy. (Agarwal 1993)

Laloo Prasad Yadav is, in effect, shifting the parameters of the discourse on language in North India. For Laloo Prasad Yadav and his supporters on his English language policy, the debate on language needs to be indigenised, just as the English language itself has been indigenised in India according to Kachru (1983) and others. It is also being de-colonised: by claiming to appropriate English for the masses, the 'other' for Laloo Prasad Yadav is not the British colonialists but rather his political opponents. An example of this 'shifting' of the parameters of discourse, this new 'othering', is the following statement made in support of Laloo Prasad Yadav's proposal: 'Those who are opposed to English would naturally be treated as persons opposed to the very concept of reservation' (Yadav 1993). According to this statement, anti-English language equals anti-Laloo Prasad Yadav equals anti-reservations equals anti-OBCs and -Dalits.

There is nothing in this statement that equates English with the coloniser, although opponents to Laloo Prasad Yadav's proposal within his own party did invoke such past imaginings by proclaiming that 'Hindi is our mother while English is a beautiful prostitute' (Lal 1993). For them, English remained an instrument of colonialism and subjugation, and class privilege. Some of them wove in the traditional/communalist threat into their anti-English arguments: the chief minister was reminded not only of indebtedness to Mohandas K. Gandhi, Rammanohar Lohia, Jayaprakash Narayan and Karpoori Thakur, but also to Purushottam Das Tandon and Madan Mohan Malviya, the latter two being the epitome of the revivalist/traditionalist elites in favour of Sanskritised Hindi (Verma 1993). Others, equally opposed to Laloo Prasad Yadav's proposal, did however recognise the importance of 'liberat[ing] Hindi from the anti-Urdu and anti-Muslim agenda of revivalist politicians' (Kumar 1991: 46) and blamed Rajiv's renewal of the 'foul contract': it was ' "English culture" [that] was responsible for the demolition of the Babri Masjid as well as continuation of casteism in society' (Verma 1993). In the end, the chief minister was forced to back down from his proposal by members of his own administration and party.

The irony is that the revivalists/traditionalists (called communalists today) are both for and against English, both part of and opposed to an alternative discourse on language to the Nehruvian discourse as enunciated more recently by Rajiv Gandhi. The BJP opposed Laloo Prasad Yadav's proposal while the Bihar Congress supported it. Yet the BJP leader Advani, recognising the BJP's appeal to the urban-caste middle class, admonishes the 'Banish English' advocates within his party (Sonntag 1996: 11). Confusion is likewise apparent in linking the language issue to the reservations (preferential treatment) issue. Laloo Prasad Yadav was warned by one of his Janata Dal colleagues that those who were pushing for re-introducing English in the school curriculum were opposed to the extension of the reservations policy and 'have been at work since the very beginning to suppress the movement for the uplift of Sudras and Dalits' (Verma 1993). Another of his colleagues issued the opposite warning: 'Those who are opposed to English would naturally be treated as persons opposed to the very concept of reservation' (Yadav 1993). Indeed, there is evidence supporting both contentions among today's revivalists, the BJP (Sonntag 1996: 18).

THE CURRENT POLITICAL MOVEMENT

Thus, an alternative politics, a politics of linguistic sub-alternity, entails more than a mechanical anti-English, pro-Hindi plan does. Indeed, 'language planning' in North India is far from being a technical, rational, apolitical activity, despite the Nehruvian propensity towards such planning. Instead, language planning in North India is a function of elite competition (whether it is Nehru versus Tandon in the 1950s or the Yadav movement in the 1990s), and political rhetoric tapping India's inner domain (whether by the revivalists or the Yadavists). The result is a messy plan, differing from state to state to Centre. And it is intensely political.

I do not want to suggest that the politics of linguistic sub-alternity is moral or ideal. For example, while illiteracy and infant mortality have decreased under Laloo Prasad Yadav's administration (Prasad, 1995), corruption and sycophancy are widespread, as the recent animal husbandry scandal and the textbook escapade (*Indian Express*, 1994) suggest. Indeed, Laloo Prasad's administration may not even qualify as an alternative in any structural sense: Hauser (1996) has suggested that the Bihar chief minister lacks the ability to even conceive of structural change, let alone implement it. In Uttar Pradesh, the second Mulayam Singh Yadav government, which was a coalition between Yadav's Samajwadi party and the Dalit BSP, fell after internal bickering, only to have the BSP form a short-lived government on its own – with support from the BJP! In North India, politics is not moral, it is democratic: 'The elite conflict illustrated by the language debate is an outgrowth of the democratic process of politics' (Sheth 1990: 35). Rural-based backward castes, frequently in alliance with Muslims and Dalits, are challenging the English-speaking Nehruvian urban-based elite and attempting to sideline the communally inspired upper-caste Hindutva elite in the process. It is a conflict between what Sheth calls the 'vernacular elite', the English-speaking elite, and the Sanskritised Hindi elite.

That the newly emerging vernacular elite is winning in the current round of competition is apparent from the outcome of the recent general election. The Congress party, widely regarded as the bastion of the English-speaking urban professional elites, lost significantly. The BJP, representing the upper-caste Hindutva (communalist/revivalist) elite, emerged as the largest party and attempted to form a government. Vajpayee, the BJP Prime Minister, took his oath in Hindi rather than English, as was the tradition among the Nehruvian elite, while other BJP MPs took the oath in Sanskrit. But the BJP could find few coalition partners and lasted in office for less than two weeks, with Vajpayee resigning rather than facing a vote of confidence he was sure to lose.

The new government is a leftist coalition ranging from Laloo Prasad Yadav's Janata Dal to Mulayam Singh Yadav's Samajwadi Party to regional parties (for example, in Tamil Nadu, Assam, and Andhra Pradesh) to dissident Congressmen (for example, the new finance minister's party broke from Congress shortly before the election). One of the two Indian Communist parties joined the governing coalition, while the other is supporting it without joining. The defeated Congress party is also supporting the new government. It is, in essence, an anti-BJP alliance. The new Prime Minister, Deve Gowda, is from Karnataka, comes from backward caste peasant background, and speaks very little Hindi. The new defence minister is Mulayam Singh Yadav, the Banish English warrior from UP, whose English is limited. Apparently cabinet meetings are difficult linguistically, with Mulayam Singh Yadav not able to communicate with Gowda in English and Gowda unable to communicate in Hindi. Gowda has agreed to try to improve his Hindi (Adam 1996).

Even the seamier side of the politics of change in North India is running into linguistic difficulties. One of the coalition supporters is the JMM, Jharkhand Mukti Morcha, a party based in the Jharkhand tribal area of south Bihar along the border with Orissa and West Bengal. The JMM and other Jharkhandi parties have engaged in the politics of resistance in their attempts to win social justice for the tribals. But they play politics as well. One JMM MP, not long before the election, went public with the accusation that Congress PM Narasimha Rao had, through an intermediary, bribed him to vote against a no-confidence vote that the opposition had organised. His public statement regarding this bribe was released by the BJP to whom he had defected. He subsequently rescinded his defection, claiming that the BJP had bribed him to make this false accusation against the Prime Minister. As the plot thickened and this JMM MP looked sleazier and sleazier, he mounted his defence: 'I didn't sign it [the BJP-released statement alleging the bribe]. It was in English. I do not know what it said' (*India Today*, 1996). One can bemoan a political system that not only condones, but also seems to encourage, such corruption. Or one can celebrate the fact that it is credible that a non-English-speaking tribal would be bribed – that is, he is part of the political process, however seamy, not excluded from it.

The political centre is shifting in India. This change at the Centre was possible because of changes at the state levels in North India in the last several years, represented by the chief ministerships of Laloo Prasad Yadav in Bihar and Mulayam Singh Yadav in UP. Although their overt language policy preferences regarding English differ, they represent a new politics of linguistic subalternity.

REFERENCES

ADAM, SUNIL

1996 Stars appear to dictate Gowda's first week in office. *India Abroad* (Los Angeles), 14 June. 8.

AGARWAL, KAILASH S.

1993 English, Laloo: A Bihari story. *The Independent* (Bombay), 23 September.

ANNAMALAI, E.

1991 Satan and Saraswati: The double face of English in India. *South Asian Language Review*, vol. 1, no. 1. 33–43.

AUSTIN, GRANVILLE

1966 *The Indian Constitution: Cornerstone of a nation*. Bombay: Oxford University Press.

CHATTERJEE, PARTHA

1993 *The nation and its fragments*. Princeton: Princeton University Press.

DAS GUPTA, JYOTIRINDRA

1970 *Language conflict and national development*. Berkeley: University of California Press.

DASGUPTA, PROBAL

1993 *The otherness of English: India's auntie tongue syndrome*. New Delhi: Sage Publications.

GEERTZ, CLIFFORD

1973 *The interpretation of cultures*. New York: Basic Books.

GRAHAM, BRUCE

1993 *Hindu nationalism and Indian politics*. New York: Cambridge University Press.

HAUSER, WALTER

1996 Peasant surprise. *The Telegraph* (Calcutta), 21 May. 8.

INDIAN EXPRESS (NEW DELHI)

1994 Laloo's good books. 23 January. 3.

Pro-Laloo author put under arrest. 24 January. 1.

Pro-Laloo author denies arrest. 25 January. 9.

INDIA TODAY
1996 Voices. North American Social Edition, 31 March.

KACHRU, BRAJ
1983 *The Indianisation of English: The English language in India*. New Delhi: Oxford University Press.

KAVIRAJ, SUDIPTA
1990 Capitalism and the cultural process. *Journal of Arts and Ideas*, vol. 19. 61–75.

KUMAR, KRISHNA
1990 Quest for self-identity. *Economic and Political Weekly*, 9 June. 1247–55.
1991 Foul contract. *Seminar*, January, no. 377. 43–6.

LAL, BISHWANATH
1993 English stokes row in Bihar. *Tribune* (Chandigarh), 23 September.

LIMAYE, MADHU
1988 *Birth of non-Congressism*. Delhi: B.R. Publishing Corporation.

LOHIA, RAMMANOHAR
1966 *Language*. Hyderabad: Navakind.

MCLANE, JOHN R.
1988 The early Congress, Hindu populism, and the wider society. In Richard Sisson & Stanley Wolpert (eds.), *Congress and Indian nationalism*. Berkeley: University of California Press. 47–61.

MISHRA, GIRISH and BRAJ KUMAR PANDEY
1992 *Rammanohar Lohia: The man and his Ism*. New Delhi: Eastern Books.

OMVEDT, GAIL
1993 *Reinventing revolution: New social movements and the socialist tradition in India*. Armonk, New York: M.E. Sharpe.

ORSINI, FRANCESCA
1995 Why Tulsi? *Seminar*, August, no. 432.

PRASAD, BINOY
1995 "Laloo does it!" Consolidation of backward class leadership in Bihar: An analysis of 1995 election to the State Legislature. Paper presentation at the 24th Annual Conference on South Asia, 20–22 October. Madison, Wisconsin.

PURI, BALRAJ
1990 Politics of ethnic and communal identities. *Economic and Political Weekly*, April 7. 703–5.

RAINA, BADRI
1991 A note on language, and the politics of English in India. In Svati Joshi (ed.), *Rethinking English*. New Delhi: Trianka. 264–97.

RUDOLPH, LLOYD I. and SUSANNE HOEBER
1987 *In pursuit of Lakshmi*. Chicago: Chicago University Press.

SHETH, D.L.
1990 No English please, we're Indian. *The Illustrated Weekly of India*, 19 August. 34–7.

SONNTAG, SELMA K.

1995 Elite competition and official language movements. In James W. Tollefson (ed.), *Power and inequality in language education.* New York: Cambridge University Press. 91–111.

1996 The political saliency of language in Bihar and Uttar Pradesh. *The Journal of Commonwealth & Comparative Politics*, vol. 34, no. 2. 1–18.

VERMA, NALIN

1993 English or no English, controversy rages. *The Hindustan Times* (Patna), 17 August. 7.

YADAV, RANJAN

1993 An essential knowledge. *The Hindustan Times* (Patna), 15 August (Sunday Magazine). 11.

16
Cross-cultural discourse in world Englishes

TAMARA M. VALENTINE
University of South Carolina

English has become the language of the global village. The spread of English through new technologies of communication, joint enterprises, international teams and companies, immigration patterns, and strategies of language planning compounded with the existing widespread use of English in all domains of internationalism and intra-nationalism have elevated English to what Pennycook (1995) calls the 'worldliness' of English, 'in the sense of being in the world and worldliness in the sense of being global'. Inextricably bound up with the world, English is associated with all global changes and shifts. As suggested by one unnamed linguist, the UN should simply declare English the world language and rename it 'Globalese' (Nunberg 1996).

As a result, we are looking at a new and different world from that of the past, especially in the way of studying cross-cultural and intercultural communication. One assumption has been that the great diversity of languages world wide is a barrier to communication and development, and if all speakers learn the same common language, communication would be successful and world peace and goodwill would prevail across the globe. Of course, we know that linguistic equality is unachievable. Language and society are intertwined, each shaped by the forces of education, kinship, gender, status, and ethnicity to name a few factors impacting on its speakers in different ways depending on the situation. As a result, cultures demonstrate varying degrees of interactional styles, which lead to different pragmatic behaviours and interpretations.

Scholars show that within the context of cross-cultural communication, the most subtle linguistic cues ranging from the placement of stress, to the rhetorical structure of argument, to styles of involvement, can differ not only between language varieties but between varieties of the same language as well.

Moreover, how these cues are interpreted can differ with results of misevaluation and misjudgement between participants. And using a common language whether it is English, Esperanto, or Globalese does not necessarily guarantee successful communication between speakers nor that the speakers will share the same discourse strategies and the same cultural assumptions and expectations about what is or is not appropriate language behaviour. 'Language represents the deepest manifestation of a culture, and people's value systems . . . play a substantial role in the way they use not only their first language(s) but also subsequently acquired ones.' (Clyne 1994: 1)

MODELS AND APPROACHES

Cross-cultural variation in discourse has been approached from a number of directions: the *Contrastive Approach* contrasts native discourse across cultures; the *Interactional Approach* focuses on the interaction and speech activity between and among native and non-native cultures which lead to miscommunication (Gumperz 1982, 1992; Tannen 1986); the *Interlanguage Pragmatic Approach* examines discourse of non-native speakers in a second language (Kasper and Blum-Kulka 1993); and the *Intercultural Approach* compares the discourse of speakers from different cultural and linguistic backgrounds interacting in a common language (lingua franca) (Clyne 1994; Clyne, Ball and Neil 1991).

Many of these studies show that pragmatic transference of rules for conversation, speech acts and other conventions from one language to another occurs in ways similar to other linguistic transference (lexical, phonological, syntactic). These pragmatic rules vary according to culture. A rule may exist in one language but not in another, structures used for one speech act may be realised differently in different languages, two opposing structures in different languages may be used for one speech act, and certain speech acts may vary in weight across cultures. These rules can be categorised into two main areas: one set of rules which express broad aspects and the core values of a culture consequently defining a speech community and its members based on the notion of cultural appropriateness; and one set of rules more specific to ways of speaking and discoursal patterns within the culture. The diversity of discourse patterns and the expectations of discourse are directly related to the general cultural parameters.

Many general cultural models comparing cultural values and linguistic styles have been proposed. As discussed in Michael Clyne (1994), Geert Hofstede (1991) proposes four general cultural parameters to research differences in cultural value systems: power distance, individualism versus collectivism, masculinity versus femininity, and uncertainty avoidance. Clyne summarises these contrasts, proposing that Western-English-speaking cultures share a low power distance (support of interdependence and social equality), a low uncertainty avoidance (acceptance of dissent and few rules), high individualism, and a middle index on masculinity (aggressive versus compassionate, competitive versus friendly behaviour); in contrast, South Asian cultures share a high power distance (acceptance of social inequality, and conflict between the powerful and the powerless), a high uncertainty avoidance (low risk-taking, rigidity and dogmatism, reduction of ambiguity, dependence on experts, and authority), low individualism (high collectivism, identity based on the social system, attachment to duty, expertness, and prestige) and a middle index on masculinity.

Robin Lakoff (1990) suggests three cultural strategies of *distance, deference, and camaraderie* among cultures. Distance cultures such as European and American cultures are speaker-based, placing emphasis on formality, explicitness, impersonalness, and equality; deferential cultures such as Asian cultures are hearer-based, valuing uncertainty, indecision, and ambiguity; and camaraderie cultures assume total involvement, understanding, and empathy.

Edward T. Hall and Mildred Hall (1990) propose a model of cultural communications organising cultures in terms of context, time, space, and information flow. South Asian cultures are identified as high-context and polychronistic; acting within an expansive, highly cohesive, involved network system, a speaker draws information from within the person and his/her surroundings and accepts simultaneous occurrences of events. In contrast, the American culture is identified as low context and monochronistic. Speakers act in a restricted network; information is code-dependent and explicitly provided; and time is experienced and used linearly.

And A.K. Ramanujan (1989: 47) proposes an interesting model whereby he contends that cultures 'have overall tendencies – tendencies to idealise, and think in terms of, either the context-free or the context-sensitive kind of rules'. He argues that traditional cultures such as India are bound and ruled by context sensitivity whereas the Western cultures are context-free. He views the Indian culture as a series of concentric circles nesting one within the next, each circle contextualising the next. Something only has meaning when placed in a context of something else, which only has meaning when placed in a context of something else; each circle continually interacts with one another.

Based on these general cultural models I will show that these value dimensions can account for differing equally valid communicative styles between the cultures of Indian English and Western English speakers. Only by understanding the general cultural structures that underlie a culture can the message be appropriately understood. It is a linguist's job to examine language in action to discover the parameters in which discourse is used and understood in communication and the interactional rules, which produce what seem like orderly features in conversation. The strength of the general cultural notions leads me to believe that the communicative styles will always differ.

DISCUSSION OF INDIAN ENGLISH DATA

A series of different conversations from actual spoken interactions in English between South Asian and Western speakers will be provided to illustrate two differing communicative styles – Indian English and Western English. First, I will draw attention to five interactional strategies which make the two conversational styles different from each other:

1. strategies of saving face: softening disagreements;
2. coherence and cohesive structures;
3. prosody: high pitch patterns;
4. turn expansion by repetition, syntactic parallelism, and elaboration; and
5. interruptions.

   Then I will focus on these two communicative styles in intercultural conversations.

Saving face

The notion of face and face wants has been central to speech act research and cross-cultural pragmatics. In each culture, speakers are sensitive to the rights of others according to their cultural notion of 'polite linguistic behaviour'.

In Indian English discourse, the kinds of face needs (losing, saving, and strengthening face) can be different. Acts such as agreeing, reporting, and informing are perceived as non-face threatening, whereas disagreeing, directing, and arguing threaten face. In a hearer-based culture such as India, the more indirect, digressive, or ambiguous the speaker is the more options the addressee has for not agreeing or performing the intended action. When, however, a speaker wants to show opposition to another's view, the disagreement is often softened with face-saving measures: politeness forms, apologies, honorifics, and hedges – linguistic reflections of the cultural values of low individuality and high uncertainty – values which reflect 'the bad taste of face threatening acts'. (Clyne 1994: 190)

Example I is an English conversation among five Indian adults: four men (speakers A, B, C, and D) and one woman (speaker R) at a management training institute in New Delhi. The entire conversation is over ninety minutes long; this particular chunk is well into twenty minutes or so of the conversation. The discussion deals with the subject matter of family responsibilities of men and women in India. (See the Appendix for a description of the symbols used in the examples.)

EXAMPLE I

R: What do you think? Because you acknowledged that when you come home the food is there. Right?
D: +y' see,/I'm not saying
B: /that your wife/
D: individuals and all that but generally that is the situation. —>See, maybe I'm not correct you can correct me but that is the situation that generally I see. Most often.
B: Generalising this would be rather difficult because experience would be different from person to person=
D: =that's what I say
B: I favour to talk from my own experience. I will say it's fifty-fifty anything that y' know you can talk of the domestic issues, or the matter of sharing responsibility, the matter of taking decisions, it's all very jointly done=
A: =it's jointly y'see
D: +>ne decisions, that's what I said, responsibility and decision making are two different things. Decision-making is what? Decision-making you sit together and make a decision okay we'll do it. [But the question is of sharing the workload]
B: +[no, no, I'll elaborate on it the responsibility, for instance I go home and let's say my wife is not well or she needs a hand, —well, I'll give my hand y'know in the matter of cooking y'know, assisting her in the kitchen and going to the shop, getting vegetables, or taking children out, or sitting with them. . . .
R: But if she doesn't need your assistance do you offer it? Would you say=

B: =+Well earlier y'know this is a matter of my own responsibility and other things y'know which come into your life —like y'know the children's education, the office, y'know certain things you carry home which you can't do at office have changed things a little bit. So, five six years ago, <I would volunteered y'know like I would just go in and say, "Can I do this for you" and things like that. +Now I don't think it's that way any longer. But, if she asks me "Can you just come in? Gimme a hand" and all that well, I do it. But [normal not readily forthcoming].
A: [but then over time]
[laugh]
A: [then over a period]
C: but, then another another issue, Ramesh. Suppose you are running a temperature of [ninety and hundred]
B: [But, then, but then, uh?]
C: and low grade temperature of ninety and hundred and if your wife is running a same temperature suppose between the two I will say wife will still manage with the household job and you will lie on a bed. That is
B: /agreed/ +But, no, no, no the point, +Ashok let me say here
C: /no I making/[this is what I have]
B: [you're not well and you have work to do in office and you come to the office and do your work
R: [what do you see is your area?]
B: So, it's a question of you have division of roles y'know, responsi bilities and this office work no matter y'know what, how inconvenienced you are, and you not well whatever you come in and do the job. And, similarly at home well she takes care y'know more responsibility on
A: then over a period of time, the role of women in the house and the man has also changed. Idea we had joint family system and in case one lady of the family not the housewife is sick then other ladies are taking care, so the role of gents were less . . .

In Example I, speaker R asks speaker D the question: *What do you think?* (line 1) referring to one's responsibilities in India. As I have found to be common in my earlier work (Valentine 1988, 1991, 1995), Indian speakers do not directly answer questions. Speaker D in lines 3–7, does not directly reply to R's question. Instead, D counters R's question by what appears to be a negating statement: 'I'm not saying' (line 3), then playing down his position to lessen the impact of his argument; he says: 'See, maybe I'm not correct you can correct me' (lines 5–6). This face-saving strategy is apparent later on in the conversation as well. In line 25, B does not answer R's query. And from line 36 on, after speaker C presents a sexist scenario which speaker B fits, speaker B first hedges, expressing direct agreement 'agreed', then utters 'But no no no' (line 42). As I've shown elsewhere, in Indian English, agreement components can occur as disagreement prefaces and vice versa. What appears to be happening is that Indian English speakers work very hard to support face by agreeing so as not to risk threatening face by disagreeing; they go to the trouble of redirecting their position and softening earlier threatening statements. According to Clyne (1994), such forms of politeness are demonstrated in cultures with collective thought where emphasis is on harmony, modesty, and restraint.

Coherence

Many papers contrasting written discourse in Indian languages indicate that written texts show a greater tolerance for digression in paragraphing, spiral-like structuring, and circular argument (Kachru 1983, 1985; Pandharipande 1983). In Indian English spoken discourse, too, speakers show a non-linear development of ideas not only within turns but across turns. Contributing to this digressive conversational behaviour are markers that work at the discoursal level in English. Within turns, connectors such as *and, but, or, so, then,* and *well* work to create a cohesive link between parts within the text. They do not necessarily impart meaning to the content but express an involvement of the speaker with the topic and audience. According to Deborah Schiffrin's (1987) model of English discourse markers, such elements are used to show sequential dependency, that is, they relate syntactic units into a coherent discourse context. In the discourse of Indian English speakers, however, these elements, which frequently occur in sustained, informal talk, function as more than clause co-ordinators, temporal adverbs, or syntactic cues. Used in a different way, these markers take on a more pragmatic effect indicating upcoming utterances, continued action, and a joining of ideas, hence a lengthier turn. The Indian English speaker in Example II discusses the topic of change (in boldface) in the Indian social system; she uses eleven instances of connectors (italicised) in ten sentences.

EXAMPLE II

1 A: *So,* in every social system we have lot of subsystems. Depending upon **the culture, the caste, the region, the climate, the environment, the education,** this thing. *So,* it varies from place to place so I would say the range will be from five to ninety-five, just like that. *So,* some most of the families are

in big cities and smaller cities are very advanced and forward. *And* some families are still poor and still illiterate so it varies, varies you have **fourth grade employee**, then (xxx) **grade employer**, and **a junior officer, senior officers, managers, chairmans**, many (xxx) things like that. So it varies the social pattern, the kind of living style varies from family to family, place to place. *So and then* because of that, they exposed to the media, the awareness which is every every family, in every part of the country. *So* it's upgrading. *So* development is taking place everywhere. *But* it will take time.

Across turns, these connectors signal something slightly different. It appears that speakers are not making connections; each is talking parallel to each other, each holding their own conversation, sometimes simultaneously, each asking and answering their own questions but continuing the topic and supplying details and examples to support their argument. Connectors do not necessarily tie one turn idea to the next, rather the speaker is indicating that he/she has something to say and wants to claim the floor (see Example I, lines 17, 33, 36, 38). Similarly, negative *no*, in turn opening situations, works this way. 'No' is not used by Indian speakers to contradict or negate the previous statement but to signal that they want to claim the floor. We can clearly see this strategy in action in Example I: 'no, no, I'll elaborate on it', 'no I making' in lines 19 and 43. More specifically in lines 33 and 35, after many tries to take a turn, speaker A finally claims the floor in line 52 by initiating his turn with *then* and proceeding to discuss at length the changes in the role of women and men concerning household responsibilities. The content of speaker A's turn does not relate to the previous exchange, but speaker A's use of the connector *then* sounds like he is continuing on an earlier topic. The use of such connectors contributes to the digressive, circular development of topic in Indian English discourse.

Pitch

As John Gumperz (1982: 149) notes, Indian English systematically contrasts with Western English in prosodic conventions. In Indian English, sentences are spoken as a single whole with no pauses; there are two or more sub-units separated by abrupt changes in pitch or loudness, and the pitch change on final syllables is held high and level. In addition to these observations, I find in this data that pitch and speed signal contrasts, beginnings of turns, claimings of the floor, and interruptions. Indian speakers start off with a higher than normal pitch level and come down to normal when their turn is assured; there is no contour pattern as in Western English speech where important information is stressed. For example, in lines 3–5 of Example I, speaker D begins with a high pitch which indicates he has the floor and possibly will offer new or important information. Although speaker B overlaps speaker D's talk in line 4, once speaker D is assured of his turn he lowers to normal pitch and slower speed. Other examples are illustrated with + and – marks throughout the conversation. (The increase and decrease arrows indicate speed.)

Elaboration

One observation made earlier is that Indian English speakers' use of discourse connectors contributes to Indian digressive style and to unusually long turns. To demonstrate this style in conversation, speakers tend to make many repetitions both lexically and syntactically, use a series of parallel structures, and make elaborate circular arguments – processes suggested by Indian scholars to be highly conventionalised in Indian languages to achieve positive politeness (Subbarao, *et al.* 1991). This observation is in agreement with others that Indian English speakers prefer compound and complex sentences over native English speakers' simple and direct ones. Culturally, lengthy turns reflect power distance. It has often been noted that, on the one hand, Indian English is laced with an ornate style to humble the speaker and to exalt the addressee, and on the other it is loaded with expert knowledge and a bureaucratic tone. Clyne (1994: 183) suggests that these strategies demonstrate uncertainty avoidance.

In Example I, line 14, speaker A agrees with speaker B by repeating speaker B's 'it's jointly' in line 13. Speaker B continues his talk by using a series of parallel structures in lines 11–13: 'can talk of the domestic issues, or the matter of sharing responsibility, the matter of taking decisions' and again in lines 21 and beyond: 'cooking, assisting, going, getting, taking, sitting'. Example II is an additional example demonstrating elaboration by repetition, parallelisms, and a display of expert knowledge. These face-saving strategies are so common that often the interlocutor's repetitions and digressions may not be relevant to the point being made, hence for a non-Indian hearer, the Indian speaker is viewed as repetitive, inconsistent, and off the mark.

Interruptions

Turn-taking refers to a set of procedures for organising the selection of the next speaker. In an ideal situation, turn-taking is done in an orderly fashion with no or little overlaps and interruptions. The fact that each speaker perceives the previous speaker's message as reaching a completion may cause speakers to violate each other's cues for recognising and signalling the relevant places for smooth transitions. According to Arpita Mishra (1992), interruptions in Indian English discourse do not necessarily mean disruption in an exchange.

Interruptions can supply additional information to the content of the speech of the previous speaker, function for joint production of a message, demonstrate attentive listening, and keep the flow going without pausing.

In Indian English discourse, interruptions are not made at clause boundaries as is usual in Western English conversation but within clauses and mid-utterances thus leading to simultaneous talk. For the most part, in Example I, even though a speaker is interrupted he nevertheless continues and makes his point. Throughout Example I, there are a number of instances of simultaneous talk, overlaps, and interruptions (line 3–4, 17–19, 32–35, 37–38, 42–46) (designated by / / and []). To illustrate, speaker A in Example I attempts to break in a number of times starting at line 33. Not until line 52 does speaker A finally succeed in getting the floor. To a non-Indian, speaker A's comments now seem irrelevant, and his lengthy turn unwarranted. Examples III and IV further illustrate this phenomenon. Regardless of an interruption, speakers complete their talk often simultaneously with other speakers. Interruptions and overlaps are not viewed as infringements on another speaker's turn but as co-operative talk in Indian English spoken discourse. In fact, Indian English speakers have a high tolerance for simultaneous talk.

EXAMPLE III

A: You would never use the Indian language, the word [for
B: [that's interesting]=
C: =yeah
B: I [saw a movie last night, just last night]
A: [do you guys ever notice that? always use line?]
B: **exactly same thing, exactly the same thing,** I saw a movie last night, it's a new Indian movie and this guy tells him he's got to stand in a queue. . . .

EXAMPLE IV

A: See that's to you. But you can't tell this to someone else=
B: =why not?=
C: [but culture itself has generated the pressure]
A: =[because that person's culture is not yours. I mean you don't share a culture with that person that was born here.
B: I don't know whatever you say.

Discussion of cross-cultural data

Focusing on the five strategies that run through Indian English conversation, I will now examine the dynamics of intercultural discourse. Example V is a conversation centred around the topic raised by the primary speaker, Indian English speaker 1, on the American state of Arizona and its desert-like landscape. Three other Indians and an American contribute to this discussion.

EXAMPLE V

IE1: ...+It's about an hour from Phoenix. And then in the middle of desert they made a house there=
IE2: =in the middle of desert?
IE1: +Arizona has [a strange landscape]. It's not really a desert. It's [more] more lake
IE3: [(xxx) simultaneous talk] /yeah/
IE4: [it's almost desert]
IE1: than a desert I mean not the desert
IE4: [marshy]
IE1: –no not that even
IE3: dry
IE1: >either desert probably comes to you Indian desert. Indian desert is too much like a desert because India desert everywhere you know because of heat and all that.
AE: Arizona is too, isn't it? (high pitch)
IE3: –no, Arizona is nothing compared to Indian desert.
AE: Really? I though it was quite the same (high pitch)
IE1: –no, +Arizona has saguaro cactus. Saguaro cactus plants saguaro cactus plants they say
IE4: [+(xxx) I don't know]
IE1: –it takes eighty five years just to have a sprout out of the place you'll find in Arizona twenty feet tall saguaros which mean they've probably been around for 3000 years 6000 years. +And when you talk of the wild west (hm) you know the picture which comes in front your mind wild west oh boy Hollywood picture. That's what Arizona is all about and all the Hollywood setting
AE: I call that desert=
IE1: =huh?=
AE: I call that desert.
IE1: no, no +> from an American standard yes, but I'm trying to tell you from an Indian standard.
IE4: Yes, it is different

Indian speaker 1 begins the discussion about a couple he knows who live in the desert of Arizona. In an authoritative tone at a high pitch level he states that Arizona has a strange landscape; 'it is not really a desert' (line 4). During this time other Indian speakers are talking, contributing bits of information not at the end of clauses but mid utterance here and there. After speaker 1 compares Arizona to the Indian desert, claiming it is 'too much like a desert' (line 14), the American in a high-pitched voice twice questions the Indian English speaker's thinking (lines 16 and 18). Rather than directly responding to the American speaker's suspicions, speaker 1 replies 'no, Arizona has saguaro cactus' (line 19). Then he proceeds to provide detailed information on the saguaro cactus giving unbelievable statistics on the lifespan of the desert plant (lines 22–25). At a high-pitch level he shifts the topic to that of the wild west and Hollywood. Not missing a beat, the American speaker returns to her original questioning twice stating: 'I call that desert' (lines 28 and 30). Again the Indian English speaker replies with negative 'no, no' (line 31) and with increasing speed and pitch counters the American's confrontational tone with an equivocal position: 'from an American standard yes, but I'm trying to tell you from an Indian standard', to which another Indian speaker affirms 'yes, it is different' (line 33).

All the Indian English conversational elements are present in this example: bureaucratic tone, elaboration with lexical repetition, digressions of topics, face-saving strategies, simultaneous talk, maintenance of high pitch and high speed to claim the floor, and supporting comments from other Indian speakers. In this exchange, the American speaker feels frustrated. Neither does she get her questions answered, nor is she given an opportunity to articulate her concerns.

Example VI is provided to show how in intercultural conversations, two different speakers interpret a pause. The Indian speaker is discussing a sexual harassment incident. After four seconds, the American speaker thinks her partner has completed her turn and begins: 'I hear of incidents' but is interrupted mid-utterance by the Indian speaker; the American speaker refrains from taking the floor.

EXAMPLE VI

IE: ... +But she was afraid. She was saying that they are not looking right and they are all teasing me (ahhhh) and after some time they all two guys they came and hold her legs. And she shouted very badly. Then everybody came and he got ran away from that train then <4 sec.>

AE: I [hear of incidents]

IE: +[and from that time on I am afraid of travelling alone. –I am afraid.

AE: Well I hear of incidents in Delhi. . . .

To illustrate further the differing styles in intercultural communication, Example VII between two women, an Indian and an American, is given. The discussion centres around the cultural differences between American and Indian women.

EXAMPLE VII

IE: We think we are better than American woman's in many respects. **We have a strong** emotional relationship with our spouse **we have a strong** emotional relationship with our in-laws, **we have we have a stable**, reliable, and valid sort of (pause) you can say (pause) structural build-up than most of American woman's have. We don't have such chronic disorders like they have. They have their in ah the Western countries divorce and broken families are a very common thing. But in our family if a friend if a boy is going to divorce his wife he will um think hundred times **what others will say what his family will say what his father will think what his in-laws will think** then he will unless and until his very this is in our society all these things are happening because we are imbibing those Western traditions. That is not in our inheritance and we can if we can those ah those imbibe trends in a right way we are imbibing those trends in a negative way. If we can imbibe those trends in a positive way then we can better ourselves. But we are doing it in ah the reverse ah direction that's why these pathologist social pathologies are overcoming these days.

AE: Why do you think divorce is so bad?

IE: I don't think that. I haven't said ki the West is so bad. I think ki we have seen only the bad picture of them. We don't want to we don't want to imbibe the good picture of them. We actually we Indians have an inherent tendency to have everything ready made. If we want to take anything we want it ready made. If you want to do um if you want to go for anything like if you want to ah go for shopping and ah the shopkeeper shows ki 'this is a good piece of cloth'. They they will 'no show me anything ready made that is is more lasting and cheaper'. We will go we will go for those things so this is ah this is our viewpoint. We have a false viewpoint of you. You, I'm not criticising any culture. I'm saying it is our fault if we are imbibing in the wrong way. If we can imbibe it in a right way we can better ourselves. And chances are there ki that we can better ourselves in more extremely positive way. And don't be mistaken by the notion that I have any wrong views about Westerners.

AE: Oh no, it's just that divorce is very common in America. (yeah) and it's because people find out that they can't live together and are not happy. And I'm from the school that if you're not happy then you shouldn't live together.

IE: +If you are unable to cope you will not live without spouse. And well you can give him a time to understand to make a situation better. I think you're to that view, nuh? We also have develop that view but if he doesn't want to better the situation. . . .

In the Indian speaker's lengthy turn (lines 1–17), the Indian English speaker controls the floor by initiating at a high-pitch level her turn and introducing new information. Throughout the turn she uses the elaboration strategies of parallel structures: 'we have a strong emotional relationship with our spouse, we have a strong emotional relationship with our in-laws, we have stable, reliable and valid . . . build-up' (lines 2–5); 'what others will say, what his family will say, what his father will think, what his in-laws will think' (lines 9–10), lexical repetitions, especially with the word **imbibe**, a bureaucratic tone ('chronic disorders', 'imbibing Western traditions', 'social pathologies'), non-circular development, and complex sentence structure. The American speaker seems lost (or defensive) when she asks: 'Why do you think divorce is so bad?' (line 18) to which the Indian speaker rapidly responds 'I don't think that' (line 19). Hearing disagreement, the Indian speaker backs down by criticising and faulting India for adopting Western habits and behaviour (lines 19–33). The Indian speaker digresses to shopkeeper, a false viewpoint of the West, and imbibing the wrong and right ways, before closing with 'don't mistaken by the notion that I have any wrong views about Westerners' (lines 32–33). The American woman returns to the topic of divorce defending an unhappy couple's right to divorce in lines 34–37. The Indian speaker reworks the American's view, then asks a rhetorical question before continuing on another lengthy turn (lines 38 and beyond). During most of her turn, the Indian speaker maintains a high-pitch level and rapid speed.

SUMMARY AND IMPLICATIONS

Language is embedded in the cultural context – only by understanding the general cultural meaning and the set of rules which reflect the core values of a culture and its speech communities can the message in the form of 'rules of speaking' within the culture be fully understood and interpreted. The proposed general cultural models suggest that far-reaching overall cultural values find expression in these communicative rules. As a result, when two speakers from two cultures interact, the linguistic differences observed in conversation are based on each culture's notion of appropriateness – cultural appropriateness in the sense that cultures encode their notions of values in the pragmatics of language. Within the context of cross-cultural communication, shown by the exchanges between South Asians and Westerners, we see that even among speakers who share the same language variety, different linguistic cues, and interpretations of these cues exist across cultures. At times, both sets of speakers are perplexed by the other's linguistic behaviour. Sometimes, the native cultural patterns predominate, and an insensitivity to others' linguistic needs surfaces.

In high-context cultures such as in South Asia, where speakers' information is drawn from the environment, situation, gestures, and the mood surrounding them, the conversation is filled with an inordinate amount of information and repetition of words, phrases, and ideas that low-context people hear as irrelevant information. The examples illustrate that the Indian speakers provide an abundance of information that the American speakers do not want to hear; the American speakers want only the facts that the Indian speakers are reluctant to give. Not only is there cultural variation in contexting, then, but in patterns of directness and indirectness as well.

At the same time, in South Asian cultures time is seen as non-tangible, concern is paid more closely to involvement with people than to holding to time constraints. Hence Indian conversations are subject to high-involvement strategies of interruptions, simultaneous talk, and repetition across and within turns, whereas American speakers are more concerned with following the rules of negative politeness, that is, not disturbing others and more concern for talking straight. Hence, we see in the examples that American English speakers wait for the appropriate pause, pitch, or signal to interrupt or take a turn but that insertion point never seems to open up in Indian English conversations. Similarly, we see that when Indian speakers do not conform to American cultural norms, the American speaker perceives an overlap as an interruption and stops talking.

Too, each cultural group uses their own discourse patterns to save face in terms of their own cultural values. Each culture is sensitive to face wants in different ways. To achieve positive politeness and to reduce any chance of uncertainty, Indian speakers tend towards lengthier and more complex sentences, integrating both support and contradiction into an argument, and a more repetitive and digressive style than the Western speakers whose style is a pointed, linear, single account argument. The American views the Indian as waffling and the Indian views the American as too direct and rude.

What does this mean then for the English language teacher and the second-language learner, the employee in a multicultural workplace, and the individual on the international scene? With respect to the study of world Englishes, teachers and researchers have failed to recognise that formally and functionally the indigenised varieties of English have developed their own distinct pragmatic identities and its users their own set of norms and attitudes.

This paper is one piece of evidence to confirm that speech acts do not behave in the same way in all varieties of English.

> The first language and the socio-cultural conventions of its use exert a lasting and all-pervasive influence on the learners' second language competence as well as performance at each level of the structure of the language – from phonology to discourse structure. (Kachru 1985: 229)

This observation then raises the question of awareness. With an ever-increasing emphasis on multiculturalism and diversity, wider communication, and complexity of interactions in this world today it is the responsibility of all speakers, both native and non-native English speakers, to be aware of variation in discourse patterns. Sharing a language does not necessarily mean sharing the cultural values, attitudes, and sociolinguistic norms. On the one hand, native English speakers need to be mindful of the cultural differences that exist when different cultural groups communicate in English. In the conversations in this paper the American speakers are primarily from a monolingual/monocultural background, so an understanding of cultural and linguistic variation may be limited. Such situations are not unusual ones, however, for in international domains English speakers are commonly judged by native-speaker norms and native cultural values. At the same time, the aim of second language acquisition has been for the learner to achieve the competence of a native speaker. It is well documented, however, that variation at all linguistic levels exists among all the varieties of English. Perhaps it is time, then, that less emphasis be placed on native-speaker English norms especially within global contexts such as in India where the users of English have acquired native competence in their own variety. And, given the current diverse workplace where communication breakdown is a common occurrence, understanding the different pragmatic styles of people from different backgrounds is essential to improve intercultural communication. Such efforts will lead not only to a more productive workforce but also to a happier one. For sensitivity to cultural differences and linguistic styles across speech communities is a first step in the direction to understanding the unity which underlies the diversity in this world.

APPENDIX *Transcription system*

.	final fall
?	final rise
<>	precise unit of pause
=	latching of speaker's utterances
//	overlapping of speaker's utterances
[]	interruption
...	missing conversation
(xxx)	unintelligible speech
underline	extra prominence
+	high pitch
–	low pitch
—	normal pitch
>	increased speed
<	decreased speed

REFERENCES

CLYNE, MICHAEL
1994 *Inter-cultural communication at work. Cultural values in discourse.* Cambridge: Cambridge University Press.

CLYNE, MICHAEL, MARTIN BALL and DEBORAH NEIL
1991 Inter-cultural communication at work in Australia. *Multilingua,* 10. 251–73.

GUMPERZ, JOHN
1982 *Discourse strategies.* Cambridge: Cambridge University Press.
1992 Interviewing in intercultural situations. In Paul Drew & John Heritage (eds.), *Talk at work.* Cambridge: Cambridge University Press. 302–27.

HALL, EDWARD T. and MILDRED HALL
1990 *Understanding cultural differences.* Yarmouth, ME: Intercultural Press.

HOFSTEDE, GEERT
1991 *Cultures and organizations.* London: McGraw-Hill.

KACHRU, YAMUNA
1983 Contrastive studies of English and Hindi. *Annual Review of Applied Linguistics,* 3. 50–77.

1985 Discourse analysis, non-native Englishes and second language acquisition research. *World Englishes*, 4.2. 223–32.

KASPER, GABRIELE and SHOSHANA BLUM-KULKA (eds.)

1993 *Interlanguage pragmatics*. New York: Oxford University Press.

LAKOFF, ROBIN

1990 *Talking power*. Basic Books.

MISHRA, ARPITA

1992 *English in cross-cultural communication*. New Delhi: Creative.

NUNBERG, GEOFFREY

1996 E-Babel. *Esperantic Studies*, 7, Autumn 1996. 3–4.

PANDHARIPANDE, RAJESHWARI

1983 Contrastive studies of English and Marathi. *Annual Review of Applied Linguistics*, 3. 118–36.

PENNYCOOK, ALASTAIR

1995 English in the world/The world in English. In James W. Tollefson (ed.), *Power and inequality in language education*. Cambridge: Cambridge University Press. 34–58.

RAMANUJAN, A.K.

1989 Is there an Indian way of thinking? *Contributions to Indian Sociology*, 23.1. 41–58.

SCHIFFRIN, DEBORAH

1987 *Discourse markers*. Cambridge: Cambridge University Press.

SUBBARAO, K.V., R.K. AGNIHOTRI and A. MUKHERJEE

1991 Syntactic strategies and politeness phenomena. *International Journal of Sociology of Language*, 92. 35–53.

TANNEN, DEBORAH

1986 *That's not what I mean!* New York: Ballantine Books.

VALENTINE, TAMARA

1988 Developing discourse types in non-native English: Strategies of gender in Hindi and Indian English. *World Englishes*, 7.2. 143–58.

1991 Getting the message across: Discourse strategies in Indian English. *World Englishes*, 10.3. 325–34.

1995 Agreeing and disagreeing in Indian English discourse: Implications for language teaching. In Makhan L. Tickoo (ed.), *Language and culture in multilingual societies: Viewpoints and visions*. Singapore: SEAMEO Regional Language Centre. 227–50.

17

Indian English: The reality behind the myths

JEAN D'SOUZA
Pune

There is a story about a man called Nasruddin. Someone came to him and asked him to guess what was hidden in his hand. He gave Nasruddin several clues – 'It has the shape and size of an egg. It looks and tastes like an egg. Inside it is yellow and white. It was laid by a hen.' Nasruddin said, 'I can guess. It is some kind of cake!' Like Nasruddin, researchers in the New Varieties of English (NVEs) have been given all the clues, yet they fail to come to the right conclusions, or refuse to acknowledge the obvious. Let us take Indian English as a case in point.

Indian English is one among several varieties of English, which have collectively been called the New Varieties of English. The NVEs are a phenomenon peculiar to the ex-British and American dominions where English stayed on after the colonial masters left, stayed on to become more than a second language though not really a first (at least not for the majority of the population). English in these ex-colonial contexts took on certain characteristics that seem to justify the study of these varieties as phenomena different from those in all other contexts in which English is spoken. It was in the interest of differentiating these varieties from others that they began to be called the NVEs. The adjective 'new' is not strictly correct if 'new' is taken as meaning 'of recent origin'. Some of the NVEs are older than Australian English, for

---

This is a considerably revised and updated version of a paper to appear in *English World-Wide* 18:1.

example, but Australian English is not counted among the NVEs. The adjective 'new' applies more in the sense of 'a new phenomenon' – something that has not occurred in quite this way or on quite this scale before.[1]

The NVEs in general – and particular NVEs like Indian English, Singapore English, Nigerian English – have been studied for many years now and literature about them abounds (Cheshire 1991; Kachru 1983, 1992; Ho and Platt 1993). In the course of this research, however, certain persistent myths about NVEs have arisen. The main purpose of this paper is to look at some of these myths and to try as far as possible to reveal the realities behind them. I examine five major myths, and although I refer to Indian English specifically, my arguments will apply to all the NVEs. I deliberately give no references for these myths because like all myths it is hard to say where they originate, but study of the NVE literature will show how deeply entrenched they are and how easily a great number of scholars seem to take them as given:

1. Indian English is a 'non-native' variety of English (or *the egg is a cake* syndrome).
2. Indian English has no standards.
3. Indian English lacks creativity.
4. Indian English is the language of a small but dominant elite.
5. English is the cause of most of the problems in India and in the world

INDIAN ENGLISH IS A 'NON-NATIVE' VARIETY

This first myth is a trifle tired one, but one that keeps resurrecting itself in spite of efforts to lay it to rest. The problem arises from the fact it is not easy to say what exactly the term 'non-native' means. Does it mean that English is 'not native' to India? If so, then strictly speaking English is not 'native' to America or to Australia either, yet English in these contexts is not looked on as non-native. Obviously, therefore, this is not the sense in which we talk of a 'non-native' variety. (Singh *et al.* 1995)

Do we instead mean that English is not the native language of the speakers of English in the NVE contexts? But English is the native language of a small (but growing) section of the population and there are a considerably larger number of people who learn English along with another language right from childhood. We have therefore to ask ourselves what exactly we mean by a 'native speaker' of English? If we recognise a variety of English called 'Indian English', as does *The Oxford Companion to the English Language* (1992), then are not Indians native speakers of that variety or do we want to say that Indian English is a variety of English that has no native speakers?

If we acknowledge the fact that Indians are native speakers of Indian English this is no more or less enlightening than to acknowledge the fact that Americans are native speakers of American English, and Britishers are native speakers of British English. It also follows from the above that Indians are not native speakers of American English, just as Britishers are not native speakers of Indian English. Why is this at all illuminating and therefore necessary to say?

Paikeday (1985) has very clearly shown the problems involved with the use of the term 'native speaker'. Almost all researchers in the field of NVE studies note the problems that arise when the term is used to refer to English in the NVE contexts and yet, even while noting the problems, most researchers (except for a very few) continue to use the term. Why is this so?

The main reason I believe is because it is convenient to do so. It is 'convenient' because NVE studies took on the discourse strategies of Second Language Acquisition (SLA) studies and in the course of time got trapped in the discourse of SLA. I say 'trapped' because English in the NVE contexts is more than a second language and to study it in purely second-language terms is to allow the discourse of SLA to limit our vision. Thus, terms like 'native speaker', 'second language', 'interference', 'fossilisation', 'transfer', etc., are no longer transparent (if they ever were transparent) when it comes to the acquisition of English in the NVE contexts. That the discourse trap is not an easy one to get out of is demonstrated by the fact that scholars continue to use the terms of the discourse even while being intellectually aware of its problems. I admit that it is not easy to come up with new terms, to reject the old terminology by avoiding it or by using circumlocutions. Yet, every time we use the old terminology we renew its legitimacy and tighten our own blinkers, and if those at the forefront of the field continue to subscribe to outdated and meaningless terms then the myth just grows stronger. As D'Souza (1993: 39) claims, 'The NVEs are a new phenomenon and we will never really understand them as long as we try to fit them into established categories that they render meaningless.'

The task that lies ahead is challenging but by no means impossible. With a little care and concerted effort the bogey of terminology should no longer haunt us. The term 'NVE', for example, while it does have its problems (as noted earlier), does not at least carry the unnecessary baggage that the term 'non-native varieties' does. Of all the terms used to refer to the NVEs – non-native, indigenised, transplanted – it is the least problematic and could be used until a better term is found.

INDIAN ENGLISH HAS NO STANDARDS

It is an oft-repeated myth that the standard of English in India has fallen and is falling. What is never even considered is that the wrong yardstick is being used. When the 'standard of English' is talked about it is taken for granted that the standard is that of British English. But why should this be so? English in India is acquired by Indians from other Indians, the teachers are Indian, and the textbooks are Indian. The language is not a foreign language, so how can the question of a foreign standard arise in the first place?

Once again the problem stems from the fact that we have taken certain things as given (our myths) and have resisted the need to re-examine them. The first given is that 'English is not our language'. The second given follows from this, that 'the standards are not ours to set'. What we often fail to realise is that English is our language. After more than two hundred years of constant presence and use how can it not be? And though we have been diffident about setting standards they have evolved very naturally and are in place even though they are not always acknowledged. The fact that they are not always acknowledged makes us linguistic schizophrenics and this is not a very happy situation. That is why D'Souza (1993) makes a plea for a new approach to the study of the NVEs and stresses the importance of codification and acceptance *in deed* as well as *in fact* of local standards.

What evidence is there to show that local standards have emerged in India? As I said earlier, the textbooks used in Indian schools are locally produced. Perhaps an examination of one or two of these may be interesting. I looked at two textbooks:

1. The Standard X (school-leaving year) English textbook for students offering English as a first language, and
2. The Standard XI English textbook meant for 'learners from the English medium and the non-English medium schools' (Preface).

Both books are produced by the Maharashtra State Board of Secondary and Higher Secondary Education, Pune.

In the Standard X textbook, 26 per cent of the texts given are written by Indians. The Introduction to the book says,

> The passages in the book are of a varied nature. Maximum care has been taken to see that they will help promote the students' emotional life, enrich their knowledge of English, broaden their outlook inculcate a fine social sense and develop literary taste. Most of the passages have been adopted from the original sources *in order to keep in tact the literary beauty and charm.* [emphasis mine]

The authors of the textbook do not differentiate between the Indian and the non-Indian contributions to the book. All the passages are seen to be of value and Indianness is seen as essential to literary quality as may be inferred from the quotation, especially the last phrase. The Standard XI textbook goes one step further in that 61 per cent of the texts are written by Indians. The cultural content and the language of these texts are 'very Indian'. This is not seen as a 'problem' by the editors (otherwise the texts would not have been included) but as a perfectly natural phenomenon, which indeed it is.

This Indian writing in English is therefore accepted as standard even though there are areas where it differs from standard British English. This is the English that is being taught in our schools and is generally accepted. Yet, if at any point in time 'someone in the know' points out that we do things differently from the way the British do, then there is an immediate outcry that 'standards have fallen' and 'English has gone to the dogs'. This is where the linguistic schizophrenia comes in. We use English as if it belongs to us but the minute this is brought to our attention we get into a flap and say that it is not our language. The situation is exacerbated by the fact that we have no local reference materials available (at least not in any serious sense) and are forced to turn to dictionaries and grammars based on other varieties when in doubt about items of usage or grammar. This only heightens the sense of insecurity about the language.

Good descriptions of NVE standards are important both for local use and also because they provide data for reliable descriptions of World English (D'Souza 1993). There has been much talk of World English in recent years, but no description of World English will be complete that does not draw on the NVEs. Yet, to date, not one NVE has been described in any serious sense. This is, perhaps, what leads Greenbaum (1986: 193) to say:

> No established and acknowledged standard dialect of (say) Indian or Nigerian English yet exists on which grammarians can draw for the data to be described in their grammars of the standard language.

Descriptions of local NVE standards will provide the data for dictionaries and grammars of World English. A further advantage of good descriptions is that they will allow for the possibility that tests like that of English for International Communication (TOEIC) will be less biased towards any given variety and will acquire international validity (see Lowenberg 1992 for a discussion of this point). At present these tests, though claiming to be 'international', have no input from any of the NVEs and fall far short of their claims.

The emphasis in this section has been on the acknowledgement and acceptance of local standards. Even while writing this I am aware of the problems involved with standardisation, with the elitist nature of the enterprise. However, as I see it, not to acknowledge the local standards in the NVE contexts is even more elitist because then by default British English becomes the standard and a very few can achieve that simply because very few have access to that.

INDIAN ENGLISH LACKS CREATIVITY

Of the myths discussed so far this is probably the most controversial. There are those who time and again have celebrated the creativity of Indian English (Kachru 1986, 1988, 1994a) and there are those who decry the 'sterility' of Indian English (Dasgupta 1993). So really the question here is which is myth, which reality? My phrasing of the 'myth' should make it clear to the reader what my stand is; I now try substantiate it, basing my arguments primarily on Indian 'creative' writing in English.

Indians have been writing poetry and fiction in English from about the mid-nineteenth century (see Jussawalla and Dasenbrock 1992). If we look just at fiction we have names like Mulk Raj Anand, Bhabani Bhattacharya, Upamanyu Chatterjee, Anita Desai, Bharati Mukerjee, R.K. Narayan, Raja Rao, Vikram Seth, Khushwant Singh, to cite just a few. These writers have used the English language to write about themes and topics that are Indian, and to do so have had to mould the language, to shape it to their respective needs. They are not slaves to the language; rather they have subjugated the language to their literary purposes. As a result we have a variety of styles and a nativising of the language to a greater or lesser extent depending on the author (see D'Souza 1991 for a possible classification of writers). All this literary activity cannot be written off as 'sterile'.

In addition, creativity in one domain has triggered creativity in others. Upamanyu Chatterjee's *English August*, a seemingly impossible book to film because most of the action takes place in the protagonist's mind, inspired director Dev Benegal to produce a film. A judge at the Festival of Three Continents at Nantes commented on Benegal's original style and use of new images. The film met with widespread acclaim and language plays a crucial role in its success. As one critic puts it,

> The excitement *English August* generated at the Toronto International Film Festival was therefore deserved. Shot on location in Andhra Pradesh, it uses English as its primary language, which not merely adds to its international appeal but is also honest in stating modern India's preference for the language. (Khosla 1994)

One of the grounds on which charges of sterility have been levelled against Indian English is that there is a dearth of great writing in English by

Indians when compared to the work produced in the other Indian languages. Given the range of topics that Indian fiction writers have dealt with and the fact that they have used English to talk about the Indian experience I don't see how the charge of 'sterility' per se can hold. A rejoinder to this view is the question 'Is creativity measured by greatness?' In other words, if there is no truly great writer then there is no creativity? If Indian writing in English has not produced a writer of the stature of a Tagore or a Munshi Premchand then are we to assume that Indian writing in English is not creative? I think the answer to all these questions is a resounding 'No'. India has produced far too many good writers for the creative enterprise to be written off as non-existent. Taking that as a given, let us examine some of the possible reasons for the lack of 'greatness'.

The path Indian writers in English have had to tread has by no means been an easy one. Until about the 1980s they had to deal with questions of nationalism and the criticism of the linguistic patriots who asked 'Why write in English at all?' The attitude Indian writers had to contend with was not very different from that articulated by Halpe (1976: 1):

> A Sri Lankan would surely write in Sinhala or Tamil if he could: *if he does not it is because he cannot.* [emphasis mine]

Writing in English was the subject of much criticism and was taken as evidence of either lack of knowledge of the mother tongue or alienation from the local context.

If the social climate is such that a writer has to constantly reassure himself/herself about what he/she is doing, that must constitute a very real hindrance to greatness. The Indian writer was not alone in this; the same situation arose in other NVE countries (see Wijesinha 1994 for the case of Sri Lanka). This negative attitude to Indian writing in English in part stems from the perception, totally wrong in my view, that by writing in English Indians are negating or downgrading the other Indian languages. This perception is well illustrated by the following excerpts from Tripathi (1994):

> Indians have been using it [English] for creative purposes, and, *it follows or is to be assumed, that they have no literary language of their own.* [emphasis mine] (p. 169)

> Those who summon forth the names of R.K. Narayan and other Indo-Anglian writers *possibly do not know, or do not wish to remember*, that Tagore got the Nobel Prize for Literature, earlier in the century, for his work in Bengali. The bulk of mainstream Indian literature is produced in national languages, and their literatures are self-sustaining entities, generally with a history and corpus that compare favourably with most modern literatures of the world. [emphasis mine] (p. 179)

This attitude of protectiveness towards the 'national languages' and their literatures is absolutely unnecessary. One is not less Indian because one writes in English, nor does one necessarily reject the greatness of writing in the national languages. In general the social climate in the 1990s is more accepting of English. The young writers of today feel comfortable with the English language and have no desire to apologise for their use of it. They have grown up speaking English in a country in which English is no longer a foreign language.[2] It is from this generation and those to come that we can expect truly great work. As Wijesinha, who is himself a creative writer, remarks:

> The guilt felt previously by the English educated about not participating in the life of those with stronger indigenous roots, which translated into an excessive concentration on rural scenes, has now lifted as far as the younger generation is concerned. . . . We find a satisfying confidence amongst younger writers to tackle subjects of immediate interest, without feeling obliged to retreat to areas about which their knowledge is limited. (Wijesinha 1994: 110)

India today is producing more and more writing in English. In the last five years a large number of women have entered the field of fiction:

> At first it was in ones and twos. Today, they have arrived in droves and are even threatening to outnumber their male counterparts. This is the prevailing syndrome of the women writers in India. These young ladies in their thirties and forties are keeping stride in a field which has traditionally had more men than women. It is not surprising then, that for every *Trotter Nama* there is a *Tara Lane* and for every *Suitable Boy* there is *The Thousand Faces of the Night.* (Majumdar 1994)

These young writers are using 'not a contorted version of the Queen's English but a language they have learnt in India' (Majumdar 1994), and are writing about things that stem from their own experiences and are close to their hearts. *The Thousand Faces of the Night* by Githa Hariharan won the 1993 Commonwealth Prize for the best book from the Eurasian region. It may not be long before the first 'great' work emerges.

Before I consider the myth of lack of creativity truly laid to rest let me deal with one last point. Creativity has many facets and one of the most difficult to master is humour. Unless one has a confident, assured knowledge of a language humour is almost impossible. For the last several years advertising in India has made use of English, or an easy blend of English and Hindi, to create advertisements that are humorous, clever, topical and much appreciated by the audience. This is an area which shows how much English is a part of the local scene and how little it depends on British or American norms. A few examples may help make the point (even though some of the flavour is lost by taking the advertisements out of context. 1. appeared at the time of the invasion of Kuwait; 2. when news of the outbreak of mad cow disease first hit the headlines; and 3. appeared during the 1996 general elections in India:

1. Kai Ku wait for more trouble
   For a peaceful Middle,
   feast on Amul.
2. Union Jacked by Mad Cows!
   Amul butter
   Mera Cow Mera Desh
3. Lights! Camera! E1-Action!
   Amul butter
   Stars in every Party
4. *dosti ek icy cheeze hai* [part of a TV ad for a new mint called Icy]
5. Curry the flavour of this chicken [ad for Venky's Chicken]

Examples like these abound (no glosses are given as the reader/viewer is expected to understand both languages) and in my opinion this playful, joyous use of language is inconsistent with the view that:

> . . . the presence of the [English] language in this country is a matter of keeping a standing army of English words in a state of constant readiness, wearing combat gear. When you are wearing combat gear, you cannot relax, and the arts of relaxation, including a creativity that is in touch with your community's cultural unconscious, are denied to you. (Dasgupta 1993: 217)

English is at home in India, as at home as any of the other languages that are held to be a part of the Indian heritage.

INDIAN ENGLISH IS THE LANGUAGE OF A SMALL BUT DOMINANT ELITE

This myth is so deeply entrenched, so unquestioningly accepted that even suggesting that it is a myth may seem sacrilegious to some. Yet it is precisely such taken-for-granted 'facts' that serve as mental straitjackets. Let us therefore presume to question this myth by first exploring the meaning of the phrase 'small but dominant elite'.

That English is the language of a *small* group is perhaps uncontroversial. Conservative estimates put the number of English-knowing people in India at

3 per cent of the population; less conservative estimates go up to about 5 per cent. That English is the language of a *dominant* group suggests that speakers of English hold power in India, that they constitute *an elite*. An elite is 'a group of the most powerful, rich, or talented people in a place or a community' (*Collins Cobuild Dictionary* 1987). If English is the language of a small but dominant elite then either one or both of the following statements should be true:

- All (or most of) the powerful, rich and talented people in Indian are speakers of English.
- All (or most) speakers of English in India are powerful, rich, and talented.

A little thought will show us that in India today neither of these statements is true. There are many powerful, rich, and talented people who would not describe themselves as speakers of English[3] and there are a lot of speakers of English among the lower income groups, among the powerless and among the untalented.

What I am suggesting is that we need to rethink this myth rather than accept it as fact. It may have been true in the years following independence when the English-educated held power in the country but is it true today? What we really have to ask is this – In India today how much of the day-to-day business of the government is actually carried on in English? How many of our politicians come from English-speaking homes or have gone to English-medium schools? How many of our industrialists, singers, dancers, artists, and writers have English as their first language? And, on the other hand, of those who have English as a home language or have gone to English-medium schools, how many are in politics, how many are industrialists, how many creative artists?

A look at the Secondary School Leaving Examination conducted by the Maharashtra State Board of Secondary Education is quite an eye-opener. In 1994 the merit list was dominated by students from vernacular medium schools. The English-medium schools (the so-called 'elite' schools) hardly featured at all. Out of 105 students on the merit list only 6 students were from English-medium schools. A headline in a local paper proclaimed 'PUNE CONVENT SCHOOLS FAIL TO IMPRESS' (English medium schools are called 'convent' schools even when not run by religious organisations) and the reporter went on:

> Another amazing fact was that for the last ten years no student from any convent school had topped the merit list, either general merit or the divisional merit list. This is also true for the HSC Examinations in all the seven divisional boards (*Maharashtra Herald*, 28 June 1994).

In 1996, while more students from the convent schools made it to the merit list, the top six positions still went to non-convent schools. What does this suggest? If the best students come from vernacular medium schools they are the ones who are likely to go on to positions of power in later life and constitute a part of the elite. I am not suggesting that these students do not know English; all I am saying is that a mere knowledge of English is not enough to give power. Power is not something conferred by the language or emanating from it; power comes from a combination of factors and is a relationship between people rather than an entity in and of itself. As a relationship it is subject to variation and change. Therefore, to say that English is a language of power and that English speakers form a small but powerful elite as if that holds true for all people and for all time is, I believe, to constrain our vision and limit our understanding by focusing on the language and ignoring socio-economic and other factors that play a much bigger role in conferring power in any given encounter. Let us at least presume to question this myth because if we do we may have a clearer picture of Indian English and the role it plays in the country (D'Souza in press).

ENGLISH IS THE CAUSE OF MOST OF THE PROBLEMS IN INDIA AND IN THE WORLD

And so finally to the biggest myth of all – the myth that language or more specifically the English language is the source/cause of all the problems in the world. Accusations of 'hegemony' (Kachru 1994b), 'imperialism' (Phillipson 1992), 'racism' (Ngugi 1981), etc. are levelled against the language as if it were responsible for the domination, the power play, the injustice that we find when we look around us. (If this were true then the horrible events in Rwanda and Yugoslavia should never have happened because English had little or no part to play in those political disasters.)

The role of language has increasingly been emphasised in the social sciences in recent years. Language is analysed to show how it influences people negatively, how it carries hidden agendas, how it enslaves and disempowers. 'Language is not innocent' is the cry that is raised. 'Language is a loaded weapon.' All this is true and needs to be said but in the saying we tend to forget that no weapon loads itself and that if language is not 'innocent' it is because the human beings who use it are not innocent.

The truth of the matter is that in concentrating our attention on language we almost always ignore the human beings who use the language and who make it what it is. If we want to find out why things are the way they are today it is human nature that needs to be studied. Our theories of language must derive from and be tested against our theory of the nature of humankind. Human nature *is* open to analysis and the study of human nature must form the basis of our social disciplines if they are to have any explanatory adequacy. The questions we need to address are – What are the laws of our nature? Why do we behave in certain ways? What aspects of our nature have guided the course of history, have contributed to the formation of our social institutions, to our use of language, etc.? Human beings are not just helpless creatures at the mercy of history and society but are active creators of both. Language is an instrument used in the process but we must remember that it is *used*, there always has to be a human agent. History and society are what they are because human beings are what they are. This simple fact must be recognised because nothing will change if human beings are not willing to change.

To have validity our academic disciplines have to be based on a theory/theories of the human being. These theories must be tested against the data provided by history, against the evidence provided by our studies of human societies and institutions. There is so much data available yet we seem to learn nothing from it. If the constant laments among language scholars have been that 'applied linguistics leaks', that 'sociolinguistics is a discipline in search of a theory' and so on it is because to this day no sociolinguist/psycholinguist has based his/her observations on a coherent theory of the nature of humankind. Until we have such a theory and are not afraid of looking into ourselves and seeing both our great capacity for good and our enormous potential for evil, all our social disciplines will leak. Sadly, even current approaches that emphasise 'critical awareness' direct that awareness at language rather than the species that uses language. Why do we use language as our whipping boy? Is it because we are afraid of looking at ourselves?

CONCLUSION

The main aim of this paper has been to raise certain questions about the study of the NVEs in general and Indian English in particular. I suggest that perhaps the time has come to question some of the givens, to see things afresh and to jettison some of the deadwood we have been carrying around.

Terminology is an area that has continued to cause problems for the study of the NVEs and we must make a concerted effort to rid the field of inappropriate and loaded terms. English now belongs to the world and multilinguals who speak English do not need to apologise for their bilingualism. Terms like 'non-native', 'second-language', etc. can no longer be used in NVE contexts unless one defines them anew in every instance of use. Their meanings cannot be taken for granted.

In the NVE contexts, English can only be understood if it is seen as indigenous. In India, for example, it shares some of the features of the other minority languages in that it is spoken by a small group. It also shares some of the features of the majority languages in that it has a wide reach. Seeing English as indigenous and therefore available to all Indians will perhaps help us understand: what it is that enables a rickshaw-puller speaking in Hindi to use words like 'value' and 'knowledge'; why the titles of so many television programmes are an easy blend of English and Hindi, for example, *Business Baatein, Samachar Diary, Hello Zindagi, Superhit Muqabla;* what is it that has led to the widespread use of terms of address like 'uncle' and 'aunty'.[4] All these uses of English cannot be understood if it is seen as a foreign language. The attitude of the linguistic patriots, which is a kind of reverse snobbery, cannot but obfuscate the issue.

Let me conclude by making a few disclaimers. It has been no part of my purpose in writing this paper to point a finger at anyone or to adopt a holier-than-thou attitude. All scholars in the field have subscribed to some or all of the myths discussed above at some point in time. This is why no references are provided in many places where the reader may expect them. To cite individuals would be to pick scapegoats and that is not necessary. What is necessary is that all researchers in the field make an immediate and concerted effort to rid their own work of these myths; otherwise the danger is that we will keep going round in circles and ultimately get nowhere.

NOTES

1. For a discussion of the origin of the term NVE see Platt (1988). For a discussion of the features that characterise the NVEs see D'Souza (1992).
2. In a recent interview R. Raja Rao was asked why he wrote only in English. His response was that it was the only language he knew well enough to express himself creatively in, and added that if he wanted to be a little aggressive he might well ask 'Why not?' (*Maharashtra Herald,* 7 July 1996) It is interesting to note that there is no hint of apology here, as one might have found with older writers, just an acceptance of the fact.
3. A good example is Laloo Prasad Yadav, the Chief Minister of Bihar and at one time even seen as a contender for the post of Prime Minister. When questioned by the press about his small knowledge of English he replied that he had grown up as a grazer of cattle. What relevance did English have for him?
4. This is a fascinating area for study. These terms are not only used by middle-class children to address the parents of their friends (Sridhar 1989), but are used by

domestic servants to address their employers and by the children of the employers to address the domestics!

REFERENCES

CHESHIRE, JENNY (ed.)

1991 *English around the world: Sociolinguistic perspectives*. Cambridge: Cambridge University Press.

COLLINS COBUILD ENGLISH LANGUAGE DICTIONARY

1987 London and Glasgow: Collins.

DASGUPTA, PROBAL

1993 *The otherness of English: India's Auntie Tongue syndrome*. New Delhi: Sage Publications.

D'SOUZA, JEAN

1991 Speech acts in Indian English fiction. *World Englishes,* 10: 3. 307–16.

1992 On the relationship between code-mixing and the new varieties of English: Issues and implications. *World Englishes,* 11: 2/3. 217–23.

1993 Varieties of English old and new: A matter of standards. In Anne Pakir (ed.), *The English language in Singapore standards and norms*. Singapore: UniPress. 32–46.

in press *The powerless face of a 'powerful' language: English in NVE contexts.*

GREENBAUM, SIDNEY

1986 English and a grammarian's responsibility: The present and the future. *World Englishes,* 5: 2/3. 189–195.

HALPE, ASHLEY

1976 Editorial. *Navasilu* 1.

HO, MIAN-LIAN and JOHN T. PLATT

1993 *Dynamics of a contact continuum: Singaporean English*. Oxford: Clarendon Press.

JUSSAWALLA, FEROZA and REED WAY DASENBROCK

1992 *Interviews with writers of the post-colonial world*. Jackson and London: University Press of Mississippi.

KACHRU, BRAJ

1983 *The Indianization of English: The English language in India*. New Delhi: Oxford University Press.

1986 *The alchemy of English*. Oxford: Pergamon Press.

1988 Towards expanding the English canon: Raja Rao's 1938 credo for creativity. *World literature today.*

1992 *The other tongue English across cultures*, second edition. Urbana and Chicago: University of Illinois Press.

1994a The speaking tree: A medium of plural canons. In James E. Alatis (ed.), *Educational linguistics, crosscultural communication, and global interdependence*. Washington DC: Georgetown University Press. 2–22.

1994b English and contact linguistics: Dimensions of the linguistic hegemony of English. In Thiru Kandiah & John Kwan-Terry (eds.), *English and language planning: A Southeast Asian contribution*. Singapore: Times Academic Press. 19–49.

KHOSLA, MUKESH

1994 An Indian's English August. *Sunday Herald* (supplement of the *Maharashtra Herald*), 25 December 1994.

KRISHNAMURTHY, Y., S.B. JOSHI, H.R. KADEPURKAR and A. OESCH

1984 *Kumarabharati Standard X*. Pune: Maharashtra State Board of Secondary and Higher Secondary Education.

LOWENBERG, PETER

1992 Testing English as a world language: Issues in assessing non-native proficiency. In Braj Kachru (ed.), *The other tongue English across cultures*, second edition. Urbana and Chicago: University of Illinois Press. 108–21.

MAHARASHTRA HERALD, THE

28 June 1994

7 July 1996

MAJUMDAR, SUBHRA

1994 Women authors: The writing's on the wall. *Women's Herald* (supplement of *The Maharashtra Herald*), 5 October 1994.

MCARTHUR, TOM

1992 *The Oxford companion to the English language*. Oxford: Oxford University Press.

NGUGI WA THIONG'O

1981 *Writers in politics*. London: Heinemann.

PAIKEDAY, THOMAS

1985 *The native speaker is dead*. Toronto and New York: Paikeday Publishing Inc.

PATIKURKANI, C.T., Y. KRISHNAMURTHY, A.P. VITTHAL, V. JOSHI and Z.N. PATIL

1994 *Yuvakbharati Standard XI*. Pune: Maharashtra State Board of Secondary and Higher Secondary Education.

PHILLIPSON, ROBERT

1992 *Linguistic imperialism*. Oxford: Oxford University Press.

PLATT, JOHN

1988 The nature of indigenized Englishes: Interference–creativity–universals. Paper presented at the First Hong Kong Conference on Sociolinguistics.

SINGH, R., J. D'SOUZA, K.P. MOHANAN and N.S. PRABHU

1995 Discussion note on new/non-native varieties: A quartet. *Journal of Pragmatics*, 24. 283–94.

SRIDHAR, KAMAL K.

1989 English in Indian bilingualism. New Delhi: Manohar.

TRIPATHI, P.D.

1994 English: "The Chosen Tongue". *Navasilu*, 11 & 12. 164–74.

WIJESINHA, RAJIVA

1994 Forms of alienation: Sri Lankan fiction in English. *Navasilu*, 11 & 12. 102–13.

18

Monistic pluralism: Language ideology in a language movement

KAILASH S. AGGARWAL
Imphal

This paper attempts to construct the language ideology covertly informing the two-decade-long movement for the inclusion of Meiteilon (Manipuri language) in the Eighth Schedule of the Constitution of India. It looks at the movement's spokesperson's conceptualisation of language as a predominant marker of ethnic identity within a feature cluster that includes culture, history, literature, script, etc. While the movement represents a struggle for mother tongue valorisation and greater pluralism, a closer look at it reveals that it is a hierarchical ethnolinguistic pluralism and not a balanced, democratic pluralism that informs most of the scholarly and popular assertions justifying constitutional recognition of Meiteilon. To that extent it is a doctrinaire of hegemonism or, to use a paradox, of a monistic pluralism, and not of a democratic pluralism at all.

Our main database comprises a collection of clippings (news reports, feature articles and editorials) on the Meiteilon movement from the most popular local English weekly, *The Resistance*. Additional documents like memoranda to the Prime Minister of India and a monograph on Naga tribal ethnolinguistic concerns have been included in the corpus. Such a database is bound to be interrogated. Clearly, our problem is directly related to, to use Hobsbawm's words, the habit of historians to 'confuse editorials in select newspapers . . . with public opinion' (1990: 11). We have tried to overcome this problem by attaching greater weight to the implicit frame of reference and the implied common world of beliefs than to the explicit statements per se.

It needs to be pointed out here that research into language ideology and ethnolinguistic identity is an area beset with confounding complexities. Without entering into the polemics of the area, we intend to provide snapshots of recent Meiteilon-speakers' mainstream thinking as it is revealed to us by the various assertions and reassertions during the language movement. As these assertions construct language ideology space of the state, specifically in respect of language status and language valuations in official-public domains, all of the state's languages and language varieties are automatically drawn into relations with one another. Further, language movements are bound up with the politics of ethnicity in as much as they maintain, or challenge, dominant linguistic practices.

LANGUAGE IDEOLOGY

In this preliminary attempt to explore a relatively new area of inquiry, we have adopted a simplified notion of language ideology. Alan Rumsey's definition is a useful starting point: linguistic ideologies are 'shared bodies of common-sense notions about the nature of language in the world' (1990: 346). We may pause here a moment to address a fundamental question: why choose language ideology as a framework for the study of language movements. A simple reason is that the term itself has been appearing with increasing frequency in studies of language (see Silverstein 1985; Woolard 1989). The work subsumed under 'language ideology' covers a range of disciplines which have asked a variety of different questions about language. If we look beyond the term itself, we find a wealth of studies that encompass social, cultural, ethnic, and political conceptions of the nature of language, under the guise of attitudes, loyalty, values, prestige, stigma, beliefs, norms, standards, hegemony, etc. From this wealth of studies, it becomes apparent that this is an interesting and challenging field of inquiry, under whatever name.

Unfortunately, scholars working on more social and less formal linguistic concerns in ethnically complex societies have often given only token recognition to language ideology. More often than not, a view of language as the expression or definition of identity has been acknowledged as central in coming to terms with ethnic relations and nationalism (Fishman 1972). Just as, by now, social context is clearly established as an essential dimension of linguistic analysis, so also ideology is becoming more central to accounts of language produced from various perspectives. In fact, context and ideology came in together. In even the most quantitative, correlational sort of sociolinguistics, from the early important work of Labov (1972), the motive force of linguistic variation lay in conceptions and evaluations of languages and language varieties. These surely fit into the broad notion of 'ideology' used here.

Scholars working under the banner of 'ethnography of speaking' have long given systematic attention to language ideology. Examining the social conditioning of ideology, ethnographers of speaking have frequently related language beliefs to other cultural and social forms in a society. For example, Heath (1983) has tied ideology and language socialisation to formal education. Such authoritative social institutions as schooling (Scollon and Scollon 1981), law (Conley and O'Barr 1990), and the mass media (Spitulnik 1992) have provided the terrain for some of the most pointed studies of the dimension of power in language ideology.

A number of recent studies of language politics (for example, Sonntag and Pool 1987; Woolard 1989) specifically examine the content and signifying structure of language ideologies, taking them not just as the background to the investigation of ethnicity and language, but as a *central* topic. Still more recently, there has been a reconsideration of specific Western ideologies of language (Romaine 1994), fuelled in large part by Foucaultian and post-Gramscian interest in discourse.

In light of the foregoing backgrounder to an emerging field of inquiry, we might hope to develop a more systematic and grounded approach, which could lead to sounder characterisations of language ideology in specific settings in specific time. In advancing characterisations of the cultural conceptions of language and the ideology of the people we study, we might be able to grapple with the interlinkages in various kinds of ideology – from the overt, organised system, through the covert, gut level of the habitués, to the 'lived' ideological implications of linguistic practice itself.

THE MEITEILON MOVEMENT

Since the Meiteilon setting is comparatively lesser known within India itself, it might be useful to provide the history and geography, politics and economy, and the ethnic and religious composition of the state of Manipur. However, as accounts on these and related dimensions are available in the literature (Aggarwal 1992, 1994, 1995; Pramodini 1989), I will refrain from repeating them here.

It is worth pointing out, however, that even though the context here is highly fluid and new and newer developments take place almost every month, the fundamentals of the sociolinguistic dynamics as provided in the papers referred to remain as valid as they were.

Yet, a brief note on Meiteilon is in order. Meiteilon has been reported in the Indian census reports since 1881. Grierson (1904–29) classified Meiteilon, or 'Meithei' as he called it, under the Kuki-Chin group of the Tibeto-Burman language sub-family, although for lack of adequate diachronic and synchronic information on the language and an apparent gap in the features of Meiteilon and other languages of the Kuki-Chin group, 'Meithei-Chin' was considered a more appropriate name. Later, on the basis of contrastive studies on Tibeto-Burman languages, it was suggested that there were predominant affinities between Meiteilon and Kuki-Naga (Benedict 1972). The subjection of Meiteis to Hinduism not only led to the introduction of Sanskrit and Bengali vocabulary into Meiteilon, it also led to the replacement of the archaic Meitei script by Bengali script (Aggarwal 1994).

LANGUAGE AS A DISTINCTIVE FEATURE

As a nodal topic, worthy of an explicit treatment in its own right, language is strikingly conspicuous in most of our corpus as *the* 'overarching core value' (Smolicz 1989) of ethnic identity. Almost all ethnic leaders, directly and/or indirectly involved in the movement for inclusion of Meiteilon in the Eighth Schedule (hereafter the 'Meiteilon movement') project their own mother tongue as the overarching core value and, interestingly, not simply for the dominant majority (Meitei) ethnic group but also at a multiethnic level, totally encompassing all other native ethnolinguistic minorities, who may or may not speak Meiteilon as a second language. This is particularly palpable whenever reference is made to non-Meiteilon speaking communities, particularly the tribal groups and especially the various Naga communities, even though the issue in question is to be situated in the Meitei ethnolinguistic community. A case in point is a memorandum submitted to the Prime Minister of India by the office bearers of ten Meitei ethnic NGOs:

> We, the undersigned representatives, on behalf of the Meiteis and *those who speak Meiteilon as lingua franca*, urge the Government of India to take positive, immediate measures to kindly see that the following *demands of the Meitei Community* be fulfilled at the earliest to avoid unwanted consequences. Demand No. 1: An official bill be placed in the coming monsoon session of the Parliament for inclusion of Meiteilon in the Eighth Schedule of the Indian Constitution. Demand No. 2: The word Manipuri, being the name of the language and the Bengali script, being the script of Meiteilon, as against the Government accepted

> and recognised script of Meiteilon be discontinued forthwith, and Demand No. 3: Meiteilon with its original script recognised and accepted by the Government of Manipur in 1980 be maintained and included in the Eighth Schedule of the Indian Constitution. [all emphasis mine] (6 July 1992)

In this quote, the issue is focused in terms of the name and script of the language, which in itself is a sufficiently interesting phenomenon deserving special attention. On the one hand, in the multiethnic context of Manipur, the Meiteilon movement is taken to represent not only the Meiteis but also all other ethnic groups who use the language as a 'lingua franca' (such use being taken for granted), the demand is to rename Manipuri as Meiteilon – the language of the Meiteis. No doubt, this demand symbolises a cultural crisis, that is, the Hinduisation of Meiteis in the eighteenth century and the subsequent Sanskritisation of Meiteilon. 'The term *Manipur* is a misnomer', they argue, 'since it neither signifies that it is the language of the Meiteis nor can it signify that it is the language of all the inhabitants of Manipur.' (Aggarwal 1992: 31–32) The intrinsic contradiction in identity definition and assertion is only too obvious.

However, the force of the argument derives from the apocryphal projection of Meiteilon as reflecting the linguistic practice of *all* native ethnic groups of Manipur, implicitly signifying the idea that the coherence and strength of a geopolitical unite is contingent upon the legitimate existence of just one language. It is not accidental that the Meiteilon movement from the beginning vindicates the dominant language's exclusivity while at the same time asserting its compendious status:

> Meiteilon is the lingua franca of Manipur. It is often argued that its status of the lingua franca carried with it grave responsibilities. The apologists of Manipuri may argue that it is less offensive to tribal sensibilities whereas the term 'Meiteilon' may be resisted by the hill people as the term itself connotes a strong Meitei bias. However, nothing could be more wrong. From time immemorial, people in the hills have known the language of the Meiteis as Meiteilon. For them, there is no other term for this language. They are neither concerned with the aesthetics of the language nor are they swayed by the Sanskritisation mania that fathered the term 'Manipuri'. Meiteilon through centuries of association has merged into their bloodstream whereas Manipuri is still an alien term and for this simple reason they reject it outright. We have yet to understand this basic fact [that] our brothers in the hills know and speak Meiteilon because it is the only medium of exchange and understanding between the diverse groups inhabiting Manipur. The act of changing the name of the language from Meiteilon to Manipuri alone therefore will not make Meiteilon any more acceptable to non-Manipuris. (*Resistance*, 9 January 1976: 2)

The assertion with regard to the unquestionable status of Meiteilon as the 'only medium of exchange and understanding' among the linguistically diverse tribal groups has been equally strongly contested:

> How widely then is Meitei language used in Manipur? To be sure, it's still a foreign language to thousands of tribals within the state of Manipur. For example, most of the tribals in Churachandpur district can't even speak Meiteilon; in many areas in North District (Mao), the tribals don't understand Meiteilon at all though they speak Nagamese freely. Even in many remote villages in Ukhrul district, Meitei is hardly understood; and so is the case in many remote villages of Tamenglong district. And what about hundreds and even thousands of Nepalese and other non-Meiteis in Manipur who do not know Meitei language? (Shishak 1992: 3–4)

The argument of Shishak (1992) has been conceded, albeit indirectly, by even influential Meitei statesmen:

> The need for an English version of the life history of Jananeta Comrade Irabat, the pioneer revolutionary of Manipur, has long been felt, *especially for the tribal people and the reading public who are not well-versed in Manipuri.* (Jhochouba Singh 1983)

The crux of the matter is not whether Meiteilon is the lingua franca or not, but the fear among the protagonists of the movement that opposition to Meiteilon by other ethnolinguistic groups, particularly the tribal Naga population of the state, could weaken the ideological force of the Meiteilon movement.

This dubious apologia of the Meiteilon movement is apparent in the dialectic of exclusivity and inclusivity throughout. On 31 March 1978, when the Manipur Official Language Bill was passed in the State Legislative Assembly, *Resistance* rejoiced, 'With the passing of the Bill, the long-standing aspirations of the Meiteis have been realised.' (4 April 1978: 1) Thus, the multiethnic assertion in support of Meiteilon ultimately boils down to the 'long-standing aspirations of the *Meiteis.*' [emphasis mine] The subterfuge lies in the fact that for the dominant, majority community, one's own mother tongue is indisputably envisioned as a distinctive feature of ethnic identity and at the same time it is empowered to assume the role of a unifying and encompassing force in a multi-ethnic, multilingual state.

What is most intriguing is that the 29 tribal languages spoken in the state (Census of India 1981) have been denied an equally valid status of being markers of distinctive ethnic identity for their respective speech communities, on trumped-up grounds of lack of distinctive script, written literature and 'standardisation'. Hence, the question of the archaic Meiteilon script assumes great significance. It has been argued that the replacement of the ancient

Meitei script by Bengali script had blurred the 'historical moorings of the Meitei community' and that it was ignominious to demand the constitutional recognition of a language with a borrowed script. Let me refer only to the statement in the State Assembly of Mr R.K. Dorendra, then a Janata Party MLA, and later a Congress (I) Chief Minister of the state twice, who emphasised the revival of the old script on two grounds:

> 1. Script is a vital instrument in defining our identity. 2. In the whole of the north-eastern region, barring the Assamese and Bengali area, ours is the only existing script which has nurtured and consolidated a nature civilisation. It is an index of our Mongoloid roots as well as our oriental affinities. (*Resistance,* 4 July 1978: 1–6)

A number of tribal MLAs, belonging particularly to different Naga communities, 'dismissed the cause of the Meitei script' as a manifestation of Meitei ethnocentrism and characterised it as a retrogressive step. Some of the Naga MLAs warned the government that

> any attempt at compulsion on such a sensitive issue might revive in turn the demands for the integration of Naga-inhabited and Mizo-inhabited areas into Nagaland and Mizoram respectively. (Aggarwal 1992: 31)

In fact, most Naga tribal ethnic leaders and scholars have argued in favour of adoption of Roman script for Meiteilon. They also counter-assert that 'if the Meitei people were not willing to accept simply an alien script, they could not expect the tribal people to accept the whole of their language' (Aggarwal 1992)

These conflicting contentions reveal the complexities and ambivalence of linguistic definitions of ethnic identity. They not only reflect the language ideologies of the ethnolinguistic communities concerned, they envision and enact connections between linguistic and socio-political phenomena. Though the political dimension of the issues remain by and large unarticulated, the assertions and counter-assertions on the script issue illustrate the extent to which linguistic differences can be politicised. In fact, throughout this emotionally charged negotiation over orthography and related issues, intolerance happens to be the dominant note. In that sense, it is dominance by the majority, not pluralistic democratic co-existence that is being negotiated.

LANGUAGE IN A FEATURE CLUSTER

Language is only one, among a cluster of features, marker of ethnic identity. Descent, history, culture, religion, written literature, etc. constitute a feature cluster which, separately or in combination, function as identity markers. Their identificational function implies separability, a *natural discontinuity*, in the real world. These discontinuities refer to natural groups of people, defined in our case in terms of ethnicity, the popular perceptions of which rationalises in much the same way as species in the animal kingdom. If feathers are predictive of beaks, eggs and an ability to fly, so is a distinctive language predictive of an authentic history and culture (Blommaert and Verschueren 1992). Windisch (1990) has also observed such an ideological phenomenon in his study of Swiss nationalism. Windisch calls it 'essentialism', which he describes as follows:

> Every system of political and social representation is organised around essences, natures or noumena which are regarded as, by nature, transcendent, unalterable and historical (1990: 40)

The ideological implication of the notion of natural discontinuity, as well as linguistic essentialism, is that the absence of a 'distinct language' tends to cast doubts on the legitimacy of claims to distinctive ethnicity and/or nationality. Consider these two statements relating to Sanskritisation of Meiteilon:

> To understand Meiteilon as it is, the historical events that led to the cultural influence of Bengal among the Meiteis should not be forgotten. The conversion of Meitei kings to Vaishnavism and the imposition of the new royal faith on the Meiteis in the 18th century brought inevitable additions to the cultural vocabulary of the Meiteis. To look more cultured, they ('the self-styled scholars') want to identify Meiteilon as far as possible with Sanskrit, the primary source of Indo-Aryan language in India. . . . Their unhealthy brains tend to forget the distinctiveness of Meiteilon as a Sino-Tibetan language. (*Resistance,* 3 February 1976: 3)

> The . . . process of Sanskritisation of our language is still carried on indiscriminately. The only difference is that the mantle has now fallen on the shoulders of a new class of elites whose intellectual staple is still Bengali literature or whose outlook and sensibilities are still Bengali oriented. (*Resistance*, 9 January 1976: 2)

In both these statements, the issue is not the lack of a clearly distinct language, but the effacement of the erstwhile distinct language by alien vocabulary which is seen as the first item in a list of insidious indicators of the erosion of ethnic-cultural-linguistic identity. So far, language alone, in its pure form, is offered as the distinctive trait of the group. And since a distinctive language is adequately predictive of a distinct group identity, inferentially other features are not really needed.

Such a strategy is typically crucial for the valorisation of relatively smaller and little-known groups as that of the Meiteis in a vast country like India. Hence, the vandalisation of the internal (formal) distinctiveness of the group's language, seen as being violated by the Hinduisation of its speakers and its Sanskritisation, is perceived as a real and serious threat to the linguistic discontinuity of the group. Let us look at some assertions:

> During the ascendancy of Hinduism, the influence of Brahmins in all spheres of our life was absolute. Our successive kings since Pamheiba being under their thumbs, this was accomplished easily. Then with cold calculation they started replacing local names by Sanskrit ones . . . (*Resistance,* 9 January 1976: 2)

> The injustice done to Meitei literature is apparent in the syllabi of the colleges and the university in Manipur. Translated books from Sanskrit, Bengali and English are the major textbooks. . . Masterpieces of Tagore, Kalidas, Shakespeare etc. in a Meitei bamboo framework pass for the bright jewels of new Meitei literature. (*Resistance*, 3 February 1976: 7)

> Another handwork of these scholars is the so-called books on Meiteilon grammar. Some of them adopt the English style of sentence patterns into Meiteilon; some even go to the extent of correcting the Meitei forms of certain words to suit the Sanskrit words. Attempts have also been made to replace all the familiar terminologies of Meitei grammar by new outlandish terms from Sanskrit grammar. (*Resistance,* 3 February 1976: 7)

> Meiteilon belongs to the Sino-Tibetan phylum; it has its own phonetic system and everything should be subservient to the system. (*Resistance*, 13 April 1976: 1)

From the foregoing quotes, it is clear that linguistic discontinuity is perceived to embrace a wide spectrum, including orthography, vocabulary, grammar, phonology, and literature. The view that language ideology is not totally independent of language structure is also strengthened. Further, while culture and religion do represent trace elements in the feature clustering, they are not discreetly focused, and are invoked only to emphasise their negative role in vitiating the formal properties of Meiteilon. Interestingly, the forces held responsible for this process are not entirely external to the group. Along with the Hindu missionaries and pundits of the past, the Manipur Sahitya Parishad and the All-India Radio, Imphal, Meitei scholars and creative writers have been accused of the Sanskritisation mania.

The feature clustering underlying ethnic group identification is such a powerful cognitive mechanism that the presence and knowledge of just one feature is assumed to be adequate, especially when it concerns language. By this premise, groups that are distinguished solely on the basis of a distinct language are treated a priori as 'real' ethnic groups. As a corollary, groups that might actually satisfy other parameters of the feature cluster but are devoid of a distinct language can be summarily dismissed:

> This time militant tribal students felt that there was no point in keeping up appearances (of learning Meiteilon) as in the past. The tribal students under the leadership of ATSUM (All Tribal Students Union of Manipur) protested against what they regarded as 'imposition of Manipuri language' by organising an economic blockade in 1982. (*Resistance*, 14 August 1984: 2)

In most such reports 'tribal students' and 'tribal people', referred to alternatively as synonymous, are seen as an undifferentiated lot and juxtaposed with Meiteilon speakers. Here we see the dynamics of feature clustering at work very clearly.

The people belonging to the different tribal groups, particularly the Naga, could be reasonably seen to share most other features of the cluster, like descent, religion, history, habitat, food, and productive activities. And yet, invariably they are treated as a residual category, an extremely heterogeneous group of people united only by their opposition to the 'imposition of Meiteilon'. The absence of a distinctive language renders the presence of all other elements of the feature cluster infructuous and, the group forfeits its right to natural discontinuity:

> Mr. Khelchandra [then President of Manipur Sahitya Parishad] is however convinced that whether the tribal students learn Manipuri in the schools or not, they cannot do without the language in their social life. It was a mark of the indispensability of Manipuri that the tribal students could not hold a public meeting after they had taken out a public rally in June 1984 at Imphal, he said. According to him, the tribal students had to forgo the meeting in order to save themselves the embarrassment of having to speak in Manipuri, which is the common medium among the tribes. (*Resistance*, 4 September 1984: 2)

The working of feature clustering is further illustrated by another characteristic in our corpus; after the investment of language as the criterion, additional features are invoked, but without attributing the identificational function to them. This leads to polemics such as this:

> But as the base of education in the hill areas expanded along with greater accessibility to Christian missionary-run English medium schools in Manipur and neighbouring states, the raison d'être for the tribal students to learn Manipuri began to be seriously undermined. (*Resistance*, 14 August 1984: 2)

Here, though Christianity emerges as a distinguishing feature of the tribal groups (juxtaposed to Meitei Hindus), apropos the Meiteilon movement, it is not the religious antimony as such but the symbiotic relationship between religion and language, which is the staple of the argument. Religion has played a kinetic role in bringing about substantive lingua-cultural changes among both the Meiteis and the tribal groups.

The Meitei Hindus and Pangans (Meitei-speaking Muslims) also observe extensive food taboos, with one despising the tribals for eating beef, the other for eating pork. Commenting on the relationship between the Meiteis and the tribals, Shimray *et al.* state that the

> . . . practices of segregation, extensive food taboos and the treatment of Naggers as unclean and savages brought about a deadlock in developing any kind of goodwill between the kingdoms of the plains and the sovereign Naga country (1994: 7).

Brazo, a Meitei scholar, regrets,

> Today the Meiteis seem to be nowhere since they embraced Hinduism. Being baptised into Vaishnavism by a crafty Santidas, the Meiteis had been gulled out of their ignorance into rearing up a strong prejudice and hatred against the Muslims and the Hill people of Manipur. (*Resistance*, 1978: 7)

Lastly, ethnicity and territoriality have been used as supplementary parameters justifying the inclusion of Meiteilon. These two features are projected as establishing the dominant group's natural discontinuity (from Memorandum submitted to the Prime Minister of India by all Political Parties in Manipur, February 1992: 2):

> As the State of Manipur was merged in the Dominion of India on October 15, 1949, it was not separately represented in the Constituent Assembly during the framing of the Constitution. As a result, the case of including Manipuri as a national language in the said schedule could not be considered. Since the said merger, the people of Manipur have been making persistent demands for the inclusion of Manipuri in the Eighth Schedule. But this legitimate demand has not been met favourably so far. More than one million people speak Manipuri in the Manipur valley as their mother tongue while more than half-a-million people freely use this language in the Hill Areas as a means of communication with members of other tribes and their brethren in the valley.

The status of Meiteilon as 'the Official Language of a State of India' and its function as the 'lingua franca of the State of Manipur' have been repeatedly emphasised in this memorandum, thereby invoking the feature of territoriality. The feature of ethnicity is invoked most directly in relation to the demographics of Meiteilon speakers:

> There are, besides (one million people who speak Manipuri as a mother tongue . . . in the State . . .), several lakhs of people speaking Manipuri as their mother tongue in Assam, Tripura, Bangladesh and Burma. There are Manipuri settlements in West Bengal and Uttar Pradesh also. (Manipur Sahitya Parishad 1987: 38–9)

In sum, natural discontinuities are defined in terms of features like language, descent, history, culture, religion, and territoriality, which are so manifestly clustered that even one of them may be adequate to characterise a distinctive group entity. Given such a definition of an ethnolinguistic group, homogeneism becomes the norm within the natural discontinuities (Blommaert and Verschueren 1992: 362). Since such a view is so obviously ingenuous, most advocates of it are most likely to abjure themselves of their adherence to it when challenged. As a matter of fact, here we touch upon a deeply ingrained doctrinaire which is very coherently – though mostly implicit – present in the majority community's discourse on their language rights, identity and movement. Such a doctrinaire of homogeneism, with its various surface faces, is a prototype of a society in which differences are seen as dangerously centrifugal and in which the 'best' society is predicated to the lack of intergroup differences.

Thus, the ideal prototype of society is monolingual, mono-ethnic, mono-religious, mono-cultural and mono-ideological. Ethnolinguistic movements, interpreted as the struggle to conserve groups as pure and homogeneous, are envisaged to be a legitimate vocation within the insidious doctrine of homogeneism. In turn, pluralistic societies are seen as hydra-headed because they make demands on the state that run counter to the natural groupings of people. Such a doctrine, which has for long dominated the mainstream Western intellectual tradition (Romaine 1994), is used as an ideological frame of reference by the dominant, majority groups throughout India.

NEGOTIATION OF PLURALISM

It is a truism that language creates identity and discontinuity. It is also a truism that language unites as well as divides. Hence, it can be turned into a battlefield of intergroup strife. Given the context of multidimensional diversities – linguistic, social, caste, class, religious, ethnic, and racial – India's modern history (particularly since the 1920s) is replete with short- and long-term physical and psychological conflicts and antagonisms between distinctive ethnolinguistic groups and communities.

Since 'language' is often projected as the distinctive feature of 'natural' groups of people, its divisive potential is manipulated to function as an instrument of oppression and discrimination, leading to gross linguistic inequality. In such an Indian context of linguistic inequality, the language movements and conflicts may be tendered as the backwash of the systematic denial by the State of the 'legitimate' linguistic, socio-cultural and political rights of a vast number of 'natural' but 'minority' groups. These 'muted' groups (Aggarwal 1995) have been for decades engaged in different struggles to protect and assert their 'natural' right to use their respective languages in an increasing number of public domains and resist the official-institutional hegemony of a handful of dominant majority languages.

During the Meiteilon movement, the Indian Government has been accused of linguistic imperialism. In November 1991, the All Manipur Students Union (AMSU) spearheaded a civil disobedience movement which included, among others, the boycott of all scheduled languages in educational institutions, rebuffing the national anthem and a ban on the screening of Hindi films particularly. Mr S. Saratchandra, then President of AMSU, reportedly warned that if their demand was not conceded, 'it might harm the integrity of India'. (*The Hindustan Times*, 29 April 1992)

It seems pertinent to point out here that the entire North-East region of India represents a case where the Central Government is faced with explicit and direct secessionist demands. Various tribal and non-tribal groups and communities in the region feel threatened about their identity because of the Indian State's centralising drives, policy of lingua-cultural hegemony and the increasing military response to their demands and aspirations. The denial of the Central Government to recognise the linguistic rights of the Meiteis provokes a quid pro quo response in terms of the rejection of all symbols of Indian nationhood:

> . . . the MPP (Manipur People's Party) has forced the issue by declaring that the Party will boycott the Republic Day Celebration as a first step in the protest against the non-inclusion of Manipuri language in the Eighth Schedule (*Resistance,* 23 January 1979: 1)

The temporising response of the Centre and the tenacious assertion of the leaders of the Meiteilon movement continued throughout the 1970s and 1980s. Fundamentally, what underlies the political volatility of the Eighth Schedule as the primary and sole constitutional dispensation on language policy is that its listing of the country's 14–18 languages (out of 1652 mother tongues) is intended to represent both the Indian nation-state and its internal diversity at the same time. The Government's stated policy of egalitarianism, as encapsulated in the national motto of Unity in Diversity, has been interrogated by invoking the feature of 'language family':

> A glance at the list of languages in the Eighth Schedule of the Constitution of India reveals that the languages listed therein are restricted to Indo-Aryan and Dravidian linguistic families only, with the Tibeto-Burman languages of India being excluded altogether. (Memorandum submitted to Prime Minister of India

by all political parties of Manipur, 6 February 1991)

The implicit threat contained in this Memorandum is trenchant enough:

> Non-inclusion may create alienation. The inclusion, therefore, will promote national integration by creating in the minds of Manipuris a sense of belonging to India. (Memorandum . . . 6 February 1991)

The same threat is echoed more explicitly in another Memorandum submitted to the Prime Minister by the Manipur University Students' Union (MUSU) on 6 February 1991:

> The youth of Manipur would like to emphasise the fact that they are born Indians, though they live in a remote corner of India which is more than 2000 kms. away from New Delhi. They, therefore, hope that their genuine desires and aspirations should not be dampened in any way by political chicanery. Moreover, the age old problem of insurgency in the State originated from the alienative feelings which can be counteracted by giving a proper place in the Indian Mainstream.

The Centre made a complete turn-around on 20 August 1992, when the Indian Parliament passed the 71st Constitution Amendment Bill that included Konkani, Manipuri and Nepali in the Eighth Schedule. Intriguingly, this historic Bill was passed without any debate or discussion whatsoever, by a consensus to waive all parliamentary procedures (Aggarwal 1993). While this gratifies the cupidity of the Meiteilon (as well as Konkani and Nepali) speakers, what is a matter of worry is that this Amendment Act manifests a sharp contrast to the Centre's stubborn refusal to even appreciate the demand during the nearly two-decade-long Meiteilon movement, during which period there was enormous loss of human life and public property.

The success of the Meiteilon movement further reveals the doctrine of homogeneism *ne plus ultra.* This *succes d'estime* has in fact resulted in substantive changes in the language attitudes in the Meitei community, attitudes that represent a virtual mirror image of the Central Government's language ideology. Look at this editorial comment:

> The ground reality is quite disheartening. The in depth analysis on this controversial issue (the use of Meiteilon in public domains) clearly shows that the non-Meitei IAS and IPS, MCS and MPS officers, and other high officials including technical persons are not in favour of implementing the historical decision to use the Manipuri language in the offices of the Government of Manipur due to so many factors. . . . The tribals of Manipur are not interested in learning the Manipuri language though it is their lingua franca. The ethnic identity crisis has played havoc in the development of Manipuri language. (*Freedom,* 22 April 1994)

This editorial comment is in sharp contrast to the earlier position with regard to the 'imposition' of Meiteilon on non-Meiteis:

> The misgivings, if there be any, that the inclusion of Manipuri in the Eighth Schedule will give rise to the imposition of this language on those in the State of Manipur whose mother tongue is not Manipuri, and that such step would be detrimental to the growth of other languages or dialects in the State is unfounded. Manipuri has never been imposed on the speakers of other languages in the State. (Memorandum to the Prime Minister, 6 February 1991)

It needs to be underscored that the radicalism of the Meiteilon movement is not a product of any pluralistic ideology as such. It rather represents the speech community's hyper-nationalist reaction to the linguistic hegemony of the Indian State, which however, threatens the possibilities of future democratic and pluralistic collaboration among distinctive ethnolinguistic groups in the state. While fighting against the hegemonistic lingua-cultural policies of the Central Government, a regionally dominant group stretches its ethnolinguistic fervour to the point of encompassing all other minorities within its own identity framework, thereby directly negating a pluralistic framework.

This clearly is the case in most Indian states, organised on lopsided linguistic criteria. The Meiteilon movement makes this specially clear, as here, the justification and proposed legislative measures are supported by insidious arguments associating state authority with state language, which in turn, are used to vindicate higher levels of legislation (that is, listing in the Eighth Schedule).

Threatened by the Meitei-speaking community's touting of Mendel's Law as *vox populi* and the implications of such vigilante legitimisation, the tribal groups, particularly those within the Naga umbrella, have grown restive over time and vindicated their own response (Shishak 1992: 3):

> Already Meiteilon is compulsory in elementary and high schools; as a result many tribal boys and girls are deprived of higher education just because they happen to fail in Meiteilon in the secondary board examination. The worst is yet to come. If Meiteilon is included in the so called 'Eighth Schedule' of the Constitution of India, it is likely to be the medium of instruction in schools and colleges, and tribal students may even be compelled to study Meiteilon in Manipur colleges. What a nightmare just to think about such a possibility! If the tribals do not flex their muscles and fight now they will become a bunch of Meiteis before long. Is this what the tribals in Manipur want?

All this indicates an obvious paradox: while the legitimacy of each group's preoccupations with its own distinctive ethnolinguistic identity implying the natural discontinuities is never challenged, the hierarchical concentric circles of monistic linguistic hegemony seem to find explicit and implicit legitimisation in the Meiteilon movement and ultimately in the language ideology of the State and Central Governments.

In sum, the foregoing illustrations and discussion invoke the image of a body of concentric empires, each comprising a wide variety of linguistic, ethnic, religious, and socio-cultural groups, each of which is oppressed by the hegemony of the immediately superordinate empire and all of which are *altissimo* oppressed by a monolithic globalised state. Because the oppression of the empire(s) is directed against features which are sacred, representing the inalienable characteristics (objectively and/or subjectively) of the natural groups, the resistance of these groups is seen as *ipso facto* legitimate. And hence, the struggle for each group's language rights can only be conceptualised in terms of freedom or liberation. The protagonists of the Meiteilon movement have not dissembled such a conceptualisation as is evident from these lines of the Memorandum of MUSU: 'In other words, we lost our political without losing the linguistic freedom. But when we attained the political freedom, we lost our linguistic freedom.' (Shishak 1992: 2)

It is only natural that people revolt when they are deprived of their own linguistic freedom. Consequently, the natural, normal and ideal society is one in which these forms of deprivation and oppression are absent: the state in which people sharing a language live within a territorially defined geo-political unit:

> Manipuri language plays a vital role as a potent instrument of promotion of integration, understanding and amity among the people, tribal and non-tribal in the State of Manipur. (Memorandum to the Prime Minister by all political parties, 6 February 1991: 2)

The inclusion of non-native speakers of Meiteilon within the Meitei natural group makes it clear again that homogeneism is the underlying premise of the movement. Of course, the deeper level legitimacy of homogeneism (which alternatively can be called monistic pluralism in a macro context) remains complex and obscure in most of the arguments. However, the repeated emphasis on the use of Meiteilon, as a mother tongue of the dominant majority and a lingua franca of the 'mated' minority, unravels the sutures of the argument that successful society-building requires as high degree a uniformity as possible.

CONCLUSION

The conceptual problems involved in our preliminary attempt to construct the language ideology of the Meiteilon movement in terms of feature clustering and the doctrinaire of homogeneism, alternatively called monistic pluralism, should be clear. Using the Chomskian distinction of deep and surface structure, one could argue that in the Meiteilon movement, inasmuch as in other ethnolinguistic movements in India and elsewhere, beneath the surface structure of pluralism is a deep structure monistic ideology, if one takes into account the dynamics of micro-macro contexts in totality. No doubt, ethnolinguistic homogeneism as a synoptic perspective on society rules out a number of social considerations. Class and gender differences, differences in socio-economic status, political affiliations and interests and the like do not emerge as factors contributing to social coherence or conflict, except as 'natural' criteria for identifying and separating whole groups in the building of a peaceful, harmonious society. This is, to say the least, a partial picture obscured by monocausalism. Second, the direct and naive association of (monistic) ethnolinguistic identity with freedom or liberation is certainly not vindicated by facts. Every minority has its own minority. And for members of minority groups, be they indigenous or immigrant, the dominance of the majority at each successive level of the concentric empires may be as stifling as that of the *ne plus ultra* giant empire at the centre. In each case, the 'natural' rights of minorities are denied in a scheme of linguistic hierarchy and monistic pluralism.

The explicit language ideology embodied in the Meiteilon movement evidently negotiates a hierarchical, and thereby monistic, not a democratic, balanced structuring of linguistic pluralism. The struggle for 'legitimate' and 'natural' ethnolinguistic rights emerges as such a powerful and central concern that ideologically it eclipses all other concerns, including similar rights of one's counterpart. It also displays a remarkable consistency with regard to monism as a widespread ideological premise, as manifest in seemingly trivial, emotional statements and suggestion. The doctrinaire of homogeneism is rationalised not in terms of an ideological critique, not even in terms of an economic or a political critique, but in terms of the supposedly 'natural' necessity of a single language.

Lastly, it needs to be emphasised that in our study of the Meiteilon movement, sketchy and preliminary though as it might be, language comes out as the most important element in the *feature cluster*. Further, the conceptualisation of a 'natural' correspondence between a language and a political administrative unit makes it such a powerful mobilising force that it obliterates all other socio-political dimensions of language. Language may not only equally characterise all members of one ethnic group (though within the group the linguistic and non-linguistic resources may be unevenly distributed along different dimensions), but also across ethnic groups. One or more elements comprising a feature cluster of culture, history, script, literature, territoriality, etc. may be opportunistically invoked to function as powerful frame(s) of reference. Less romantic features such as economic-class differences, virtually disappear from the picture, or their relevance is gravely downplayed.

Though our analysis of the language ideology of language movements is based on the Meiteilon movement, it is hoped that such attempts can provide a significant empirical tool for the investigation of elusive phenomena like language ideologies, popular perceptions, ideas and opinions on the role of language, and views about language policy and planning. Certainly in popular ideology, language tends to be a much more fundamental, natural and inalienable aspect of ethnic or group identity in general.

REFERENCES

AGGARWAL, K.S.

1992 To include or not to include: An attempt to study the language conflict in Manipur. *Language Problems and Language Planning*, vol. 16, no. 1. 21–7.

1993 Crisis of identity: The linguistic quagmire. *Independent*, 23 April.

1994 Language in the plural context of Imphal: An empirical and multidimensional perspective. Unpublished Ph.D. dissertation, New Delhi: Jawaharlal Nehru University.

1995 Epilogue. In R.S. Gupta, A. Abbi & K.S. Aggarwal (eds.), *Language and the state: Perspectives on the Eighth Schedule*. New Delhi: Creative Books.

BENEDICT, P.D.

1972 *Sino-Tibetan: A conspectus*. Cambridge: Cambridge University Press.

BLOMMAERT, J. and J. VERSCHUEREN

1992 The role of language in European nationalist ideologies. *Pragmatics* 2: 3. 355–75.

CENSUS OF INDIA

1981 *Manipur, Series 13, Part III*. New Delhi: Manager of Publications.

1991a *India, Series 1, Part II of 1992*. New Delhi: Registrar General and Census Commissioner.

1991b *Manipur, Series 15, Paper 1 of 1991*. Imphal: Director of Census Operations.

CONLEY, J.M. and W.M. O'BARR

1990 *Rules versus relationships*. Chicago: University of Chicago Press.

FISHMAN, J.A.

1972 *Language and nationalism: Two integrative essays*. M.A. Rowley: Newbury House.

GRIERSON, G.A.

1904–29 *The linguistic survey of India, Vol. III, Part I*. Calcutta Government Press.

HEATH, S.B.

1983 *Ways with words*, New York: Cambridge University Press.

HOBSBAWM, E.J.
1990 *Nations and nationalism since 1780: Programs, myth, reality*. Cambridge: Cambridge University Press.

JHOCHOUBA, S.
1983 *Comrade Irabot: A tribute*. Imphal: Publisher not mentioned.

LABOV, W.
1972 *Language in the inner city: Studies into Black English vernacular*. Oxford: Blackwell.

MANIPUR SAHITYA PARISHAD
1987 *Glimpses of Manipuri language* (second revised edition). Imphal.

PRAMODINI, N.
1989 *A social grammar of Meiteilon*. Unpublished Ph.D. Dissertation, Imphal: University of Manipur.

ROMAINE, S.
1994 *Language in society: An introduction to sociolinguistics*. Oxford: Oxford University Press.

RUMSEY, A.
1990 Wording, meaning and linguistic ideology. *American Anthropologist*, 92. 346–61.

SCOLLON, R. and S.P.K. SCOLLON
1981 *Narrative, literacy and face in interethnic communication*. Norwood, NJ: Ablex.

SHIMRAY, G.A., S. LUITHUI and T. BOSE
1994 An introduction to the ethnic problem in Manipur. *North East Voice*, vol. 1, no. 2. 6–12.

SHISHAK, T.A.
1992 *North-Eastern tribals and language issues*. Ukhrul: The Tangkhul Theological Association.

SILVERSTEIN, M.
1985 Language and the culture of gender. In E. Mentz & R. Parmentier (eds.), *Semiotic Mediation*. Orlando: Academic Press. 219–59.

SMOLICZ, J.
1989 Personal cultural systems in a plural society. *Media Asia*, 6 (1). 43–52.

SONNTAG, SELMA K. and J. POOL
1987 Linguistic denial and linguistic self-denial: American ideologies of language. *Language Problems and Languages Planning*, vol. 11, no. 1. 46–65.

SPITULNIK, D.
1992 Radio time sharing and the negotiation of linguistic pluralism in Zambia. *Pragmatics*, 2: 3. 335–54.

WINDISCH, U.
1990 *Speech and reasoning in everyday life*. Cambridge: Cambridge University Press.

WOOLARD, K.A.
1989 *Double talk: Bilingualism and the politics of ethnicity in Catalonia*. Stanford: Stanford University Press.

IV

SYNTAX AND SEMANTICS

19
Grammar and 'others'

PRAMOD KUMAR PANDEY
M.S. University of Baroda

My purpose in this paper is to argue for the linguistic appropriation of the individual speaker's awareness of 'others' in his knowledge of language. When appropriated, this awareness, I am proposing, is located in a component being called the C(onsensual) Component that is crucially involved in the organisation of social aspects of linguistic knowledge in relation to internalised aspects.

The paper is organised as follows. Sections 1 and 2 discuss the origin of the term 'grammar' and its efficacy for the cognitivist view of language. Section 3 shows how, contrary to their assumption, analyses in Transformational Generative Linguistics (TGL) fail to adhere to the criteria of grammar. Sections 4 and 5 present external and internal evidence for a function of 'others' in the speaker's internalised knowledge of language. Section 6 discusses the ideological implications of the 'other' concept in linguistic knowledge.

1. 'GRAMMAR' AND 'LANGUAGE'

TGL now maintains that what is loosely called knowledge of language involves the knowledge of 'grammar' and its interaction with other cognitive systems.

I wish to thank Probal Dasgupta and P.G. Patel for their useful comments on an earlier draft of this paper.

A grammar, also called 'I-language' ('I' for 'internalised'), is the tacit knowledge of language internalised by the mind/brain (Chomsky 1986). It is an instance of an innate endowment called Universal Grammar. Knowing a grammar must be distinguished from knowing how to put it to use – 'E-language' ('E' for 'externalised'), which is independent of the mind/brain. Similarly, knowing a grammar must be distinguished from knowing a language such as Arabic or Pashto. In fact, the notion 'language' is an 'epiphenomenon' and entirely dispensable. In Dasgupta's (1996) account, the development in TGL leading to the disuse of the notion 'language' is a reversal to the Cartesian programme for the study of language.

The Cartesian influence notwithstanding, the story of the importance of the notion 'grammar' in TGL is worth recounting for the purpose at hand. Its origin lies in the official cognitivist doctrine to which generative linguistics adheres, namely, that the workings of one mind are not accessible to other observers (Lewis 1941). The only criterion for the existence of 'other minds' is the 'creative aspect of language use' which is 'a mystery that eludes our intellectual grasp' (Chomsky 1980: 222). The cognitive abilities of an individual or, in TGL terminology, grammar, on the other hand, presents problems that can be addressed for explanation.

Considering the complex network of internal systems that operate in a variety of conditions and determine the linguistic behaviour of individuals, the only method that could make a serious study of our knowledge of language possible is a series of abstractions and idealisations. The first step in this direction was the decision for TGL to be 'concerned primarily with an ideal speaker-listener, in a completely homogeneous speech community, who knows its language perfectly and is unaffected by' memory limitations, distractions, etc. (Chomsky 1965: 3). The next step was to confine the theory to the study of grammar, in the sense explained earlier.

The choice of 'grammar' as the object of study also follows from the effort in TGL to grapple with two types of problems that were inherent in structural linguistics. One had to do with the speech community as the locus of language. The notion of speech community is not completely verifiable, and so linguistic statements based on it are not falsifiable and completely verifiable, the main criteria of scientific statements, within the Deductive Nomological model of explanation. If the locus of language is assigned to the individual speaker-listener, then linguistic statements based on the data drawn from his linguistic behaviour can be validated in natural or experimental conditions.

Secondly, the data drawn from a speech community cannot be brought under the control of the theory. There is the difficulty in separating variant from invariant phenomena. The linguist can never be sure about the variation resulting from a principle of grammar. This goes against the grain of autonomous linguistics, whose main inspiring question has been how language is possible amidst data in so much confusion, flux and imperfection (for example, Braine 1971). As Jakobson has pointed out, 'It is only by consistently taking the invariants into our account that we will be able to free ourselves from blind empiricism . . .' (Jakobson and Pomorska 1983: 50). The concept of a grammar successfully frees a linguistic description from 'blind empiricism' in that its rules function not merely to give a psychologically real account of linguistic phenomena, observed in an individual's productions, but also to predict that despite observed variation, there is a common core around which the variations nucleate.

2. COGNITIVIST AND COMMUNICATIONIST CONCEPTIONS OF LINGUISTIC KNOWLEDGE

The distinction between 'grammar' and 'language' significantly brings to focus several such conceptual distinctions about the linguistic reality, such as language as 'a medium of cognition' or as 'a means of communication', as private or public knowledge, and so on. The opposing points of view, which nonetheless share the explanation of the human individual's knowledge of language as their theoretical goal, can be presented in the form of statements in (1) and (2), the former usually ascribed to TGL:

(1) i. Language is a means of cognition.
ii. The knowledge of language is a form of mental representation.
iii. Language is a natural object; the ability to know a language is innate.
iv. The knowledge of language is private, and interacts with other aspects of cognition such as belief, knowledge about the external world, etc.
v. Linguistic issues relating to problems such as language change, language variation, and translation relate to the use of language, and are not central to the theory of linguistic knowledge.
vi. The main goal of a theory of language is to explain invariant properties of linguistic structure.
vii. The 'scientific methodology' for linguistics is the same as that for natural sciences.

(2) i. Language is a medium of communication (Strawson, Halliday).
ii. The knowledge of language is a mental activity (Dummet, McDonough).

iii. Language is a social object; the ability to know a language is acquired along with other social aspects of behaviour (Bernstein, Quine, Labov).

iv. The knowledge of language is public (Wittgenstein, Kripke).

v. Linguistic issues relating to problems such as language change, language variation, and translation relate to indeterminate aspects of linguistic form and meaning and are of intrinsic interest to a theory of language (Labov, Moore and Carling).

vi. The goal of a theory of language is to explain both invariant and variant properties of linguistic structure (for example, the Prague School, Weinreich *et al.*).

vii. The 'scientific methodology' for linguistic research is the same as that for social sciences (for example, Quine, Hymes).

It is easy to see that the concept of 'grammar', assumed to be a natural kind (that is, innate), consisting of linguistic rules and representations internalised by the human child under the impetus of social exposure, and amenable to scientific investigations properly fits the cognitive view of language characterised in (1), but not the functionalist view characterised in (2).[1] The approaches exemplifying opposite persuasions are sometimes assumed to be complementary, for example, in the view that language is both a 'means of cognition' and a 'medium of communication' (Kelkar 1992), or both a 'natural 'and 'social' kind (Pateman 1987), or investigatable using the methodology of both natural and social sciences (Quine 1972).

TGL keeps the two approaches separate on the modular view that the linguistic faculty is a distinct cognitive faculty with its specific properties of principles and mental representations, as compared to the unitary view according to which individuals have uniform capacities for all cognitive faculties. The notion 'language' is found to be a misfit for the modular view of the linguistic faculty on account of its socio-cultural connotations.

The move in TGL to focus on the notion 'grammar' shows that it has come closer to philosophy and to psychology, in both of which the notion 'idiolect' is found to be sufficient.[2] This move is particularly suited to its empirical research programme. It is more restrictive and focussed, to begin with, than the empiricist unitary approach and, if found to be unsuccessful in the face of complex data, its schematism can be expanded. Its failure or success will still be judged by the criteria of science, as compared to the research into the concept 'language', a non-empirical concept.

3. LINGUISTIC ANALYSES

Since the distinction between 'grammar' and 'language' is crucial in TG linguistic theory, it is pertinent to enquire whether the criteria of 'grammar' are adhered to in the works of TG linguists. There are at least three aspects of TG linguistic analysis which do not conform to the criteria of 'grammar'.

First, the data are always representative, and never idiosyncratic. What is irreducible to a commonly observed fact of the language and is the individual's own, is of no theoretical significance and interest (Lyons 1991).

Secondly, TG linguists continue to depend for evidence for the physical reality of grammars primarily on intuitive judgements. The latter are needed to establish the 'truth' of grammars, but not their physical reality, for which external evidence from domains such as language acquisition, language disorders, historical change, and language contact is needed. Research in the latter areas is carried out without any support from claims regarding the accountability of TG theory to explanations of their problems.[3]

Thirdly, TGL usually finds it necessary to make two kinds of generalisations – universal ones and language-specific ones. For instance, Malayalam has two syllable structure constraints, among others – one, known as the No-Coda Constraint,[4] is a language-specific constraint, not found, for example, in Sanskrit; and the other, known as the Sonority Sequencing Principle,[5] is a universal constraint, common to most languages. It might be argued that language-specific constraints should be regarded as grammar-specific constraints. This description however stretches the notion of grammar to the extent that it obliterates the distinction between what the speaker has inherited as part of his innate endowment and what he has inherited on account of growing up belonging to a specific language community. If everything is a part of grammar then the distinction between universal principles and anything like language-specific principles is rendered trivial.

4. EXTERNAL EVIDENCE FOR 'OTHERS'

The source of the misdirection in TGL in meeting the criteria of grammar in linguistic analyses is a certain element in the individual's knowledge of language, namely, other-concept – the idea that individuals cognise the presence of other linguistic facts apart from those that are amenable to generalisation.

The other-concept is a home area in the notion 'language', especially the creative aspects of language use as envisaged in Pragmatics, and in normative approaches to meaning. (for example, Kripke 1982: 22, 24, 30–31n). Meaning in these approaches is determined not by a person's internal dispositions or mechanisms, but the linguistic institutions of a culture that have in them enshrined the 'functions' which determine the use of language.

The presence of such linguistic institutions is rationalised by the 'other' concept. It is necessary, I am proposing, as an interface area between the internalised grammar and language. Consider, for example, questions commonly asked by speakers in admittance of their lack of knowledge of forms existing as an external reality, for example, 'What does the phrase mean?', 'How is the word pronounced?' When a speaker's, typically a child's, wiring connecting a linguistic form to its mental representation is missing or broken, and both possibilities must be envisaged in any natural system, he automatically turns to others – people who 'know' it. This happens because there is in-built harmony between what the child knows and what others in whose ambience he uses it know. 'Others' help an individual plug the hole in his mental representation of linguistic forms.

The automatic turning to others for help regarding 'wiring' problems is not a part of one's culture, acquired through experience, arbitrarily varying with different language communities, but rather a natural reflex common to all learners, regardless of their languages and individual talents. Promulgation of a particular form representing a certain language variety is a matter of culture, but not the individual's disinterested instinct cognising 'others' sharing his knowledge. At least not at the present stage of human evolution, whatever might have been the case in the early stages.

The presence of others in the grammar is vindicated especially in those cases where there is no logical basis to knowing an aspect of language, for example, how the compound *dancing doll* means 'a doll that dances', but the compound *dancing master* does not only mean 'a master who dances' but also or rather 'one who teaches dancing'. No method of induction can help the learner form generalisations about such aspects of grammar.[6] The child, of course, learns them as individual items and incorporates them as part of her grammar via the transduct of 'others'. Non-inductively generalisable data, that is, data that make up broken families of generalisations, for example, word-formation rules, are organised by the innate cognitive devices operating within the mental space connected with 'others'.

On a conventional interpretation of facts such as nominal compounds and word-formation rules it is easy to see that UG without the notion of 'others' would certainly account for creativity but not for what makes grammar non-esoteric and sensitive to alterity. That there is some meaning in using the term 'Universal Grammar' in the revised sense to include the ontological presence of 'others' is not so difficult to concede if we bear in mind that the root 'know', in relation to language, means both 'understand sentences produced by others' and 'produce sentences that can be understood by others'. The awareness of others is assumed, and is thus a primitive notion, in relation to knowledge of language.

The word 'awareness' is crucial here. It should be understood in the sense of the Indian Navya-Nyaya system of logic (Matilal 1985), where it includes both propositional acts such as believing, judging, perceiving, intuiting etc., and non-propositional acts such as sensing – for example, our knowledge of sandalwood, whose identity rests both with the smell and the material wood.

It is important to bear in mind that the relation between 'grammar' and 'others' is not one of causality in the sense that A causes B, notwithstanding the historical fact that a speaker appropriates his grammar from others. If it were not so, we could explain the grammar of A in terms of the grammar of B. But the fact is that we don't. 'Other' here should be understood in the idealised sense to mean 'other speakers' as well as written and spoken productions by other speakers. It should be understood as a general term of the sortal type (for example, dog, river, etc.), not as a singular term (for example, Bill Clinton, that stool, M.G. Road, etc.), nor as a general term of the mass type (for example, sugar, crowd, etc.).[7] We assume that Universal Grammar has cognitive space for 'others' understood in the sortal sense but subject to interpretation as a general or singular term by the individual speaker.

5. INTERNAL EVIDENCE

The preceding section discussed externalist arguments for the linguistic appropriation of 'others' in the grammar, based on the assumption that an individual speaker depends on the outside environment for the full creativity of his knowledge of language. Let us now turn to internal evidence for a general phenomenon of indeterminacy in grammars, such as optional rule application and exceptions to rules and constraints.

Optional application of rules causes difficulty in language learning (Baker 1979; Dell 1981). A grammar G with optional rules is less learnable than grammar G' without optional rules, yet G, not G', characterises natural language. This is a paradox that has no clear solution in the learnability theory. The difficulty that optional rule applications create for the learnability of grammars consists in giving rise to over-inclusive grammars, that is, grammars containing both correct and incorrect forms. Thus, a rule R that changes a set of forms X to a set of forms Y optionally, gives rise to two sets of forms.

In actuality, however, not all the members of the set that form a natural class may have both the forms. In that case our grammar will be over-inclusive, as it may give rise to a non-existing form.

TGL proposes alternative ways to prevent grammars from being over-inclusive. One of the common devices is marking a given lexical or phonological form for its exceptional feature in the lexicon, that module of the grammar that includes, among other things, idiosyncratic information about words. For example, the ungrammaticality of (4b) is accounted for by marking the ditransitive verb 'suggest' in the lexical entry as disallowing the frame [__NP(Indirect Object) + NP(Direct Object)], so that a sentence with the verb 'suggest' does not undergo the optional Dative Movement.

(3) a. Mary gave a shock to her boss.
b. Mary gave her boss a shock.

(4) a. John suggested the idea to his boss.
b. *John suggested his boss the idea.

The possibility of over-inclusiveness of phonological forms is much greater, especially on account of lexical (roughly, phonemic) rule applications (Pandey 1991). At any rate, resort to the lexical entry is a common solution to the problem of over-inclusiveness.

The question of exceptions and irregularities is different from that of optionality. First of all, exceptional and irregular forms do not pose a serious difficulty of learnability as they are acquired with primary data, although generally later than regular ones.

However, exceptions and irregularities do cause overgeneration in intermediate grammars when learners tend to generalise rules to apply to even those forms that are exceptions to them. Thus, we hear of *foots* and *fishes* in learners' grammars, on the analogy of *book-books*, *bus-buses*, and so on. It is well known that one of the processes of morphological change involves the paradigm uniformity of forms (Kiparsky 1971). Yet children do end up acquiring exceptional and irregular forms of the language.

The question that is of interest here is, considering the enormity of the deductive gap between the primary linguistic data and the adult intuitions that he has to acquire, why does a child finally go for a complex grammar? It is difficult to find an answer that assumes a solipsistic view of grammar. The only plausible *raison d'être* for exceptions and optional rule application in the grammar is the cognizance of alterity – other speakers, other forms.

What is the relationship between linguistic generalisations owing their allegiance to 'others' and the truly productive, inductively derived generalisations in the grammar? There is a tradition of basic research in this area to show that the former are given precedence in the derivation of forms. Panini had enjoined that in the case of the derivational meanings of forms competing with popular usage, the latter should supersede the former (Raja 1990: 111). Kiparsky's Elsewhere Condition (for example, Kiparsky 1982), based on Paninian grammar, requires that given a less general rule X and a more general rule Y applying to a form ø, X has precedence over Y. It appears then that properties of grammar relating to 'others' are ordered before those inductively generalised by the individual.

The picture of linguistic reality that emerges from a consideration of the evidence discussed above supports the addition of consensuality to the individual nature of innate human rationality. As against the view of rationality in which others are a mere part of the environment on which depends the maturation of the linguistic faculty, the revised view incorporates the awareness of others in the linguistic faculty.

Accounting for the linguistic appropriation of the awareness of facts relating to others will need spelling out the principled basis of the sub-component dealing with consensual facts. As far as I can see, this issue will require a detailed investigation of the structure of the lexicon, the various pathways involved in speech production and reception connecting it. Evidence from neurolinguistics appears to have a crucial role to play here.

The proposed Consensual(C)-component ultimately questions the basic assumption of UG, namely, that it is an independent innate system in the mind-brain determining the common properties of languages.

There are aspects of linguistic structure however that seem to reflect the worldly reality in ways that clearly cannot be attributed as originating in the mind, but only organised there. The binary hierarchical nature of the prosodic structure of words and higher units, for example, have quite directly to do with the unidimensional nature of time in which units can be distinguished as 'long' versus 'short', or 'weak' versus 'strong', or some such dichotomous set, and not with the structure of the mind which is capable of very complex distinctions. The mind simply organises the material in the manner in which it can be used with facility.

A possible internalist (= individualist) response to the proposal for incorporating 'others' in the grammar may be to treat it as belonging to Periphery (Chomsky 1981), covering odd facts of a language that a speaker has to learn and that have nothing to do with UG. Thus claims of connectionism for learning irregular forms by associationist networks rather than by rules are dismissed as irrelevant to UG (Cook and Newson 1996: 71). The internalist arguments, however, have to account for such facts as relevant to the organisational principles of UG. A principle such as the Elsewhere Condition is as much a part of the natural endowment as say the property of syntactic operations to be structure-dependent (Chomsky 1975). If EC is not assumed to be a part of UG, grammars can treat all less general facts as peripheral. EC ensures their place in the grammar. The presence of a principle such as EC offers strong evidence for UG allocating a space for 'other' facts. This recognition provides the basis for further enquiry into the phenomena that have a bearing on the organisational, not merely acquisitional facts.

6. IDEOLOGICAL IMPLICATIONS

Are there general implications of the finding regarding the situation of the other-concept in the grammar? In what ways does the revised ontology affect our understanding of grammar? In several ways. First of all, it relieves the notion of grammar from hypostatisation. Its ontological weight can be ignored only at the risk of condemning generative linguistics to a state of solipsism that does not accord with the facts of linguistic explanation and theory-building. Yet, the explanation of the other concept proposed here supports a reductionist rather than a cultural approach.

It is assumed that the awareness of others in grammar is possible because of an in-built consensual component in them. The extent to which the outer world affects the composition of the grammars by interacting with them is however a matter for deeper investigation, possibly within a broader approach along the lines of evolutionary biology (Wilson 1995). A purely cultural account of the knowledge of others in grammars that assumes that knowledge of language is collective and social rather than individual is flawed on familiar grounds (Pateman 1987).

The fundamental problem with TG linguist in accepting the innate social aspect of linguistic reality arises from the fact that the concept of Universal Grammar is grounded in biology. The study of individual grammars consequently assumes them as the linguistic apparatus in the mind/brain. The knowledge of language, however, although grounded in biology exists in consciousness. The other-concept is homogeneous with linguistic knowledge at the level of consciousness. The later view of Universal Grammar as a subject matter of the cognitive science,[8] a field of study inspired mainly by the work of Chomsky, should have no difficulty in coming to terms with the concept. The proposal of the paper is that grammar, as a module of cognition, includes a mental space for 'others' that has a bearing on its internal organisation. The main evidence for the other-concept has come from the phenomena of exceptions and optional rule applications, which are a problem for learnability theory, and all those properties of a grammar that put a check on the creative ability of 'homo loquens'.

In what ways is the other-concept revealing about reality and human nature? It supports the scientific view of reality. Like the world as known to science, grammar too is subject to dual or multiple control (for example, Prigogene and Stengers 1984): on the one hand, the innate principles of UG, and on the other hand, external facts funnelled via the instinct for 'others'. The other-concept rationalises our ability to reach beyond our private selves. At the same time, in so far as individual grammars allow 'others' to bear on them, human individuals have a mutual dependency relation even at the level of consciousness, which is where grammars dwell. This fact accounts for the continuity of knowledge, scope for change in the knowledge, and the spread of change.[9] Diversity is thus innately ingrained in the mental dispensation for knowledge of language.

NOTES

1. A great deal of German and French work on philosophy of language falls in this camp, especially that of Gadamer, Habermas, Derrida and Foucault. Despite its great interest, it has not yet established a working relation with linguistic investigations, and is thus not being discussed here.
2. See Dummet (1993) on how philosophy can do with the notion 'idiolect' even for advocates of the communication-intension approach to the explanation of linguistic knowledge.
3. See Pandey (1989) for a discussion of this issue.
4. The No-Coda Constraint in Malayalam (Mohanan 1982) prevents syllables from ending in consonants. This leads Malayalam speakers to break words like *bhakti* 'devotion' and *campa* as bha-kti and ca-mpa, unlike, for example, Hindi speakers who break it as bhak-ti and cam-pa.
5. According to the Sonority Sequencing Principle (Kiparsky 1979), segments of a syllable progressively decrease in sonority from peak to the margin, for example, in *prank*, the vowel is the most sonorous segment occupying the peak position; the flanking segments gradually decrease in sonority towards the margin.
6. Some linguists (for example, Di Sciullo and Williams 1987) may find these aspects of linguistic knowledge of little interest, while others (Halle 1973) may find them to be significant. In the later approach, all idiosyncratic words are assigned to the dictionary or the 'conventional lexicon' (Corbin 1989), while non-words are kept out by a 'filter' or 'selector', interposed between the rest of the grammar and the lexicon.
7. See Griffin (1977) for a discussion of these terms.
8. Lyons (1991: 220–36) discusses at some length on how psychologism in TG linguistics is of later development.

9. A generative linguistic account of language variation and change must be based on showing how the macro-level reality of language relates to the micro-level reality of grammar. Positing the other-concept in the grammar appears to be the only plausible way to do this.

REFERENCES

BAKER, C.L.

1979 Syntactic theory and the projection problem. *Linguistic Inquiry* 10. 533–81.

BRAINE, MARTIN D.S.

1971 On two types of models on the internalization of grammars. In D. Slobin (ed.), *The ontogenesis of grammar*. New York: Academic Press. 153–86.

CHOMSKY, NOAM

1965 *Aspects of the theory of syntax*. Cambridge: MIT Press.

1975 *Reflections on language*. New York: Pantheon.

1980 *Rules and representations*. New York: Columbia University Press.

1981 On the representation of form and function. *Linguistic Review,* 1. 3–40.

1986 *Knowledge of language: Its nature, origin and use*. New York: Praeger.

COOK, VIVIAN and MARK NEWSON

1996 *Chomsky's universal grammar*. Oxford: Blackwell.

CORBIN, D.

1989 Form, structure and meaning of constructed words in an associative and stratified lexical component. In Geert Booij & J. van Marle (eds.), *Yearbook of morphology*. Dordrech: Foris. 31–54.

DASGUPTA, PROBAL

1996 Cartesian linguistics wins in three moves. *Indian Philosophical Quarterly* 23 (1–2). 187–200.

DELL, FRANCOIS

1981 On the learnability of optional phonological rules. *Linguistic Inquiry* 12. 31--7.

DI SCIULLO, ANNA MARIA and EDWIN WILLIAMS

1987 *On the definition of word.* (LI Monographs 14) Cambridge, MA: MIT Press.

DUMMET, MICHAEL

1993 Language and communication. In A. George (ed.), *Reflections on Chomsky*. Oxford: Basil Blackwell.

GRIFFIN, NICHOLAS

1977 *Relative identity*. Oxford: Clarendon Press.

HALLE, MORIS

1973 Prologomena to a theory of word-formation. *Linguistic Inquiry* 4. 3–16.

HYMES, DELL (ed.)

1964 *Language in culture and society*. New York: Harper & Row.

JAKOBSON, ROMAN and K. POMORSKA

1983 *Dialogues*. Cambridge: Cambridge University Press.

KELKAR, ASHOK R.

1992 Conceptions of language and of language use. *Journal of Indian Council of Philosophical Research* 9 (3). 1–28.

KIPARSKY, PAUL

1971 Historical linguistics. In William Dingwall (ed.), *A survey of linguistic science*. College Park, Maryland: University of Maryland.

1979 Metrical structure assignment is cyclic. *Linguistic Inquiry* 10. 421–40.

1982 From cyclic phonology to lexical phonology. In Harry van der Hulst & Norval Smith (eds.), *The structure of phonological representations* II. Amsterdam: Foris. 131–76.

KRIPKE, SOL

1982 *Wittgenstein on rules and private language*. Oxford: Blackwell.

LABOV, WILLIAM

1972 *Sociolinguistic patterns*. Philadelphia: University of Pennsylvania Press.

LEWIS, C.

1941 Some logical considerations concerning the mental. *Journal of Philosophy* 38.

LYONS, JOHN

1991 *Natural language and universal grammar: Essays in linguistic theory*, vol. I. Cambridge: Cambridge University Press.

MATILAL, BIMAL K.

1985 *Logic, language and reality: An introduction to the Indian philosophical studies*. New Delhi: Motilal Banarasidass.

MCDONOUGH, RONALD

1993 Linguistic creativity. In Ron Harre & Roy Harris (eds.), *Linguistics and philosophy: The controversial interface*. Oxford: The Pergamon Press.

MOHANAN, K.P.

1982 *Lexical phonology*. MIT doctoral dissertation. Distributed by Indiana University Linguistics Club.

MOORE, TERENCE and CHRISTINE CARLING

1982 *Understanding language*. London: Macmillan.

PANDEY, PRAMOD K.

1989 Review of special issue on linguistic theory and external evidence. Rajendra Singh (ed.), *Canadian Journal of Linguistics* 33 (4). *Indian Linguistics* 50. 192–98.

1991 Optional rules in lexical phonology. In W. Bahner *et al.* (eds.), *Proceedings of the XIV International Congress of Linguists*. Berlin: Akademie Verlag. 510–13.

PATEMAN, TREVOR

1987 *Language in mind and language in society*. Oxford: Clarendon Press.

PRIGOGINE, L. and I. STENGERS

1984 *Order out of chaos*. New York: Bantam Press.

QUINE, WILLIAM V.

1972 Methodological reflections on current linguistic theory. In Donald Davidson & G. Harman (eds.), *Semantics of natural language*. New York: Humanities Press.

RAJA, KUNJUNNI

1990 Philosophical elements in Panini's Ashtadhyayi. In H.G. Coward & K.K. Raja (eds.), *Encyclopedia of Indian philosophies*. New Delhi: Motilal Banarasidass. 111–13.

WEINREICH, URIAL, M. HERZOG and W. LABOV

1968 Empirical foundations for a theory of language. In W.P. Lehmann & Y. Malkiel (eds.), *Directions for historical linguistics*. Austin: University of Texas Press.

WILSON, EDWARD O.

1995 *Naturalist*. London: Penguin Books.

WITTGENSTEIN, LUDWIG

1972 *Remarks on the foundations of mathematics*. Cambridge, Mass: MIT Press.

20
Ergative case licensing in a split ergative language

ALICE DAVISON
University of Iowa

In this paper, I focus on the ergative case marker *–nee*, which marks subjects in Hindi/Urdu, provided that a number of separate conditions are met. The conditions for the syntactic licensing of the ergative marker include syntactic position, values of tense and aspect as well as transitivity of the verb, and the exception properties of the main verb and its compounded forms. This pattern does not fit immediately into the familiar lexical/structural Case dichotomy (Chomsky 1981, 1986), or semantically linked versus default case. I will argue that ergative is not a semantically linked, lexically determined case, and because it is dependent on conditions ranging from the verb to the highest functional projections within the clause, it does not have the stability or invariance of a lexical Case. To represent in concrete detail the role of licensing conditions in different parts of the clause, I take the basic clause to be a series of lexical/functional projections, as in Chomsky (1995), with movement of the ergative DP from inside VP to subject position, motivated by the requirement

---

An earlier version of this paper was presented in the Syntax and Semantics panel of the 18th meeting of the South Asian Language Analysis Roundtable, Jawaharlal Nehru University, New Delhi, 6–8 January 1997. I am grateful to the University of Iowa for travel support, to the NSF (grant RI-88-00534) and AIIS for fellowships which made possible the earlier stages of this research, and for helpful comments and discussion to Elena Bashir, Chris Culy, Probal Dasgupta, Bill Davies, Paula Kempchinsky, Anoop Mahajan, and Carlota Smith.

that Case and other features be checked by specific morphological affixes. I contrast ergative licensing on subjects with reflexive coindexing, which requires a subject antecedent, and verbal agreement, which may refer to the subject, but may be quite independent of subjects. I show that ergative Case, reflexive coindexing and agreement are dependent on different conditions for licensing, which converge on the subject.

POSTPOSITIONAL AND NULL CASE MARKING IN HINDI/URDU

Independently of the lexical/structural distinction (see 2.2), Case in Hindi/Urdu may also be categorised as null (nominative) or postpositional. Postpositional Case includes the genitive *-kaa*, the ergative *-nee* and other postpositions with some dependent semantic content, *-koo* dative, 'to/for', *-par* 'on, at', *-see* 'from, with' and *-kee liyee* 'for the sake of'. Objects of PP in general, and Kase Phrases in particular, have oblique morphological form.

I treat nominative subjects and objects as having no K marker of Case (as does Mohanan 1993). Only nominative NPs trigger verb agreement; the f-features NUMBER and GENDER marked on both finite and non-finite forms, and PERSON marked on finite forms. All NP/DPs have f-features, but these features are not inherited by PP (or DP and postpositional Kase marker) and so agreement is blocked.

The dative *-koo* on definite/specific objects has this property also. If nominative NPs had a null K suffix (as in Bittner and Hale 1996; Laka in press), and if we assume a null accusative K, we lose generalisations about Hindi/Urdu: only P assigns oblique morphological case morphology to NP, and only direct morphological case NPs trigger agreement. There are bare oblique NPs which express locatives of place and time without an overt Kase postposition and without triggering agreement (Khan 1989); if there is a null K, it aptly characterises these NPs.

ERGATIVE AS STRUCTURAL OR LEXICAL CASE

If ergative is a structural Case, in the sense of Chomsky (1981, 1986), rather than a lexical Case, then it is not linked to a specific theta roles, and it is not specially associated with individual lexical items. It should be associated with a grammatical function such as subject, and dependent on the presence of a Case assigner like finite tense. But some writers have treated ergative as a lexical Case, linking it with the Agentive semantic role (Mohanan 1990), or with the perfective form of the verb, like a passive derivation (Mahajan 1990). The normal association of ergative and transitivity presents another set of problems for both views (Marantz 1991; Laka in press).

THE FUNCTIONAL CATEGORIES WHICH LICENSE ERGATIVE

The ergative is licensed by the functional categories ASPECT and TENSE, in some ways like other structural Cases, the nominative and genitive. Lexical Case, represented by the dative, is stable and less dependent on the syntactic environment. The local clause with a *-nee* subject must be perfective. Nominative Case on the subject is ungrammatical in the perfective aspect for the verb *deekh* 'see, look at' (1b), though grammatical elsewhere. The ergative is ungrammatical except in the perfective:

(1) a. *maiN-nee wahaaN kooii billii bhii nahiiN deekh-ii*
I-ERG there some cat-NOM-FSG EMPH not see-PF-FSG
'I didn't see a single cat there.'

b. **maiN wahaaN kooii billii bhii nahiiN deekh-ii*
I-NOM there some cat-NOM-FSG EMPH not see-PF-FSG
'I didn't see a single cat there.'

(2) a. *tum wahaaN kooii billii bhii nahiiN deekhoogee*
you-FAM-NOM there some cat EMPH not see-FUT.-FAM-2SG-M
'You won't see a single cat there.'

b. **tum-nee wahaaN kooii billii bhii nahiiN deekhoogee*
you-FAM-ERG there some cat EMPH not see-FUT-2SG-FAM-M
'You won't see a single cat there.'

Verbs that do not allow ergative subjects may have nominative subjects, or lexical dative Case, which does not depend on Tense/Aspect. The subject in (3b) remains dative, whether the verb is imperfective (present) or perfective:

(3) a. *billii*$_i$ *apnii*$_{i/*j}$ *baccee laaeegii /laaii*
cat-F-SG-NOM self's children bring-FUT.3SG-F /bring-PF-FSG
'The cat$_i$ will bring/brought its$_{i/*j}$ kittens.'

b. *baccooN*$_i$*-koo apnii*$_{i/*j}$ *billii dikhaaii dee-tii /dii*
children-DAT self's cat-FSG sight give-IMPF /give-PF-F-SG
'The children$_i$ see/saw, glimpsed their own$_{i/*j}$ cat.'

In non-finite clauses, the ergative is not possible on the subject, whether the non-finite clause is implicitly perfective (and has a perfective finite counterpart), as in (4). In (5) and (6), the participle corresponds to a *–nee* finite clause.

(4) a. *raadhaa$_i$-nee [apnee$_{i/*j}$ bhaaii-kaa aisee logooN-see baat kar-naa]*
Radha-ERG self's brother-GEN such people-with talk do-INF
pasand nahiiN kiyaa
liking not do-PF
'Radha$_i$ did not like [self's$_{i/*j}$ brother talking to such people].'

b. *us-kee bhaaii-nee aisee loogooN-see baat kii*
3SG-GEN brother-ERG such people-with talk do-PF
'Her brother talked to such people.'

c. **raadhaa$_i$-nee [apnee$_{i/*j}$ bhaaii-nee aisee loogooN-see baat*
Radha-ERG self's brother-ERG such people-with talk
kar-naa] pasand nahiiN kiyaa
do-INF liking not do-PF
'Radha$_i$ did not like [self's$_{i/*j}$ brother talking to such people].'

(5) a. *[[pulis-kaa e$_i$ pakR-aa hu-aa] coor$_i$ jeel-see bhaag ga-yaa*
police-GEN seize-PF be-PF thief jail-from run go-PF
'The thief$_i$ [whom$_i$ [the police arrested e$_i$] escaped.' (Subbarao 1984: 181)

b. *pulis-nee/*0/*kaa coor-koo pakR-aa/pakaR li-yaa*
police-ERG/NOM/GEN thief-DAT seize-PF/seize take-PF
'The police arrested the thief.'

c. **[[pulis-nee e$_i$ pakR-aa hu-aa] coor$_i$] jeel-see bhaag ga-yaa*
police-ERG seize-PF be-PF thief jail-from run go-PF
'The thief$_i$ [whom$_i$ [the police arrested e$_i$] escaped.'

(6) a. *(mujhee) [raam saarii rooTii khaa-yaa hu-aa] lag-taa*
I-DAT Ram-NOM-MSG all bread-F-SG eat-PF be-PF strike-PF-MSG
'Ram seems (to me) to have eaten all the bread.'

b. *raam-nee saarii rooTii khaa-yii hai*
Ram-ERG all bread-FSG eat-PF-FSG is
'Ram has eaten all the bread.'

c. **/?raam-nee saarii rooTii khaa-ii hu-ii] lag-tii*
Ram-ERG all bread-FSG eat-PF-F be-PF-F strike-IMPF-F
'Ram seems to have eaten all the bread.' (cf. Mahajan 1990)

Ergative Case varies with nominative and genitive Case on subjects, depend on values of TENSE and ASPECT. While ergative marking depends on finite tense and perfective aspect, lexical dative case is very stable in non-finite, non-perfective contexts. Subjects with lexical case are not sensitive to the licensing conditions for structural case, including ergative.

(7) a. *baccee-koo* *bukhaar* *aa-yaa*
child-DAT fever-M come-PF-M
'The child got a fever.'

b. *[baccee-koo/*kaa/ *baccaa* *bukhaar* *aa-yaa* *hu-aa]* *jaan paRaa*
child-DAT/GEN/ child-NOM fever come-PF be-PF seem-PF
'The child seemed to have gotten a fever.'

(8) a. *usee* *ham-see* *gussaa* *aa-taa/aaeegaa/aa-yaa*
3SG-DAT us-with anger come-IMPF /come-FUT/come-PF
'He/she gets angry/will get angry/got angry with us.'

b. *usee /*us-kee* *gussaa* *aa-tee hii,* *woo* *ghar-kee* *andar*
3SG-DAT/ 3SG-GEN anger come-IMPF-EMPH 3SG house-GEN in
'As soon as he got angry, he went into the house.'

DOES ERGATIVE CASE HAVE SEMANTIC CONTENT?

I will propose that it does not, except for implied contrast with lexical, theta related Case. ergative is often assumed to mark the sentence Agent. Some writers (Hook 1979) use this term synonymously with sentence subject to include just the terms which can be antecedents of reflexive pronouns and of controlled null subjects of conjunctive participles. For others, the role Agent has to do with volitionality, or conscious choice (Mohanan 1993). This association is not implausible. Transitive verbs have at least two arguments with distinct roles, distinguished by factors such as those discussed by Dowty (1989). The external argument or the subject quite often refers to a volitional or effective force, which acts in some way upon a more passive entity.

Yet there are numerous examples of ergative-marked subjects which are not agents except in the structural sense used by Hook. The ergative marks Cause or Source (9a,c,) Experiencer (10a), and Goal (11a), as well as Agent.

(9) a. *paristhitiyooN-nee* *usee* *ghabraa* *di-yaa* CAUSE/SOURCE
circumstances-ERG 3SG-DAT confound give-PF
'The circumstances confounded him/her.' (Bahri 1992: 169)

b. *is* *samasya-see* *woo* *ghabraa* *ga-yaa/* *uTh-aa*
this problem-from 3SG be-confounded go-PF/ rise-PF
'He got perplexed by this problem.' (Bahri 1992: 169)

c. *[us-kee duur rah-nee]-nee mujhee nahiiN khiiNc-aa*
3SG-GEN far stay-INF-ERG I-DAT not draw-PF
'His staying far off didn't attract me.' (Shah, p.c.)

(10) a. *aurangzeb-nee un-kii maut-par afsoos ki-yaa* EXPERIENCER
Aurangzeb-ERG 3pl-GEN death-LOC regret do-PF
'Aurangzeb felt regret/regretted his death.' (Hook 1979: 196)

b. *mujhee [is tarah gussaa dikhaa-nee]-kaa afsoos hai*
I-DAT this way anger show-INF-GEN regret is
'I regret (showing my anger this way).' (Hook 1979: 75)

(11) a. *maiN-nee naukarii baRii muSkil-see paa-ii hai* GOAL
I-ERG employment big difficulty-with obtain-PF is
'I got employment with much difficulty.' (Barz and Yadav 1993: 135)

b. *usee kaam mil-aa hai*
3SG-DAT work obtain-PF is
'He got work.' (Barz and Yadav 1993: 135)

There are other corresponding constructions with different Case marking on the non-agent – the dative *–koo* on Experiencers and goals, and *-see* 'from' on causatives. Related lexical items like these are common in Hindi/Urdu (see discussion in Montaut 1991). The differences between related lexical items might appear to be in agentivity, but as Montaut notes, there is only a weak tendency to associate the ergative with agentivity, because of alternations of the type given in (10), and because the association cannot be maintained in non-perfective or non-finite sentences (Montaut 1991: 102–4). Hook (1979) and Barz and Yadav (1993) of compare related expressions, which differ in Case marking, but apparently not in meaning. The explanation may lie in differences of Aktionsart (states, activities), and in the fact that lexical Case is constant, unambiguously marking a subject as non-agentive. By contrast, ergative subjects appear to be agentive by contrast, though they need not be interpreted as agentive. The *–nee* verb *pahcaan-naa* 'recognise' has a non-volitional Experiencer subject:

(12) *maiN-nee us-kii aawaaz pahcaan lii*
I-ERG 3SG-GEN voice recognise take-PF
'I recognised his/her voice.' (Bahri 1992: 382)

Perfective agentive *-nee* verbs like *khaa-naa* 'eat' may also lose *-nee* if combined with an intransitive light verb, which conveys a particular aspectual meaning, without losing the Agent role.[2] If there were a constant association of volitionality with *-nee* it would be hard to explain how it can be absent on agentive subjects even in the perfective (13b), and why it is required on non-agentive subjects in perfective/finite clauses (12) (but see note 2 and Davison to appear).

(13) a. *us-nee/*woo* *rooTii* *khaa-ii*
3SG-ERG 3SG-NOM bread-FSG eat-PF-FSG
'He/she ate the bread.' (OBJECT AGREEMENT)

b. *woo / *us-nee* *rooTii* *khaa* *ga-yaa/ga-ii*
3SG-NOM-M/F / 3SG-ERG bread eat go-PF-M /go-PF-F
'He/she ate up the bread (completely).' (SUBJECT AGREEMENT)

SUBJECT FUNCTION AND REFLEXIVE BINDING

Reflexive coindexing, like ergative Case, requires a subject antecedent, whether the subject has the Agent role or Experiencer/Goal role (see Mohanan 1990, Montaut 1991 and Davison in press for discussion). The reflexive, which is formally invariant for person, number and gender is *apnaa* 'self's, and *apnee (aap)* (postposition) '(self's) self'. In a single clause, the reflexive picks out the subject rather than another argument (14):

(14) *baccee*$_i$*-nee* *duusree* *baccee*$_j$*-see* *apnaa*$_{i/*j}$ *khilaunaa* *chiin* *li-yaa*
child-ERG other child-from self's toy snatch take-PF
'The child$_i$ snatched self's$_{i/*j}$ toy from another child$_j$.'

In sentences that allow long-distance as well as local coindexing (15), the reflexive is coindexed with subjects, whether they are null PRO, nominative, or ergative:

(15) *maaN*$_i$*-nee* *raam*$_j$*-koo* *[PRO*$_j$ *apnee*$_{i/j}$*-koo* *gumnaam* *patra*
mother-ERG Ram-DAT self-DAT anonymous letters-NOM-MPL

likh-nee]-kee liyee *manaa* *kiyaa*
write-INF-BENEFACTIVE forbidden do-PF-MPL
'Mother$_i$ forbade Ram$_j$ [PRO$_j$ to write self$_{i/j}$ anonymous letters.'

Both ergative licensing and reflexive binding are a consequence of the Extended Projection Principle (EPP), which guarantees a syntactic subject (Chomsky 1986, 1995). It is enforced by a feature of TENSE, one of the ergative licensers. The EPP functional projection cannot be AGR, because reflexive binding and verbal agreement may be independent:

(16) *monaa*$_i$*-nee (apnee)* *aap*$_{i/*j}$*-koo* *gumnaam* *ciTThiyaaN* *bheej diiN*
Mona-ERG self's self-DAT anonymous letters-NOM-FPL send give-PF-FPL
'Mona$_i$ sent herself$_{i/*j}$ anonymous letters.'

The verb has the feminine plural features agreeing with the direct object *ciTThiyaaN* 'letters', rather than the feminine singular matching the subject antecedent of the reflexive, Mona.[3] I will represent the TENSE functional projection as follows:

(17) [$_{TP}$ Spec (DP) [$_{T}$¢ ASP-P Tns$_{[D]}$]]

TENSE enforces the Extended Projection Principle requirement for a syntactic subject by requiring a nominal element (NP/DP) to move to its Specifier position. This [D] feature is strong, requiring overt movement of the whole DP to check the [D] feature, which is then deleted on TENSE (Collins 1997). Note that this principle guarantees not only a syntactic subject, which have its ergative Case checked by TENSE, but also a subject antecedent for a reflexive. I will use the proposal in Cole and Sung (1994) by which the reflexive is adjoined to a functional projection, here TENSE, and gets referentially identified by Specifier-Head agreement.

(18) [$_{TP}$ KP/DP$_{i}$ [$_{T}$¢ ASP-P [$_{Tns}$ REFL$_{i}$ TNS$_{[N]}$]]]

Reflexive identification, ergative licensing and the Extended Projection Principle are all associated with TENSE, and distinct from the nominative licensing-verb agreement function of AGR.

AGREEMENT AND NOMINATIVE CASE

In most Indic languages, the presence of ergative or any other postpositional Case on the subject blocks subject-verb agreement. If the subject is not a possible antecedent, then the direct object (19) or nominal part of an N-V complex predicate (20) is a possible agreement antecedent.

(19) a. *baccooN*$_{i}$*-nee* *apnii*$_{i/*j}$ *billii* *nahiiN* *deekh-ii*
children-MPL-ERG self's cat-NOM-FSG not see-PF-FSG
'The children$_{i}$ did not see self's$_{i/*j}$ cat.'

b. *baccee*$_{i}$*-koo* *apnee*$_{i/*j}$ *kuttee* *dikhaaii* *diyee*
child-MSG-DAT self's dog-NOM-MPL sight give-PF-MPL
'The children$_{i}$ caught sight of self's$_{i/*j}$ dogs.'

(20) a. *moohan*$_{i}$*-nee* *apnee*$_{i/*j}$ *maaN-baap-kii* *yaad* *kii*
Mohan-MSG-ERG self's mother-father-GEN memory-F do-PF-FSG
'Mohan$_{i}$ remembered self's$_{i/*j}$ parents.'

b. *moohan$_i$-koo* *apnee$_{i/*j}$* *maaN-baap-kii* *yaad* *aa-ii*
Mohan-MSG-DAT self's mother-father-GEN memory-F come-PF-F
'Mohan$_i$ remembered self's$_{i/*j}$ parents.'

Lack of subject agreement is not a special property of ergative subjects, nor is object agreement specific to perfective aspect:

(21) *moohan$_i$-koo* *apnee$_{i/*j}$* *maaN-baap-kii* *yaad* *aa-eegii*
Mohan-MSG-DAT self's mother-father-GEN memory-F come-FUT-FSG
'Sita$_i$ will remember self's$_{i/*j}$ parents.'

There is a single set of f-features on a verbal complex that agrees with the f-features of some nominative NP. We can equate nominative with the ability to trigger verb agreement. Since agreement is required where it is possible, I will assume that one AGR projection per sentence is strong, and that strong features take precedence over weak features in deciding which set of features are overtly manifested. For concreteness, I will represent agreement as the following structural configuration (but see Chomsky 1995; Collins 1997):

(22) [$_{AGRP}$ DP$_{[NOM [PNG]]}$ [$_{AGR¢}$ XP AGR $_{[NOM [PNG]]}$]]

Agreement is concretely represented as a sub-case of Specifier-Head agreement, allowing the NP Case features and PNG f-features to be checked by AGR. The formal feature NOM is erased on both AGR and DP. The f-features including plural are retained on DP as they enter into interpretation. AGR may fail to have the features [NOM[PNG]] if it is formed in the lexicon with the default features 3pSGM:

(23) a. *baccooN-nee* *us-billii-koo* *deekh-aa*
children-ERG that cat-DAT see-PF-MSG
'The children saw that cat.'

b. *baccooN-nee* *woo billii* **deekh-aa / deekh-ii*
children-ERG that cat-NOM see-PF-MSG see-PF-FSG
'The children saw that cat.'

The default features are possible (23) a. just when no NOM case remains to be licensed and deleted on a DP. Otherwise the derivation is ill formed because nominative Case is not checked, as in one version of (23b) (Chomsky 1995).

THE STRUCTURE OF VERB PHRASE

On the assumption that theta role and lexical Case assignment are local (Speas 1990), I represent the VP in (24) as (25):

(24) *maiN-nee* *us-kii* *aawaaz* *pahcaan* *lii (hai)*
I-ERG 3SG-GEN voice (FSG) recognise take-PF-FSG is[4]
'I recognised his/her voice.' (Bahri 1992: 382)

(25) $[_{VP}$ *maiN-nee* $[_{AGRP}$ *uskii aawaaz*$_i$ $[_{VP}$ t_i *pahcaan* t_V $[_{AGR}$ $AGR_{[NOM]\ [3FSG]}$ $t_V]]]$ lii]

The subject is separated from the verb and object by some internal function projection; here it is AGR (Koizumi 1995).[5] The VP internal AGR represents the ability of *pahcaan* to assign structural nominative Case, and also checks the 3PFSG agreement features of the object *us-kii aawaaz* 'his/her voice'. These object features are not overtly expressed unless the subject f-features are blocked by being within a KP, and the object is Nom, as in (23b).

The verb *pahcaan* 'recognise' and all its semantic as well as syntactic and morphological information is copied onto AGR and then the higher null V. The ergative Kase feature of the subject is consistent with the lexical properties of *pahcaan*. In this sentence, there is another main verb, *lee-naa* 'take', which is used as a compounded auxiliary, here expressing orientation of the event towards the subject, for the benefit of the subject referent. As an independent verb, *lee-naa* 'take' also has an ergative subject. The combination pahcaan *lee-naa* 'recognise-take' inherits the ergative marking property of both constituents [but see (28)–(29)].

THE ROLES OF FUNCTIONAL PROJECTIONS IN LICENSING ARGUMENTS

Licensing has been treated as feature checking in a local relation, head-specifier agreement (and we could resolve the KP feature [ERG] into [[FINITE] PERFECTIVE]). The sub-tree in (25) is combined with the relevant functional projections in (26) to represent (24):

(26) $[_{TP}$ *maiN-nee*$_j$ $[_{ASPP}$ t_j $[_{VP}$ t_j $[_{AGRP}$ *us-kii aawaaz*$_i$ $[_{VP}$ t_i *pahcaan* $t_V]$ $[_{AGR}$ $AGR_{[NOM]\ [3FSG]}$ $t_V]]$ $[_V$ $t_V]]$ $[_{ASP}$ $ASP_{[PERFECTIVE]}$ $t_V]]$ $[_{TNS}$ $TNS_{[D]\ [PRESENT]}$ $lii_V]]$

The projection stops with TP, and does not include a higher AGR:

(27) $[_{AGRP}$ $KP_{[ERG]}$ $[_{TP}$ t_{KP} $t_{Tns}]$ $[_{AGR}$ $AGR_{[NOM^*\ [1PNSG\ M/F]]}$ $TNS_{[D]}]]$

If the derivation continued as in (27), the [Nom] feature on AGR could not be checked by KP in its specifier, which has the feature [Erg]. There are no match of f-features either: A [Nom] subject would not be licensed by the verbal complex. The object f-features in (24)–(26) are realised on the TENSE-AGR complex, since the KP subject cannot match any AGR features. The object f-features (checked by the lower AGR along with [Nom] Case) get realised on the higher AGR just when the KP subject fails to have f-features (23a); see 5.

RELATIONS OF FEATURES TO LICENSERS IN ERGATIVE CLAUSES

TENSE and ASPECT are heads of functional categories, which may license ergative on a subject, but do not require ergative on a DP. Future tense disallows ergative, while intransitive verbs and some exceptional transitive verbs do not have ergative subjects in perfective sentences. TENSE does however also enforce the Extended Projection Principle; all values of TENSE attract a DP (Chomsky 1995: Chapter 4) to the Specifier of TENSE.[6] The [D] feature of TENSE is discharged.

If the ASPECT value is not perfective, or if TENSE is not finite, then [Erg] is not licensed, as we saw in sentences (1)–(5). Future tense disallows ergative, while intransitive verbs and some exceptional transitive verbs do not have ergative subjects in perfective sentences. It appears that ergative Case checking does not satisfy a requirement of the host TENSE/ASPECT. but the reverse: [ERG] must find the right values of TENSE/ASPECT. Yet movement of the [ERG] nominal phrase will be guaranteed because this phrase has DP features which satisfy the EPP.

NOMINATIVE LICENSING OF TRANSITIVE SUBJECTS.

Let us compare the derivation and the Case licensing in (27) with the derivation from the same VP structure in (28)–(29), but with different functional projections above it.[7]

(28)	*maiN-(*nee)*	*us-kii*	*aawaaz*	*pahcaan*	*lee-taa*	*(huuN)*
	I-NOM/-ERG	3SG-GEN	voice-FSG	recognise	take-IMPF.MSG	am

'I recognise his/her voice.'

(29) [$_{\text{AGRP}}$ *maiN*$_j$ [$_{\text{TP}}$ t_j [$_{\text{ASPP}}$ t_j [$_{\text{VP}}$ t_j [$_{\text{AGRP}}$ *us-kii aawaaz*$_i$ [$_{\text{VP}}$ t_i*pahcaan* t_V] [$_{\text{AGR}}$ AGR$_{\text{[NOM][3FSG]}}$ t_V]] [$_{\text{ASP}}$ ASP$_{\text{[IMPERFECTIVE]}}$ *letaa*$_V$]] [$_{\text{TNS}}$ TNS $_{\text{[PRESENT]}}$ *huun*]] [$_{\text{AGR}}$ AGR$_{\text{[NOM][1SG]}}$]]

The verb *pahcaan* 'recognise' allows [Nom] or [Erg] on its subject. The [Erg] feature would not be licensed because ASPECT is imperfective. Agreement refers to the nominative subject. The [NOM] DP subject is attracted to ASP/TENSE to supply the DP specifier, which discharges its [D] requirement for the EPP. The subject raises further to AGRP to meet its [Nom] requirement and to check f-features. The DP object is also [Nom]; it raises to the Specifier of the lower AGR to check the [Nom] case and the f-features [3p.SG.f]. In a sentence like this, the 'higher' set of f-features are realised on the verb, as there is only one set of inflectional suffixes per verb in Hindi (unlike Marathi [Gair and Wali 1988] or some of the 'eastern' Hindi languages [Mahto 1989]).

Two identical AGR heads are represented, requiring independent checking of both nominative Case and f-features on subjects and objects. If only one DP has nominative Case checked by the AGR projection, as in Mahajan (1990), this DP could be the subject, in sentence (28), or the object in (24). If this AGR is the highest projection, over TP, then the object would be higher than the subject, even if the subject moves to TP.

REFLEXIVES AND THE NOTION OF SUBJECT

Nominative subjects may antecede reflexives and also trigger agreement (3a), but there is no intrinsic connection between reflexivisation and agreement [see (14b)–(15b) and (14a)–(15a), (19)–(21)]. Accordingly, I use AGR to represent the association of agreement/nominative Case, and TENSE to serve as the host for reflexive cliticisation and enforcer of the EPP subject requirement:

(30) *baccooN*$_i$*-nee* *apnii*$_{i/*j}$ *kitaabeeN* *paRhiiN*
children-3PL-M-ERG self's books-3PL-F read-PF-3PL-F
'The children$_i$ read their$_{i/*j}$ (own) books.'

(31) [$_{\text{TP}}$ *baccooN-nee*$_j$ [$_{\text{ASPP}}$ t_j [$_{\text{VP}}$ t_j [$_{\text{AGRP}}$ t_x *kitaab*$_{\text{i [NOM]}}$ [$_{\text{VP}}$ t_i*paRh*$_{\text{[V-ERG]}}$] [$_{\text{AGR}}$ AGR$_{\text{[NOM]}}$]]] [$_{\text{ASP}}$ ASP$_{\text{[PERFECTIVE]}}$ [*-ii*]$_{\text{[FSG]}}$]] [$_{\text{TNS}}$ TNS $_{\text{[3SG]}}$ *apnii*$_x$ *hai*]]

Note that the reflexive clitic is coindexed with the external argument ergative KP, but the agreement is controlled by the nominative object. TENSE/ASPECT are more consistently present and identify the subject more consistently than AGR. There is an interesting consequence of this language-specific separation of subject properties and agreement. Reflexives in this language are not inflected by lexical PNG-features (like many languages with long-distance reflexives), and in this language, the reflexive arguments have neither nominative form nor agreement features, for example the predicate nominal (32a):

(32) a. **raam*$_i$ *apnaa* *aap*$_i$ *nahiiN* *hai*
Ram self's self-NOM not is
'Ram is not himself.'

b. *raam*$_i$ *apnee* *aapee*$_i$ *-meeN* *nahiiN* *hai*
Ram self's AAPAA-in not is
'Ram is not in his right mind, is not himself.'

As Yamabe (1990) notes, the dative experiencer construction in (33a) is not possible if the nominative theme is itself a reflexive (33b).

(33) a. *apnii*$_{i/*j}$ *maaN-koo* *kumaar*$_i$ *acchaa* *lag-taa* *hai*
self's mother-DAT Kumar-NOM good strike-IMPF is
'His$_{i/*j}$ mother likes Kumar$_i$.' (Yamabe 1990: 115)

b. **raam*$_i$*-koo* *sirf* *apnaa* *aap*$_{i/*j}$ *acchaa* *lag-taa* *hai*
Ram-DAT only self's self-NOM good strike-IMPF is
'Ram likes only himself.'

c. *raam*$_i$ *sirf* *apnee* *(aap)*$_{i/*j}$*-koo* *acchaa* *lag-taa* *hai*
Ram only self's self-DAT good strike-IMPF is
'Only Ram likes himself.'

Rather, there must be a reversal (optional elsewhere), in that the reflexive must be in the dative KP, while the nominative theme is a name (and as the antecedent of the reflexive, it is also the subject by movement to Spec/TENSE).

SUMMARY AND CONCLUSIONS

In this paper, I have proposed that the *-nee* ergative postposition marks subjects as a structural Case, licensed primarily as a subject. It is dependent on conditions at different points in the clause structure: the case assigning properties of the verb, and the verbal complex, as well as functional projections of TENSE and ASPECT. Ergative licensing is represented here as an example of the displacement property of language (Chomsky 1995).

The ergative DP/KP fulfills the Extended Projection Principle requirement for a DP, a strong feature of TENSE/ASPECT, which attracts the subject from within VP before Spellout. In this position, the special requirements of nee to be licensed by perfective aspect and finite tense are automatically met. The EPP also guarantees that there will be a subject antecedent, regardless of Case, to identify the reflexive which cliticises at LF to TENSE (or ASPECT). The agreement system is independent of subject properties, as both subjects and objects have nominative Case and can trigger agreement, and morphological agreement is not correlated with referential identity. If two agreement triggers are available, the subject AGR has priority, probably because of the strong EPP feature, which is always checked before Spellout.

NOTES

1. This sentence is possible for some speakers, but most of those I have consulted require a nominative embedded subject. Mahajan (p.c.) suggests that the Ergative may be licensed by the perfective aspect of the local clause and the finite tense of the matrix, assuming a Raising operation.
2. Some exceptional intransitives allow either Nominative or Ergative subjects, like *khaaNs-naa* 'cough' and *bhauNk-naa* 'bark' (ia,b), with subject-verb agreement blocked in (ia) but required in (ib). The same licensing conditions (finiteness, perfectivity) hold for these verbs as for the transitive verbs that take ergative subjects (ic).

   i. a. *raat-koo* *kuttee*0/-nee* *zoor-see* *bhauNk-aa* *hai*
   night-DAT dogs-M.PL-NOM/-ERG force-with bark-PF-MSG is
   'Dogs barked loudly at night.'

   b. *raat-koo* *kuttee/*-nee* *zoor-see* *bhauNk-ee* *haiN*
   night-DAT dogs-M.PL-NOM/-ERG force-with bark-PF-MPL are
   'Dogs barked loudly at night.'

   c. *kuttee/*-nee* *zoor-see* *bhauNk-tee* *haiN/* *bhauNkeeNgee*
   dogs-MPL-NOM/-ERG force-with bark-IMPF are/ bark-FUT-MPL
   'Dogs bark/will bark loudly.'

   The sentences with *-nee* and those without *-nee* do not differ in agency. For example, one may cough involuntarily or to get someone's attention, but the choice of *-nee* does not necessarily coincide with the intention to convey conscious choice.
3. If reflexive coindexing and verbal agreement took place in the same projection outside the VP, AGR, then it would be possible for the reflexive itself to be syntactically higher than its antecedent.

   i. a. *baccooN$_i$-nee* *apnii$_{i/*j}$* *kitaabeeN* *paRhiiN*
   children-ERG self's books-FPL read-PF-FPL
   'The childrenı read their$_{i/*j}$ (own) books.'

b. *baccooN$_i$-kii kitaabeeN apnooN$_{i/*j}$-nee paRhiiN
children-GEN books-FPL self-ERG read-PF-FPL
'The childreni read their$_{i/*j}$ (own) books.'

The Ergative NP remains in VP (Mahajan 1990), while the object NP raises to AGR to check NOM Case in (i), reversing the normal c-command relation of antecedent and reflexive, otherwise not possible (ii).

4. The present tense copula may be omitted; there is a slight meaning difference between the perfective alone (like past tense of English) and the perfective + copula (like the present perfect). I will assume that there can be null finite tense.
5. Bowers (1993) and Collins (1997) each propose that the subject is separated from the rest of the verbal projection by a functional projection with a null head. Bowers (1993) defines PR as the head of Predicate Phrase, which has the semantic function of relating the predicate VP to an external argument. Collins (1997) proposes TR which checks the Case of objects, but also has feature-checking properties also found on T. Laka (to appear) uses ASPECT to check Case of the VP internal NP in Ergative languages. In this paper I use AGR within VP, in order to focus on the association of Nominative Case and agreement features, which is independent of subject properties.
6. Clauses must have subjects without even non-finite tense infection. ASPECT, as well as whatever head is present in Small Clauses (Haegeman 1995) must be able to attract DP to enforce the EPP.
7. If the main verb is linked with a non-ergative aspectual verb, the combination also fails to license an Ergative subject:

i. *ham(*-nee) kaThoorii-see usee pahcaan paaee*
we(-ERG) difficulty-witH 3SG-DAT recognise manage-PF-1PL.M
'We managed to recognise him/her with difficulty.' (Bahri 1992: 382)

This aspectual verb *paa-naa* 'to manage, obtain' like *sak-naa* 'be able' and *cuk-naa* 'to complete' may be a separate verb head because of its independent contribution of meaning to the sentence (see Porizka 1963). In this case, we can explain the failure of Ergative licensing with an intervening functional projection which does not license Erg if DP/KP moves locally to the nearest specifier. If DP/KP moves over this projection headed by paa and goes directly Spec/ASPECT, then the Shortest Move condition will be violated. This explanation is similar to the one expressed in terms of Government in Singh (1993); if there is an intervening modal/aspectual verb projection between Perfective ASPECT and the Ergative subject in VP, then Perfective cannot govern and check the Ergative Case on the subject. Alternatively, the modal/aspectual verbs could be treated like the compound or vector verbs in (24).

REFERENCES

BAHRI, HARDEV

1992 *Siksaarthii hindii-angreezii SabdkooS / Learner's Hindi-English Dictionary*. Delhi: Rajpal Sons.

BARZ, R and Y. YADAV

1993 *An introduction to Hindi-Urdu*. Delhi: Munshiram Manoharlal.

BITTNER, MARIA and K. HALE

1996 The structural determination of case and agreement. *Linguistic Inquiry*, 27. 1–68.

BOWERS, JOHN

1993 The syntax of predication. *Linguistic Inquiry*, 24. 591–656.

CHOMSKY, NOAM

1981 *Lectures on government and binding*. Dordrecht: Foris Publications.

1986 *Knowledge of language*. New York: Praeger.

1995 *The minimalist program*. MIT Press.

COLE, P. and L-M. SUNG

1994 Head movement and long-distance reflexives. *Linguistic Inquiry*, 25. 355–85.

COLLINS, CHRIS

1997 *Local economy*. Cambridge: MIT Press.

DAVISON, ALICE

(in press) Lexical anaphors in Hindi/Urdu. In Kashi Wali, K.V. Subbarao, Barbara Lust & James Gair (eds.), *Lexical anaphors and pronouns in some South Asian languages: A principled typology*. Berlin: Mouton de Gruyter.

(in press) Ergativity. In Edith Moravcsik & Michael Noonan (eds.), *Proceedings of the Symposium on Formalism and Functionalism*. Amsterdam and Philadelphia: John Benjamins.

DOWTY, DAVID

1989 Thematic proto-roles and argument selection. *Language*, 67. 547–619.

GAIR, JAMES and KASHI WALI

1988 On distinguishing AGR from AGR: Evidence from South Asia. *Chicago Linguistics Society*, 24. Parasession on Agreement. 87–104.

HAEGEMAN, LILIANE

1995 *Introduction to government and binding theory*, second edition. Oxford: Basil Blackwell.

HOOK, PETER

1979 *Intermediate Hindi structures*. Ann Arbor: University of Michigan, Center for South Asian Studies.

KHAN, BABER S.

1989 A note of disagreement on verb agreement in Hindi-Urdu. *Linguistics*, 27. 71–87.

KOIZUMI, M.

1995 *Phrase structure in minimalist syntax*. MIT dissertation.

LAKA, I.

(in press) Theta-blind case: Burzio's generalization and its image in the mirror. In Eric Reuland (ed.), *Papers from the Workshop on Burzio's generalization.*

MAHAJAN

1990 *The A/A-bar distinction and movement theory.* MIT dissertation.

MAHTO, PANCHANAN

1989 *On the nature of empty pronominals.* Hyderabad: CIEFL unpublished dissertation.

MARANTZ, ALEC

1991 Case and licensing. ESCOL '91. 234–53.

MOHANAN, TARA

1990 *Arguments in Hindi.* Stanford University dissertation.

1993 Case alternation on objects in Hindi. *South Asian Language Review,* 3.1. 1–30.

MONTAUT, ANNIE

1991 *Aspects, voix et diatheses en hindi moderne.* Paris and Louvain: Editions Peeters.

PORIZKA, V.

1963 *Hindi language course.* Prague: Statni Pedagogicke Nakladatelstvi.

SINGH, JOGA

1993 Case dependencies in Hindi. In A. Davison & F. Smith (eds.), *Papers from the XV SALA meeting,* 296–321. Iowa City, Iowa: South Asian Studies Program, University of Iowa.

SPEAS, MARGARET

1990 *Phrase structure in natural language.* Dordrecht: Kluwer Academic Publishers.

SUBBARAO, K.V.

1984 *Complementation in Hindi syntax.* Delhi: Academic Publications.

YAMABE, JUNJI

1990 *Dative subject constructions in Indic languages.* University of Tokyo, Department of Linguistics, unpublished Master's thesis.

21
Tense and negation in Bengali

GILLIAN CATRIONA RAMCHAND
University of Oxford

Bengali possesses two negation markers, which occur in different morphosyntactic contexts, and with different aspectual consequences. The existence of these two negation markers poses a number of puzzles for linguistic theory. Negation, as a functional element within sentential structure, has not received the kind of treatment that would predict this kind of variability in both semantics and morphosyntax.

The negative particle *na* in Bengali occurs sentence-finally with a tensed verb, as in (1).

(1) *Ram* *am-Ta* *khacche* *na*
Ram mango-CLASS. eat-PRES/3RD NEG
'Ram isn't eating the mango.'

The negative particle *ni* is only found with morphologically untensed, non-aspectual forms of the verb, but has the semantic effect of negating an event in the past, as in (2).

(2) *Ram* *am-Ta* *khay* *ni*
Ram mango-CLASS. eat-3RD NEG
'Ram didn't eat the mango.'

The challenge here lies in explaining firstly the morphosyntactic distribution of these two forms of negation and providing an explicit semantic framework that will account for their interpretation. In doing so, we must also provide an account for a long-standing puzzle in the negation of complex predicates in the language. It is well known among South Asian linguists that the negation of a completive complex predicate in Bengali (and many other North Indian languages) using the *na* element is systematically ungrammatical (3).

(3) **Ram* *am-Ta* *kheye* *phello* *na*
Ram mango-CLASS. eat-PERF. throw-PAST/3RD NEG
'Ram didn't eat up the mango.'

However, using the alternative negation strategy *ni*, also produces ungrammatical results for sentential negation. The only possible reading for (4) is the discoursally marked 'negation of completion' reading.

(4) *Ram* *am-Ta* *kheye* *phaeli* *ni*
Ram mango-CLASS. eat-PERF throw-3RD NEG
i. 'Ram didn't *completely* eat up the mango (but he did eat some of it).'
ii. *'Ram didn't eat the mango up.'

The purpose of this paper is to propose a theoretical framework which can make sense of the morphosyntactic and semantic differences between the two negation strategies, and thus to solve the puzzle of the completive complex predicates' interaction with negation.

THE DATA

Bengali is an SOV language. Arguments may scramble with considerable freedom, but elements cannot generally appear to the right of the verb, except under very marked discourse conditions. The verb itself is complex consisting of a head, an aspectual marking and tense, in that order. The verbal complex agrees with the subject of the sentences in person only. The following examples illustrate this.

(5) PRESENT PROGRESSIVE
ami *am-Ta* *khacch-i*
I-NOM mango-CLASS. eat-PROG-PRES-1ST
'I am eating the mango.'

(6) PRESENT PERFECT
ami *am-Ta* *kheye-ch-i*
I-NOM mango-CLASS. eat-PERF-PRES-1ST
'I have eaten the mango.'

(7) SIMPLE PAST
ami *am-Ta* *khelam*
I-NOM mango-CLASS. eat-PAST/1ST
'I ate the mango (either perfective or imperfective).'

Bengali has two distinct sentence-final negation elements, which are in complementary distribution depending on the aspectual class of the verb phrase to be negated. In the non-perfective tenses (simple and progressive present, simple past, and future tenses), the particle *na* is used to negate the sentence, as shown in examples (8) and (9).

(8) *ami* *am-Ta* *khacchi* *na*
I-NOM mango-CLASS. eat-PROG-PRES-1ST NEG
'I am not eating the mango.'

(9) *ami* *am-Ta* *khelam* *na*
I-NOM mango-CLASS. eat-PAST-1ST NEG
'I didn't eat the mango.'

All of these tenses are compatible with imperfectivity, as the standard tests show.

(10) *ami am-Ta khacchi ektu khonner jonno*
'I am eating the mango for a short while.'

(11) *ami am-Ta khelam ektu khonner jonno*
'I ate the mango for a short while.'

However, when the sentence to be negated is in the perfect tense, as in (12), the sentence-final negation marker is *ni*, and the verb form reverts to a simple untensed form, as in (13). Despite this untensed form of the verb, the sentence is interpreted unambiguously as a past-tense negative.

(12) *ami* *am-Ta* *kheyechi*
I mango-CLASS. eat-PERF/PRES/1ST
'I have eaten the mango.'

(13) *ami* *am-Ta* *khai* *ni*
I mango-CLASS. eat-1ST NEG
'I didn't eat the mango.'

BACKGROUND ASSUMPTIONS: MORPHOSYNTAX

Bengali is a straightforwardly head-final language in all its projections. I will assume a binary branching structure with Spec positions on the left, containing tense, aspect and negation functional projections, as in (14). Following the hypothesis in Chomsky (1993), I will assume that lexical items come specified for their inflectional features, and must raise to the head of the relevant functional projection to check those features. However, unlike Chomsky (1993),

I will not be assuming the existence of explicit ACR projections. The features that the verbs in this language come specified for are

- an aspectual feature which I will notate [+/-bound], and
- a tense feature which in its simplest form will have [+Past, +Pres, +Fut] specification.

(14)

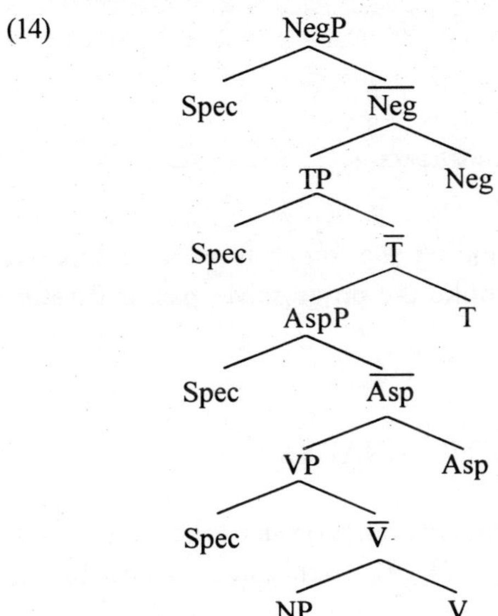

In addition, there is one verbal form which does not carry any tense or aspect marking at all, *kha-*, which is used on its own only as an habitual (realis) tense underspecified for tense and compatible with a non-bound interpretation. The form *kheye,* which is found in the perfect tense, I will assume to be specified unambiguously for [+bound]. However, it has no tense features and may appear on its own in nonfinite clauses.

The simple verbal forms of Bengali are specified in the lexicon as follows for the verb *khaoya-* 'to eat':

(15)

MORPHOLOGICAL FORM	INFLECTIONAL FEATURES
khacch-	([-bound], [+pres])
Khel-	([+past])
khab-	([+bound], [+future])
kheye	([+bound])
kha-	no features to check

In the perfect, there is an independent lexical element which carries tense information. This is an element that descends from the verb 'to be' in the language. Evidence that the tense-carrying element in the perfect in independent, while it is clearly part of the verbal form in the progressive, comes from the intrusion of emphatic particles between *kheye-* and *chi* in (16). This intrusion is impossible in the progressive between *kha* and *-chi* in (17).

(16) *ami* *am-Ta* *kheye-o-chi*
I-NOM mango-CLASS. eat (PERF)-*EMPH*-PRES-1ST
'I have EATEN the mango.'

(17) **ami* *am-Ta* *kha-o-chi*
I-NOM mango-CLASS. eat (PROG)-*EMPH*-PRES-1ST
'I am EATING the mango.'

This is the justification for including the *kheye* form as a separate morpheme underspecified for tense, unlike the progressive, past and future tense forms.

MORPHOSYNTACTIC ANALYSIS

My analysis of the distributional facts crucially relies on an explicitly aspectual projection, AspP. The simple sentences (7)–(9) would have the structure in (18)–(20), respectively.

(18)

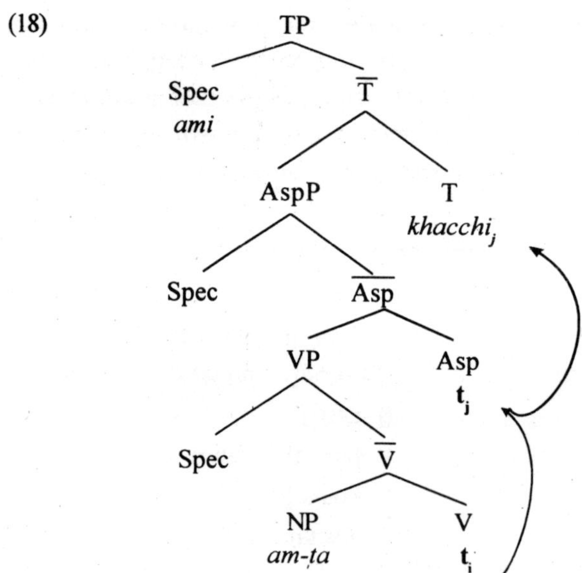

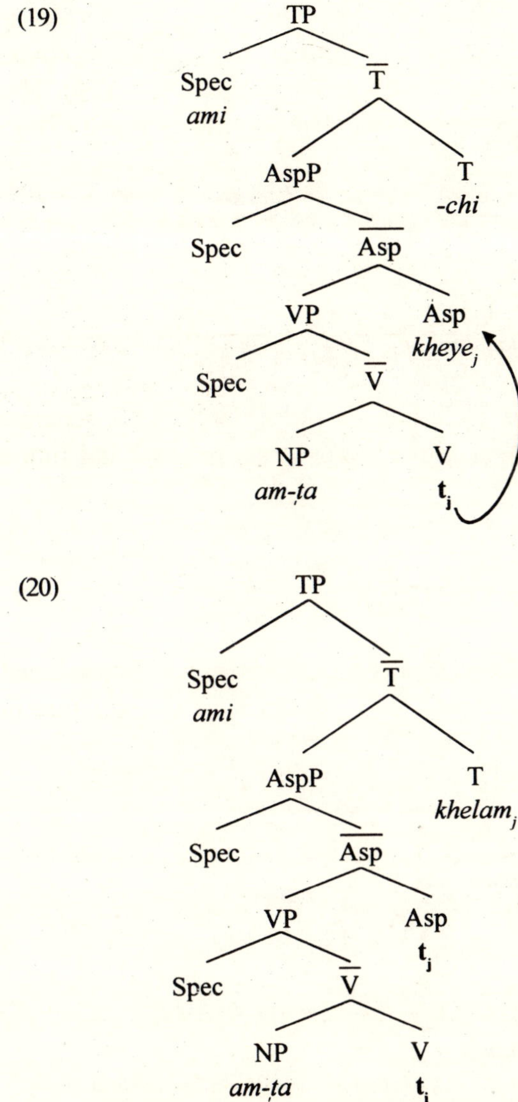

Under this analysis, the negation marker *na* is base generated as the head of NegP, giving the phrase structures in (21) and (22) for the negated sentences (10) and (11), respectively.

(21)

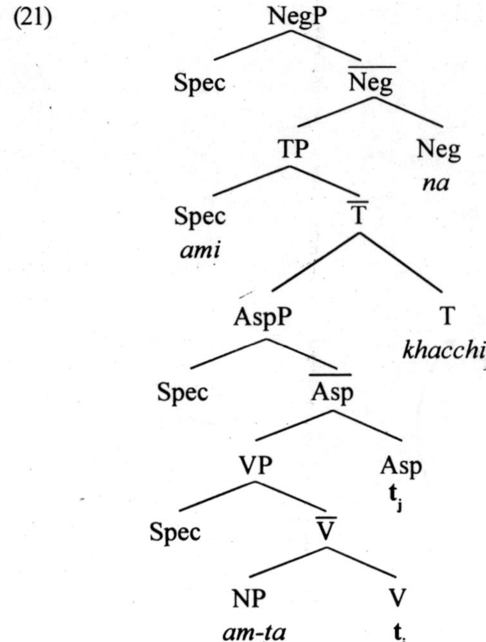
NegP
Spec
Neg
TP
Neg
na
Spec
ami
T
AspP
T
khacchi_j
Spec
Asp
VP
Asp
t_j
Spec
V
NP
am-ṭa
V
t_i

(22)

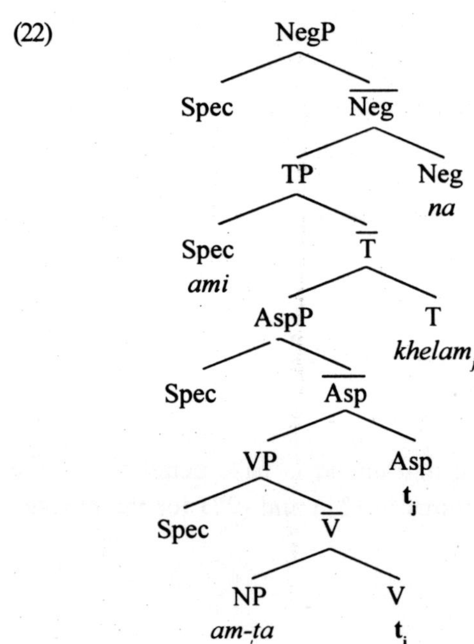
NegP
Spec
Neg
TP
Neg
na
Spec
ami
T
AspP
T
khelam_j
Spec
Asp
VP
Asp
t_j
Spec
V
NP
am-ṭa
V
t_i

On the other hand, the *ni* marker is actually responsible for contributing both aspectual and tense information to the interpretation of the sentence. I will assume that this element is base generated as the head of an aspectual projection: it is morphologically specified for perfectivity, past tense as well as negation and undergoes head-to-head movement obligatorily to check these features. The resulting phrase structure is as shown in (22).

(23)

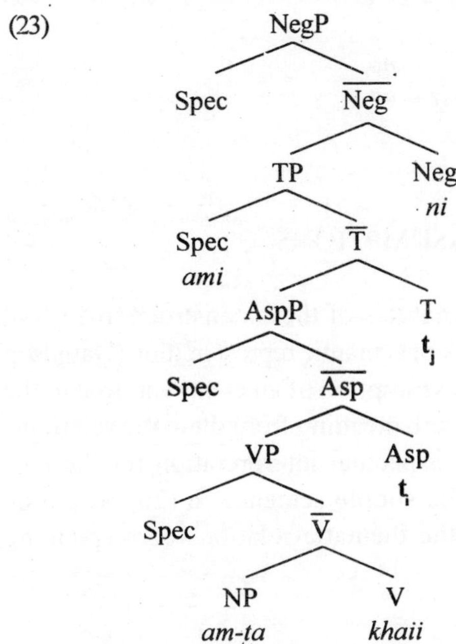

As further confirmation of the analysis that it is the *ni* particle which is specified for tense and aspect features, we find that the form of the verb that must appear in this construction is the form that is correspondingly *un*-specified for these features, namely *kha-* at the bottom of (15). Adding the negative forms to our morphological list, we get the table in (24).

(24)

MORPHOLOGICAL FORM	KIND OF HEAD	INFLECTIONAL FEATURES
khacch-	Verb	([-bound], [+pres])
khel-	Verb	([+past])
khab-	Verb	([+future])
kha-	Verb	no features to check
kheye	Verb	([+bound])
-ch-	Tense	[+pres]
-chil-	Tense	[+past]
na	Neg	[+neg]
ni	Asp	([+bound], [+past], [+neg])

I have argued for a particular view of the phrase structure of these constructions, essentially from morphosyntactic facts. However, more is needed if we are to solve the problem of the interaction of complex predicates with negation. In particular, we do not yet have an explanation for why the *na* form of negation should be incompatible with the aspectually perfective form of the verb. For this, we need to examine the semantics of these constructions more closely.

(25) **ami* *am-ṭa* *kheyechi* *na*
I mango-CLASS. eat-PERF/PRES/1ST NEG
'I have not eaten the mango.'

SEMANTIC ASSUMPTIONS

In making specific claims about the semantics of these constructions, I will be adopting a neo-Davidsonian framework of semantic representation (Davidson 1967; Parsons 1990). This involves the assumption of an event variable in the semantics, and the separability of basic verb meaning from thematic relations. Thus, abstracting away from tense and aspectual interpretation for the moment, the semantic representation for the simple sentence in (26) would be as shown, where Θ_1 and Θ_2 represent the thematic relations corresponding to 'subject' and 'object', respectively.

(26) John is eating the mango.
eating (e) & Θ_1 (e, 'John') & Θ_2 (e, 'the mango')

It is not the purpose of this paper to defend any position regarding the number or nature of the thematic relations that are appropriate to natural language. I will therefore continue to use these vague Θ labels for those relations. Nothing I argue for here hinges on this choice. Also, this representation is neutral with respect to whether one believes that the thematic relations are introduced as part of the verb meaning itself, or as a result of constructional effect due to particular functional heads.

I will also assume that the representation contains a time variable, t, which is the argument of the tense predicates, PAST, PRESENT and FUTURE. In addition, there is a tight relation between this time introduced in the course of predication and the event variable. I assume that t and e are related formally by a temporal trace function τ(e) as found in Krifka (1992) which maps an event to the 'time line' that it occupies. In any actual predication, the event introduced by the predicate is constrained to overlap with the time introduced by the predicate. We can see this as a kind of coherence requirement automatically met in verbal extended projections. In formal terms, we can represent this restriction as

(27) $\tau(e) \odot t$ (the time line of the event e overlaps t)

We can also define as primitives the event moments t_f and $t_i \in \tau(e)$ as the final and initial moment respectively of an event. Only a bounded ([+bound]) event will necessarily have a t_f.[1] With these preliminaries out of the way, we are in a position to be specific about the semantic contributions of the purely formal features introduced here. The tense features [+past], [+pres] and [+fut] can be seen to relate the t of predication to the speech time t* in the obvious ways.

[+present] contributes a restriction on the t variable such that
$t \odot t^*$

[+past] contributes a restriction on the t variable such that
$t < t^*$

[+future] contributes a restriction on the t variable such that
$t > t^*$

The aspectual feature [+bound] can also be given a specific interpretation in this system. Following the traditional description of perfective and imperfective events (see Smith 1991), I will assume that the imperfective events result from viewing the event internally, as a process, while perfective events result from viewing the event as a completed whole, from the point of view of its final moment. Thus, while the imperfective (default) case involves merely stating that the time trace of the event overlaps with the predication time t, I will assume that the perfective requires the *final moment* of the event to overlap the time of predication, specifying the existence of a final moment t_f in the temporal trace of the event. In the perfect tenses, this final moment is also specified to precede the time t of predication.

[+bound] contributes the restriction [t_f=t], where t_f is the final moment in $\tau(e)$

There are only two more assumptions to be made explicit. I assume that the level at which the event variable of the predication gets bound is AspP, and that this is done by existential closure in the default case (as in Diesing 1988). I also assume that the t variable must be bound and that this happens at the level of TP. The binding of the time variable can be subject to default existential closure, but it can also be anaphoric to previous time variables set up in the discourse (see Partee 1984 for a discussion of this possibility in a natural language).

Given this semantic framework, the semantic representation of a simple (non-negated) sentence in Bengali, would be as shown in (28).

(28) *Ram* *am-Ta* *khelam*
Ram mango-CLASS. eat-PAST/3RD
'Ram ate the mango.'

$\exists t{:}t < t^*,\ \exists e{:}\tau(e) \odot t$ [eating (e) & Θ_1 (e,'Ram') & Θ_2 (e, 'the mango')]

Here, the time variable t is usually linked anaphorically with some contextually salient discourse time in the past in the context of conversation. The past-tense marking merely provides a felicity constraint: it is used when the time picked out is before the speech time.

ANALYSIS

How do we then represent the force of the negation element in these sentences? To semantically negate a sentence such as the one presented in (28), we are faced with at least two choices. Since we have represented both the event variable and the tense time variable as separate elements in our ontology, and since they are linked by a coherence condition, it seems that we could negate the existence of either variable with the same semantic results. If this is true, then it is a problem for a theory that aims for parsimony of description. However, I will argue that the choice between negating the event and negating the time variable is not neutral, but does have semantic consequences in certain situations. The following minimal pair in Bengali will make this clearer.

(29) *ami* *am-Ta* *khelam* *na*
I-NOM mango-CLASS. eat-PAST-1ST NEG
'I didn't eat the mango.'

(30) *ami* *am-Ta* *khai* *ni*
I mango-CLASS. eat-1ST NEG
'I didn't eat the mango.'

Both the examples seem to be past-tense negations of the same event. And it is clear that in many situations, either one or the other may be used with equal felicity.[2] The question is whether the two expressions actually differ in their semantics at a subtler level, and in particular, whether there are *any* contexts at all where one is more felicitous than the other. I think this is indeed the case. I have found at least two contexts where the (29) type of negation is clearly preferred over the (30) type. Consider a simple narrative where a hungry boy enters a room and finds a mango lying on the table. He has been told by his mother that he mustn't eat anything before dinner, so he refrains from eating it just then.

(31) *Ram ghore dhuklo. Or khub khide pacchilo. O tabeler upore am-Ta dekhlo. Amta khello na . . .*

While the *ni* form is certainly possible here, it seems that the *na* form is preferred. Even clearer is the following situation. Suppose Ram has a car that is always giving trouble. In particular, the car quite often refuses to start. When that happens, he has to call in his neighbour, who is a mechanic, to fix it. If Ram is reporting that it was only one day this week that his car did not start, someone might felicitously ask him the following:

(32) *kon* *dine* *gari* *'start'* *holo* *na*
Which day car start become-PAST/3RD NEG
'On which day did the car not start?'

In this case, it would not be felicitous to use the *ni* form, because it would mean that the car did not start at all for the day. Thus, sentence (33) means that the car did not start at all yesterday, while (34) means that there was *some* event of the car not starting that occurred yesterday, but then perhaps the neighbour fixed it and Ram was able to drive to work.

(33) *kalke* *gaṛi* *'start'* *hoi* *ni*
yesterday car start become-3RD *ni*
'Yesterday the car didn't start at all.'

(34) *kalke* *gaṛi* *'start'* *holo* *na*
yesterday car start become-PAST/3RD *na*
'Yesterday the car didn't start (but then my neighbour came and fixed it).'

This relates to the fact that in general, speakers will translate the *ni* negations using the phrase 'at all', and report that the *ni* type is 'more emphatic'.

I argue that these two negation strategies in Bengali reflect different semantic quantifiers in the representation. While their effects are quite often indentical, they have different consequences in discourse. Specifically, I wish to argue that in the case of *na*, what we have is a simple negation of events. The time variable is linked, as usual, via context, to some particular time in the past, and the negation merely says that no event of the specified type occurred at that moment.

(35) *Ram* *am-Ta* *khelam* *na*
Ram mango-CLASS. eat-PAST/3RD *na*
'Ram didn't eat the mango.'

$\exists$t:t< t*, ¬ $\exists$e:τ(e) $\odot$ t [eating (e) & Θ_1 (e,'Ram') & Θ_2 (e, 'the mango')]

However, with the *ni* marker, what we have is a quantifier that binds the time variable directly. A sentence with this sort of negation states that for no time at all (in the discourse context) did an event of the specified type occur.

(36) *Ram* *am-Ta* *khay* *ni*
Ram mango-CLASS. eat-3RD *ni*
'Ram didn't eat the mango at all.'

For No t:t< t*, $\exists$e:τ(e) $\odot$ t [eating (e) & Θ_1 (e,'Ram') & Θ_2 (e, 'the mango')]

It is easy to see that in many cases these two logical forms give the same truth conditions. Both types of negation are strongly influenced by context: in the case of *na* the location of t is specified by the discourse, and similarly in the case of *ni* the set of time variables that are considered the 'universe' of variables captured by the negative quantifier is controlled by the discourse context. However, there are differences. In the case of a narrative where the time variable is saliently linked to a context where each sentence advances the discourse time, a form which allows the sentence to pick up the narrative time variable, and then predicate something of it is more felicitous (the *na* type). In the case of the non-starting car, the existence of the adverbial 'yesterday' provides the universe of discourse for the time variable and means that in the *ni* sentence, every single time within that frame must be times at which there was no car-starting. On the other hand, the *na* type of sentence allows one moment within the discourse time to be picked out, and then the non-starting event predicated of just that moment. More generally, the feeling of emphaticness that speakers report for the *ni* form is related to this universal negation of *all* the times in the context.

NEGATION AND COMPLETIVE COMPLEX PREDICATES

With this semantic analysis in hand, let us now turn to the problem of the completive complex predicates. These predicates are a particularly striking instantiation of the prohibition of [+bound] forms with the *na* negation marker. And, in addition, they also seem to reject the *ni* marker for pure sentential negation.

These complex predicates consist of a 'light' verb (LV) which carries tense and agreement marking, and which is semantically bleached; and a 'heavy' verbal participle that contributes the semantic content of the predication. The aspectual complex predicates I am concerned with here are obligatorily perfective in nature. An example is given in (37).

(37) *ami* *am-Ta* *kheye* *phellam*
I-NOM mango-CLASS. eat-PERF throw (LV)-PAST-1ST
'I ate up the mango.'

As stated before, these complex predicates interact with negation in a rather surprising way. The crucial examples are repeated here as (38) and (39).

(38) **ami* *am-Ta* *kheye* *phellam* *na*
I-NOM mango-CLASS. eat-PERF throw (LV)-PAST-1ST NEG
'I didn't eat up the mango.'

(39) *ami* *am-Ta* *kheye* *phaeli* *ni*
I-NOM mango-CLASS. eat-PERF throw (LV)-1ST NEG
'*I didn't eat up the mango.'
'I didn't *completely* eat the mango.'

In fact, we now have the machinery in place to account for both classes of ungrammaticality. The ungrammaticality of sentence negation in (39) can be understood if we assume a particular view of the phrase structure of complex predicates. Rather than take the view that complex predicates are constructed in the lexicon and then inserted straightforwardly under V in the phrase structure, the two components are actually base-generated at different functional levels in the phrase structure. This allows us to maintain a unified view of the *kheye* forms and say that it is a verbal form that must raise to Asp to check its [+bound] feature, but which crucially goes no higher. The light verb *phæla* under this view is the tense head which is distinctive in that it selects for a [+bound] AspP as its complement.[3] In fact, the only semantic contribution of *phæla* seems to be the tense of the construction, and the fact of completiveness accruing to the whole sentence. The following tree diagram shows the structure I assume for the complex predicates.

(40)

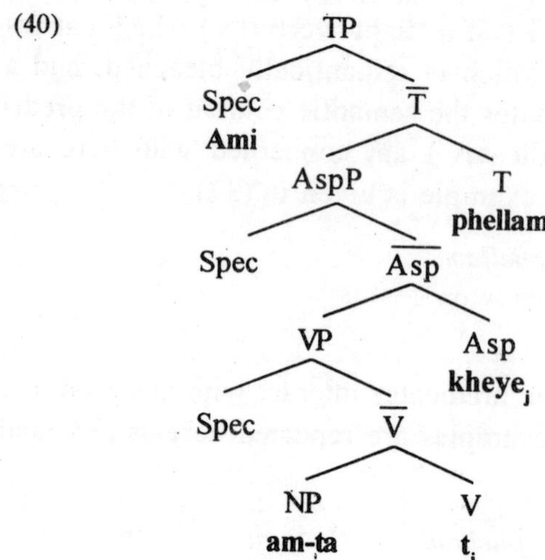

The semantic representation for this sentence would be:

(41) $\exists$t:t< t*, $\exists$e: t_f (in τ(e) = t [eating (e) & Θ_1 (e,'I') & Θ_2 (e, 'the mango')]

Notice that here, in the completive sentence, the requirement that τ(e) merely overlap with t is replaced by a condition that the final moment of τ(e), defined as t_f, is equal to t. The light verb *phæla* is responsible for introducing this restriction on the relationship between the event and the time variable. Notice too that this restriction incorporates the presupposition that such a terminal point actually exists for the event in question.

It is now clear why the *ni* particle is not possible in this construction. There is simply no place for it in the structure. If it were base-generated in the head of AspP it would block the raising of *kheye* to that position. It also could not itself raise through tense to the head of NegP since this movement would be blocked by the *phæla* verb in the head of TP.

What about the felicitous reading for *ni* negation that we do obtain? This reading is derived most plausibly under reanalysis of the 'kheye phæla' verb, inserted as a unit under V (the other possible analysis discarded for the case above). Consider what would happen if such a reanalysis were possible. The tree structure for the sentence would be as shown in (42).

(42)

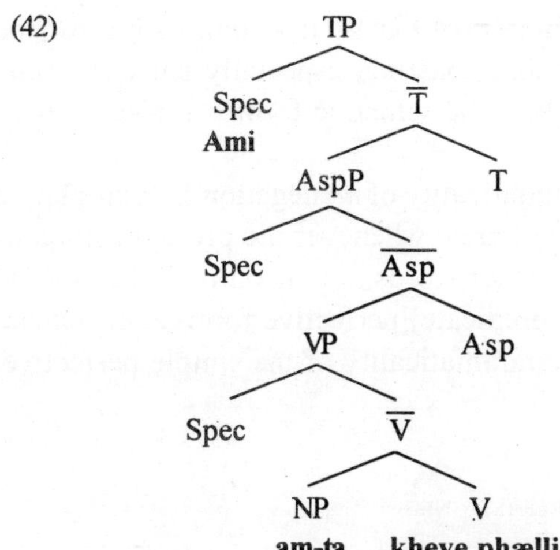

In this case, the *ni* particle can be inserted legitimately into the tree structure (42) under Asp, and then raises to T and Neg to check its features. In addition, the reanalysis forces a lexicalisation of the meaning of the *phæla* verb in that it no longer represents a pure functional element. Now, we have a new verb *kheye phæla* which means 'to completely eat'. This gives rise to a negated sentence of the form.

(43) For No $t{:}t< t^*$, $\exists e{:}\ t_f\ (\text{in}\ \tau(e)) =$ [complete–eating (e) & Θ_1 (e,'I') & Θ_2 (e, 'the mango')]

Thus, the only meaning available for this construction is that of negating a 'completely eating' event, not of negating the eating altogether.

Now we turn to the ungrammaticality of the *na* form of negation with these complex predicates. It should be clear from the phrase structure tree that there should be no morphosyntactic impediment to introducing the *na* negation element in the tree structure. Instead, we will see the ungrammaticality as arising from an essentially semantic source. Let us consider the semantic representation of the non-negated complex predicate.

(44) $\exists t{:}t< t^*$, $\exists e{:}\ t_f\ (\text{in}\ \tau(e)) = t$ [eating (e) & Θ_1 (e,'I') & Θ_2 (e, 'the mango')]

The *na* negation marker, recall, negates the event variable directly, in contrast with the *ni* marker which negates the time variable. Thus, we would expect to get the following semantic form for the complex predicate negated with *na*.

(45) $\exists t{:}t< t^*$, $\neg\exists e{:}\ t_f\ (\text{in}\ \tau(e)) = t$ [eating (e) & Θ_1 (e,'I') & Θ_2 (e, 'the mango')]

However, negating the event contradicts a major presupposition of this logical form: namely that an endpoint $\tau(e)$ exists. It is impossible for the endpoint to exist without the event also existing, especially since the time variable it is linked to also exists. Thus, the semantic form is logically incoherent.

This explanation of the ungrammaticality of *na* negation for completive complex predicates predicts that it will arise whenever the presupposition of the endpoint of an event is made. In other words, the incompatibility should arise even for simple (non-complex predicate) perfective forms. This expectation is justified, as seen by the ungrammaticality of the simple perfective, repeated here as (46).

(46) **ami* *am-Ta* *kheyechi* *na*
I mango-CLASS. eat-PERF/PRES/1ST NEG
'I have not eaten the mango.'

The reanalysis option cannot be invoked here to save the structure. Reanalysis would potentially remove the offending presupposition by making the *phæla* verb not a felicity-inducing element, but simply part of the lexical content of a potentially non-completive verb. However, this will fail because the resulting structure will have no tense or aspect specification, since *na* is a pure negation marker.

CONCLUSION

In this paper, I have argued that both morphosyntactic and semantic facts are implicated in the differences between the two forms of negation in Bengali. In particular, I have argued that *na* is a pure negation marker, and *ni* is specified for both tense and aspect features ([+past] and [+bound], respectively). In the case of *na*, negation occurs with explicit tense marking, and the time variable *t* associated with the construction is subject to existential closure and discourse anaphora. The *na* negation directly negates the existence of an event of a particular type. With the negation marker *ni*, on the other hand, the negation operator directly binds the *time* variable and no discourse anaphora is possible.

Thus, negation of completive complex predicates fails for separate reasons for the two forms of negation. In the case of *na* negation, the semantic representation of completiveness produces a presuppositional structure which contradicts the direct 'event negation' that the *na* form effects. This results in a strong feeling of contradiction often reported by speakers. In the case of *ni*, the problem is morphosyntactic: for sentence negation, the *ni* particle must be inserted in the head of AspP in the phrase structure, a position which I argue is already filled by the light verb of the complex predicate. In the acceptable reading of *ni* negation, the complex predicate is reanalyzed as a simplex predicate structure with completion as the main verbal head, producing the required interpretation.

The analysis proposed here has consequences for both the semantic and syntactic representation of negation in natural language. On the syntactic side, it argues that negative element (for example, *ni*) can be the morphological realisation of more than one syntactic head (Asp, T and Neg). From the semantic point of view, a distinction is drawn between negative elements which negate the existence of events *na* and those which directly bind time variables *ni*.

NOTES

1. See (Krifka 1992) on the difference between a terminal point and a set terminal point. All events in the world eventually have the former, but only a few have the latter, which is a terminal point inherent to the lexical meaning. It is the latter that I am referring to here with t_f
2. Speakers will often claim that the *ni* version is more emphatic, but that there is no other difference.
3. In fact, the selectional properties of *phæla* must be somewhat more specific than this, since there are many different light verbs in the language, all of which seem to have very particular sets of main verbs they occur with. Transitivity matching also appears to be at work here. I will not deal with these co-occurrence restrictions in this paper, but see Ramchand (1990) for an account. I assume that these facts can be made to fall out of constraints on argument structure merger in these languages.

REFERENCES

CHOMSKY, N.

1993 A minimalist program for linguistic theory. In K. Hale & S. Keyser (eds.), *The view from Building 20: A Festschrift for Sylvain Bromberger*. Cambridge, Massachusetts: MIT Press.

DAVIDSON, D.

1967 The logical form of action sentences. In N. Rescher (ed.), *The logic of decision and action.* Pittsburgh: University of Pittsburgh Press.

DIESING, M.

1988 Bare plural subjects and the stage/individual level contrast. Technical Report 88-42, Genericity in Natural Language SNS-Bericht, Universität Tubingen.

KRIFKA, M.
1992 Thematic relations as links between nominal references and temporal constitution. In I. Sag & A. Szabolcsi (eds.), *Lexical matters*. Stanford: Centre for the Study of Language and Information (CSLI).

PARSONS, T.
1990 *Events in the semantics of English.* Cambridge, Massachusetts: MIT Press.

PARTEE, B.
1984 Nominal and temporal anaphora. *Linguistics and Philosophy*, 7(3). 243–86.

RAMCHAND, G.
1990 Complex predicate formation in Bangla. In *Proceedings of the Ninth Annual West Coast Conference on Formal Linguistics*.

SMITH, C.
1991 *The parameter of aspect*. Dordrecht, The Netherlands: Kluwer.

22

Negating dynamic and deontic modality in Hindi-Urdu and Bangla

JOHAN VAN DER AUWERA
University of Antwerp

Languages may express necessity and possibility with auxiliary verbs and negation with particles. Necessity and possibility can sensibly combine with negation in two ways: either the modal has the negation in its scope or the other way round. When in a language that has both modal auxiliaries and negative particles the speaker combines a modal auxiliary and a negative particle, the resultant combination may be vague between the two scope readings or it may have one of the scope readings as the preferred or even exclusive reading. An example of vagueness of scope is Southern Dutch deontic *moeten* 'must' in combination with *niet* 'not'.

For expert advice I am most grateful to V.P. Mohammed Kunju Methar (Ghent),Thakur Dass (Agra), and especially to Chris de Lauwer (Ghent). For native speaker judgements I also wish thank Kamlesh Singh and Samir Kumar-Singh for Hindi-Urdu, and Chandra Chatterjee, Nivedita P. Haran, Susmita Ray, and Saranindra N. Tagore for Bangla, and the audiences at the Central Institute of Indian Languages at Mysore and the University of Hyderabad. All of the Hindi-Urdu and Bangla examples have been discussed with native speakers. I have tried, as much as possible, to use examples from the linguistic literature, though often excerpted from an analysis that did not concern modality or negation. If the Hindi-Urdu and Bangla examples bear no source indication, it means that the sentences resulted from the interaction with the informants. I am also grateful to the India Study Centre of the University of Antwerp for financial help.

(1) SOUTHERN DUTCH

Jan	*moet*	*dat*	*niet*	*doen.*
Jan	must:PRS.SG	that	not	do:INF

'Jan mustn't do that.' or 'Jan needn't do that.' ['□ ¬ p' or '¬ □ p']

In the translation 'John mustn't do that' we have a necessity operator ('□') with scope over a negation operator ('¬'), that is, '□ ¬ p'; with the translation 'John needn't do that', negation has scope over necessity, that is, '¬ □ p', but *moet..niet* as such is vague between the two readings. The German and English counterparts are not. The German cognate *müssen* 'must', when combined with *nicht* 'not', prefers the '¬ □ p' reading, and the English cognate *must,* when combined with *not,* essentially only allows '□ ¬ p'.

(2) GERMAN

Der	*Fritz*	*muss*	*das*	*nicht*	*tun*
DEF.NOM.M.SG	Fritz	must:PRS.3SG	that	not	do:INF

'Fritz needn't do that.' ['¬ □ p'] (*preferred*)

(3) ENGLISH

John *must not* do that. ['□ ¬ p']

The moral of this introduction is double. First, we see that even in closely related languages, which use very similar cognate markers of modality and negation and similar or, for German and Dutch, very similar word order patterns, combining these markers does not necessarily yield the same meanings. Second, some languages may support a measure of vagueness in the area of the collocation of modality and negation. Southern Dutch is a language that allows vagueness, German much less, and English least. In a language such as English we see that it is the choice of a lexical item that disambiguates the two readings. English expresses '□ ¬ p' with the ordinary *must* modal, but it can express '¬ □ p' with a specialised negative polarity modal *need* – the translation in (1) and in (2) – or, another possibility, with *have to* as in (4).

(4) ENGLISH

John *does not have to* do that. ['□ ¬ p']

What we see with *must* versus *need/have to* could be called 'lexeme-bound scope'. There is a second major strategy of marking scope, in (5) – through word order (De Haan 1994: 160–164; Palmer 1995). This could be called 'position-bound scope'.

(5) FRENCH

a. *Tu* *ne* *peux* *pas* *mang-er.* [NEG AUX NEG V]
2.NOM.SG not can:PRS.3SG not eat-INF
'You can't eat.' ['¬ ◇ p']

b. *Tu* *peux* *ne* *pas* *mang-er.* [AUX NEG NEG V]
2.NOM.SG can:PRS.3SG not not eat-INF
'You cannot eat.' ['◇ ¬ p']

The point of this paper is to investigate some of the facts in Hindi-Urdu and Bangla. The scope of the study is limited in four important ways.

First, I will only analyse markers of dynamic and deontic modality, that is, expressions of capacity, permission and obligation. The most important category left out of consideration is thus epistemic modality, the modality that targets a speaker's (strong or weak) commitment to the truth value of the proposition expressed.

Second, I will restrict the attention to auxiliaries. I will not, however, discuss to what extent these elements are truly auxiliaries rather than simply complement taking verbs and I will also not discuss modal elements of adjectival or nominal nature or origin, for example, Hindi-Urdu *zarūrat* 'necessity' (McGregor 1977: 77) or Bangla *darkār* 'necessity' (Radice 1994: 172).

Third, in both languages, modal markers can differ with respect to various nuances. A necessity marker, for example, may differ as to whether the necessity is internal, external or moral, and an ability marker may or may not imply some effort on the part of the participant. I will not discuss these semantic components, supposing them irrelevant for an understanding of what happens when they combine with negation.

Fourth, with respect to negation, I will restrict attention to what have been called 'negative particles'. Hindi-Urdu has three – the imperative *mat*, the default negative *nahīṃ*, and the more restricted *na*. Because of the nature of this study, the imperative element *mat* will not be discussed, and I will not investigate the possible relevance of the choice between *nahīṃ* and *na*, my suspicion being that the choice is irrelevant. Bangla also has various negative particles – default *nā*, 'existential' *nei*, and 'perfective' *ni*. I will ignore *ni*, mostly restricting attention to default *nā*. The element *nei* will be of relevance too, as it has a special modal use (see Section 3.2).

The comparison between Hindi-Urdu and Bangla is bound to be of interest, not in the least because the basic word order facts are different. Hindi-Urdu and Bangla are both essentially O V and V AUX, but they differ with respect to the position of the negative. In Hindi-Urdu it is essentially preverbal (see Bhatia 1977: 22–26), but in Bangla it is postverbal in simple declarative main clauses, preverbal in other types of clauses (for example, conditionals) and in one type of clause, that is, correlatives, it can be both preverbal and postverbal. (6)–(7) illustrate main clause declaratives and conditionals.

(6) HINDI-URDU

a. *rām nahīṃ jā-e-gā* [NEG V]
Ram not go-SBJ.3SG-FUT.M.SG
'Ram will not go.'

b. **rām jā-e-gā nahīṃ* [*V NEG]

c. *yadi āp na ā-eṃ to maiṃ ā-ū-gā* [NEG V]
if 2HON not come-SBJ.3PL then 1SG.NOM come-SBJ.1SG-FUT.M.SG
'If you do not come, I will come.'

d. **yadi āp ā-eṃ na, to maiṃ ā-ū-gaa* [*V NEG]

(7) BANGLA (Singh 1976: 296, 301)

a. *rām jā-be ā.* [V NEG]
Ram go-FUT.3 not
'Ram will not go.'

b. **rām nā jā-be* [*NEG V]

c. *tumi yodi na aśh-o, āmi āsh-bo* [NEG V]
2.NOM.SG if not come-PRS.2 1SG come-FUT.1
'If you do not come, I will come.'

d. **tumi yodi āśh-o nā, āmi āśh-bo* [*V NEG]

The situation in Bangla has attracted a fair amount of attention (Singh 1976; Wen 1979; van der Wurff 1989). It is clear that the postverbal pattern is more recent and it has been suggested that it is due to areal influences (cf. Klaiman 1987: 511–12).

This paper, to some extent, takes account of the variation within Bangla, in that it considers both simple declarative main clauses (the *unmarked clause type*) and conditionals (the *marked clause type*). Section 1 tries to do justice to the facts of Hindi-Urdu and Bangla, and Section 2 attempts to explain some of these facts, in part with reference to what is known about the typology of negative modals. In the end I have summarised the conclusions.

1. POSSIBLE FACTS

The hedge 'possible' in the section title refers to the real fact that the kinds of things at issue here are not described in any detail in the literature[1] and that the account is essentially based on the clues which this literature provides combined with the judgements, not always in full harmony, of altogether seven informants.

1.1 *Possibility*

1.1.1 DYNAMIC POSSIBILITY

Both languages have two sets of dynamic modals. The first contains *sak-* in Hindi-Urdu and *par-* in Bangla. The Hindi-Urdu verb combines with a verbal stem, the Bangla one with an infinitive.

(8) HINDI-URDU (McGregor 1977: 88)

maiṃ	*hindī*	*bol*	*sak-tā*	*hū*
1SG.NOM	Hindi	speak	can-PRT.PRS.M.SG	be:PRS.1SG

'I can speak Hindi.'

(9) BANGLA

o	*gai-te*	*par-e*
DIST.SG.NOM	sing-INF	can-PRS.3

'He can sing.'

The second set comprises *pā-* in both Hindi-Urdu and Bangla, sometimes better glossed as 'manage, succeed, get' than 'can' (original meaning = 'find, get'). The Hindi-Urdu verb combines with an oblique infinitive or with a bare stem, the latter apparently more and more so (Hacker 1958: 252–53; McGregor 1977: 134). Everyone seems to agree that Hindi-Urdu *pā-* is predominantly used in combination with negation (see Hacker 1958: 252–53; McGregor 1977: 134; Shapiro 1989: 104), but as (10) shows, positive occurrences have been testified.

(10) HINDI-URDU (Kachru 1980: 49)

vah	*baṛī*	*koshishoṃ*	*ke bād*	*kalkatte-*	*se*	*nikal*	*pā-yā*
3SG.NOM	much	effort:OBL	after	Calcutta-	from	emerge	manage-PRT.PF.M.SG

'He managed to leave Calcutta after much effort.'

The Bangla counterpart *pā-* combines with the infinitive, probably mostly or only those of verbs of visual perception (Zbavitel 1970: 17; Radice 1994: 212). The examples I have seen (Masica 1991: 377; Radice 1994: 212) are all negative, yet the native speakers consulted all accept a positive (11), too.

(11) BANGLA

o-r *kathā* *śhun-te* *pāy*
DIST.SG-GEN word hear-INF manage.PRS.3
'I can hear his words.'

Another construction that should be mentioned here is the 'modal passive'. The exact status of this construction need not concern us here. Suffice it to say that the Hindi-Urdu modal passive employs the auxiliary *jā-* and the main verb takes the form of a perfective participle. It is agreed that it prefers negative uses (Gatzlaff-Hälsig 1978: 106; Kachru 1980: 105; Davison 1982: 175; Montaut 1990: 107), yet Kachru (1980: 107) claims that it can occur without negation in questions and answers.

(12) HINDI-URDU (Kachru 1980: 107)

— *rājan* *se* *makke* *kī* *rotiyā̃* *khāī* *jā-eṃ-gī?*
Rajan by corn of bread.PL eat:PRT.PF.F.PL go-SBJ.3PL-FUT.PL
— *zarūr* *khāī* *jā-eṃ-gī?*
certainly eat:PRT.PF.FSG go-SBJ.3PL-FUT.PL
— 'Will Rajan be able to eat corn bread?
— He will certainly be able to.'

In Bangla the modal passive takes the main verb as a verbal noun, and the auxiliary is either *jā-* 'go' or *ho-* 'be'. There is no claim that the construction prefers negative contexts, though this may have been the case in earlier Bangla, at least for the *jā-* construction.[2] I will use the *jā-* construction for illustration, as it seems more common (Zbavitel 1970: 43; Radice 1994: 147).

(13) BANGLA (Dasgupta 1980: 92)

chobi-ṭa *āk-ā* *ge-lo*
picture-DEF draw-VN go-PST.3
'It was possible to draw the picture.'/'They were able to draw the picture.'

When it comes to negation, the languages differ more. Hindi-Urdu *sak-* allows two orders, V NEG AUX as well as NEG V AUX, but in both the meaning is 'incapacity'.

(14) HINDI-URDU (McGregor 1977: 88; cf. Kachru 1980: 106; Shapiro 1989: 104)

maiṃ *so* *nahīṃ* *sak-ā* [V NEG AUX]
1SG.NOM sleep not can-PRT.PF.M.SG
'I couldn't sleep.' ['¬ ◇ p']

(15) HINDI-URDU (McGregor 1977: 88; cf. Hook 1974: 85)

maiṃ	*nahīṃ*	*so*	*sak-ā*	[NEG V AUX]
1SG.NOM	not	sleep	can-PRT.PF.M.SG	

'I couldn't sleep.' ['¬ ◇ p']

McGregor (1977: 88) comments on this variation: he claims NEG V AUX to be neutral and V NEG AUX to be 'somewhat affective in character'.

The Hindi-Urdu verb *pā-* shows the same picture: the negation has invariably wide scope, but there are two orders: NEG V AUX and V NEG AUX. Again McGregor (1977) is aware of the difference when he claims NEG V AUX to go with 'neutral style and emphasis' (see Hacker 1958: 253; McGregor 1977: 134; Gatzlaff-Hälsig 1978: 153). With the Hindi-Urdu *jā-* passive the situation is similar again. The meaning is invariably '¬ ◇ p' and there are two orders, with McGregor (1977: 126) once more claiming that NEG V AUX goes with neutral style and emphasis (examples in Scholberg 1950: 150; McGregor 1977: 117; Kachru 1980: 105).

For Bangla I make a distinction between unmarked clauses (main declaratives) and marked ones (here illustrated with conditionals). As mentioned, when there is just one verb, the negation follows it in unmarked clauses but precedes it in marked ones. Of course, now we are considering two verbal forms, the full verb V and the AUX verb. In main clauses with *par-*, the order is obligatorily V AUX NEG and the interpretation is '¬ ◇ p'.[3]

(16) BANGLA (Dasgupta 1980: 113)

o	*manso*	*cibo-te*	*par-e*	*nā*	[V AUX NEG]
DIST.SG.NOM	meat	chew-INF	can-PRS.3	not	

'He cannot chew meat.' ['¬ ◇ p']

In conditionals, we see some variation. The order can be either V NEG AUX or NEG V AUX, and in the latter case NEG and V do not even have to be contiguous, but in all cases the interpretation remains constant.

(17) BANGLA (Dasgupta 1987: 70; cf. van der Wurff 1989: 187)

a.	*tumi*	*kaj*	*śeṣ*	*kor-te*	*nā*	*par-le, . . .*	[V NEG AUX]
	2.NOM.SG	job	end	do-INF	not	can-PST.2	

'If you cannot finish the job ...' ['¬ ◇ p']

b.	*tumi*	*kaj*	*śeṣ*	*nā*	*kort-te*	*par-le . . .*	[NEG V AUX]
c.	*tumi*	*kaj*	*nā*	*śeṣ*	*kor-te*	*par-le . . .*	[NEG X V AUX]

The word order does not seem to score any semantic effect. The word order rules for the *pā-* verb and the passive are the same and so is the interpretation (examples in Radice 1994: 212; Klaiman 1981: 75).

We can summarise by saying that in both languages the effect of combining dynamic possibility and negation is always '¬ ◇ p'. This can be achieved by both NEG V AUX and V NEG AUX orders, in Hindi-Urdu as well as in Bangla marked clause types. In Bangla unmarked clause types, however, only V AUX NEG is possible.

1.1.2 DEONTIC POSSIBILITY

In both languages the main dynamic verbs, Hindi-Urdu *sak-* and Bangla *par*, allow deontic uses.

(18) HINDI-URDU (Nespital 1980: 134)

hā,	*śukriyā,*	*ab*	*tum*	*jā*	*sak-te*	*ho*
yes	thanks	now	2PL.NOM	go	can-PRT.PRS.M.PL	be:PRS.2PL

'Yes, thanks, you may go now.'

(19) BANGLA

tumi	*nac-te*	*par-o*
2.NOM.SG	dance-INF	can-PRS.2

'You may dance.'

I have no evidence for positive deontic uses for either Hindi-Urdu or Bangla *pa-* verbs or for the *jā-/ho-* passives.

When it comes to negation, the languages differ again, as we saw with dynamic modality. In Hindi-Urdu, *sak-* shows up again, as do *pā-* and the *jā-* passive. The meaning is again always '¬ ◇ p' and judging from the examples I dare to assume that the three structures exhibit the same word order freedom as found with dynamic uses.

(20) HINDI-URDU (Nespital 1980: 135)

tum	*mere*	*sāth*	*aisa*	*bartāv*	*nahīṃ*	*kar*	*sak-te*	[NEG V AUX]
2PL.NOM	1SG.GEN	with	such	behaviour	not	do	can-.PRS.M.PL	

'So you cannot deal with me like that.' ['¬ ◇ p']

(21) HINDI-URDU

maiṃ	*bol-ne*	*na*	*pā-yā*	[V NEG AUX]
1SG.NOM	speak-INF.OBL	not	manage:PRT.PF.M.SG	

'I couldn't speak.' 'I was not allowed to speak.' ['¬ ◇ p']

(22) HINDI-URDU (Davison 1982: 159).

baccõṃ	*ko*	*is*	*tarah*	*bigāṛā*	*nahīṃ*	*jā-tā*	[V NEG AUX]
children	to	this	way	spoil:PRT.PF	not	go-PRT.PRS.M.SG	

'One should not spoil children like this.' ['¬ ◇ p']

First, Bangla is different from Hindi-Urdu in that it generally lacks constructions that are specialised for combining deontic possibility and negation. There seems to be one exception. Zbavitel (1970: 17) mentions a deontic use of *pā-*, a corpus example, and it happens to be negative.

(23) BANGLA (Zbavitel 1970: 17)

binu	*tomār*	*ghar-e*	*khe-te*	*pā-be*	*nā*	[V AUX NEG]
Binu	2SG.GEN	room-LOC	eat-INF	manage-FUT.3	not	

'Binu will not get to eat in your room.'

Second, the positive verb *par-* does combine with negation, but it can do so in two ways. The first type is shown in (24).

(24) BANGLA

karāj	*o*	*gai-te*	*par-be*	*nā*	[V AUX NEG]
today	DIST.SG.NOM	sing-INF	can-FUT.3	not	

'Today he cannot sing.' ['¬ ◇ p']

(24) has the expected V AUX NEG order and the expected '¬ ◇ p' reading (the only surprising thing is that the deontic reading seems to prefer a future verb). In the second type *nā* precedes the infinitive and it means '◇ ¬ p'. With a bare *nā* it is marked, but it appears to be fully acceptable when followed by the emphasiser *o* 'also'.

(25) BANGLA

tumi	*nā*	*o*	*nac-te*	*par-o*	[NEG V AUX]
2.NOM.SG	not	also	dance-INF	can-PRS.2	

'You may also not dance.' ['◇ ¬ p']

Deontic readings, however, whether '¬ ◇ p' or '◇ ¬ p', do not occur in the marked conditional clause type. One only gets the dynamic reading, already illustrated in (17), and the meaning is always '¬ ◇ p'.

Summarising, in Hindi-Urdu, negating deontic possibility works the same way as negating dynamic possibility. We have the same set of three constructions (*sak-*, *jā-*, and *pā-*), the same semantics ('¬ ◇ p') and the same word order variation (NEG V AUX, V NEG AUX). In Bangla, however, only one of the dynamic constructions clearly lends itself to a deontic use (*par-*) – with *pā-* as a marginal case – and only in the unmarked sentence type. The meaning can be '¬ ◇ p' or '◇ ¬ p', a distinction associated with different word orders (V AUX NEG versus NEG V AUX).

1.2 *Dynamic and deontic necessity*

For necessity, a distinction between dynamic and deontic uses does not seem to be required. In the positive uses, both languages employ an invariable relic form of a verb 'want'. The Hindi-Urdu main verb is normally an infinitive, which usually precedes, but may also follow as a subjunctive introduced by the conjunction *ki* (McGregor 1977: 79). Bangla employs a cognate, which combines with a verbal noun.[4] Both languages also employ forms of the verb 'to be/become', preceded by infinitives, which in Hindi-Urdu may agree, and in Bangla may bear an emphatic clitic *-i*.[5] As a third possibility Hindi-Urdu employs forms of a verb meaning 'fall'.

(26) HINDI-URDU (Verma 1974: 127)

Mohan	*ko*	*jā-nā*	*cāhiye*
Mohan	to	go-INF	should

'Mohan should go.'

(27) BANGLA (cf. Chatterji 1957: 188)

āj	*o-r*	*paṛ-ā*	*cai*
today	DIST-SG.GEN	study-VN	should

'Today he should study.'

(28) HINDI-URDU (Kachru 1980: 50)

mujh	*ko*	*agle*	*sāl*	*banāras*	*zarūr*	*jā-nā*	*hai*
1SG.OBL	to	next	year	Banaras	certainly	go-INF	be:PRS.3SG

'I must go to Banaras next year.'

(29) BANGLA (Klaiman 1981: 12)

āmā-ke	*ekhon*	*bāṛi*	*je-te*	*habe*
1SG-OBL	now	house	go-INF	be:FUT.3

'I shall have to go now.'

(30) HINDI-URDU (Kachru 1980: 50)

śādī	*meṃ*	*jā-nā*	*hi*	*paṛ-e-gā*
wedding	in	go-INF-	EMPH	must-SBJ.3SG-FUT.M.SG

'I will have to attend the wedding.'

Let us now see what happens when these auxiliaries combine with negation. In Hindi-Urdu for each of the three forms the negation normally precedes the main verb (see explicit statements in McGregor 1977: 78, 80). The alternative order, AUX NEG V, however, has not appeared in any example discussed in the literature nor did the informants feel as comfortable with it as with the corresponding possibility cases. As to the meaning, the three modals differ. Whereas *cāhiye* has wide scope, *ho-* and *paṛ-* take narrow scope.

(31) HINDI-URDU (cf. McGregor 1977: 78; Shapiro 1989: 133).

āp	*ko*	*hindī*	*nahīṃ*	*bol-nā*	*cāhiye*	[NEG V AUX]
2.HON-	to	Hindi	not	speak-INF	must	

'You shouldn't speak Hindi.' ['□ ¬ p']

(32) HINDI-URDU

un	*logoṃ*	*ko*	*ab*	*nahīṃ*	*jā-nā*	*hai*	[NEG V AUX]
those	people	to	now	not	go-INF	be:PRS.3SG	

'Those people do not have to go now.' ['¬ □ p']

(33) HINDI-URDU (McGregor 1977: 80)

mujhe	*ghar*	*nahīṃ*	*jā-nā*	*paṛ-ā*	[NEG V AUX]
1SG.OBL.to	home	not	go-INF	must-PRT.PF.M.SG	

'I didn't have to go home.' ['¬ □ p']

In Bangla only the verb *ho-* can occur with negation and like its Hindi-Urdu cognate, it takes only narrow scope, and as it befits normal Bangla syntax, the negation goes at the end in the unmarked clause type, and it can go in various preverbal positions in the umarked sentence type.

(34) BANGLA (Dasgupta 1980: 111)

āmā-r	*karor*	*songe*	*kotha*	*bol-te*	*ho-lo*	*nā*	[V NEG AUX]
1-GEN.SG	anyone.GEN	with	word	say-INF	be-PST.3	not	

'I didn't have to speak with anyone.' ['¬ □ p']

(35) BANGLA

a.

āj	*yodi*	*o-ke*	*paṛ-te*	*nā*	*hay . . .*	[V NEG AUX]
today	if	DIST-SG.OBJ	study-INF	not	be.PRS.3	

'If he needn't study today, then . . .' ['¬ □ p']

b. *āj yodi o-ke nā paṛ-te hay . . .* [NEG V AUX]

Interestingly, *cai* cannot occur with negation at all, not even in the unmarked clause type with negation in its canonical final position.

(36) BANGLA

**āj*	*o-r*	*par-ā*	*cai*	*nā*	[V AUX NEG]
today	DIST-SG.GEN	study-VN	must	not	

'Today he needn't/mustn't study.' ['□ ¬ p' or '¬ □ p']

Bangla does, however, have a specialised negative verb, that is, *nei,* a univerbation of the negative particle *nā* and the existential *āche* 'be'. This uniquely expresses prohibition. It is also remarkable that it cannot occur in conditionals.

(37) BANGLA (Klaiman 1981: 99; cf. also Masica 1991: 382)

dāri-ye *khe-te* *nei* [V NEG AUX]
stand-CONV eat-INF is.not
'One shouldn't eat standing up.' ['□ ¬ p']

We can summarise as follows. In Hindi-Urdu each of the three necessity verbs can combine with negation. For one of the verbs the reading is '□ ¬ p', for the other two it is '¬ □ p'. There is no connection with word order, which is said to vary between NEG V AUX and V NEG AUX. Bangla has two necessity verbs, and of these only one can occur with negation at all, the reading is '¬ □ p', in the unmarked clause type the negation goes at the end, and in the marked clause types it varies between NEG V AUX, V NEG AUX. Bangla also has a specialised negative modal, a univerbation uniquely meaning '□ ¬ p'. It only occurs in the unmarked clause type.

2. GENERALISATIONS AND EXPLANATIONS

2.1 *Lexeme-bound versus position-bound scope*

The first thing to note is that Hindi-Urdu and Bangla always disambiguate scope in combinations of modality and negations. No case has been found which displays the vagueness illustrated with Southern Dutch *niet moeten* in example (1). I also recalled that languages typically mark scope in one of two ways: they associate wide or narrow scope with the choice of a lexical item – 'lexeme-bound scope' – or with the choice of word order pattern – 'position-bound scope'.

This brings me to the second generalisation: in Hindi-Urdu, scope is always lexeme-bound and in Bangla nearly always so. For Hindi-Urdu this claims means that for each combination of modal and negation documented in §1, one can predict the scope relation from the choice of the modal. If it is, for example, the modal *sak-* that combines with negation, one knows that the modal will have narrow scope. In Bangla, scope is largely lexeme-bound as well, but there is one exception. In the unmarked clause type deontic *par-* can have both wide and narrow scope – compare (24) and (25). As here the relative position of the modal and negation disambiguates, Bangla has position-bound scope.

The interesting question is why is it that only Bangla, and not Hindi-Urdu, exploits word order to signal scope. Why should that be so? On the one hand, one could point out, Bangla has a greater degree of variation with respect to the position of the negation anyway. Whereas with non-auxiliarised simple verbs, Hindi-Urdu normally only allows a preverbal negation, Bangla has two options, postverbal and preverbal, depending on the clause type – see (6) and (7). This contrast is of course real enough, but it does not yet throw any light on why Bangla would exploit this greater degree of variation, defined in terms of clause type, for the purpose of signalling scope.[6] The crux of the matter, I propose, is that the Bangla unmarked clause postverbal position can itself be taken as a scope indicator. We need only say that the default Bangla unmarked clause VP is, depending on one's theory, consistently head-final or right-branching (see, for example, Dryer 1992) or consistently having scope-bearing elements follow (for example, Functional Grammar in the sense of Dik 1989). See Table 1.

TABLE 1 *Order, dependency, branching and scope in the Bangla default unmarked clause VP*

ORDERS	DEPENDENCY THEORY	BRANCHING DIRECTION THEORY	FUNCTIONAL GRAMMAR
O V	O is dependent	O branches	O in scope of V
V AUX	V is dependent	V branches	V in scope of AUX
V NEG	V is dependent	V branches	V in scope of AUX
AUX NEG	AUX is dependent	AUX branches	AUX in scope of NEG

One could state that the Bangla default unmarked clause VP has a high degree of cross-categorial harmony, as of any two VP elements it is always the first element which is dependent, branching, or has narrow scope. The harmony is cross-categorial, because it concerns various grammatical categories (O, V, AUX for the first element, and V, AUX, NEG for the second). This cross-categorial harmony thus enables the statement that in the Bangla default unmarked clause VP, scope is position-bound.

If the order in the default unmarked clause VP is indicative of scope, it follows that any deviation from AUX NEG order should be indicative of a different scope. This is what we find. When variation occurs – which is rarely so – it is indicative of scope: whereas deontic '$\neg \Diamond$ p' is conveyed by V AUX NEG order, deontic '$\Diamond \neg$ p' uses NEG V AUX. Contrast this with the Hindi-Urdu VP: while wide scope V follows O and wide scope AUX follows V, wide scope NEG does not follow V. Hindi-Urdu NEG does not therefore partake in the cross-categorial harmony. One cannot attach scopal properties to the position of NEG in the Hindi-Urdu VP. When NEG and AUX co-occur, there is in fact a fair amount of variation, but this is not indicative of scope. The VP in the Bangla marked clause type has the same properties: NEG precedes AUX, word order is not indicative of scope, and there is a fair amount of variation, too.

2.2 *Wide and narrow scope*

A third generalisation is that lexeme-bound scope nearly always involves a wide scope negation, in Hindi-Urdu as well as in Bangla, for possibility as well as for necessity. There is only one exception, that is, Hindi-Urdu *cāhiye*. Both the rule and the exception need to be explained.

For the possibility modals the explanation may be pragmatic. There is hardly any need for a dynamic use with scope over negation. One is not normally interested in not being able to do something or in the circumstances that make it possible that something does not happen. Or, for the deontic use, permissions are normally permissions to do something rather than to not do something. Why then do most necessity modals take narrow scope too? Perhaps we can appeal to analogy here. With necessity modals *ceteris paribus* following the model of the possibility modals, one constitutes a class of elements that when they determine scope, all do it in the same way. From this point of view the only the only element left to 'explain' then is Hindi-Urdu *cāhiye*. It should mean '¬ □ p' but in fact means '□ ¬ p'.

The incongruity between an expectation of a '¬ □ p' meaning and the fact that the meaning is '□ ¬ p' is, however, a familiar one. It is widespread in the languages of Europe. French (38) is a case in point.

(38) FRENCH

Il	*ne*	*faut*	*pas*	*que*	*tu*	*meures*
3SG.NOM.N	not	must	not	that	2SG.NOM	die.PRS.2SG

'You mustn't die.'
(lit. 'It is not necessary that you die.') ['□ ¬ p' (lit.'¬ □ p')]

The phenomenon has been studied since Tobler (1882), the example in (38) is from Horn (1989: 261–62), and I accept his explanation. In the fourteenth century, Horn claims, both the '□ ¬ p' and '¬ □ p' interpretations existed and that the latter began to disappear, even though in the modern language the negation syntactically still goes with the modal. This development makes sense, Horn (1989: 261–62) argues, in a scenario of '¬ □ p' originally having the '□ ¬ p' reading as an implicature, more particularly a so-called 'Informativeness' or 'Relation' implicature (Atlas and Levinson 1981; Horn 1984), a mechanism whereby one statement implicates a more informative one. This implicature would then conventionalise and oust the original literal meaning. From this point of view it makes sense to hypothesise the '¬ □ p' reading of *cāhiye* as an erstwhile implicature, too. Note the kind of indirect diachronic argumentation I am engaging in here: I am making a claim about the possible history of *cāhiye* using circumstantial cross-linguistic evidence.

2.3 *Specialised negative modals*

Hindu-Urdu has two modals that are more or less specialised for negative uses, viz. *pā-* and the modal passive with *jā-*. Bangla, on the other hand, has the inherently negative modal *nei*. I will first discuss *nei*. I assumed in §1.2 that *nei* is a '□ ¬ p' expression. This is not self-evident. First, as a univerbation of negation and *ache* 'be' one would expect it to mean '¬ □ p' rather than '□ ¬ p'. But it does not and again, as for Hindi-Urdu *cāhiye*, it seems one has to take to resource to an implicature hypothesis. Second, '□ ¬ p' is equivalent to '¬ ◇ p'. Can it be excluded that *nei* actually expresses '¬ ◇ p' rather than '□ ¬ p'? Under this hypothesis, we would be dealing with wide scope negation, which goes well with the claim that nearly all lexeme-bound scope in Hindi-Urdu and Bangla has wide scope negation. This hypothesis assumes that a positive 'be' construction can express possibility. Languages indeed show this, not of course English, in which *to be to* expresses necessity. In German, however, the cognate construction can express both necessity and possibility (for other cases, see Bybee, Perkins, and Pagliuca 1994: 188).

(39) GERMAN (Drosdowski 1984: 106)

Wesens-probleme	*sind*	*mit*	*den*	*Mitteln*
being.GEN-problem:NOM.PL	be:PRS.3PL	with	DEF.DAT.PL	mean:PL

der	*Ontologie*	*zu*	*lösen*
DEF.GEN.FSG	ontology	to	solve:INF

'Problems of being can/must be solved with the means of ontologie.' ['◇' / '□ p']

Against the '¬ ◇ p' hypothesis it should be mentioned that Zbavitel (1970: 16) and Masica (1991: 381) report on a necessity use of the assumed positive component of *nei*, that is, *ache* and, even though the native speakers consulted could not confirm this use, this does not prove its non-existence. Also, there is proof of a necessity use of another 'be' verb, that is, *ho-* [see (29)], while there is none for a possibility use of a 'be' verb. I conclude that both the '¬ ◇ p' and the '□ ¬ p' hypotheses have their pluses and minuses and I will not make a choice here. I will instead explore both hypotheses in the light of some general theorising on the appearance of univerbations in modal systems.

The work on univerbations comes from Horn (from 1972 onwards, most impressively in 1989). As early as in (1972: 244) (see also Horn 1989: 260), Horn formulates the universal in (40).

(40) [. . .] if a language contains a lexicalisation of ¬ □, it will also contain a lexicalisation of ¬ ? (but not necessarily the reverse) [. . .]

The notion of lexicalisation is of course wider than that of univerbation, but since *nei* is both, we need not worry about this distinction here. How then does (40) relate to the '¬ ◇ p' and the '□ ¬ p' hypotheses for the univerbation *nei*? First, it licenses the '¬ ◇ p' hypothesis, for the reason that the implicational universal is true if the consequent is true. Second, with respect to modern Bangla, (40) also licenses the '□ ¬ p' hypothesis but in a trivial way because the universal does not talk about '□ ¬ p'. The relation between (40) and the '□ ¬ p' hypothesis is more interesting with respect to older Bangla. Recall that the '□ ¬ p' hypothesis assumes that *nei* must have meant '¬ □ p' at an earlier stage. For that earlier stage, (40) predicts that Bangla should also have a '¬ ◇ p' lexicalisation. If this lexicalisation indeed existed, then the universal remains unfalsified. If it did not, then either the universal or the '□ ¬ p' hypothesis for *nei* is wrong. Now what is interesting is that the desired '¬ ◇ p' form may well have existed, for Singh (1976: 302) reports an archaic form *n-ār* < *nā-par-* '¬ ◇ p'.

Hindi-Urdu, it will be recalled, does not have modal univerbation. But it has have modals that are more or less specialised for negative uses, that is, *pā-* and *jā-*. Note that what Bangla *nei* has in common with Hindi-Urdu negativised *pā-* and *jā-* is that they all serve the '¬ ◇ p'–'□ ¬ p' meaning. This supports the idea underlying Horn's universal (40), that is, that of the two types of negative modal meaning, '¬ □ p'–'◇ ¬ p', on the one hand, and '¬ ◇ p'–'□ ¬ p', on the other, the latter is cross-linguistically more successful in attracting specialised lexemes. Only, these specialised lexemes can be of different types:

- they may be lexicalisations, possibly univerbations, of the modal and the negative – the type envisaged in Horn's (40) and exemplified by Bangla *n-ār* and possibly *nei* (under the '¬ ◇ p' hypothesis); or
- they may be conventionalisations of implicatures of earlier '¬ □ p'–'◇ ¬ p' meanings – a type possibly exemplified by Bangla *nei* (under the '□ ¬ p' hypothesis); or
- they may constitute suppletives, marshalling lexical materials from a non-modal field – exemplified by Hindi-Urdu negativised *pā-* and *jā-*.

Note, finally, that Bangla does not only have a negatively specialised modal, but also a positively specialised one, *cai*. Modals that cannot occur with negation, whatever the scope relation, seem cross-linguistically more rare. Interestingly, the only cases I have seen discussed in the literature are necessity modals, like Bangla *cai*, but they are all epistemic necessity modals (David-Nielsen 1990: 87 on Danish *må;* Jensen 1987: 66 on Danish *måtte*; Tottie 1985 on British English *must*; Silva-Corvalán 1995 on Spanish *tiene que*). I will shelve this point for future research.

CONCLUSIONS

This paper had two goals. First, it attempted to describe how Hindi-Urdu and Bangla dynamic and deontic modals combine with negative markers, and what the resulting meanings are. To this purpose, the description in §1 has provided ample illustration, with full gloss and interpretation, so as to make the account eminently falsifiable. Second, I attempted to generalise over the data obtained, relying in part on hypotheses about what is known about combinations of modality and negation in other languages.

Hindu-Urdu and Bangla have been found to be languages that always disambiguate collocations of modality and negations. They do this in partially different ways. In Hindi-Urdu scope is lexeme-bound. In Bangla it is usually lexeme-bound as well, but there is one context that allows scope to be marked by word order. The reason why only Bangla and then only in unmarked clauses allows word order to convey scope is that the Bangla unmarked clause type exhibits a higher degree of cross-categorial harmony than Hindi and than the Bangla marked clause type. Lexeme-bound scope has further been shown to involve a wide scope negation, in both languages, and I have suggested that the explanation here involves pragmatics and analogy. The one exception is Hindi-Urdu *cāhiye*, the narrow-scope negation of which makes cross-linguistic sense as an implicature from an earlier wide-scope reading.

Finally, I discussed whether Bangla *nei* should be considered as meaning '□ ¬ p' or '¬ ◇ p', and I related both hypotheses to a 25-year-old universal of Horn's on the lexicalisation of negative modals. The existence of negatively specialised modals in Hindī-Urdu was related to this universal as well.

NOTES

GENERAL NOTE: In the glosses and tables I use the following abbreviations and symbols: 1, 2, 3 'first, second, third person', ¬ 'negation', ◇ 'possibility', □ 'necessity', AUX 'auxiliary', CONT 'continuous, CONV 'converb', DAT 'dative', DEF 'definite', DIST 'distal', F 'feminine', FUT 'future', GEN 'genitive', HON 'honorific', INF 'infinitive', LOC 'locative', M 'masculine', N 'neuter', NEG 'negation', NEGAUX 'negative auxiliary', NOM 'nominative', O 'object', OBJ 'object', OBL 'oblique', PF 'perfective', PL 'plural', PRS 'present', PRT 'participle', PST 'past', SG 'singular', SBJ 'subjunctive', V 'verb', and VN 'verbal noun'.

1. The literature also contains conflicting statements. Compare Kachru (1980: 112), 'It is not possible to negate modals or explicator verbs' with Hook (1974: 95), 'In contrast to vector verbs *sak and paa* occur freely with negative elements', a

statement accompanying examples in which the modals are negated.

2. At least it is striking that all the examples Klaiman (1981: 69–70) supplies for Middle Bangla are negative (cf. also Chatterji 1970: 924–25 and Zbavitel 1970: 23–24).
3. The claim that the order is necessarily V AUX NEG is controversial, in view of the fact that Dasgupta (1980: 113) claims that *par-* can also take a negated infinitive. However, the one example offered may well only have a deontic or epistemic reading – it translates 'He may not eat fish, but he eats fish all right'. It is also true that Dasgupta discusses a construction with a negated conjunctive participle or, as I will call it with a handy one-word term, a 'converb', but this is a construction that also has a negated modal, without which the sentence is ungrammatical.

(a) BANGLA (Dasgupta 1980: 114)

o	*nā*	hase	*par-lo*	*nā*	[NEG V AUX NEG]
DIST.SG.NOM	not	laugh:CONV	can-PST.3	not	

'He couldn't help laughing.'

4. Interestingly, Masica (1991: 381) does not mention Bangla *cai*, and it remains unmentioned elsewhere too. Chatterji (1957: 188) does list it, a listing approved of by all of my native speakers. On the other hand, Masica (1991: 381) as well as Zbavitel (1970: 16) – mentions a necessity use of *āche* 'be', but none of my native speakers recognised this.
5. Bangla has three 'be' verbs. The one used here is the equational 'be' verb *ho-*. According to Masica (1991: 381) the existential 'be' verb *āche* ought to be possible. No native speaker consulted could confirm this, however. The form *nei*, taken to be a fusion of *nā* and *āche*, was however accepted. See §2.3.
6. It is instructive to bring in Marathi here. In Marathi the negation seems much more strictly postverbal than in Bangla (Bhatia 1977: 26), yet it also exploits word order to signal scope in combinations of modal and negation (Wali 1973: 382).

REFERENCES

ATLAS, JAY DAVID and STEPHEN C. LEVINSON

1981 *It*-clefts, informativeness and logical form. In Peter Cole (ed.), *Radical pragmatics*. New York: Academic Press. 1–61.

BHATIA, TEJ KRISHAN

1977 *A syntactic and semantic description of negation in South Asian languages.* Dissertation, University of Illinois at Urbana-Champaign.

BYBEE, JOAN, REVERE PERKINS and WILLIAM PAGLIUCA

1994 *The evolution of grammar. Tense, aspect and modality in the languages of the world.* Chicago: University of Chicago Press.

CHATTERJI, SUNITI KUMAR

1957 *Bengali self-taught.* London: Marlborough.

1970 [1926] *The origin and development of the Bengali language in two parts.* Part II: Morphology, Bengali index. London: Allen & Unwin.

COMRIE, BERNARD (ed.)
1987 *The world's major languages*. London: Routledge.

DASGUPTA, PROBAL
1980 *Questions and relative and complement clauses in a Bangla grammar*. Dissertation, New York University.
1987 Sentence particles in Bangla. In Elena Bashir, Madhav M. Deshpande & Peter Edwin Hook (eds.), *Select papers from SALA-7*. Bloomington: Indiana University Linguistics Club. 49–75.

DAVID-NIELSEN, NIELS
1990 *Tense and mood in English. A comparison with Danish*. Berlin: Mouton de Gruyter.

DAVISON, ALICE
1982 On the form and meaning of Hindi passive sentences. *Lingua*, 58. 149–79.

DE HAAN, FERDINAND
1994 *The interaction of negation and modality: A typological study*. Dissertation, University of Southern California.

DIK, SIMON C.
1989 *The theory of functional frammar*. Part I: The structure of the clause. Dordrecht: Foris.

DROSDOWSKI, GÜNTHER (ed.)
1984 *Duden*. Grammatik der deutschen Gegenwartssprache. Mannheim: Dudenverlag.

DRYER, MATTHEW S.
1992 The Greenbergian word order correlations, *Language*, 68. 81–138.

GATZLAFF-HÄLSIG, MARGOT
1978 *Grammatischer Leitfaden des Hindi*. Leipzig: VEB Verlag Enzykopädie.

HACKER, PAUL
1958 Zur Funktion einiger Hilfsverben im modernen Hindi. Mainz: Akademie der Wissenschaften und der Literatur.

HOOK, PETER EDWIN
1974 *The compound verb in Hindi*. Ann Arbor: University of Michigan, Center for South and Southeast Asian Studies.

HORN, LAURENCE R.
1972 *On the semantic properties of logical operators in English*. Dissertation, University of California at Los Angeles.
1984 Toward a new taxonomy for pragmatic inference: Q-based and R-based implicature. In Deborah Schiffrin (ed.), *Meaning, form and use in context: Linguistic applications*. Washington DC: Georgetown University Press. 11–42.
1989 A natural history of negation. Chicago: The University of Chicago Press.

JENSEN, HELLE ØSTKJÆR
1987 *Eine kontrastive Analyse der dänischen Modalverben BEHØVE UND MÅTTE und ihrer deutschen Äquivalente BRAUCHEN, DÜRFEN, MÖGEN UND MÜSSEN*. Odense: Odense University Press.

KACHRU, YAMUNA
1980 *Aspects of Hindi grammar*. Delhi: Manohar.
KLAIMAN, M.H.
1981 *Volitionality and subject in Bengali. A study of semantic parameters in grammatical processes*. Bloomington, IND: Indiana University Linguistics Club.
1987 Bengali. In Comrie (ed.). 490–513.
MASICA, COLIN
1991 *The Indo-Aryan languages*. Cambridge: Cambridge University Press.
MCGREGOR, R.S.
1977 *Outline of Hindi grammar*. Delhi: Oxford University Press.
MONTAUT, ANNIE
1990 La construction passive en hindi moderne. *Bulletin de la Société Linguistique de Paris*, 85. 91–136.
NESPITAL, HELMUT
1980 Zur Semantik und Syntax der Kategorien Modalität, Modus und Modalverben - ein Beitrag zur Sprachtheorie, dargestellt am Modalsystem des Hindi und Urdu unter teilweiser Konfrontation mit dem Deutschen, *Münchner Studien zur Sprachwissenschaft*, 39. 85–156.
PALMER, FRANK
1995 Negation and the modals of possibility and necessity. In Joan Bybee & Suzanne Fleishman (eds.), *Modality in grammar and discourse*. Amsterdam: Benjamins. 453–71.
RADICE, WILLIAM
1994 *Bengali: A complete course for beginners*. London: Teach-Yourself Books.
SCHOLBERG, H.C.
1950 *Concise grammar of the Hindi language*. Oxford University Press.
SHAPIRO, MICHAEL C.
1989 *A primer of modern standard Hindi*. Delhi: Motilal Banarsidass.
SILVA-CORVALÁN, CARMEN
1995 Contextual conditions for the interpretation of 'poder' and 'deber' in Spanish. In Joan Bybee & Suzanne Fleishman (eds.). Amsterdam: Benjamins. 67–105.
SINGH, UDAYA NARAYANA
1976 Negation in Bengali and the order of constituents. *Indian Linguistics*, 37. 295–303.
TOBLER, ADOLF
1921 [1882] *il ne faut pas que tu meures* 'du darfst nicht sterben', Vermischte Beiträge zur französischen Grammatik. Leipzig: Hirzel. 201–5.
TOTTIE, GUNNEL
1985 The negation of epistemic necessity in present-day British and American English. *English World-Wide* 6. 87–116.

VAN DER WURFF, WIM

1989 Scope and movement in Bengali negation. In Hans Bennis & Ans van Kemenade (eds.), *Linguistics in the Netherlands 1989*. Dordrecht: Foris. 185–94.

VERMA, SHIVENDRA K.

1974 The semantics of caahiye. *Foundations of Language,* 12. 127–36.

WALI, KASHI

1973 Negation dependent idioms, and the structure of Marathi modals. *Papers in Linguistics,* 5. 382–401.

WEN, TAN

1979 The syntax of the negative particle in Bengali, *Indian Linguistics,* 40. 246–51.

ZBAVITEL, DUŠAN

1970 *Non-finite verbal forms in Bengali.* Prague: Oriental Institute.

23
Wh-Scope extraction in Malayalam

K. SRIKUMAR
M.S. University of Baroda

In this paper I shall deal with Wh-Scope extraction facts from clausal complements in Malayalam. The analysis I propose here is largely based on my earlier account in Srikumar (1992, 1993). The account therein, formulated within the theory of Barriers (Chomsky 1986), would be recast here in terms of the Minimalist assumptions (Chomsky 1992, 1994, 1995).

Long extractions of question-words across clausal complements in Malayalam appear prima facie evidence for an analysis based on Huang's (1982) condition on extraction domain (CED). As Manzini (1996) and Chomsky (1995) note, CED cases which are contingent on lexical government of the extraction domains have been left open without an account within the minimalist theory of Chomsky (1992, 1995). However, these cases reinforce the need to retain some notion of barrier contingent on lexical selection to restrict extraction facts.[1]

THE BASIC ANALYSIS

First, by way of preliminaries, mention must be made of a few facts. As often noted (Madhavan 1987; Jayaseelan 1989; Srikumar 1992), Clefting forms the

Thanks are due to K.A. Jayaseelan, Anoop Mahajan, Probal Dasgupta, Alice Davison, James Gair and Gennaro Chierchia for useful comments and criticism on this paper. The usual disclaimers however apply.

principle strategy for producing wh-questions in Malayalam. Thus, clefted questions such as (1b) are preferred over unclefted questions like (1a).

(1) a. *kuTTiye* *nuLLiyata* *aarA* *aaNA?*
child ACC. pinch NOMN who FOC
'Who is it that pinched the child?'

b. *kuTTiye* *aarA* *nuLLi?*
child ACC. who pinched

Following my proposal elsewhere (Srikumar 1992, 1993), I shall assume a biclausal structure for clefts in Malayalam which is very much the same as the structure they have in English (cf. Rochemont 1986). And clefting we assume, is an instance of focussed movement as in Srikumar (1992, 1994a, 1994b).[2] However, following Jayaseelan (1995) I shall assume Kayne's (1992) Universal Base Hypothesis for clause structure in Malayalam. Then, following a variety of proposals in Jayaseelan (1989, 1995), Brody (1990) and Srikumar (1994a, 1994b), focussed movement (cf. Hoh and Chiang 1990) is understood as the application of the operation 'move' to [Spec, FP].

In accordance with my earlier thesis, focus (FOC) is base generated as an inherent feature of the verb 'be' *aaNA* and as an optional feature for other verbs in Malayalam.[3] Both the verbal features and 'NP' features of the F in FP are strong in Malayalam and therefore need checking-off before spell-out.[4] Hence, the operation 'move' triggers raising of the FOC feature endowed constituent to the Spec, FP and the verb to F to facilitate checking-off of their features against the V and 'NP' features of F.

(2)

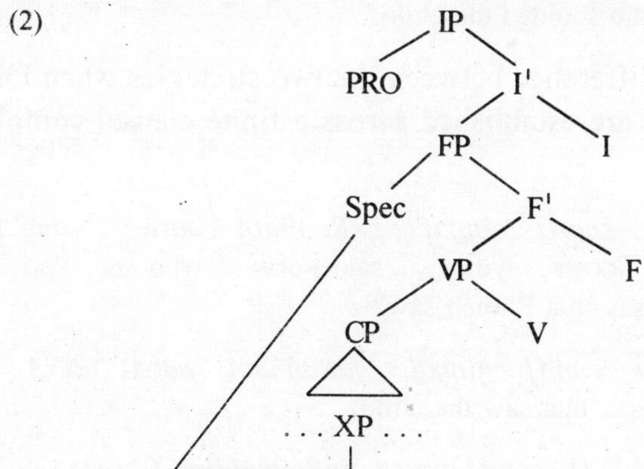

There are two ways for obtaining long-distance dependencies of question-words across sentential complements in Malayalam: one, through direct extraction of the WH-; and two, through pied-piping of the clausal complement containing the WH-.

(3) a. *[raamant kaNDu ennA] niŋŋaL paRaññatA aare aaNA*
Raman saw COMP you said NOMN who ACC FOC

b. *[raaman aare kaNDu ennA] aaNA niŋŋaL paRaññatA*
'Who did you say that Raman saw?'

Both of these strategies employ movement to [Spec, FP] in the matrix clause. But the pied-piping strategy also involves an additional movement, that is, a clause-internal question-word movement to the [Spec, FP] of its own clause. And it is the latter which perhaps triggers pied-piping. This is demonstrated by the unacceptability of the pied-piped sentence, unaccompanied by a clause-internal movement to Spec, FP.

(4) a. t_i *kuTTiye aarA*$_i$ *nuLLi ennA aaNA niŋŋaL paRaññatA*
child ACC. who pinch COMP FOC you said NOMN

b. **aarA kuTTiye nuLLi ennA aaNA niŋŋaL paRaññatA*
'Who did you say that pinched the child?'

The obligatoriness of question-word movement to [Spec, FP] in its own clause is also shown by the preference for preverbal positioning of WH- in indirect questions.

(5) a. **aarA kuTTiye śakaariccu ennA amma coodiccu*
Who child ACC. scolded COMP mother asked

b. *kuTTiye aarA śakaariccu ennA amma coodiccu*
'The mother asked who scolded the child.'

However we notice a difference between the two strategies when long question-word dependencies are established across a finite clausal complement.

(6) a. *?[raaman t kaNDu ennA] niŋŋaL paRaññatA aare aaNA*
Raman saw COMP you said NOMN who ACC FOC
'Who did you say that Raman saw?'

b. **[t kuTTiye kaNDu ennA] niŋŋaL paRaññatA aarA aaNA*
'Who did you say that saw the child?'

c. **[raaman t kuTTiye kaNDu ennA] niŋŋaL paRaññatA eviTe veccA aaNA*
'Where did you say that Raman saw the child?'

d. **[raaman t kuTTiye viLiccu ennA] niŋŋaL paRaññatA entinA aaNA*
'Why did you say that Raman called the child?'

(7) a. *[raaman aare kaNDu ennA] aaNA niŋŋaL paRaññatA*

b. *[kuTTiye aarA kaNDu ennA] aaNA niŋŋaL paRaññatA*

c. *[raaman kuTTiye eviTe veccA kaNDu ennA] aaNA niŋŋaL paRaññatA*

d. *[raaman kuTTiye entinA viLiccu ennA] aaNA niŋŋaL paRaññatA*

Whereas question-word dependencies employing direct extraction strategy show the familiar complement-non-complement asymmetry effects, the pied-piping strategy is not subject to them.[5] That is while direct extraction is permitted only for complements, the pied-piping strategy is free to apply irrespective of the complement-non-complement distinction of the question-words as exemplified by the contrasts between the sentences in (6) and (7).

By contrast, long-distance question-word dependencies across non-finite clausal complements are equally accessible through adopting either strategy, irrespective of the complement-non-complement distinction of the question-words contained as exemplified in (8) and (9).

(8) a. *saaRA kuTTiyooTA [PRO t vaayikkaan] paRaññatA entA aaNA*
teacher child to read to said NOMN what FOC
'What did the teacher tell the child to read?'

b. *raaman hariyooTA [PRO t varaan] paRaññatA entinA aaNA*
raman hari to come to said nomn why FOC
'Why did Raman tell Hari to come?'

c. *raaman hariyoooTA [PRO t varaan] paRaññatA eviTe aaNA*
'Where did Raman tell Hari to come?'

(9) a. *saaRA kuTTiyooTA [PRO entA vaayikkaan] aaNA paRaññatA*

b. *raaman hariyooTA [PRO entinA varaan] aaNA paRaññatA*

c. *raaman hariyooTA [PRO eviTe varaan] aaNA paRaññatA*

Thus, there is a curious asymmetry here between finite and non-finite sentential complements when question-words contained within them are subjected to direct extraction in Malayalam. The pied-piping strategy on the other hand is equally felicitous with both kinds of clausal complements. The complement-non-complement asymmetry observed with direct wh-extraction from finite clausal complements is strikingly similar to the asymmetries holding on extractions from adjuncts and subject noticed first by Huang (1982). Hence the absence of such an asymmetry when clausal pied-piping is adopted supports the idea that finite sentential complements are probably structural islands for extraction purposes and the pied-piping mechanism occurs as a mechanism to overcome the resulting violations.

CLAUSAL PIED-PIPING

Let us go through the evidence which argues for my proposals. First, we shall present Huang's analysis of the adjunct island cases. Then the possibility of pied-piping in other languages is examined with a view to finding out the reason why the strategy exists at all.

The complement-non-complement asymmetry holding on wh-extraction across finite sentential complements in Malayalam reminds one of the CED cases noted by Huang (1982). Noting the contrasts exemplified by sentences in (10), Huang (1982) observed that not only should the extracted position be properly governed but the domain over which elements undergo extractions also needs to be properly governed. This requirement was formulated in terms of the Condition on Extraction Domain (CED) defined as in (11):

(10) a. To who did they leave [before speaking]?
 b. Who did they leave [before speaking to]?
 c. *How did you leave [before fixing the car]?
 d. *Who left [before fixing the car how]?
 e. Who left [before fixing what]?

(11) CED
A phrase A may be extracted out of a domain B only if B is properly governed.

CED as a separate condition was however replaced with the unified notion of Barrier in Chomsky (1986) which restricts both movement and government across categories. Thus, given a configuration such as (12) typical of the sentences above, the theory of Barriers predicts that adjuncts being not L-marked constitute Blocking Categories and therefore Barriers for extraction purposes.[6] The matrix IP will also be a barrier since it inherits barrierhood from the adjunct, whereby the resulting extraction violates subjacency by 2-barriers.

(12) $[_{CP}$ Wh_i $[_{IP}$ [Adjunct . . . t_i . . .]]]

The sentences (10a and 10b) are marginally okay because the traces left behind by the extracted WH-phrases are lexically properly governed by the verb and preposition respectively, satisfying ECP.[7] Similarly, in (10e) the sentence is ruled in as legitimate by the grammar because the WH- *in situ* which gets extracted to the [Spec, CP] of the matrix clause at LF is the complement of the verb, whence properly governed for ECP. However for the adjunct WH-phrases in (10b and 10c) since the option of lexical proper government to satisfy ECP is not available, the only way they can satisfy ECP is through antecedent government. The antecedent government option however fails in these cases due to the intervening barriers: the adjunct and the matrix IP. Hence these sentences violate not only subjacency but the ECP, hence the severity of the violation.

Pied-piping of clausal complements to effect long-distance dependency for question-words contained in them also exists in languages like Basque and Imbabura Quechua (cf. Ortiz de Urbina 1989; Cole and Hermon 1981; Cole 1982). In Basque, for instance, besides direct question-word extraction from the embedded clause to the Spec, CP of the matrix clause, the wh-movement may also be effected to the Spec, CP of the embedded clause which in turn triggers pied-piping of the embedded clause to the Spec, CP of the matrix clause. Thus, in the following sentences while the (a) sentences illustrate the direct extraction strategy, the (b) sentences illustrate their parallels adopting the pied-piping strategy.

(13) BASQUE

a. *nor esan duzu [entzun du-ela peru-K [joango dela paris-a]]?*
who (A) say AUX. hear AUX.-ELA Peter-E go AUX-ELA Paris-to

b. *[Nor joango d-ela] esan du Jon-ek?*
who go AUX-ELA say AUX John E
'Who has John said will go?'

(14) IMBABURA QUECHUA

a. *ima-ta-taq ni-nki pay ranti-sqa-n-Ta?*
what-ACC-Q say-2 he buy-PRF-3-ACC
'What do you say he bought?'

b. *ima-ta ranti-sqa-n-ta-taq ni-nki?*
What ACC buy-PRF-3-ACC-Q say-2
'What do you say he bought?'

Although no subject-object asymmetry is observed with respect to either strategies, as Ortiz de Urbina (1989) Cole (1982) and Cole and Hermon (1981) note, pied-piping rescues those structures where direct WH-extraction would have led to subjacency violations, that is, the complex NPs and adjuncts.

(15) BASQUE

a. *[zeri ikusi] ondoren joan ziren hemen-diK*
what (A) see after go AUX. here from
'They left after seeing what?'

b. **zer joan ziren hemendik [t ikusi ondoren]?*
'What did they leave after seeing?'

(16) a. *[norK idatzi-ta-ko liburo-a] irekurri du peru-K?*
who-E write-ADC. of book-A read AUX Peter-E
'The book written by who did Peter read?'

b. **norK irakurri zuen Peru-K [t idatzi-ta-ko liburu-a]?*
'Who did Peter read the book written by t?'

(17) IMBABURA QUECHUA
ima-(ta) ranti-na-y-paq-taq qolqe-ta qo-wa-n?
what buy NOMN-1-for-Q money ACC give-1?
'In order to buy what has he given me the money?'

(18) a. *ima ranti-sqa-n-ta-taq apamu-sqayki?*
what buy-PRF. 3-ACC-Q bring-1 P2
'What that he has bought will I bring you?'

b. **ima-ta-taq apamu-sqayki ranti-sqa-n-ta?*
'What will I bring you that he has bought?'

(19) *pe-q wasi ruwa-sqa-n-taq sumaq?*
who-GEN. house make-PRF-3-Q good
'The house built by who is good?

Even in Malayalam, pied-piping is known to rescue subjacency effects and ECP for wh-extractions from Complex NPs (cf. Madhavan 1987) and adjuncts as exemplified in (20).

(20) a. *[aarA ezutiya pustakattinA] aaNA sammaanam kiTTiyatA*
wrote COMP book DAT. FOC award received NOMN.
'The book that who wrote received the award?'

b. *[raaman eŋŋane vaaŋŋiya pustakam] aaNA niŋŋaL vaayiccatA*
Raman how bought COMP book FOC you read nomn
'You read the book that Raman purchased how?'

c. *niŋŋaL [aarA vannatinA seeSam] aaNA sthalam viTTatA*
you who come NOMN. DAT. after FOC place left NOMN.
'After who came did you leave?'

The option of clausal pied-piping strategy to obtain long-distance dependency for embedded question-words is found only in a few languages. Therefore, this phenomenon makes us wonder as to why it is available only in these languages and not in others. According to an explanation offered by Ortiz de Urbina (1989), the pied-piping option for clausal complements in Basque and other similar languages perhaps owes to the base-generability of CP in Spec,

CP in these languages which is however not an available option in other languages and hence the difference follows. However, since a functional projection like Spec, CP is capable of hosting any maximal projection by substitutions resulting from the operation move, Ortiz de Urbina's speculation is counter-intuitive and stipulative in character. Hence, the variety of maximal projections permitted by individual languages to occur in Spec, CP must be reducible to properties specific to the moved constituents and therefore predictable from independently motivated principles.

Lending support to this argument are the following observations. Cole (1982) notes that finite clausal complements in Imbabura Quechua appear as nominals bearing overt case-markers and therefore are perhaps dominated by an NP node which would inevitably add a barrier for any kind of long dependency across them. And in Basque also, as Ortiz de Urbina observes, the tensed subordinator *(e)la* functions as the marker of adverbial adjuncts.[8] This observation may be taken to imply that finite clausal complements in Basque are not held in an argument position.

Returning to wh-extractions from finite complements in Malayalam the curious asymmetry calls for an explanation. In other words, why should finite complement clauses in particular block extraction for non-complements while non-finite complements do not do so? This is also curious since their equivalents in English and several other languages are perfectly legitimate. An answer is provided if we subject the nature of finite sentential complementation in Malayalam to closer scrutiny. There are two noteworthy characteristics associated with the nature and form of the finite sentential complementiser *ennA* in Malayalam. Firstly, it is obligatory in finite sentential complements, and secondly, the shwa ending on the complementiser *ennA*, which is itself historically a derivative of the verb meaning 'to say', though no longer in current use, is characteristically the ending on verbs when they are participial adverbials as exemplified in (21).[9]

(21) a. *raaman naTannA vannu*
Raman walk came
'Raman came by walk.'

b. *raaman kaseerayil ninnu caaTi ezuneeRRu*
Raman chair jumped stood up
'Raman jumped and got up from the chair.'

Further shwa-adjunct like all adjuncts in Malayalam are cleftable as the sentences in (22) indicate.

(22) a. *raaman naTannA aaNA vannatA*
'It is by walk that Raman came.'

b. *raaman kaseerayil ninnu caaTi aaNA ezuneeRRatA*
'It is by jumping that Raman got up from the chair.'

These facts taken together would suggest that perhaps finite clausal complements contra non-finite clausal complements in Malayalam are held in an adjoined position. This assumption, if true, would readily be explained by a natural extension of Chomsky's (1986) reformulation of Huang's CED. That is, they involve extraction across an adjoined position, which is a barrier, and therefore ought to be violations of subjacency, and if non-complements are involved, ECP too.

The plausibility of the pied-piped clauses disregarding the complement-non-complement distinction of the WH-words contained in them now receives a natural explanation. As commonly observed in the literature, violations of the subjacency condition by itself do not cause total unacceptability of a sentence, but would at best result in marginality. However, when ECP is also violated besides subjacency, the resultant is definitely odd. Thus, while complement extractions are marginally okay, the extractions of non-complements cause total rejection of the wh-questions. The pied-piping strategy however comes to bail out these wh-questions, since the question-words need not be extracted out of the clausal complement.

Given minimalist assumptions (Chomsky 1992, 1995), these cases must be handled by Minimal Link Condition (MLC) which requires movements to be composed of shorter moves if possible. The operation 'move' deriving direct extraction from finite clausal complements is in fact composed of a chain comprising of shorter links. None of the links composing it bypass an A'-position where the shortest move would have been possible. That is, given the assumption following Kayne's (1994) theory, if we assume clause final complementiser to be a consequence of the raising of IP to spec of CP, Spec, CP would no longer be available for intermediate landings. We would then be forced to assume successive cyclical movement through Spec, FP of the intermediate clauses. The resulting movement would be composed of a combination of shorter moves. But still the complement-non-complement asymmetry persists.

A plausible reason for this could be the barrier due to extraction across an adjoined position that intervenes one of the links composing the chain here. The requirement could be that the minimal link must not be formed across a barrier. If such a link is formed, then if the moved question-word is a complement its initial trace at the LF interface is legitimate. Therefore, the derivation converges although with interpretive deviance (cf. Chomsky 1991). However, if the moved question-word is a non-complement, at the LF its trace is not licit due to the intervention of a barrier in the link connecting it to its antecedent. (cf. Manzini 1996 for a similar account). Therefore, the derivation would crash.

The pied-piping strategy on the other hand succeeds because it involves a shorter move inside the complement clause and another move resulting in pied-piping of the clause, both obeying MLC. So, following Srikumar (1992) and Chomsky (1995), I would assume that it is the morphosyntactic property of the finite clausal complement which perhaps triggers a pied-piped movement, that is, a movement motivated by bare output conditions at the interface PF. The lack of complement-non-complement asymmetry with question-words when extracted from infinitive clauses on the other hand suggests that they are held in argument positions. The pied-piping strategy is perhaps a rescue mechanism to evade subjacency violation in the case of finite complements.

ARGUMENTS AS ADJUNCTS

Assuming that finite clausal complements are held in an adjoined position, the question naturally arises as to why finite clausal complements which are arguments are held in an adjoined position. In my earlier work (Srikumar 1992, 1993), this was analysed to follow from a differential base generation account of arguments contingent partly on whether they are NPs or not and also on whether or not the language is morphologically rich in case. The guiding principle to ensure this was the parametrisation of Case Filter across the different levels of syntactic derivation, that is, DS, SS, and PF. Thus, in languages which are morphologically rich in case only NPs could be base-generated in argument positions since Case Filter was supposed to apply at DS. But in language impoverished in morphological case-inflections, Case Filter was supposed to apply at PF. Therefore, all arguments, irrespective of their categorial membership, may be base-generated in their respective positions, with the proviso that non-NPs be displaced to an adjoined position by PF. DS application of Case Filter results in base-generation of finite clausal complements as adjuncts in Malayalam and Basque and in Imbabura Quechua as NPs. The argument position of the finite sentential complements in Malayalam and probably Basque is that we assume occupied by an empty pronominal coindexed with the displaced sentential complement to receive the case due for it. An alternative analysis would be to assume base-generation of finite complements in the argument position and later extraposition to an adjoined position, *à la* Stowell (1981) analysis.

Under the minimalist assumptions, case theory has been reduced to checking theory contingent on spec-head agreement in AGRP. Also, following

Chomsky (1995), we assume that in the absence of overt agreement morphology the AGRP is unmotivated and case checking for the object NP can be accomplished under spec-head agreement in the upper stair of the Larsonian VP shell illustrated in (23). That is, the case of the object NP can be said to reside as the NP-features of the V_1.

(23)

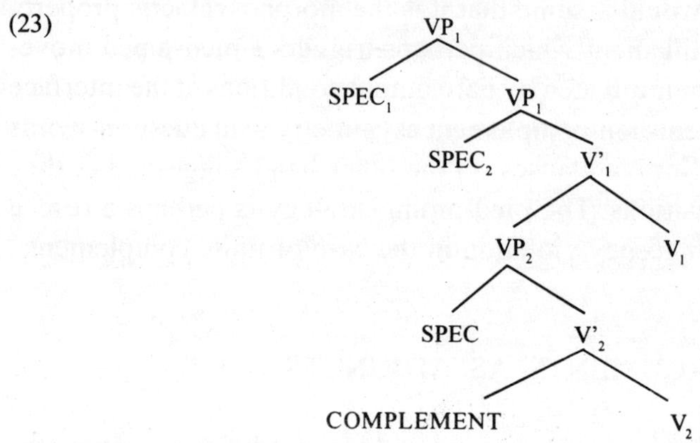

Let us assume accusative case on object NPs which is overt in Malayalam to correlate with strong NP-features of V_1. The object NP would then have to raise to spec of VP_1 to check-off its strong NP-features. For, otherwise, the strong NP-features on V_1 would survive to LF where it is uninterpretable causing the derivation to crash. Accepting Chomsky's proposal to allow multiple specs, we assume the spec of VP_1 moved into by the object NP to be the internal spec, leaving the external spec for the base-generation of subject NP. This movement is allowed for in principle since both $spec_1$ and $spec_2$ are equidistant from the complement of V_2 once V_2 raises to the light verb position V_1 because they are both contained in the minimal domain formed by the V-chain. Clausal complements, on the other hand, cannot however raise to spec of VP_1 for case-checking if they are not NPs. Hence let us suppose that they are adjoined instead to a non-visible position like V'_1, either base-generated thus or moved into to avoid case-checking valid for only NPs. If the former option is taken, an empty pronominal coindexed with the V'_1-adjoined finite clausal complement is required in the complement position to check-off the strong-NP features of V_1. However, if the latter option is adopted, then the base-generated finite sentential complement can be assumed to move to the V_1'-adjoined position to avoid checking with the strong-NP features of V_1, allowing instead its trace to check-off the strong-NP features of V_1 by copying into its spec. The second option however appears dubious for the trace is a CP-trace. Hence we assume the former option as in Srikumar (1992, 1993).

Next, we have to consider how the question-word within the pied-piped clause receives wide scope. In order to receive scope as May's (1985) principle of scope requires, the WH-words must C-Command its scopal domain, that is, whole clause. At spell-out, the WH-word is contained in the Spec, FP of the pied-piped clause which is in the Spec, FP of the matrix clause. From this position, however, the wh-word cannot C-command the whole clause. Therefore, let us assume that the wh-word raises to the matrix Spec, CP at LF. Even though extraction from the base-generated position of finite clausal complements is not permitted due to its adjoined position, the extraction is permitted at the interface LF once the focussed movement, that is, pied-piping has already taken place. The movement thus is straightaway effected to the Spec, CP of the matrix clause from where it can C-command the clause as shown in (24) (suppressing irrelevant details).

(24) $[_{CP}\, wh_i\, [_{C'}\, [_{IP}\, pro [_{I'}\, I\, [_{FP} [_{CP} \ldots t_i \ldots]_j [_{F'}\, F\, [_{VP} \ldots t_j \ldots]]]]]]]]$

Similarly, in the case of direct extractions too, the moved question-word in the Spec, FP at spell-out must raise to the Spec, CP of the matrix clause.[10]

CONCLUSION

This paper has examined the possibilities for wh-extractions from clausal complements in Malayalam. We found that an asymmetry exists between finite and non-finite clausal complements when question-words are extracted out of them. While WH-extractions from finite clausal complements are sensitive to the complement-non-complement distinction of the question-words, WH-extractions from non-finite clausal complements are not sensitive to them. This, we have argued on the strength of morphological evidence, to follow from differential base generation of clausal complements due to the strong object NP-features of V_1 in Malayalam. The finite clausal complements are held in a structurally adjunct position while the non-finite clausal complements are held in the argument position due for them. Hence WH-extractions from finite clausal complements will invite subjacency violations for they move across a non-selected position, which is a barrier and so the extractions are limited to the complements by the ECP.

The clausal pied-piping option however succeeds in circumventing the asymmetry *vis-à-vis* extractions from finite clausal complements because it does not involve movement across a barrier. As Manzini (1996) notes following Cinque (1990) and Rizzi (1990), only operator-variable chains are subject to island restrictions. In pied-piping instances, the pied-piped constituent is not an operator binding a variable trace. The trace left by pied-piping operation is an empty pronominal. Therefore, their relations are not sensitive to island restrictions. For receiving scope, however, the question-words from pied-piped clauses must move to Spec, CP at LF for C-Commanding the whole clause.

NOTES

GENERAL NOTE: The abbreviations used in this paper are as follows:
ACC = accusative, DAT = dative, COMP = Complementiser,
E = ergative, NOMN. = nominaliser

1. See however Takahashi (1994) for an approach which dispenses with the need for barriers.
2. The Focussed Movement account for clefts in Malayalam proposed in Srikumar (1992) assumes a VP-adjunction analysis.
3. The verb *be* is always associated with focus (cf. Heggie 1989).
4. This explains the preverbal position of question-words in Malayalam. The 'NP' feature of F is better construed as XP feature since any maximal projection is cleftable in Malayalam.
5. This is in fact a general restriction, as Madhavan (1987) notes, holding on clefting in Malayalam.
6. L-marking, Blocking Category and Barrier are defined as follows:
   L-MARKING: a L-marks b iff a is a lexical category that q-marks b
   BLOCKING CATEGORY (BC): a is a BC for b iff a is not L-marked and a dominates b.
   BARRIER: g is a barrier for b iff (a) or (b)
   a. g immediately dominates d, d a BC for b
   b. g is a BC for b, g ¹ IP. (Chomsky, 1986: 14).
7. EMPTY CATEGORY PRINCIPLE (ECP)
   An empty category must be properly governed, where X properly governs Y iff: X governs Y and
   a. X is a lexical category, or
   b. X is coindexed with Y (Chomsky 1981)
8. Observe the following sentence.
   [kala-tik nentorr-ela] ikus ninduen
   street-by came-ELA see AUX
   'He saw me when I was coming down the street.'
9. Jayaseelan (1984) terms these as shwa-adjuncts.
10. The WH-movement at LF may be restricted to the [+interpretive] WH-feature raising as Chomsky (1995) proposes since features are the only legitimate objects for 'move' at the interface LF.

REFERENCES

BRODY, MICHAEL
1990 Some remarks on the focus field in Hungarian. *UCL Working papers in Linguistics* 2. Department of Linguistics, University College of London.

CHOMSKY, NOAM
1981 *Lectures on government and binding*. Dordrecht: Foris.
1986 *Barriers*. Cambridge, MA: MIT Press.
1991 Some notes on economy of derivation and representation. In Freidin, ed., *Principles and parameters in comparative grammar*. Cambridge, MA: MIT Press.
1992 *A minimalist program for linguistic theory*. MIT occasional papers in Linguistics 1. Department of Linguistics and Philosophy, MIT.
1994 *Bare phrase structure*. MIT occasional papers in Linguistics 5. Department of Linguistics and Philosophy, MIT.
1995 *The minimalist program*. Cambridge, MA: MIT Press.

CINQUE, GUGLIELMO
1990 *Types of A-bar dependencies*. Cambridge, MA: MIT Press.

COLE, PETER
1982 On defining bounding nodes for subjacency. *Linguistic Inquiry*, 13. 139–45.

COLE, PETER and GABRIELLA HERMON
1981 Subjecthood and islandhood: Evidence from Quechua. *Linguistic Inquiry*, 12. 1–30.

HEGGIE, LORY
1989 Constructional focus and equative sentences. WCCFL, 8. 154–66.

HOH, P.-S and WEN-YU. CHIANG
1990 A focus account of moved wh-phrases in S-structure in Chinese. *Lingua*, 81. 47–73.

HUANG, C.-T.J.
1982 *Logical relations in Chinese and the theory of grammar*. Cambridge, MA: MIT dissertation.

JAYASEELAN, K.A.
1984 Control in some sentential adjuncts of Malayalam. BLS, 10. 623–33.
1989 Question-word movement in Malayalam. CIEFL, ms.
1995 Question-word movement to focus in Malayalam. CIEFL, ms.

KAYNE, RICHARD S.
1994 *The antisymmetry of syntax*. Cambridge, MA: MIT Press.

MADHAVAN, P.
1987 *Clefts and pseudoclefts in Malayalam*. Hyderabad: CIEFL dissertation.

MANZINI, M. RITA
1996 Minimalism and the theory of locality. In Lecture notes, Girona summer school, Spain.

MAY, ROBERT
1985 *Logical form*. Cambridge, MA: MIT Press.

ORTIZ DE URBINA, JON
1989 *Parameters in the grammar of Basque*. Dordrecht: Foris.

RIZZI, LUIGI
1990 *Relativized minimality*. Cambridge, MA: MIT Press.

ROCHEMONT, MICHAEL
1986 *Focus in generative grammar*. Amsterdam: John Benjamins.

SRIKUMAR, K.

1992 *Question-word movement in Malayalam and GB theory*. Hyderabad: Osmania University dissertation.

1993 Unbounded question-word movement, clausal pied-piping and case filter parameter. *IJDL* XXII, 2. 29–41.

1994a Clefts in Malayalam: a focussed movement approach. In Alice Davison & Frederick M. Smith (eds.), *Papers from the Fifteenth South Asian Language Analysis Roundtable Conference 1993*. Iowa City: South Asian Studies Program, University of Iowa. 322–30.

1994b Clefts in Malayalam: A focussed movement perspective. Osmania University, ms.

STOWELL, TIM

1981 *Origins of phrase structure*. Cambridge, MA: MIT dissertation.

TAKAHASHI, DAIKO

1994 *Minimality of movement*. Connecticut: University of Connecticut dissertation.

24

Anaphoric orientation in Hindi

RITA BHANDARI
State University of New York

Hindi is well known as a scrambling language. The ditransitive sentence in (1a), for example, admits all of the permutations shown in (1b–f) (Dayal 1994):

(1) a. *Ram-ne Mohan-ko kitab dii*
Ram-ERG Mohan-DAT book gave
'Ram gave a book to Mohan.'

b. *kitab Ram-ne Mohan-ko dii*

c. *Mohan-ko kitab Ram-ne dii*

d. *kitab Mohan-ko Ram-ne dii*

e. *Mohan-ko Ram-ne kitab dii*

f. *Ram-ne kitab Mohan-ko dii*

As has been discussed by a number of authors (Mahajan 1990, 1994; Jones 1993; Dayal 1994), scrambling in Hindi interacts with binding phenomena in complex ways. For example, although clause-bounded scrambling of a reflexive does not change binding possibilities (2a–b), scrambling of a pronoun (3) or a reciprocal (4) may:

I thank Dan Finer and Richard Larson for their comments, suggestions, and guidance while I was writing this paper. I also think the faculty and students of the Linguistics department at Stony Brook for their support and input. I alone am responsible for all errors.

(2) a. *Ram-ne$_i$ Mohan-ko$_j$ apni$_{i/*j}$* kitab dii
Ram-ERG Mohan-DAT self's book gave
'Ram$_i$ gave his$_i$ book to Mohan.'

b. *Mohan-ko$_j$ Ram-ne$_i$ apni$_{i/*j}$ kitab dii*

(3) a. *Ram-ne$_i$ Mohan-ko$_j$ uski$_{*i/j}$ kitab dii*
Ram-ERG Mohan-DAT his book gave
'Ram$_i$ gave Mohan$_j$ his$_{*i/*j}$ book.'

b. *Ram-ne$_i$ uski$_{*i/*j}$ kitab Mohan-ko$_j$ dii*

(4) a. *laRkiyō$_i$-ne laRkō-ko$_j$ ek duusre$_{i/j}$-ki kitabeN dii*
girls-ERG boys-DAT each other's books gave
'The girls$_i$ gave the boys$_j$ each other's$_{i/j}$ books.'

b. *laRkiyō$_i$ neek dusre$_{i*j}$-ki kitabeN laRkō-ko$_j$ dii*

In this paper, I focus on the inability of scrambling to change the subject orientation of reflexives and the anti-subject orientation of pronouns in Hindi. I show that by combining an analysis of scrambling as adjunction to Agr projections with an account of Hindi reflexives and pronouns as LF-clitics (following Chomsky 1986; Pica 1987; Hestvik 1990), many of the interaction facts fall out straightforwardly. In Section 1, I briefly sketch the background assumptions of this paper. In Section 2, I address the binding effects using the approach to reflexive and pronominal binding developed by Pica and Hestvik, in which these elements move to T.

1. BACKGROUND

In order to discuss the interaction of Hindi word order with scrambling and binding, it is necessary to make some guiding assumptions about each. Below I sketch these assumptions and also indicate where more detailed justification may be found.

1.1 *Hindi word order and scrambling*

The basic and derived structure of Hindi scrambling has been widely discussed in the literature (Mahajan 1990, 1994; Jones 1993; Dayal 1994). For purposes of this paper I will adopt the general Minimalist framework of Chomsky (1995), in which subject, direct object and indirect object arguments originate within VP but move to Agr(eement) projections in order to check case features prior to Spell-out. Overt movement of the arguments to the Spec of Agr projections is induced by a strong feature of Agr in Hindi. The verb also raises to check off its features. Under these proposals the structure of (5a), for example, is as in (5b) prior to Spell-out:[1]

(5) a. *Ram-ne* *Mohan-ko* *kitab* *dii*
Ram-ERG Mohan-DAT book gave
'Ram gave a book to Mohan.'

b. $[_{TP}$ $[_{AGRSP}$ ram-ne$_j$ $[_{AGROP}$ mohan-ko$_i$ $[_{AGROP}$ kitaab$_k$ $[_{VP}$ t_j t_i t_k $t_V]]][_{AGRO}$ AGRO $t_V]]$ $[_{AGR\text{-}O}$ AGRO $t_V]]$ $[_{AGRS}$ AGRS $t_V]]$ $[_{TNS}$ TNS dii$_V]]$

Here *Ram-ne* 'Ram' has raised to Spec of AgrSP, *Mohan-ko* 'Mohan' has raised to Spec of AgrO, and *kitab* 'book' has raised to a distinct Spec of AgrO. The verb *dii* 'gave' has raised to higher Agr heads. Assuming that the T feature is weak in Hindi, the subject raises to Spec of TP at LF following the principle of 'procrastinate' (Chomsky 1995). I will later give arguments that such raising does in fact take place at LF in Hindi.

I also adopt the widely-held view that scrambling permutes basic word order by Chomsky-adjoining arguments to maximal projections. In particular, I assume here that scrambling operates on pre-Spellout structures like (5b) and adjoins phrases to maximal Agr projections.[2] Under these assumptions, (6a), a scrambled version of (5a), is obtained by adjoining *kitab* 'book' to AgrSP, as in (6b):

(6) a. *kitab* *Ram-ne* *Mohan-ko* *dii*
book Ram-ERG Mohan-DAT gave
'Ram gave a book to Mohan.'

b. $[_{TP}$ kitab$_k$ $[_{AGRSP}$ Ram-ne$_j$ $[_{AGROP}$ Mohan-ko$_i$ $[_{AGROP}$ t_k $[_{VP}$ t_j t_i t_k $t_V]]][_{AGRO}$ AGRO $t_V]]$ $[_{AGR\text{-}O}$ AGRO $t_V]]$ $[_{AGRS}$ AGRS $t_V]]$ $[_{TNS}$ TNS dii$_V]]$

The exact properties of the adjunction involved in scrambling are controversial. Dayal (1994) assumes that scrambling in Hindi is fundamentally a form of A-bar movement; accordingly, such movement creates the equivalent of operator-variable structures. Others, including Jones (1993), assume that scrambling is analogous to A-movement, as it involves a chain that is active at its head. Mahajan (1990) argues that Hindi scrambling may be either A-movement or A-bar adjunction. Issues raised by this dichotomy will be addressed as the discussion proceeds.

1.2 *Binding and functional categories*

The analysis of binding assumed here derives from proposals by Chomsky (1986) and Lebeaux (1983), according to which reflexive anaphors undergo cliticisation at LF. On this account, the example in (7a) receives the analysis in (7b), in which the anaphor moves at LF and assumes a highly local relation with its antecedent:

(7) a. Ram [$_{VP}$ respects himself]

b. Ram himself$_i$ [$_{VP}$ respects t_i]

As discussed in Chomsky (1986), this proposal has the virtue of assimilating constraints on anaphora to familiar constraints on movement structures. For example, the unavailability of reflexives in subject position of a tensed clause, illustrated in (8a), can be explained as a violation of the empty category principle (ECP): after LF movement, the trace (t_i) of the reflexive in (8b) fails to be properly governed:

(8) a. *Ram said [$_{CP}$ that himself was tired].

b. Rasm himself$_i$ said [$_{CP}$ that t_i was tired].

The general analysis also brings languages English more closely into line with languages like Spanish and French, in which reflexive cliticisation is overt.

In recent years, the LF cliticisation analysis has been developed and extended in a number of interesting ways. Pica (1987) draws an important distinction between bi-morphemic anaphors that are fully phrasal (XPs) and anaphoric elements that are simply heads (X^0s).[3] Pica proposes that the class of X^0 reflexive elements cliticise to INFL, whereas XP elements adjoin to the Spec of their governor at LF. Under Pica's proposal, the Norwegian example in (9a), containing the X^0 monomorphemic possessive reflexive *sin,* involves LF movement of the clitic to INFL where it comes into the local domain of the matrix subject. By contrast, in the example in (9b) the possessive reciprocal *hverandres*, which is an XP, does not raise to INFL and can be bound by either the subject or the object.

(9) a.	*John$_i$*	*fortalte*	*Ola$_j$*	*om*	*[sin$_{i/*j}$*	*kone]*
	John	told	Ola	about	REFL	wife
b.	*De$_i$*	*fortalte*	*dem$_j$*	*om*	*[hverandres$_{i/j}$*	*koner]*
	they	told	them	about	each other's	wives

This analysis neatly explains the very frequent subject-orientation found with reflexives that are monomorphemic clitic elements. X^0 clitic reflexives move to INFL where their only local antecedent is the subject. Hence such anaphors must have subject orientation.

Hestvik (1990) further extends Pica's general idea to pronominals, arguing that pronouns too are plausibly divided into X^0 and XP classes. Hestvik's motivation is the anti-subject nature of Norwegian pronouns, which, unlike their English counterparts, are forbidden from coreferring with a subject:

(10) a. *John*$_i$ *liker* *hans*$_{*i/j}$ *bil*
John$_i$ likes his$_{i/j}$ car

b. *John*$_i$ *kikket* *bak* *ham*$_{*i/j}$
John$_i$ looked behind him$_{i/j}$

Hestvik proposes that whereas English anaphors and pronouns are all XPs, their Norwegian counterparts are all clitic X^{0}s. Since the latter move to INFL at LF, and hence into the local domain of the subject, Norwegian reflexives are forced to be subject-oriented (that is, subject-bound), and Norwegian pronouns are forced to be anti-subject-oriented (that is, subject-disjoint) [compare (11) and (9a)].

(11) *John*$_i$ *fortalte* *Ola*$_j$ *om* *[hans**$_{i/j}$ *kone]*
John told Ola about his wife

In the following sections, I will assume the general family of proposals by Chomsky, Lebeaux, Pica and Hestvik. More precisely, I will assume that Hindi reflexives and pronouns are X^0 clitics that obligatorily move to (the equivalent of) INFL at LF. For concreteness, I will follow the versions of the binding conditions given by Chomsky (1986), for the relevant local domain D, at LF.

(12) Condition A: An anaphor must be bound in D.

Condition B: A pronominal must be free in D.

Condition C: An R-expression must be free.

Note that since anaphoric elements form chains after LF movement, these binding conditions must be understood as relativised to chains. Thus, when we assert that reflexives must be bound in their local domain, we are understanding this to apply to the head of the clitic chain (13a). Likewise, when we assert that pronouns must be free in their local domain, we understand this to apply to the chain-head (13b), and so on.

(13) a. Ram$_i$ (*apni*$_j$ . . . t$_j$) (i = j, with *Ram* and *apni* 'himself' in the relevant local domain)

b. Ram$_i$ (*us*$_j$ . . . t$_j$) (i ≠ j, with *Ram* and *us* 'him' in the relevant local domain)

2. INTERACTIONS BETWEEN SCRAMBLING AND BINDING

2.1 *Reflexive binding*

Hindi reflexives and pronouns pattern analogously to those in Norwegian: the former are subject-oriented and the latter are anti-subject-oriented. Hindi reflexives and pronominals are thus in strict complementary distribution, unlike their English counterparts. The following sentences illustrate the contrast:

(14) a. *Ram-ne*$_i$ *uske*$_{*i}$*/ apne*$_i$ *aage* *piichhe* *dekha*
Ram-ERG him/self front back looked
'Ram$_i$ looked around him*$_i$/himself$_i$.'

b. *Ram-ne*$_i$ *Mohan-ko*$_j$ *apni*$_{i/*j}$*/ uski**$_{i/j}$ *tasveer-ke* *aage* *rakha*
Ram-ERG Mohan-DAT self /his picture of front put
'Ram$_i$ put Mohan$_j$ in front of a picture of him*$_{i/j}$/himself$_{i/*j}$.'

These facts can be explained by directly extending the Pica-Hestvik analysis to Hindi. We illustrate with the somewhat simpler example in (15):

(15) *Ram-ne*$_i$ *Mohan-ko*$_j$ *apni*$_{i/*j}$ *kitab* *dii*
Ram-ERG Mohan-DAT self's book gave
'Ram$_i$ gave his$_i$ book to Mohan.'

Assume that in this sentence, the reflexive *apni* raises at LF and adjoins to T, the equivalent of INFL for our purposes. Assuming also that the subject raises to Spec of TP, the LF representation of (15) is in (16):

(16) [$_{TP}$ ram-ne$_j$ [$_{AGRSP}$ *ram-ne*$_j$ [$_{AGROP}$ mohan-ko$_i$ [$_{AGROP}$ apni kitaab$_k$ [$_{VP}$ t$_j$ t$_i$ t$_k$ t$_V$]][$_{AGRO}$ AGRO t$_V$]] [$_{AGR\text{-}O}$ AGRO t$_V$]] [$_{AGRS}$ AGRS t$_V$]] [$_{TNS}$ TNS dii$_V$]]

Note that after movement, the subject is the only c-commanding[4] NP accessible to the reflexive (that is, in its local domain). Neither the direct object nor the indirect object are in a position to c-command *apni*. Hence strict subject orientation is required.

Consider now example (17), which is the same as (15) except that the indirect object *Mohan-ko* 'Mohan-DAT' has scrambled to the pre-subject position.

(17) *Mohan-ko*$_i$ *Ram-ne*$_j$ *apni*$_{*i/j}$ *kitab dii*

The indexing patterns show that scrambling does not affect the coreference possibilities of the reflexive. This too is accounted for on the reflexive clitic movement hypothesis. (18) is the LF representation of (17):

(18) [$_{TP}$ ram-ne$_j$ [$_{AGRSP}$ mohan-ko$_i$ [$_{AGRSP}$ *ram-ne*$_j$ [$_{AGROP}$ t$_i$ [$_{AGROP}$ apni kitaab$_k$ [$_{VP}$ t$_j$ t$_i$ t$_k$ t$_V$]][$_{AGRO}$ AGRO t$_V$]] [$_{AGR\text{-}O}$ AGRO t$_V$]] [$_{AGRS}$ AGRS t$_V$]] [$_{TNS}$ TNS dii$_V$]]

In (18), the indirect object scrambles and adjoins to AgrSP. At LF, the subject raises out to Spec of TP where it now once again c-commands the reflexive *apni*. Although Mohan c-commands *apni* the two arguments cannot be coindexed given the fact that *apni* also c-commands[5] Mohan. Hence coindexation would lead to a Condition C violation.

Note that our analysis of anaphoric phenomena in (15) and (16) hinges crucially on the assumption that the subject raises to a higher position (here identified as TP spec) at Logical Form. Simply raising of *apni* to the local domain of *Ram* would place it outside the c-command domain of *Mohan* in (15) [see (15')]. However, this would not be sufficient to explain the coreference facts of (17). Since scrambling has moved *Mohan* to a position higher than the subject *Ram*, local movement of *apni kitab* 'self's book' would leave it within the binding domain of the scrambled object [see(17')]:

(15') *Ram-ne apni kitab$_i$ [Mohan-ko t$_i$dii]*

(17') *Mohan-ko [Ram-ne apni$_i$ kitab [t$_i$dii]]*

Our analysis assumes that there is a further raising of the subject to position higher than that occupied by Mohan in (17), and that *apni* raises into the domain of this high locale. It is for this reason that scrambling is unable to affect binding with reflexives: scrambling never raises an argument higher than AgrSP, and this is too low (at LF) to affect reflexive binding.

We see then that under the LF clitic analysis, scrambling will never affect the subject orientation of reflexives. The subject will be the only local C-commanding antecedent available at LF, scrambling of arguments prior to LF will have no consequences for reflexive binding.

2.2 *Reciprocal binding*

The behaviour of reflexives under scrambling contrasts sharply with that of reciprocals. The sentences in (19) and (20) show that scrambling with reciprocals *does* alter binding relations. In (19a), the direct object cannot be the antecedent of the reciprocal, *ek duusre*, but scrambling the direct object makes it a potential binder in (19b):

(19) a. *laRkiyõ-ne$_i$ ek duusre-ko$_{i/*j}$ laRke$_j$ dikhaye*
girls-ERG each other-DAT boys showed
'The girls$_i$ showed each other$_{i/*j}$ to the boys$_j$.

b. *laRkiyõ-ne$_i$ laRke$_j$ ek duusre-ko$_{i/*j}$ dikhaye*
girls-ERG boys each other-DAT showed
'The girls$_i$ showed the boys$_j$ to each other$_{i/j}$.

In (20a) the indirect object argument can bind a reciprocal embedded in the direct object NP. But if the direct object NP is scrambled to a position higher than the indirect object, the latter is no longer available as a binder.

(20) a. *laRkiyõ-ne*$_i$ *laRkõ-ko*$_j$ *ek duusre*$_{i/j}$*-ki* *tasveereN* *dikhayiN*
girls-ERG boys-DAT each other's-GEN pictures showed
'The girls$_i$ showed the boys$_j$ pictures of each other$_{i/j}$.'

b. *laRkiyõ-ne*$_i$ *ek duusre*$_{i/*j}$ *ki tasveereN* *laRkõ-ko*$_j$ *dikhayiN*
'The girls$_i$ showed each other's$_{i/*j}$ pictures to the boys$_j$.'

The reciprocal *ek duusre* in Hindi is a bi-morphemic element consisting of *ek* 'one' and *duusre* '(an)other'. Under the general Pica approach, the Hindi reciprocal is naturally analysed as a phrasal item rather than a clitic: that is, as an XP rather than an X^0, As such, reciprocals do not move to T at LF, and hence any c-commanding NP in the relevant local domain would constitute a potential antecedent. This predication is illustrated by the LFs in (21a) and (21b), corresponding to (19a) and (19b):

(21) a. [$_{TP}$ laRkiyoN-ne$_j$ [$_{AGRSP}$ *laRkiyoN-ne*$_j$ [$_{AGROP}$ laRkoN-ko$_i$ [$_{AGROP}$ [$_{DP}$ ek duusre-ki tasveereN]$_k$ [$_{VP}$ t$_j$ t$_i$ t$_k$ t$_V$]][$_{AGRO}$ AGRO t$_V$]] [$_{AGR-O}$ AGRO t$_V$]] [$_{AGRS}$ AGRS t$_V$]] [$_{TNS}$ TNS dikhayiiN$_V$]]

b. [$_{TP}$ laRkiyoN-ne$_j$ [$_{AGRSP}$ *laRkiyoN-ne*$_j$ [$_{AGROP}$ [$_{DP}$ ek duusre-ki tasveereN]$_k$ [$_{AGROP}$ laRkoN-ko$_i$ [$_{VP}$ t$_j$ t$_i$ t$_k$ t$_V$]][$_{AGRO}$ AGRO t$_V$]] [$_{AGR-O}$ AGRO t$_V$]] [$_{AGRS}$ AGRS t$_V$]] [$_{TNS}$ TNS dikhayiiN$_V$]]

In neither case does the reciprocal raise to T. In the former, pre-scrambling structure, both *laRkiyõ-ne* 'girls' and *laRke* 'boys' c-command *ek duusre-ko* 'each other-DAT', and hence both are potential antecedents of the reciprocal. In the latter, post-scrambling structure, 'each other-DAT' is c-commanded only by *laRkiyõ-ne* 'girls', hence *laRkiyõ-ne* is the only possible antecedent.

The distribution of reciprocals carries an interesting implication for the LF raising of the subject that we have assumed. Consider the contrast between (22a) and (22b):

(22) a. **Ek duusre*$_i$*-ke* *bacchõ-ne* *[Ram aur Sita]*$_i$*-ko* *dekha*
each other's children-ERG Ram and Sita-DAT saw
'Each other's$_i$ children saw Ram and Sita$_i$.'

b. *[Ram aur Sita]*$_i$*-ko* *ek duusre*$_i$*-ke* *bacchõ-ne* *dekha*
Ram and Sita-DAT each other's children-ERG saw

In (22a) binding between the NP *ek duusre-ke*, 'each other's' and the object *Ram aur Sita*, 'Ram and Sita', is not possible, presumably because the latter does not c-command the former. In (22b), however, where the object is scrambled to presubject position it may bind the reciprocal. Although straightforward on the surface, in fact this data is problematic for our twin assumptions that scrambled element is adjoined to AgrSP and that the subject LF-raises to Spec of TP. Note that under these assumptions, the LF for (22b) is as in (23), where *ek duusre-ke bacchõ-ne* raises around *Ram aur Sita*, destroying the c-command relation necessary for binding (23):

(23) *[ek duusre$_i$-ke bacchõ-ne]$_j$ [Ram aur Sita]$_i$-ko t_j dekha*
each other's children-ERG Ram and Sita-DAT saw

To account for the grammaticality of (22b) I will retain our two guiding assumptions about scrambling and subject movement but suggest that what is actually raised at LF is different than what is shown in (23). More precisely, I propose that what raises to TP Spec in (22b) is not the entire DP, but rather only the NP *bacchõ-ne* (the nominal head of the construction) it contains. Under this proposal, the LF of (22b) is not (23) but rather (24):

(24) *[bacchõ-ne]$_j$ [Ram aur Sita]$_i$-ko [ek duusre$_i$-ke t_j] dekha*
children-ERG Ram and Sita-DAT each other's saw

Here the raising of only *bacchõ-ne*, 'children-ERG', preserves the crucial c-command relation between *ek duusre* and its antecedent, correctly predicting the possibility of binding.

The partial raising proposal largely follows under the Minimalist framework assumed here. Chomsky (1995) proposes that movement be recast in terms of copying, so that movement of a phrase [α [β γ]] yields a chain of the general form in (25a). Chomsky further assumes that constraints prevent the realisation of duplicate phonological material, and hence that redundant portions of a chain like (25a) must be made 'silent'. Assuming [α [β γ]] to be structurally complex, there will be a number of possibilities for silencing duplicate material, for example those in (25b–d):

(25) a. [α [β γ]] . . . [α [β γ]]

b. [α [β γ]] . . . *e*

c. *e* . . . [α [β γ]]

d. [*e* [β γ]] . . . [α [*e*]]

Notice now that what we are proposing in (24) essentially matches the situation in (25d). That is, we can view the 'partial raising' in (24) as in fact the product of full raising, as shown in (26), with the elements shown in boldface rendered silent (and hence syntactically inactive):

(26) ***[ek duusre-ke*** *[bacchõ-ne]]* *[Ram aur Sita]$_i$-ko*
children-ERG Ram and Sita-DAT
[ek duusre$_i$-ke ***[bacchõ-ne]]*** *dekha*
each other's saw

More particularly, we can view the LF raising of the subject as leaving only the NP core of the complex DP active in the TP Spec. That is, only the portion of DP that featurally interacts with agreement (T) remains active in the subject position, the residue is rendered silent and inactive.

2.3 *Pronominal binding*

We have seen why Hindi reflexives are subject-oriented. Let us now consider the anti-subject orientation of Hindi pronominals, and how this behaviour interacts with scrambling. As in Hestvik's (1990) analysis of Norwegian, I assume that Hindi pronominals also move to T at LF. Since the subject in Spec of TP always c-commands them, pronouns are always disjoint from the subject of a clause. This is illustrated by (27a) and its LF (27b):

(27) a. *Ram-ne$_i$* *Mohan-ko* *us-ki$_{*i}$* *kitab* *dii*
Ram-ERG Mohan-DAT his book gave
'Ram$_i$ gave Mohan his$_{*i}$ book.'

b. [$_{TP}$ ram-ne$_j$ [$_{AGRSP}$ *ram-ne*$_j$ [$_{AGROP}$ mohan-ko$_i$ [$_{AGROP}$ [$_{DP}$ uskii kitaab]$_k$ [$_{VP}$ t$_j$ t$_i$ t$_k$ t$_V$]][$_{AGRO}$ AGRO t$_V$]] [$_{AGR\text{-}O}$ AGRO t$_V$]] [$_{AGRS}$ AGRS t$_V$]] [$_{TNS}$ TNS dikhayiiN$_V$]]

In the latter, *us* 'his' has raised to T, and the subject has raised to Spec of TP. The pronoun is in the local domain of the c-commanding subject, and hence cannot be bound by it.

Pronominal binding provides further evidence for 'partial subject raising' discussed in connection with reciprocals. We have noted that a subject NP may never bind a pronoun because the subject in Spec of TP always c-commands the pronoun. A pronoun may however by coreferential with an argument embedded within an NP in subject position:

(28) *[Ram-ki$_i$ behen-ne]$_j$* *us-ko$_i$/*$_j$* *dekha*
Ram's sister-ERG him-DAT saw
'Ram's$_i$ sister saw him$_i$.'

But consider now (29), where the indirect object pronoun is scrambled to the presubject position. Coreference between the pronoun and the embedded NP in the subject is no longer possible:

(29) *Us-ko*$^{*}_{i}$/$^{*}_{j}$ *Ram-ki*$_i$ *behen-ne*$_j$ *dekha*

Notice that if the entire subject NP raises to Spec of TP at LF, this fact is not predicted. The pronoun in T would not c-command the argument *Ram*, hence no Condition C violation would occur. At the same time, *Ram* would not c-command the pronoun so no Condition B violation would occur. The unacceptability of coindexing in (29) shows that these results are not correct.

The correct results are obtained if we assume that only *behen-ne*, the NP contained in the genitive DP *Ram-ki behen-ne*, is active in Spec of TP at LF (30). If *Ram* is active only in the lower position, then the pronoun in T does c-command it. Coindexation between the pronoun and the NP *Ram*, would thus cause a Condition C violation. Hence conference between *us-ko* and *Ram* is correctly blocked:

(30) $[_{TP}$ $[_{DP}$ ram-kii behen-ne$]_j$ $[_{AGRSP}$ usko$_i$ $[_{AGRSP}$ *$[_{DP}$ ram-kii behen-ne$]_j$* $[_{AGROP}$ t_i $[_{VP}$ t_j t_i $t_V$$]]$$[_{AGRO}$ AGRO $t_V$$]]$ $[_{AGRS}$ AGRS $t_V$$]]$ $[_{TNS}$ TNS dekhaa$_V$$]]$

SUMMARY

The analysis presented here provides a unified account of binding and its interaction with scrambling in Hindi. It is shown that without taking recourse to the notion of precedence as a property of the binding principle (Jones 1993), the subject orientation of reflexives and the anti-subject orientation of pronouns can be explained in terms of a structural mechanism.

This analysis is premised on the following guiding assumptions. Firstly, following proposals made by Lebeaux (1983), Chomsky (1986), Pica (1987), and Hestvik (1990, 1992) reflexives and pronouns are analysed as X^0 clitics which raise to T^0 at LF. In Hindi, the subject orientation of reflexives and the anti-subject orientation of pronouns follows from the fact that the subject, which raises at LF to Spec, TP to check weak nominal features of T^0, is the only argument that always c-commands both reflexives and pronouns in T^0 at LF. So while reflexives must always be coreferential with the subject, pronominals must always be disjoint from it. Scrambling of arguments to presubject position makes no difference to the orientation of reflexives and pronouns with respect to the subject because it involves adjunction to an Agreement projection prior to Spellout. Since the subject raises to Spec, TP at LF, it is the only argument in position to c-command the element in T^0. All other arguments are too low. In contrast to reflexives and pronouns, reciprocals are XP anaphors (following Pica 1987) and do not raise to T^0. They may thus be coreferential with any c-commanding antecedent and scrambling of arguments alters binding possibilities of reciprocals.

An interesting effect that was observed in the discussion of binding was the 'partial raising' of the subject. This provides empirical evidence for Chomsky's (1995) proposal that only those elements, which interact with Agr features, are featurally active for the purposes of raising or copying.

NOTES

1. The phrase structure I assume here has Tense Agreement. There is no morphological evidence in Hindi that suggests that Tense must be inside Agreement.
2. Although, in principle, it is possible to adjoin phrases to TP by scrambling, I argue that this in fact never happens. The Spec-TP position is licensed only at LF due to the weak T feature.
3. Note that while bi-morphemic elements are always XPs, monomorphemic elements may be either X^0 or XP. Thus while pronouns in both Norwegian and English are mono-morphemic, only the former are X^0. Hestvik (1990) points out that a crucial difference between the Norwegian pronouns and their English counterparts is the fact that while the former allow restrictive modification, the latter do not.

   i. *han med rfd hatt*
   'he with the red hat'

   ii. *hun som gar der*
   'she that walks there'

   Hestvik accounts for the unacceptable English translations of the Norwegian phrases by arguing that since English pronouns are 'inherently maximal projections', there is no place for the restrictive modifiers to occur. Hindi pronouns like those in Norwegian allow restrictive modification, as shown in (iii-iv), and are thus analysed as X^0:

   iii. *vah lal topi vala*
   he red hat one
   'he with the red hat' (Lit: 'He with the red hat's mother')

4. The definition of c-command adopted here is from Chomsky (1995):
   X *c-commands Y if (a) every Z that dominates X dominates Y and (b) X and Y are disconnected.*
   In this case the lowest Z that dominates both *apni* and *Mohan* is AgrS'. *Mohan* which is adjoined to TP is not dominated by TP since it is only dominated one segment of the category. Similarly, *apni* is not dominated by both segments of AgrS. (See May 1985 for discussion of the notions of segment versus category.) Following Chomsky (1995), 'X and Y are disconnected if X¹Y and neither dominates the other.'
5. A possible alternate explanation is based on Chomsky's (1995:270) assumption that 'covert operations are pure feature raising'. IN this case only the features of the syntactic subject *bacchoN-ne* 'children' would move to Spec-AgrSP to check

the N features of AgrS. Conditions of Economy would prevent any extra material from moving.

REFERENCES

CHOMSKY, NOAM

1986 *Knowledge of language*. New York: Praeger.

1995 *The minimalist program*. Cambridge, MA and London: MIT Press.

DAYAL, VENEETA

1994 Binding facts in Hindi and scrambling phenomenon, in Miriam Butt, Tracy Holloway King & Gillian Ramchand (eds.), *Theoretical perspectives on word order issues in South Asian languages*. Stanford: CSLI.

HESTVIK, ARILD

1990 LF movement of pronouns. *North-East Linguistic Society,* 20. 200–14.

1992 LF movement of pronouns and antisubject orientation. *Linguistic Inquiry,* 23.557–94.

JONES, DOUGLAS

1993 *Binding as an interface condition: An investigation of scrambling.* MIT dissertation.

LEBEAUX, DAVID

1983 A distributional difference between reciprocals and reflexives. *Linguistic Inquiry,* 14: 723–30.

MAHAJAN, ANOOP

1990 *The A/A-Bar distinction and movement theory*. MIT dissertation.

1994 Toward a unified theory of scrambling. In Norbert Corver & Henk van Riemsdijk (eds.), *Studies on scrambling: Movement and non-movement approaches to free word-order phenomena.* Berlin and New York: Mouton de Gruyter. 301–30.

MAY, ROBERT

1985 *Logical form.* Cambridge, MA: MIT Press.

PICA, PIERRE

1987 On the nature of the reflexivization cycle. *North-East Linguistic Society*, 17. 483–99.

25

Reflexivity in Kannada: Implications for universal grammar

JEFFREY LIDZ
University of Delaware

It is well known that Kannada and other Dravidian languages have more than one way of expressing reflexivity. These languages have both a special anaphoric pronoun as well as a verbal indicator of reflexivity (Bhat 1978, Amritavalli 1984). The anaphoric pronoun has been somewhat of a mystery because it has unusual locality restrictions. In particular, the anaphoric pronoun, *tannu*, does not permit binding by a coargument. However, when the verbal reflexive, *koL*, is present, this condition is obviated.

(1) a. *Raamu Shyaamu tann-annu priitis-utt-aane anta namb-utt-aane*
Ram-NOM Shyam-NOM self-ACC love-NPST-3SM that believe-PRES-3SM
'Ram believes that Shyam loves self.' (self = Raam only)

b. *Raamu Shyaamu tann-annu priit-i-koLL-utt-aane anta namb-utt-aane*
Ram-NOM Shyam-NOM self-ACC love-PP-REFL-NPST-3SM that believe-PRES-3SM
'Raam believes that Shyam loves self' (self = Shyam only)

This observation led Lidz (1995a) to argue that Kannada provides support for Reinhart and Reuland's (1993) theory of reflexivity, which states that coargument binding must be licensed. Such licensing can come about in two ways: lexically/morphologically or syntactically, where syntactic reflexive-marking comes in the form of morphologically complex reflexives. Kannada also has a morphologically complex reflexive, *tannu-tannu*, which can be bound by a coargument and thus seems to support this theory.

(2) *Raamu* *tann-annu-tann-e* *priitis-utt-aane*
Raam self-ACC-self-EMPH love-NPST-3SM
'Ram loves himself.'

In this paper, I will argue against the reflexivity approach of Reinhart and Reuland (R&R) and Lidz for its failure to adequately characterise the semantic difference between syntactically reflexive-marked sentences and morphologically reflexive-marked sentences in Kannada and other languages. In its place I will argue for an interface condition between the semantics and the lexicon which states that all semantically reflexive sentences are lexically reflexive. Any sentence, which is not lexically reflexive, is not semantically reflexive. This condition is superior to the R&R binding conditions because it not only provides a better characterisation of the Dutch and Kannada facts, but also better predictions about the range of cross-linguistic variation in the anaphoric system.

The paper is organised as follows.

Section 1 discusses R&R's theory of reflexivity and discusses three major problems with it, notably the semantic distinction between lexically and syntactically reflexive-marked predicates.

Section 2 introduces the concept of Near-reflexivity, a property of predicates which is introduced by certain anaphors.

Section 3 discusses Condition R, the requirement that all semantically reflexive predicates be lexically reflexive. Two predictions of this condition with respect to the range of cross-linguistic variation in the anaphoric system are examined and shown to be borne out.

Section 4 discusses some conclusions and consequences of the view presented here.

1. REINHART AND REULAND'S THEORY OF REFLEXIVITY

Reflexivity as a property of predicates
Reinhart and Reuland (1993) observe that the Dutch morphologically simplex anaphor *zich* resists binding by a coargument while the Dutch morphologically complex anaphor *zichzelf* does not:

(3) a. *Max* *haat* *zich*
Max hates self
'Max hates himself.'

b. *Max haat zichzelf*
Max hates selfself
'Max hates himself.'

This property of *zich*, however, is not maintained with all verbs. With verbs that are lexically reflexive, *zich* may be bound by a coargument:

(4) a. *Max wast zich*
Max washes self
'Max washes himself.'

b. *Max schammt zich*
Max shames self
'Max is ashamed.'

Since the domain in which the anaphor finds an antecedent is constant in these examples but the ability for the simplex anaphor to be bound differs across verbs, R&R conclude that the binding theory should be stated in terms of predicates rather than in terms of anaphors. Kannada provides evidence for this claim, as here the simplex anaphor *tannu* can only be bound by a coargument if the verb is marked reflexive via the affix *koḷ*.

(5) a. **Hari tann-annu hode-d-a*
Hari self-ACC hit-PST-3SM
'Hari hit himself.'

b. *Hari tann-annu hode-du-koND-a*
Hari self-ACC hit-PP-REFL.PST-3SM
'Hari hit himself.'

Since the syntactic relationship between the anaphor and its antecedent is the same in these two sentences but the binding possibilities diverge, it looks as though a binding theory based on properties of predicates rather than syntactic structure alone is required.

R&R's binding conditions

R&R take sentences like (3) and (4) as indicative that an anaphor-centred binding theory should be replaced by a predicate-centred binding theory. That is, while the standard binding conditions are conditions on when anaphora is possible, R&R hold that binding facts are facts about reflexive predicates and not about anaphora at all. (I will ignore R&R's distinction between syntactic and semantic predicates here since it has no bearing on the following arguments.) They propose the binding conditions in (6) (to replace the standard binding conditions of Chomsky 1981/1986). (7) lists the definitions these conditions depend on.

(6) Condition A: A reflexive-marked predicate is reflexive.
Condition B: A reflexive predicate is reflexive-marked.

(7) a. A predicate is *reflexive* iff it has two coreferential arguments.
b. A predicate is *reflexive-marked* iff
i. it is lexically reflexive; or
ii. one of its arguments is a SELF anaphor

A SELF anaphor is a morphologically complex anaphor and contrasts with SE anaphors which are morphologically simplex.

The basic intuition behind these conditions is that there is a one-to-one mapping between a particular semantic property (reflexive) and a particular formal property (reflexive-marked), where there are two ways to realise the formal property. A predicate can be reflexive-marked if it is lexically reflexive (that is, if it has two elements on its theta-grid marked as coreferential) or if one of its arguments is a SELF anaphor.

In Kannada, lexical reflexivity is morphologically expressed via the verbal affix *koḷ* (Lidz 1995a). If a predicate is lexically reflexive, then this affix is present. Let us now see how R&R's binding conditions explain the distribution of the Kannada anaphors. In (5a) we find a reflexive predicate which is not reflexive-marked. The predicate is reflexive because it has two coreferential arguments. It is not reflexive-marked because neither argument is a SELF anaphor and the predicate is not lexically or morphologically reflexive. Since the reflexive predicate is not reflexive marked, (5a) violates R&R's Condition B.

In (5b), however, the predicate is both reflexive and reflexive marked. It is reflexive because the two arguments are coreferential; it is reflexive-marked because the verb is morphologically reflexive-marked. Both Condition A (the requirement that reflexive-marked predicates be reflexive) and Condition B (the requirement that reflexive predicates be reflexive-marked) are satisfied. (2) also satisfies both conditions. In this case the reflexive predicate is reflexive-marked via the SELF anaphor, *tannu-tannu*, and therefore satisfies both conditions. The long-distance interpretation of (1a) meets both requirements trivially because there are neither reflexive predicates nor any reflexive-marked predicates. Finally, in (1b) the long-distance interpretation is blocked because the embedded predicate is reflexive-marked but not reflexive.

Problems with R&R

There are several reasons to believe that R&R's theory does not accurately capture the facts about anaphora cross-linguistically. First, R&R predict that all monomorphemic reflexives will be antilocal. Second, they predict that all morphologically reflexive-marked predicates are semantically reflexive. Third, they predict the semantic equivalence of syntactically and morphologically reflexive-marked predicates.

LOCALLY BOUND SIMPLEX ANAPHORS

R&R predict that all monomorphemic anaphors will be antilocal. That is, since a predicate can be reflexive-marked only by a SELF anaphor or lexically, then in the absence of lexical reflexivity no SE anaphors should be able to be bound by coarguments. This prediction is not borne out. For example, in Hindi, Chinese and Russian (among a great many other languages) the morphologically simplex anaphor may be bound by a coargument:

(8) HINDI: *Raam-ne apne-ko maara*
raam-ERG self-ACC beat
'Raam beat himself.'

(9) CHINESE: *Lisi piping ziji*
Lisi criticise self
'Lisi criticised himself.'

(10) RUSSIAN: *On zastrelil sebja*
He shot self
'He shot himself.'

These anaphors also allow binding over a clause boundary. In order to explain the distribution of simplex anaphors in these languages, R&R would have to say either that some simplex anaphors are ambiguous between being SE anaphors or SELF anaphors or that all verbs can be inherently reflexive in these languages. That is, they might first try to explain these anaphors by saying that they are really SELF anaphors and that the difference between SELF anaphors and SE anaphors is not a matter of morphological complexity. However, this tack runs into immediate trouble since these anaphors allow long-distance binding, an impossibility if they reflexive-mark the predicates that they are arguments of. The alternative is thus to say that these anaphors are ambiguous between SE and SELF. This tack makes the theory unfalsifiable, however, since it takes away any criteria for determining which category of anaphor any given element belongs to. A second tack that might be taken by R&R to explain these data would be to say that any verb in these languages can be lexically reflexive. This tack is also unfalsifiable since it gives no way to determine lexical reflexivity.

NON-REFLEXIVE REFLEXIVE-MARKED PREDICATES

A second problem for the R&R theory concerns the morphological reflexive-marker *koL* in Kannada. If *koL* is a reflexive-marker, then we expect any verb marked with that morpheme to be semantically reflexive. If such a verb were not semantically reflexive, then Condition A would be violated; we would have a reflexive-marked predicate, which was not semantically reflexive. Such cases are readily available (Lidz 1995b, 1996):

(11) a. *baagil-u* *much-i-koND-itu*
door-NOM close-PP-REFL.PST-3SN
'The door closed.'

b. *Hari* *kannu-gaL-annu* *tere-du-koND-a*
Hari eye-PL-ACC open-PP-REFL.PST-3SM
'Hari opened his eyes.'

A discussion of the possible solutions that could be offered for these cases by R&R is beyond the scope of this paper, but see Lidz (1996) where several such solutions are examined and shown to be untenable. The important thing to note here is that the verbal reflexive does not entail semantic reflexivity but rather occurs in a wide range of constructions that correspond to a single argument structure representation. Semantic reflexivity often gives rise to the verbal reflexive but neither requires the other.

THE DISUNITY OF REFLEXIVE-MARKED PREDICATES

R&R's theory predicts that reflexive-marked predicates are semantically uniform since the two types of reflexive-marking are collapsed in the binding conditions. Since the binding conditions apply at LF and only make reference to reflexive-marking and not to the manner of reflexive-marking, it follows that these predicates are indistinguishable at LF.

However, predicates that are reflexive-marked by SELF anaphors have different semantic properties from predicates that are lexically reflexive-marked. That is, the one-to-one mapping between the semantic property of being reflexive and the formal property of being reflexive-marked breaks down when we examine the semantic properties of these two types of predicates more closely. Consider the Madame Tussaud context first discussed in Jackendoff (1992). Here, a famous person goes into the wax museum and looks into the mirror. If the speaker describing this situation says (12a), then we get the interpretation that the person saw his own reflection in the mirror. But, if the speaker says (12b), we get either the interpretation that the person saw his own reflection or the interpretation that the person saw a reflection of his statue:

(12) a. *Hari* *tann-annu* *nod-i-koND-a*
Hari self-ACC see-PP-REFL-PST-3SM
'Hari saw himself.' (= Hari, statue)

b. *Hari* *tann-annu-tanne* *nod-id-a*
Hari self-ACC-self see-PST-3SM
'Hari saw himself.' (= Hari or statue)

When the predicate is syntactically reflexive-marked, the range of possible interpretations of that predicate is greater than when the predicate is morphologically reflexive-marked. Such a situation should not arise given R&R's claim that reflexive-marking (no matter how it is achieved) corresponds to semantic reflexivity.

2. NEAR REFLEXIVES

What the Madame Tussaud examples illustrate is that SELF anaphors allow an interpretation in which the anaphor is referentially dependent on its antecedent but not necessarily identical with it. That is, the anaphor can pick out an entity from the domain of discourse that is related to and similar to its antecedent. We will call such anaphors 'Near-reflexives'. The difference between near-reflexive predicates (that is, predicates which have a near-reflexive as an argument) and semantically reflexive predicates is given in (13).

(13) a. $\lambda x[P(x,x)]$ (*semantic reflexive*)

b. $\lambda x[P(x, f(x))]$ (*near-reflexive*)

(13a) indicates that the two arguments of the predicate P are identical. In (13b), the second argument is a function of the first argument. These representations are formally distinct, although in most cases they are extensionally equivalent. That is, the near-reflexive function does not prohibit the antecedent and the anaphor from being the same entity in the world, although in the semantic representation they are distinguished. On the other hand, in a semantically reflexive sentence, the anaphor and its antecedent must be completely identical, both in the world and in the semantic representation. Since lexically reflexive predicates do not allow a non-identity interpretation, it follows that they are semantically reflexive, that is, that they have the representation (13a). Predicates that are reflexive-marked via a morphologically complex anaphor do permit the non-identity interpretation, and so implicate the semantic representation (13b).

3. CONDITION R

Given that the coargument restriction on anaphors like *tannu* is obviated in the presence of lexical reflexivity and that lexical reflexivity is semantic reflexivity (that is, not near-reflexivity), I have proposed the following principle (Lidz 1996):

(14) CONDITION R
$\lambda x [P(x, x)]$ $\leftrightarrow$ $(\theta_i = \theta_k)$
semantics theta-grid

The left side of this formula depicts the semantic representation of reflexivity. The right side depicts the representation of the theta-grid of a lexically reflexive predicate. The condition states that is a predicate is semantically reflexive, then it must be lexically reflexive. Similarly, if a predicate is lexically reflexive, then it must be semantically reflexive. Let us now see how Condition R gives us the desired results. Consider (15):

(15) a. **Hari* *tann-annu* *hode-d-a*
Hari self-ACC hit-PST-3SM
'Hari hit himself.'

b. *Hari* *tann-annu* *nod-i-koND-a*
Hari self-ACC see-PP-REFL.PST-3SM
'Hari saw himself.' (= Hari, ≠ statue)

(15a) is ruled out in violation of the left-to-right implication of Condition R; the sentence is semantically reflexive but not lexically reflexive. The near-reflexive interpretation is ruled out in (15b) because the predicate is lexically reflexive and so must be semantically reflexive, by the right-to-left implication of Condition R.

All coargument-bound anaphors are near-reflexives

Condition R makes an interesting prediction: if an anaphor can be bound by a coargument (in the absence of lexical reflexivity), then that anaphor is a near-reflexive. This prediction follows from Condition R because if a predicate is not lexically reflexive, then there is no way for it to be semantically reflexive. This prediction appears to be borne out in languages as diverse as English, Hindi and Russian. We consider these in turn. First, it is well known that the English anaphor *himself* can be bound by a coargument:

(16) John hit himself.

That this anaphor allows the near-reflexive interpretation is clear (see

Jackendoff 1992). Consider the situation in which there is a statue depicting John and he throws a football at it and hits it with the football. Here it is natural to say (17) and mean that John hit the statue that depicts him.

(17) John hit himself with the football.

Hindi, as we saw, has a morphologically simplex anaphor, which can be bound by a coargument, a prima facie counterexample to R&R's binding theory. Condition R correctly predicts that this anaphor is a near-reflexive. Here, imagine the situation where someone goes into the wax museum and becomes enraged at seeing the statue depicting him. Here, we can say (18) to mean either that this person committed suicide (shooting himself) or vandalism (shooting the statue).

(18) *Ram museum gay-aa. Vahaan us-ne apnii statue dekh-ii*
Ram museum go-PFV. There he-ERG self's statue saw-PFV.
'Ram went to the museum. There he saw his statue.'

a. *Us-ne apne-ko goli maar-dii*
He-ERG self-ACC bullet kill-PFV.
'He shot himself.' (= Ram or statue)

b. *Us-ne apne-aap-ko goli maar-dii*
He-ERG self-self-ACC bullet kill-PFV.
'He shot himself.' (= Ram or statue)

Russian is a further interesting example from this perspective because, like Kannada, it has both an affixal reflexive as well as a morphologically simplex anaphor. Unlike Kannada, however, the morphologically simplex anaphor can be bound by a coargument in the absence of the affixal reflexive. Since the affixal reflexive is taken to indicate lexical reflexivity, it follows that when the verbal reflexive is absent the predicate cannot be lexically reflexive and thus is not semantically reflexive. So, sentences with the anaphor bound by a coargument must have a near-reflexive interpretation.

This prediction is borne out. Imagine the situation described above in Hindi, but with Boris Yeltsin as the protagonist. When the verbal reflexive is present, the near-reflexive interpretation is blocked (as predicted by Condition R). When the anaphor is present, the near-reflexive interpretation is available.

(19) a. *Yeltsin zastrelil-sja*
Yeltsin shot-REFL
'Yeltsin shot himself.' (= Yeltsin, ≠ statue)

b. *Yeltsin* *zastrelil* *sebja*
Yeltsin shot self
'Yeltsin shot himself.' (= Yeltsin or statue)

Variation in lexical reflexivity

A second prediction made by Condition R has to do with the extent of lexical reflexivity found in a given language. Dutch and Kannada differ in that in Kannada any verb can be made lexically reflexive through the affixation of the verbal reflexive, while Dutch allows only a small set of lexically specified verbs to be lexically reflexive. We might thus expect to find a language that allowed no predicates to be lexically reflexive. Such a language, if it had an anaphor that did not permit a near-reflexive interpretation, might block binding by a coargument across the board. That is, in a language where there is no lexical reflexivity, we predict the existence of an anaphor that can never be bound by a coargument. Malayalam is such a language. The Malayalam simplex anaphor, tan, cannot be bound by a coargument whereas the complex anaphor *tan-ne-tanne* can (Mohanan 1982; Jayaseelan 1995):

(20) a. **moohan* *tan-ne* *aaraaDhik'k'uNNu*
mohan self-ACC worships
'Mohan worships himself.'

b. *moohan* *tan-ne-tanne* *aaraDhik'k'uNNu*
mohan self-ACC-self worships
'Mohan worships himself.'

This generalisation holds even with verbs which are lexically reflexive in other languages (Jayaseelan, personal communication).

(21) a. **raaman* *tan-ne* *kshauram* *ceytu*
raaman self-ACC shaving did
'Raman shaved.'

b. *raaman* *tan-ne-tanne* *kshauram* *ceytu*
raaman self-ACC-self shaving did
'Raman shaved himself.'

Note also that (21b) allows the near-reflexive interpretation that Raaman shaved a portrayal of himself, as predicted by Condition R. We can conclude that Malayalam has no lexical reflexivity. The fact that *tan* can never be bound by a coargument indicates that this anaphor does not express near-reflexivity and follows from the combination of lexical properties of Malayalam with Condition R.

Under this conception, all variation in the behaviour of reflexive forms found among the world's languages reduces to lexical variation. The syntactic binding theory is constant, as is Condition R. What varies is the extent of lexical reflexivity permitted by a language and the range of anaphors found in that language. The remaining question is what properties of the lexicon or of lexical items determines the extent of lexical reflexivity and whether a given anaphor allows a near-reflexive interpretation.

CONCLUSION

In this paper I have argued that the theory of reflexivity of Reinhart and Reuland (1993) does not explain certain semantic facts associated with reflexive-marked predicates. In particular, lexically reflexive-marked predicates have different semantic properties from syntactically reflexive-marked predicates. Such differences are predicted by R&R not to exist. In place of the R&R binding conditions, I have proposed Condition R which forces semantic reflexivity to be lexically expressed. Any cases of coargument binding in the absence of lexical reflexivity were shown to involve near-reflexivity, a semantic representation which involves a dependence between two elements rather than complete identity between them.

This theory recognises the existence of two types of anaphor: those that introduce the near-reflexive function and those that do not. It is interesting to note from this perspective that the anaphors which resist local binding are in some sense more reflexive than the ones which do not. That is, the anaphors which do not introduce the near-reflexive function cannot be coargument-bound because of Condition R. These anaphors have been taken by some to be some sort of cross between a pronominal and an anaphor (Mohanan 1982; Jayaseelan 1995), but the data discussed here seems to implicate their anaphoric properties to be stricter than other anaphors or pronominals.

REFERENCES

AMRITAVALLI, R.
1984 Anaphorization in Dravidian. *CIEFL Working Papers* 1. 1–31.
BHAT, D.N.S.
1978 *Pronominalization*. Pune: Deccan College.
CHOMSKY, N.
1981 *Lectures on government and binding*. Dordrecht: Foris.
1986 *Knowledge of language: Its nature, origin and use*. NY: Praeger.
JACKENDOFF, R.
1992 Madame Tussaud meets the binding theory. *NLLT*, 10. 1–31.

JAYASEELAN, K.A.
1995 Anaphors as pronouns. ms. Hyderabad: CIEFL.
LIDZ, J.
1995a Morphological reflexive marking: Evidence from Kannada. *Linguistic Inquiry*, 26. 705–10.
1995b On the non-reflexive nature of the Kannada verbal reflexive. Paper presented at SALA, 17.
1996 *Dimensions of reflexivity*, Ph.D. dissertation, University of Delaware.
MOHANAN, K.P.
1982 Grammatical relations and anaphora in Malayalam. In A. Marantz & T. Stowell (eds.), *MIT Working Papers in Linguistics, Papers in Syntax*. Cambridge, MA: MIT. 163–90.
REINHART, T. and E. REULAND
1993 Reflexivity. *Linguistic Inquiry*, 24. 657–720.

26
Morphological causatives, UTAH and monoclausality

R. Amritavalli
Central Institute of English and Foreign Languages

Following Marantz (1984) and Baker (1988), there has been a revival of interest in morphological causatives in the generative tradition (Li 1990; Alsina 1992; Guasti 1993, 1996; Fujita 1996). This subsequent work, along with the evolution of the theory, has led to some modifications in Baker's original treatment of causatives, while yet continuing to preserve certain issues as central to the causative agenda. In this paper I review some issues pertinent to Kannada, and show how the causative agenda needs to be broadened. I focus mainly on two questions: the nature of the causative complement, that is, whether the 'inner', causativised clause is a full clause, a small clause VP, a mere VP, or something else; and the case realisations of the noun phrases that are ostensibly arguments of the 'inner' clause, in particular, the causee. These issues will be seen to have a crucial bearing on the nature of case and theta-role assignment in causative sentences. I shall not here enter into a detailed description of the Kannada morphological causative and its place in a causative typology, for which I refer the reader to Amritavalli (in press).

CLAUSAL DOMAINS AND VERBAL PROJECTIONS

Baker's Verb Incorporation account of morphological causatives continued a tradition in generative grammar (and relational grammar) of a biclausal analysis of these structures: 'The idea that morphological causatives are derived from a source containing two verbs and two clauses is far from original . . .' (Baker 1988: 154). Baker's larger concern was to explain what were often analysed as 'Grammatical Function (GF) changing rules' in terms of independently motivated principles of Government-Binding theory; hence an analysis of causatives in terms of GF-changing was implicitly assumed. The aim was to reduce the differences between periphrastic causatives (with a full, lexical causative verb) and morphological causatives (with a bound morpheme as a causative) to a single difference: the affixal nature of the causative morpheme, which forced the 'inner verb' to move. Subsequent work has attributed affixal status to full causative verbs that appear to form complex predicates; for example, Italian *fare* (Guasti 1996).

I shall argue against the GF-changing assumption. Let us begin by noting that the persistence of the 'clause union' approach to causatives led to the neglect of two sets of related facts: one, the complement to the causative morpheme is never a full clause with the functional projections of Infl (such as tense) (Li 1990); and two, the putative biclausal structure of the causative sentence is not always reflected in its syntactic behaviour. In Kannaḍa, the entire causative sentence behaves as a single domain for binding and passivisation; the 'inner clause' cannot passivise, nor can the 'inner subject' act as a binder or create an opaque domain to prevent binding by the upper, surface subject. The Kannada causative appears simply to be a single clause.

This fact is worth stressing, because even analyses which have recognised the absence of a fully articulated biclausal structure for causatives have assumed, or argued for, some residual features typical of biclausality. Li (1990) assumes the causative complement to be a small clause VP complement. Crucially, this VP has an optional 'inner clause' syntactic subject position. (Intriguingly, though, this position is not occupied by the 'inner' subject, for Kannada-type languages. The putative 'inner' subject is in fact generated as an adjunct. It is assigned its theta role by a special principle of Argument Demotion; as for its case, 'an oblique case can be assigned to it' (Li 1990: 414). Thus, the only function of the empty lower subject position is to let the 'lower' *object* move into it, to receive accusative case!)

Guasti (1993, 1996) advances an argument from the scope of adverbials. Consider the following example from Lebanese Arabic (Guasti 1993: 13). The example is designed to show that an adverb can modify either the causative affix or the verb stem.

(1) *Hanna* *massak* *xa:Lid* *lshunta* *bi* *bejt* *lzira:n*
Hanna held-CAUS Khalid the suitcase in house DET neighbours
'Hanna made Khalid hold the suitcase in the neighbours' house.'

The PP *in the neighbours' house*, on one reading, modifies the holding: the suitcase is held in the neighbours' house. According to a second reading, Hanna was in the neighbours' house when she caused Khalid to hold the suitcase. Guasti (1996: 298) gives a similar example from Italian:

(2) *Adele ha fatto cuocere il maiale con un limone in bocca*
Adele has made cook the (suckling) pig with a lemon in mouth
'Adele made the suckling pig cook with a lemon in its mouth.'
'Adele made the suckling pig cook with a lemon in her mouth.'

She concludes that 'the causative affix and the base verb root head separate VPs' (Guasti 1993: 14); that is, 'there are two verbal projections in a causative sentence, one headed by the causative verb and the other by the base predicate' (1996: 298).

It is true that there is scopal ambiguity in (1) and (2), and similar examples can be constructed for Kannada as well. I shall agree, too, that there is more than one verbal projection in a causative sentence. The problem, however, is to determine the relation between the number of verbal projections, and the number of predicates which define syntactic domains, not only for binding and passivisation, but for case- and theta-role assignment. To see that this is a non-trivial question, consider now the following sentences in English, which parallel the data in (1) and (2) in that they show a similar scopal ambiguity for adverbial phrases.

(3) a. Mary cooked the meat in the oven.
b. Mary cooked the meat in the sun.
c. Mary parked the car in the rain.

Example (3a) is interpreted with the meat in the oven and Mary out of it. Example (3b) is ambiguous: Mary might be a votary of solar power, or she may be out in the sun, barbecuing. (3c) is again ambiguous: the car may have been left in the rain, or it might have been raining when Mary parked it. What we see is that scopal ambiguity of adverbial phrases obtains in what have traditionally been called monoclausal transitive sentences.

Is there, then, only a single verbal projection in causatives? Let us say, rather, that monoclausality is not a theory-independent notion. Under a theory of phrase structure such as Larson (1988), there are 'extra' verbal projections in a clause with a verb like *give*, traditionally a monoclausal ditransitive verb. But now the relation between multiple verbal projections and multiplicity of predicates, with multiple syntactic domains, is not as self-evident as the causative literature has assumed. (Larson's theory, a response to evidence for asymmetrical c-command in the dative and double object constructions, freely generates X-bar, that is, Specifier-Head-Complement, structures; thus VPs are generated with empty heads that serve as landing sites for head-to-head movement.)

Speas (1990) attempts to restrict such entirely free generation of V-projections by requiring these to be justified at the level of Lexical Conceptual Structure (LCS). In her account, a verb like *cook*, which (i) takes an agentive subject and (ii) participates in the transitive-inchoative alternation, has in its LCS an extra predicate CAUSE. Thus, *cook*, though not overtly morphologically marked as causative, is indeed a causative verb in this analysis (Speas 1990: 94–6). (Speas arrives at her analysis of verbs like *cook* independently of the data we note in (3), which thus now serve as further support for it.)

In short, adverbial scope variation obtains with apparently monomorphemic transitive predicates; and in a conservative theory of phrase structure, it is not in itself an argument for 'extra' verbal projections. However, developments in the theory of phrase structure allow verbal projections to be generated and justified on non-morphological grounds, such as asymmetrical c-command (Larson 1988) or Lexical Conceptual Structure (Speas 1990). These developments also entail that there is no one-to-one relation between the number of verbal projections, and the number of domains in which syntactic operations like case- and theta-role assignment apply. Thus, although the original proposal for more than one verbal projection in a causative sentence continues to be viable, this shift of perspective about clause structure necessitates the re-evaluation of certain implicit, and rather problematic, assumptions about case-marking and theta-role assignment in causative sentences.

A SINGLE DOMAIN FOR CASE AND THEMATIC ROLE ASSIGNMENT

Let us hypothesise that the causative complement is simply a VP complement, that is, an X-bar theoretic Specifier-Head-Complement structure. This structure is a complement to a causative verb/morpheme that may now be totally abstract, as in the case of *cook* (see Li 1990 for arguments that the causative complement is never a full clause). An important consequence of such a structure is that case- and theta-role assignment can now treat the entire clause (the causative sentence) as a single, unitary domain, and not as subdomains 'belonging to' the base verb and the causative morpheme.

To understand the significance of this development, let us pause to consider some current approaches to causatives. The 'clause union' mindset, revealed in the terminology 'inner subject' and 'inner object', assumes a 'cyclical' assignment of case and theta role; preserving the analogy with periphrastic causatives, where two lexically independent verbs 'do their own thing,' so to speak. In Li (1990), the causative morpheme (V1) and the base verb (V2) assign accusative case to the NPs in their domain before verb movement takes place (for 'type 2' causatives, where the causee appears with accusative case). This procedure, which results in two accusative NPs on the surface, turns out to yield the wrong results: it is supplemented by the statement that if a 'language (on the surface) allows only one accusative case, which is usually assigned adjacently, then only NP1 (the embedded subject) will have accusative case and NP2 will be marked with an oblique Case' (Li 1990: 412). (How this 'filtering out' of a double accusative is accomplished is not spelt out.)

If Li's apparently straightforward case-assignment procedure for 'type 2' causatives runs into problems, his handling of Kannada-type or 'type 1' causatives is particularly untidy. Li starts out with the untenable assumption (Amritavalli, in press) that the causative morpheme in 'type 1' languages is a non-case assigning morpheme. As a result, the lower object, though still case-marked by the lower verb, gets its case not when it and the verb are *in situ*, but after it has moved into the lower *subject* position and the lower verb has adjoined to the causative morpheme! These assumptions and movements nevertheless 'leave(s) NP1 (the causee, RA) still needing Case, but an oblique Case can be assigned to it . . .' (Li 1990: 414).

Guasti (1996) recognises the need for a more integrated approach to case and theta marking, but her approach is not without problems. The causee of intransitives, which surfaces as accusative, is case-marked by the 'complex verb' (in effect by the upper verb, since the lower verb is intransitive). Causees of transitive predicates cannot be case marked accusative, since the 'lower object' already is accusative-marked (it is unclear whether this is done by the lower verb, the causative, or both, subject to a double accusative filter, cf. the discussion of Li earlier and the CFPP as follows). Now a special lexical property of the causative verb, unique only to this construction, saves the situation: *fare* takes a benefactive argument and assigns dative case to it. But *fare* also has the option not to have this lexical property, resulting in an oblique case for the causee of transitives.

In effect, this analysis posits three causative verbs *fare*: one for intransitive and two for transitive complements. The causee of transitives is theta-marked benefactive by *fare*; but (as Guasti acknowledges) this procedure yields a patient role for the causee of intransitives, thus treating them differently.

We need not labour the point that current approaches to case- and theta-role assignment in causatives are confused, and that case assignment to the causee, in particular, is *ad hoc* and problematic. I have argued in earlier work that the causee in Kannada-type languages is not structurally case-marked as an integral argument of the 'lower' verb (or the higher verb, in Guasti 1996), but semantically case-marked in the manner of an adjunct. Indeed, the Larsonian approach to phrase structure renders the distinction between adjuncts and arguments irrelevant; what remains is the distinction between structural case assignment and semantic case assignment.

The treatment of the causee for case- and theta-marking purposes has so far been circumscribed by the view that it is an erstwhile, demoted subject of a lower verb. This is to repeat the mistake of analysing the passive *by*-phrase as an erstwhile subject which has undergone Agent Demotion. Such a 'grammatical function changing' approach has two problems. First, it obscures the semantic regularity in the choice of case-marker or preposition for the causee, just as the old analysis of the passive *by*-phrase obscured the regularity in the choice of *by* (cf. agentive *by*-phrases such as *the sonata by Mozart*). Second, it cannot allow for any semantically systematic variation in the choice of the case-marker or preposition. This is not such a problem for the English verbal passive (though the English adjectival passive does allow more than one preposition to mark the 'agent' or 'source'). In the case of the Kannada causative, we shall see, the failure to allow semantic case-marking will be a serious limitation.

CAUSEE'S CASE

Recall that across languages, there is variation only in the case marking of causees of transitive complements. In Kannada, this causee usually surfaces as instrumental *-inda*, but it can also be marked with *kaili* (again, an instrumental postposition: literally 'in hands'), or even *hatra* ('near'). Any approach to case assignment will minimally have to take this variation into account; perhaps by treating *-inda* as (optional) case assignment, and the others as optional postpositional phrases.

Our contention is that these cases and postpositions are simply assigned according to semantic appropriateness. Observe that *-inda* is the case of a source adjunct in (4). Our approach, which uses no idiosyncratic case assignment rules for causatives, allows us to generalise the causee's case marking with that of the adjunct in (4).

(4) *yamuna* *avana* *maatininda* *tallaNisidaLu*
yamuna his words INSTR. winced
'Yamuna winced at his words.' (Sridhar 1990)

Not all causees of transitives are marked instrumental, however. For a well-defined class of predicates known as 'ingestives,' the causee emerges as dative. Now this fact has been noticed, and thought to have a simple explanation (Sridhar 1990: 218): namely, that the dative case originates from the 'quirky' case of the 'lower' predicate, which induces the so-called 'dative subject' [cf. (5a)]. Thus, the dative case in (5b) has been thought to be 'consistent with deriving such sentences from underlying dative subject sentences' such as (5a) (Sridhar 1990: 218).

(5) a. *nana-ge* *siTTu* *bantu*
I DAT. anger came
'I got angry.' (LIT. to-me anger came)

b. *timma* *nana-ge* *siTTu* *bar- is- ida*
timma I DAT. anger come CAUS.
'Timma made me get angry.'

Dative case in ingestive causatives, however, appears even when the complement does not, in isolation, have dative case. In (6a), we have ingestive predicates with nominative subjects. Notice that these arguments surface as dative in (6b).

(6) a. *magu* *haalu* *kuDiyitu* *(snaana* *maaDitu)*
child NOM. milk drank bath did
'The child drank milk (took a bath).'

b. *taayi* *maguvi-ge* *haalu* *kuD-isi-daru* *(snaana* *maaD- isi-* *daru)*
mother child DAT. milk drink CAUS. bath do CAUS.
'Mother fed the child milk (gave the child a bath).'

What (5b) and (6b) show is that (i) case-assignment to the causee of ingestives is semantically regular; (ii) this regularity cannot be traced to a putative regularity in the 'source' clause, that is, the causative complement in its independent occurrence. It must be seen as a regularity in the causative clause taken as a holistic domain.

A particularly interesting variation of causee's case, even within the limited domain of ingestives, is seen in (7) (example from Cole and Sridhar 1977). The causee here is marked instrumental instead of dative.

(7) *avaninda* *tinnisiyee* *biDutteene*
he INSTR. eat CAUS. EMP. aspect
'(I) shall make him eat, get him to eat' (not = feed him)

As the gloss shows, in (7) the agentivity of the causee is important, in the (perverse) sense that a particular entity must bend to the causer's will. Thus the role of the causee is not purely ingestive; neither is there a general causation of an event of eating (as has been sometimes suggested in the discussion of causative semantics). What must be noted is that the change in the causee's case in (7) from dative to instrumental goes against the general claim in the literature (Alsina 1992; Guasti 1996) that *affectedness* of the causee corresponds to a 'promotion' up the case hierarchy (that is, to accusative or dative, from instrumental). In Kannada, what is at issue is not a hierarchy of cases, but the theta roles reflected by particular cases.

In fact, there is some evidence that even the case of intransitive causee can vary with the semantics. (8) from Cole and Sridhar (1977) is an example of instrumental case, this time on the causee of an intransitive predicate, which is expected to have accusative case.

(8) *raayaru* *balavanta* *maaDi* *magaLinda* *haaDisidaru*
Rao insistently daughter INSTR. sing CAUS.
'Mr Rao forced his daughter to sing.' ('made her sing')

Notice once again the sense of coerced agentivity. To my knowledge, the discussion about the affectedness, or otherwise, of the causee has so far been limited to the causee of transitives, which has well-known case variation.

A NEW AGENDA FOR CAUSATIVES

Empirical inadequacies apart, the lack of clarity in current approaches about whether a causative sentence is a single domain, or more than one domain, for case- and theta-role assignment has resulted in stipulative statements of an important generalisation. Consider the *Case Frame Preservation Principle* (CFPP) of Baker (1988: 122).

(9) THE CASE FRAME PRESERVATION PRINCIPLE (CFPP): A complex X^0 of category A in a given language can have at most the maximal case assigning properties allowed to a morphologically simple item of category A in that language.

Baker's observation – it remains little more than that – is a puzzle for his theory, which seeks to assimilate morphological causativisation to periphrastic causativisation. As we have seen, case marking is allowed to be sometimes independently executed by the constituent parts of the complex verb. Thus there is no independent principle of grammar which accounts for this difference of a 'case-limit' between affixal and periphrastic causativisation. The CFPP has the status of a global constraint/filter (cf. the earlier discussion of Li's and Guasti's account of case-assignment).

Now once we analyse the morphological causative predicate as a unitary predicate which, just as it is a single domain for (that is, allows only one set of) functional projections such as tense, is also a single domain for case- and theta-role assignment, we allow only one 'set' of structural cases to be assigned; and the CFPP will automatically fall out. Thus, if a language has only two structural cases, only two structural cases will be found in causatives; all other cases will be semantic cases.

I have raised in earlier work the problem of the non-iterativity of the morphological causative operation, as opposed to the complete freedom of indefinitely continuing a periphrastic causative sentence. That is, morphological causatives do not have the open-endedness of the periphrastic causative in (10).

(10) John had Mary make Jane force Morris have . . . Jerry eats pancakes.

Morphological causative affixes can be reiterated once in some languages (Malayalam *ipp-ikk*, Hindi *aa* and *vaa*); Kannada *isu* cannot be reiterated at all. But even where a 'second degree' of causativisation is allowed in the morphology, it is not always clear that there is a corresponding addition of arguments (*pace* Baker's Mirror principle, which requires strict pairing of morphological and syntactic operations). In some verbs of Hindi, for example, the *-aa* and *-vaa* forms appear to simply be free variants. Consider the double object verbs *bheej* 'send' and *dee* 'give'. Here, where the underived verb starts out with dative and accusative arguments, the addition of the instrumental appears to sanction both the first and the second causative morphemes; that is, both *bhijaa, bhijwaa* and *dilaa, dilwaa* occur in the single syntactic frame NP-nom./erg. NP-instr. NP-dat. NP-(acc.).

But while the morphological operation of causativisation is limited, the periphrastic expression of causativisation is not ruled out. Thus where there are causative morphemes without corresponding arguments, we also find causee-like arguments in structures without any morphological causatives. Consider (11) and (12) from Hindi and Kannada, respectively.

(11)	*usne*	*raam se*	*lakshman ke dwara*	*siita ko*	*jaane ko*	*kahaa*
	he ERG.	ram INSTR.	lakshman INSTR.	sita ACC.	go-INF.-ACC.	said

'He got Ram to send word through Lakshman for Sita to go.'

In (11) we see the same instrumental phrases for semantically sanctioned intermediaries, that otherwise appear with morphological causatives. A similar iterative addition of causee adjuncts is seen in (12). Notice the single causative suffix, and the use of instrumental case and other postpositions.

(12) a. *amma nanna kaili (nanninda) maguvige haalu kuDisidaru*
mother my hands (I-INSTR.) child-DAT. milk drink-CAUS.
'Mother had me give milk to the child.'

b. *gurugaLu ammana kaili nanninda maguvige haalu kuDisidaru*
the guru mother's hands I-INSTR. . . .
'The guru made mother have me give milk to the child.'

c. *deevaru gurugala moolaka ammana kaili nanninda . . .*
the lord guru through mother's hands I-INSTR.
'The lord through the guru got mother to have me give milk to the child.'

The data in (11) and (12) thus reinforce our proposal for the semantic case-marking of causee phrases.

A second important consequence of our proposal is that by assimilating the English transitive-inchoative alternation to the intransitive-transitive alternation in languages with morphological causatives, it raises two questions, hitherto unrecognised, as central to the causative agenda. Why does English have a (zero-morphological or abstract) causative structure 'in the first degree' (transitive and intransitive *cook)*, but not have non-periphrastic causatives of transitives, or causatives of causatives? The question assumes significance in light of children's errors (Bowerman 1981).

(13) She came it over here. (*intended:* brought)
Don't eat her yet. (*intended:* feed)
I'm singing him. (*intended:* making him sing)
Down your little knee. (*intended:* put down . . .)
How would you flat it? (*intended:* flatten)

As the last example shows, English has not only a zero-morpheme relating intransitive and transitive verbs; it also has an *-en* suffix that derives verbs from adjectives (*flat-flatten*). In addition, it has *-ify* and *-ise*, which derive verbs respectively from stems and adjectives (*simple-simplify, dei-deify*), and stems, adjectives and nouns (*minimise, equal-equalise, criticise/publicise*). As I show in Amritavalli (in press), the putative causative suffix *isu* in Kannada also has a similar 'verbalising' role. The question thus arises why none of these English affixes are available to derive causatives from transitive verbs.

A related question is why, in the languages of the world, causative typological variation is confined to the causatives of transitives (and 'further up' in degrees of what is known as 'adicity'). Why is there no variation between languages in the case-frame alternation relation of intransitive sentences to transitive, that is, causative, sentences? By bringing English into the causative mainstream (as I have done), it is possible to effect a second shift of perspective which might afford an answer. Take the verb *cook* in its intransitive and transitive variants:

(14) a. *The meat* cooked (in the oven).

b. Mary cooked *the meat* (in the oven).

We see in (14) the familiar correspondence between transitive object and intransitive subject. Now for English, we do not speak of the subject of intransitive *cook* becoming the object of the transitive *cook*; rather, we visualise *the meat* as always an object (a 'theme'); we generate this object *in situ*, and move it out when the verb is intransitive, in order for it to get case.

For morphological causative languages, however, this same alternation is described as the 'inner subject' becoming the 'causative object.' See (15).

(15) a. *tarkaari beeyitu*
'The vegetables cooked.'

b. *siita tarkaari (yannu) beey-is-idaLu*
'Sita cooked the vegetables.'

This reversal is very odd and disturbing for a grammar which subscribes to some version of (what Baker articulates as) UTAH. UTAH, or the Uniformity of Thematic Assignment Hypothesis, states that:

(16) Identical thematic relationships between items are represented by identical structural relationships between these items at the level of D-structure.

UTAH is a generalisation about thematic-to-syntactic mapping. However, as there is no non-circular way of ascertaining what thematic roles are present in a sentence, UTAH has sometimes been executed (if not interpreted) as a mapping from morphologically simple syntactic frames to morphologically complex syntactic frames. (We have already referred to the early treatment of the passive *by*-phrase as a demoted subject, in order to identify it as agent.) It is clearly morphological derivation which leads to intransitive theta frames being mapped into transitive frames for languages with morphological causatives. But if morphology is ignored,

- the 'intransitive subject' can simply be assimilated to the theme of unaccusatives, and generated in place as an object;

- by an extension of this logic, 'transitive subjects' can be generated in place as something other than 'subjects' of inner verbs, and therefore as something other than agents: they are probably sources, goals, instruments, locations, and so on.

I have earlier argued (Amritavalli 1980, and in press) that the direction of morphological derivation obscures regularities in the mappings of semantic roles to syntactic frames. This point (in fact) can be rather dramatically illustrated within Kannada itself. Kannada has both a morphological causativisation process, and a morphological inchoativisation process. Thus, there are transitive-intransitive pairs of sentences, where for one set of verbs the intransitive verb is morphologically basic, while for the other set it is the transitive verb which is morphologically basic. This is seen in (17) and (18).

(17) a. *magu biiLutte*
'The child falls.'

b. *niinu maguvannu biiL -is- uttii*
'You make-fall the child.'

(18) a. *baagilu haaki-koLL-utte*
'The door closes (INCHOATIVE).'

b. *niinu baagilannu haaktii*
'You close the door.'

The pair of sentences in (17) is related by the causative morpheme *isu*; and in (18) by the inchoative marker *koLLu*. Thus, while in the first pair the intransitive sentence (17a) is 'basic', it is the transitive sentence (18b) which is basic in the second pair. The correspondence between intransitive subject and transitive object, however, remains unchanged in both pairs. (Note, too, that 'fall' and 'close' are both 'unaccusative' verbs, in spite of the morphology.)

REFERENCES

ALSINA, ALEX
1992 On the argument structure of causatives. *Linguistic Inquiry* 23: 517–55.

AMRITAVALLI, R.
1980 Expressing cross-categorial selectional correspondences: an alternative to the X-bar syntax approach. *Linguistic Analysis,* 6:3. 305–343.
in press A Kannada perspective on morphological causatives. In K.G. Vijayakrishnan *et al.* (eds.). CIEFL.

BAKER, MARK C.

1988 *Incorporation: A theory of grammatical function changing*. Chicago: University of Chicago Press.

BOWERMAN, MELISSA

1981 The acquisition of complex sentences. In Paul Fletcher & Michael Garman (eds.), *Language acquisition: Studies in first language development*, 285–305. Cambridge: Cambridge University Press.

COLE, PETER and S.N. SRIDHAR

1977 Clause union and relational grammar: Evidence from Hebrew and Kannada. *Linguistic Inquiry* 8:4. 700–713.

FUJITA, KOJI

1996 Double objects, causatives and derivational economy. *Linguistic Inquiry* 27:1. 146–73.

GUASTI, MARIA T.

1993 *Causative and perception verbs: A comparative study*. Turin: Rosenberg and Sellier.

1996 Semantic restrictions in romance causatives and the incorporation approach. *Linguistic Inquiry* 27:2. 294–313.

LARSON, RICHARD K.

1988 On the double object construction. *Linguistic Inquiry*.19:3. 335–91.

LI, YAFEI

1990 X^0 binding and verb incorporation. *Linguistic Inquiry* 21. 399–426.

MARANTZ, ALEC

1984 On the nature of grammatical relations. Doctoral dissertation, MIT.

SPEAS, MARGARET

1990 *Phrase structure in natural language*. Dordrecht: Kluwer.

SRIDHAR, S.N.

1990 *Kannada*. London & New York: Routledge.

27
The significance of topic in a V2 language: Evidence from Kashmiri

KASHI WALI, OMKAR N. KOUL and ASHOK K. KOUL
University of Syracuse Central Institute of Indian Languages, Mysore

It is well known that in a V2 language almost any sentence constituent can be placed in the sentence-initial position, the finite verb occupying the second position. The fronted constituent is known as topic. An interesting and puzzling facet of the fronted constituent is that it invariably includes the subject across all V2 languages irrespective of the basic word order, which may be SVO as in Icelandic, or SOV as in German and Kashmiri. The subject-initial V2 order raises an interesting question about the position of the subject. Is the subject in the specifier position of IP as is the case in English or is it in the specific position of CP, the usual topic and operator position? This distinction is shown in (1) and (2):

(1) $[_{IP}$ Subj V...]

(2) $[_{CP}$ Subj V [IP]]

Traditional analyses of V2 assume the structure in (2). In this analysis the subject moves to the specifier of CP in both SVO and SOV languages. The analysis treats subjects on par with other constituents and primarily draws support from German and Dutch. These show a verb-final SOV order in the finite embedded clause but a verb-second SVO order in the root clause. The assumption is that the presence of a complementiser in the embedded clause blocks the verb movement and preserves the basic verb-final SOV order. In the root clause the complementiser C is absent. The absence of C motivates verb to move to C resulting in the main clause verb-second V2 order. The subject is supposed to move to the specifier of CP. A problem with this analysis is that the subject movement to the specifier of CP, that is topic, seems unmotivated. There is no reason why the subject should move to the topic position, since it already occupies sentence-initial position.

Within the current minimalist feature framework such unmotivated movements are regarded as wild and must be discarded. The theory states that every movement must have a motivation. Elements move to fulfil some morphological feature.

According to Travis (1991) and Zwart (1993), the subject in all V2 languages moves to the specifier of IP and not to the specifier of CP. The movement to the specifier of CP appears to be meaningless. The movement of other constituents to the specifier of CP is justified since they can be topics but a priori, a subject in the specifier of CP seems to serve no function. Note that under this theory, structures in a V2 language follow from the general linguistic theory and do not need any special proviso.

The hypothesis that V2 subjects move to the specifier of IP faces problems, as there is little conclusive empirical evidence from V2 languages that supports it. Most of the arguments given in favour such as clitics in Dutch and weak unstressed subjects in German are extremely marginal and have not been widely accepted (Schwartz and Vikner 1996).

The object of this paper is twofold. We show that the theoretical demands of the minimalist framework – that the subject moves to the specifier of IP – are on the right track. However, the claim that the movement of the subject to topic position is wild and unmotivated is too wild. The paper claims that it is the movement of the subject to topic position that defines a V2 language from all other languages. A V2 language does not single out subject from non-subjects. All constituents, including the subject, are equally licit in the topic position. We claim that the movement of constituents to topic position is motivated by the strong feature of the topic itself that needs to be checked by PF. This movement is driven by Altruistic or Enlightened self-interest movement (Lasnik 1993, 1995). Our claim is based on the data from Kashmiri, a V2 language with basic verb-final SOV order.

Note that in the minimalist framework, there are only two levels of representations: PF and LF. The lexical items project X-bar trees on which movement operates to reach PF and LF levels with an intermediate stage called Spellout. The movement may be guided by both PF and LF representations as in (3).

(3) LEXICAL X-bar structure → (pre Move α) → Spellout → (post Move α) → LF
(Old S-structure)
|
PF

Movement driven by PF representation is called pre-Spellout movement. It may vary from language to language and produce word order differences. Post-Spellout movement takes place to fulfil the representations at LF. Movements take place for no other reason than to check morphological features such as abstract case, tense, operator, etc., and are guided by the economy principles of Procrastinate, Greed, and Last Resort. Morphological features may be strong or weak, with strong features requiring checking by PF, which occurs in specifier-head configurations.

Consider now Kashmiri data. Unlike German, V2 structures are found in both root and finite embedded clauses, as in (4).

V-2 order: [XP V [...]] XP = subject, object, adverb, other constituents

(4) ROOT CLAUSE

a. *miraa* ***cha*** *caay* *cavaan* *baagas* *manz*
Mira is tea drinking garden-DAT in

b. *caay* ***cha*** *miraa* *cavaan* *baagas* *manz*
tea is Mira drinking garden-DAT in

c. *baagas* *manz* ***cha*** *miraa* *caay* *cavaan*
garden-DAT in is Mira tea drinking

'Mira is drinking tea in the garden.'

(5) FINITE SUBORDINATE CLAUSES

a. *jaaveedan* *l'uukh* *aslaam-as* *(zi/ki)* *tsI* ***par*** *yi* *kitaab*
Javed-ERG wrote Aslam-DAT that you read this book

b. *jaaveedan* *l'uukh* *aslaam-as* *(zi/ki)* *yi* *kitaab* ***par*** *tsI*
Javed-ERG wrote Aslam-DAT that this book read you

'Javed wrote to Aslam that you read this book.'

These sentences give us no clue as to the basic word order, in particular that of the verb. The arguments for a basic word order that locates the verb in the final position are derived from relative clauses, conditionals, alternative questions, nonfinites, etc.

(6) V-FINAL IN RELATIVE CLAUSES

su	*da:kTar*	*[yemsund*	*bI*	*dava:*	*hevan*	***chu-s]***	*gov*	*dili*
the	doctor	whose	I	medicine	eating	is-LSG-PS	went	Delhi

'The doctor whose medicine I am taking went to Delhi.'

(7) V-FINAL IN ALTERNATIVE QUESTIONS

me	*chu*	*nI*	*pata:*	*(ki)*	*mohnI*	*cay*	***ceya:***	*ya:*	*na*
I	be	not	know	that	Mohan	tea	will drink	or	not

'I do not know whether Mohan will drink tea or not.'

(8) V-FINAL IN 'IF' CLAUSE

agar	*raman*	*miraai*	*kitaab*	***ditse*** . . .
if	Ram	Mira-to	book	gave

(9) V-FINAL IN NON-FINITE CLAUSES

tAm'	*von*	*miiraayi*	*[mohnas*	*caay*	***dinI***	*khAAtrI]*
he	told	Mira	Mohan-DAT	tea	give-INF-ABL	for

'He told Mira to give tea to Mohan.'

Consider now the position of I. The inflectional element for agreement. In Kashmiri both the infinitive UN and the nonfinite past participle MUT show gender number inflection and occur in the final position supporting the argument that at least this part of I follows the verb and verb moves to I and has an SOVI structure.

(10) GENDER NUMBER FORMS OF THE INFINITIVE UN AND THE PAST PARTICIPLE MUT

	M.SG.	M.PL.	F.SG.	FPL
a.	un	In'	In'	Ini
b.	mut	mlt'	MIts	matsl

A crucial argument for I being in the final position comes from relative clauses as well.

(11) I-FINAL WITH CLITICS IN RELATIVE CLAUSES

su	*da:kTar*	*[yemsund*	*bI*	*dava:*	*kheva:n*	***chu- s]***	*gov*	*dili*
the	doctor	whose	I	medicine	eating	is-lsg-ps	went	Delhi

'The doctor whose medicine I am taking went to Delhi.'

Note that in (11) the pronominal suffix *-s* is clinging to the finite auxiliary *chu*. The same is true about the adverbial verb-final clauses as exemplified in (12).

(12) I-FINAL WITH CLITICS IN ADVERBIAL CLAUSES

harga:h	*toh'*	*tAmis*	*co:b ti*	***diy-iv***	*to:ti*	*kari*	*nI*	*yi*	*kA:m*
even though	you	him	beating	give-2PL-PS	then	do	not	this	work

'Even though you beat him up, he will not do this work.'

The final verb plus I position also draws support from the scrambling within IP, which includes adverbs. The adverb may follow the subject, as in (13b). Note that such scrambling is not available in languages like Icelandic and Yiddish where the Infl occupies the second position in subject-initial clauses.

(13) SCRAMBLING WITHIN IP

a.	*miiraa*	***cha***	*caay*	*cavaan*	*baagas*	*manz*
	Mira	is	tea	drinking	garden-DAT	in
b.	*caay*	***cha***	*miiraa*	*baagas*	*manz*	*cavaan*

Now it is well known that Kashmiri is an ergative language and has an extensive agreement system, which subsumes the pronominal suffixes or clitics. In ergative structures the verb shows agreements with the absolutive object. The spec-head theory of case and agreement requires that there be an AGR-object phrase. In nonergative structures the verb agrees with the subject providing the evidence for AGR subject phrase. We assume the structure of the inflectional verb is as shown in (14) below.

(14) STRUCTURE OF THE INFLECTIONAL VERB

V + gn agr + CL referring to SUBJ + CL referring to DO + CL referring to IO

The forms of clitics are cued to lexical cases, namely ergative, absolutive and dative, and their order is controlled by structural case (see Wali and Koul 1994). As all the clitics are aligned under inflectional nodes and as they mark the relevant information about their *pro* coreferents, namely lexical case and structural case, they must be in a spec-head relation with these coreferents at some level. We claim that the functional node AGRs, that is I, is final and the spec-head relation is obtained by moving the verb to AGRs, the subject to the specifier of AGRs, and the object to the specifier of AGRO. The basic structure is (15), where we assume an SOV structure VP-internally.

(15) $[_{IP}[_{VP}$[SOV] AGRO Tns AGRs]]

We claim that in Kashmiri V moves to AGRo and AGRs and the subject and object move to their respective specifiers and create an SOVI structure at IP level. The movements are for checking the structural case of the subject and the object as required within the minimalist framework. Note that these movements are pre-Spellout. In Kashmiri, there is no evidence either from the adverb or the negative that the verb or object movement is post-Spellout as required by the principle of Procrastinate, which states that the movement should be delayed as late as possible, that is, by LF. This is exemplified by the difference in the verb movement in English and French noted in Chomsky (1995).

A problem with our analysis is that the verb-final structure with overt subject or any other overt constituent is never found in the finite clause. The presence of an overt constituent requires the finite verb complex to be in the second position, the V2 configuration noted in (4) and repeated in (16). The sentence with the verb in the final position as in (17) is unacceptable.

(16) *tsl* *chihA:n* *parina:va:n* *su*
you AUX-2SG-3SG teaching him
'You are teaching him.'

(17) *tsl* *su* *parina:va:n* ***chihA:n***
you him teaching AUX-2SG-3SG

An interesting facet of Kashmiri is that the finite verb is thrown in the final position just in case all its arguments are null or pro, a construction that is unique to Kashmiri V2. In short, the finite verb stays in the final position in the absence of overt constituents [see (18a)]. (18b) shows that the verb in the first position is barely acceptable.

(18) a. *parlna:va:n* ***chihA:n***
teaching AUX-2SG-3SG
'You are teaching him.'

b. **chihA:n* *parlna:va:n*
AUX-2SG-3SG teaching
'You are teaching him.'

(18a) suggests that the verb and its *pro* arguments are in IP in the structure as in (19).

(19) [$_{IP}$ pro pro nonfinite verb form finite verb/aux+2sg+3sg]
you him teaching are

The structure in IP is as predicted by Zwart (1993) within the minimalist theory. The *pro* subject is in the initial position. It shows that the finite verb has moved to AGRo and AGRs through tense and the case of both the subject and the object has been checked. There is no evidence of verb-raising to C in (19). In contrast, (16) shows that the verb and the overt subject are in a specifier-head relation in CP, as in (20).

(20) [$_{CP}$ Subj$_i$ V$_j$ [$_{IP}$ t$_i$ Obj nonfinite verb t$_j$]]
you are him teaching

The subject has moved to the specifier of CP which is the topic position, and the verb to C. Note that the subject movement in (20) is not guided by any morphological feature checking requirement, such as Case. The case features have been checked in IP itself. We claim that the specifier of CP has a strong topic feature that must be checked. The topic feature may be checked by moving any constituent, including the subject, into the specifier of C head. The subject has no special status. It is licit for the subject to check the topic feature. The movement of the constituents, including the subject is not self-serving as required by the economy principle of Greed, which states that items move only to satisfy their own requirement. The movement of constituents is to satisfy the strong topic feature of the CP specifier. Such movement is currently known as altruistic or enlightened self-interest (Lasnik 1993), by which, items may move to satisfy the requirements of the position they move to. Altruism shows that the self-serving principle as stated under Greed is too strong and needs to be weakened.

What motivates the verb to move to C? Currently there are several theories. The most famous of these assumes that the verb moves for reasons of finiteness (Holmberg and Platzack 1995). Clearly that cannot be the case. The clause in (19) with all *pro* arguments is just as finite as the clause with overt arguments in (20), but the verb has not moved to C. We claim that the verb moves to C to check the topic feature. Checking the features of a specifier requires lexicalisation of the respective functional head as noted in Zwart (1993). An apparent counterexample to our claim comes from narrative inversion where the verb is often found in the initial position. We will not go into the details of the analysis of these constructions here.

The proposal that the subject moves to topic position draws support from yes-no interrogatives and imperatives. These allow the subject to move to the specifier of CP unlike other V2 languages. Yes-no questions in Kashmiri are formed by a Q marker affixed to the verb as in (22). In both the declarative (21) and the yes-no question (22), the subject precedes the verb. The low acceptability of (23) shows that topic position preferably must be filled.

(21) *tsl gatsha-kh paga:h garl*
you go-2SG-PS tomorrow home
'You will go home tomorrow.'

(22) PREVERBAL SUBJECT IN YES-NO Q (S V + CL + Q . . .)

tsl *gatsha-kh-a:* *paga:h* *garl?*
you go-CL-2SG-Q tomorrow home
'Will you go home tomorrow?'

(23) QUESTION VERB WITHOUT A PRECEDING CONSTITUENT

??[$_{CP}$ gatsha-kh-a:] *[$_{IP}$ tsl* *paga:h* *garl]?*
go-PS-2SG you tomorrow home
'Will you go home tomorrow?'

(24) PREVERBAL TOPIC IN YES-NO Q: (TOP V + CL + Q . . .)

[$_{CP}$ paga:h *gatsha-kh-a:]* *[$_{IP}$ tsl* *garl?*
tomorrow go-PS-2SG-Q you home
'Will you go home tomorrow?'

(25) PREVERBAL TOP IN IMPERATIVES

[$_{CP}$ koori *di-tav]* *[$_{IP}$ pro kitaab].*
girl-to give-2PL book
'Give the book to the girl.'

The presence of an overt NP, including the subject, in yes-no constructions comes as no surprise under the strong topic feature. We believe that the operator position in the yes-no question is empty due to the overt question marker. In the imperative the verb is in its root form and carries the imperative mark. The empty position then invites the overt NP to check the topic feature.

Kashmiri shows that it is the strong topic feature of the CP specifier that defines a V2 language. The specifier of CP allows only overt lexical elements. A condition on the CP specifier is that it must be lexicalised by PF level. Any overt constituent including the subject may fulfil the lexicalisation. The overt constituent moves before Spellout stage. The movement is altruistic. This demand of CP specifier to be lexicalised seems natural and intuitively correct. It is a mark of the V2 language. It explains the topic-like behaviour of the subject. The movement of the subject to the specifier of CP is not wild as stated in Zwart (1993) and Travis (1991). It has a function. Kashmiri finite clause allows only *pro* elements to stay in situ in IP configuration, as they cannot fulfil the lexicalisation requirement of the topic.

In sum, Kashmiri brings into focus the significance of topic in a V2 language. It is the topic that draws the verb to the second position. The function of the verb in this position is simply to check the topic feature. The verb in this position does not necessarily define finiteness as is currently assumed.

REFERENCES

CHOMSKY, NOAM

1995 *The minimalist program*. Cambridge: MIT Press.

HOLMBERG, A. and C. PLATZACK

1995 *The role of inflexion in Scandinavian syntax*. New York: Oxford University Press.

LASNIK, HOWARD

1993 Lectures on minimalist syntax. University of Connecticut: Working Papers in Linguistics. Occasional Papers: 1.

1995 Case and expletives revisited: On greed and other human failings. *Linguistic Inquiry* 26.4. 615–34.

SCHWARTZ, BONNIE D. and VIKNER STEN

1996 The verb always leaves IP in V2 clauses. In Belletti & Rizzi (eds.), *Parameters and functional heads*. Oxford: Oxford University Press. 11–63.

TRAVIS, L.

1991 Parameters of phrase structure and verb-second phenomena. In *Principles and parameters in comparative grammar*. 339–64.

ZWART, J.W.

1993 Verb movement and complementizer agreement. *The MIT Working Papers in Linguistics* 18. 297–341.